D1323587

Public
Housing
Myths

UWE BRISTOL
WITHDRAWN
LIBRARY SERVICES

Public Housing Myths

PERCEPTION, REALITY, AND SOCIAL POLICY

Edited by

Nicholas Dagen Bloom, Fritz Umbach,
and Lawrence J. Vale

Cornell University Press ITHACA AND LONDON

Copyright © 2015 by Cornell University

All rights reserved. Except for brief quotations in a review, this book, or parts thereof, must not be reproduced in any form without permission in writing from the publisher. For information, address Cornell University Press, Sage House, 512 East State Street, Ithaca, New York 14850.

First published 2015 by Cornell University Press
First printing, Cornell Paperbacks, 2015

Printed in the United States of America

Library of Congress Cataloging-in-Publication Data
Public housing myths : perception, reality, and social policy / edited by Nicholas Dagen Bloom, Fritz Umbach, and Lawrence J. Vale.
    pages cm
  Includes bibliographical references and index.
ISBN 978-0-8014-5204-8 (cloth : alk. paper)
ISBN 978-0-8014-7874-1 (pbk. : alk. paper)
1. Public housing—Social aspects. 2. Public housing—Economic aspects. 3. City planning.
I. Bloom, Nicholas Dagen, 1969– editor. II. Umbach, Gregory Holcomb, editor. III. Vale, Lawrence J., 1959– editor. IV. Heathcott, Joseph, 1968– . Public housing stands alone. Container of (work):
HD7288.77.P83 2015
363.5'85—dc23
                                                                2014029478

Cornell University Press strives to use environmentally responsible suppliers and materials to the fullest extent possible in the publishing of its books. Such materials include vegetable-based, low-VOC inks and acid-free papers that are recycled, totally chlorine-free, or partly composed of nonwood fibers. For further information, visit our website at www.cornellpress.cornell.edu.

Cloth printing   10 9 8 7 6 5 4 3 2 1

Paperback printing   10 9 8 7 6 5 4 3 2 1

CONTENTS

Introduction   *1*

I. Places

MYTH #1 Public Housing Stands Alone   *31*
Joseph Heathcott

MYTH #2 Modernist Architecture Failed Public Housing   *47*
D. Bradford Hunt

MYTH #3 Public Housing Breeds Crime   *64*
Fritz Umbach and Alexander Gerould

MYTH #4 High-Rise Public Housing Is Unmanageable   *91*
Nicholas Dagen Bloom

II. Policy

MYTH #5 Public Housing Ended in Failure during the 1970s   *121*
Yonah Freemark

MYTH #6 Mixed-Income Redevelopment Is the Only Way
to Fix Failed Public Housing   *139*
Lawrence J. Vale

MYTH #7 Only Immigrants Still Live in European Public Housing   *154*
Florian Urban

MYTH #8 Public Housing Is Only for Poor People   *175*
Nancy Kwak

III. People

MYTH #9 Public Housing Residents Hate the Police   *189*
Fritz Umbach

MYTH #10 Public Housing Tenants Are Powerless   *206*
  Rhonda Y. Williams

MYTH #11 Tenants Did Not Invest in Public Housing   *223*
  Lisa Levenstein

Notes   *235*
Acknowledgments   *277*
Contributor Biographies   *279*
Index   *281*

Public
Housing
Myths

INTRODUCTION

If American urbanists and politicians share any conventional wisdom across political divides, it is the idea that public housing failed in every possible dimension. Public housing has, indeed, come a long way from the idyllic interwar images of children frolicking in landscaped courtyards, tidy brick buildings, and presentable families. These dreamy places—and the promised step forward from decaying and crowded urban slums—sent countries around the globe down the road to public housing construction (Figure I.1). Since then, however, endless portraits of derelict towers, rampant criminality, and unchecked disorder have contrasted sharply with public housing's idealistic aspirations. And if the woeful images and narratives rarely did justice to the complexity of public housing on the ground, there is no question that public housing as it exists is usually a world away from what the movement's founders had in mind (Figure I.2).

Public housing, after all, has its roots in what we would today consider utopian ideas about urban life and human nature. The huddled urban masses could be whisked away from tenements, gangs, and disease to a paradise not only of simply sanitary housing but of better living and behavior. Beyond building modern apartments for the urban working class, both in Europe and America, the state would provide excellent schools, community centers, parks and playgrounds, close supervision, and health care. Public housing was not just replacing tenements with modern housing, but replacing urban disorder with a highly regulated, socially controlled urban community: the slumless city of the Settlement House vision. However, world war, budget realities, politics, mismanagement, racism, and social conflict undermined this broad housing vision both here and abroad after World War II. The story varied by region and nation, but the early idealism often lost out to a penny-pinching focus

1

Figure I.1 Jane Addams Houses, Chicago (ca. 1930s). The initial vision of public housing as achieved in Chicago. Courtesy of the Library of Congress.

on the quantity of units over their quality, racially biased urban politics, and an increasingly punitive welfare state. Given public housing's utopian birth, its subsequent and very public fall from grace was perhaps inevitable—there was, after all, a rather long way to tumble.[1]

Nor did it help public housing's case that from a functional perspective public housing represents one of the more complex undertakings of twentieth-century public administration. Designing and building lovely complexes, even when it did happen, guaranteed little. Intricate financing, administrative complexity, urban poverty, and challenging daily operations combined to make public housing management notoriously difficult. The most dramatic failures engendered by these challenges (such as Pruitt-Igoe, Cabrini-Green, and Ronan Point), and the growing distance over time between utopian premise and urban reality, bolstered the powerful critique of public housing from both the left and the right. This critique not only endures but until recently completely swamped any reasonable discussion of the phenomenon known as public housing.[2]

Figure I.2 After the fall from grace: the Techwood Homes awaiting redevelopment in Atlanta. Courtesy of the Library of Congress.

The range of public housing programs and motives is rarely acknowledged outside specialist circles. It is true that most traditional public housing programs, by design, funnel government funds and powers into low-cost housing for construction, renovation, and long-term operations, but there has always existed a strong private dimension to public housing, including private-sector contracting to build, maintain, and renovate public housing projects. In Europe, in particular, nonprofit managers and social housing companies have played leading roles in building and operating public housing projects for over a century. In Singapore, the vast majority of residents even have the opportunity to purchase their units. Motives have also varied greatly, despite the widespread view that public housing is always a liberal or socialist program. The pressure for public housing programs in the United States, for instance, frequently came as much from private downtown business interests, who viewed public housing as a tool for clearing poor neighborhoods, as it did from liberal idealists. Singapore's leaders, and those in China today, view public housing as a key element of economic modernization as much as a humanitarian program. Public housing, then, includes a range of institutions, actors, and aims, depending upon a particular context.

Public housing comes in more flavors than stereotypes suggest. Popular and academic attention has focused on high-rise projects in big cities, but the majority of what remains of the nation's traditional public housing (approximately 1.1 million of an original 1.4 million units) consists of low-rise complexes (including single-family homes) in small towns and cities. This smaller scale approach, in fact, predominates among the country's three thousand housing authorities. European and Asian cities, despite a few high-profile disasters, have constructed and maintained millions of low-, medium-, and high-rise public housing units. In fact, many European governments have invested heavily to renovate or reconfigure large-scale social housing projects while keeping the original residents on site. Generalizing about public housing's essential nature from Pruitt-Igoe or Ronan Point fails to capture the design diversity—and the varying quality of life over time—in such a widely distributed phenomenon.

The racial composition of public housing has been and is today also more complex than widely believed. While it is true that in the United States racial and ethnic minorities have formed the disproportionate majority of public housing residents for the last several decades, it is also the case that many housing authorities, including that of New York City, created public housing projects for a majority white tenancy. Many of these white projects subsequently tipped to minority occupancy because whites enjoyed access to subsidies for single-family homes in the emerging, racially restricted suburbs. In Europe, too, non-white immigrants also populate a sizable share of European social housing units despite public housing's roots in social democratic policies targeted at white Europeans. On the other hand, Europe's public housing continues to shelter millions of native-born white Europeans—not only that continent's "new minorities"—despite media portrayals. Likewise, in diverse cities such as New York, San Francisco, and London, the broad range of ethnic minorities calling public housing home belies popular notions of the projects as a program only for African Americans and Latinos. In Asia, too, race is not a factor in public housing in the same ways. Singapore, for instance, employs

4

strict ethnic quotas in each of its projects, thereby ensuring a substantial Chinese ethnic majority in every complex. To say that public housing is minority housing by its nature is not consonant from a global or historical perspective.

These widespread misconceptions about the true nature of public housing make the subject of public housing ripe for myth busting. Since 2000, even while many American and European public housing towers have been pulled down, and even as the reputation of public housing programs sank to new lows, historians and social scientists have quietly imploded the conventional wisdom about public housing. Addressing a range of large- and mid-sized cities, including New York, Chicago, Boston, Baltimore, and St. Louis, and identifying overlooked but crucially important themes ranging from management to tenant activism, these fresh perspectives and unexpected findings have given public housing studies a new life. At the same time, a wealth of overseas scholarship—less familiar to American audiences—has emerged that charts public housing's complex fate in several European and Asian contexts.

We are learning a lot more, for instance, about the instances in which public housing partly realized the goals of its early twentieth-century inventors through case studies that have largely been ignored by most public housing scholars. Northern Europe, Singapore, Hong Kong, many small towns, and even New York City, for example, all gave rise to decently managed public housing systems that may not be utopian but have adequately sheltered hundreds of thousands, even millions, of low-income tenants in modern apartments for decades. These communities are often rougher around the edges or more institutional than the dreamers of the interwar period had in mind—and they often throw off genteel observers today—but many publicly constructed developments convey a genuine community feeling and a quality of life that compares favorably with conditions found in urban tenements both past and present. These communities also provide needed low-rent (or low-cost ownership) housing in very expensive cities.

We also know that the real problems in even the most troubled projects can never be explained by a single causal factor. Tall buildings, superblock urban forms, or welfare concentration—factors usually blamed for all problems in public housing—constitute just part of an intertwined problem, and some places have many of these "problems" without ever becoming wholly problematic. The new scholarship does not naively celebrate public housing projects, public housing managers, and heroic residents. The reality of deeply troubled housing projects here and abroad precludes such romanticism, but the research is sufficient in depth and data to spark new questions.

The persistence of crime, poverty, and other social problems in cities such as New Orleans and Chicago—even after the elimination of most public housing projects associated with those ills—raises questions about earlier scholarship and public policy that primarily blamed housing projects for a range of urban problems in poor neighborhoods. Chicago's aggressive Plan for Transformation has erased nearly all of its highly stigmatized family high-rise public housing projects from the city's landscape, but this did not stop the city from becoming the murder capital of the United States in 2012, with five hundred killings in just one year. Perhaps there was more to the story than we thought. A new accounting is needed, one less weighted with utopian and ideological baggage, that can bring us closer to the truth about a complex and quite fascinating twentieth-century social experiment.[3]

To provoke this discussion, we have reframed the generally accepted beliefs about public housing as a series of myths. What the editors of this text mean by *myths* is that while there is much truth to public housing criticism, the hypercritical framework, like any mythology, has assumed a power far beyond the specific facts of the story. That Pruitt-Igoe failed did not, ipso facto, mean that all public housing everywhere had to (or would) go the way of that doomed place. Even the failure of multiple projects both in the United States and abroad should not be allowed to define the reputation of complex and varied government programs that still house millions of low- or moderate-income people. Nor do experts, even today, understand fully the interwoven factors that caused a project such as Pruitt-Igoe to fail. A 2011 documentary, *The Pruitt-Igoe Myth*, raises questions about the conventional wisdom surrounding the project without fixating on just one smoking gun to explain the collapse. Yet, all too often, the worst cases are allowed to become mythologized into the reigning stigmatized stereotype, even as these "worst cases" fail to be analyzed in nuanced ways.[4]

The myths that engulf public housing, like all myths, feature strong didactic elements, rooted in utopian origins and political biases that thwart rational analysis. The new housing research thus attempts to steer clear of utopian regrets but also tries to avoid reductive arguments that pit liberals against conservatives. Conservatives did not kill all public housing; liberals did not always save or even adequately defend it; tenants were not simply victims or villains; and racism was just one of many factors undermining the promise of public housing. The finger-pointing of an earlier generation missed the real, and really interesting, stories.

The Founding Myth

The tight connection between leftist modernist planning and public housing that began in the 1920s has made it nearly impossible to look at public housing as a form of urban shelter or as kind of regular government service; rather, it has taken on a deeper meaning as an expression of an ideological movement of planning and design. Because public housing arrived on the scene freighted with utopian idealism (the belief that it could *transform* both people and places) and burdened with ready-made enemies on the right, any and all blemishes in that unrealistic narrative severely damaged the claims made by early advocates. Since the 1950s, scholars and activists from a variety of different political and occupational perspectives have justifiably focused on the failure to achieve ambitious community revitalization and improved human nature through public housing. Judged by its founding standards, public housing has often fallen short.[5]

Public housing had its initial roots in straightforward housing reform in cities such as London, Paris, Vienna, New York, and Chicago. Housing activists at first saw public housing as simply the next, logical step in housing reform (after the implementation of building regulations and zoning) on their march to the creation of a healthy and sanitary metropolis. Some housing experts disagreed vehemently with this tactic, but it was hard for many housers not to believe that "market failure" in the lower end of the housing market could only be remedied through constructive government action. Housing as a municipal service was, from their view, just like city water or public parks: a necessary public provision when market failure was obvious.

The international movement in modern housing of the 1920s and 1930s, however, along with social democratic movements in many countries (Labor in Britain, Viennese socialism, or the New Deal in the United States) added a significantly more ambitious, almost magical, notion to public housing. Housing would be the vanguard of the sanitary city, organized in such a fashion as to create healthy and happy communities of working-class inhabitants regardless of the wider social forces acting upon it. Through the provision of open spaces, community facilities, and generous social services, public housing in Europe and America in the interwar period became part of planned urban districts built with increasing self-containment.

The distance between ideal and reality quickly surfaced. Proponents intended separation, for instance, to convey superiority over past forms of ill-conceived tenements and shacks. Isolated projects, however, also could come to signify unwanted difference, emphasizing the distance between modern forms of housing and the more comforting forms of conventional dwellings. The story of public housing might well have turned out somewhat differently if these complexes had been built from the beginning as regular urban buildings, part of the fabric of the city; much of today's newer "affordable housing" has sought to remedy this disjuncture.

In the United States, the community infrastructure and social democratic uplift of the New Deal era also frequently fell victim to bottom-line thinking in the 1940s and 1950s, even as the founding ideology still made grand claims about urban transformation. In the postwar period, public housing continued to be constructed in ever vaster modernist superblocks (and, in a few large cities, often with very tall towers), even as many of the more utopian notions such as community and health facilities disappeared from housing project grounds, victims of the new austerity. All too frequently local officials looked to public housing more as a patronage opportunity than as a program supplying decent housing for the working class— let alone a utopian community effort. Others could not resist the opportunity to hijack the program to serve the purposes of business-oriented urban renewal schemes. Such political interests often meant maintenance and even construction funds found their way into well-connected pockets.

Even more troubling, public housing both in the United States and elsewhere became a tool by which elites created the minority-free urban space real estate interests often demanded. As public housing shifted from a venue for housing carefully vetted members of the working class to a place for domiciling those so displaced (or too poor to live elsewhere), social exclusion became a leading part of public housing's agenda. Many projects and their increasingly minority or immigrant populations were left to rot. So much for utopia![6]

THE AMERICAN CRITICAL PERSPECTIVE

It wasn't hard to find fault with public housing as it developed, particularly in the postwar United States. By the 1950s, the critique of public housing focused almost exclusively on the failure of the community planning ideal. Sure, the apartments at first were generally of a higher standard than the old tenements, but could they really be enjoyed in peace? The urban activist Jane

Jacobs castigated tower-in-the-park planned districts not only for failing to generate community but also because they destroyed existing, functioning places under the guise of urban improvement. Jacobs had very little to say about public housing apartments as housing, perhaps because their quality was higher at the time than the standard walk-up apartments in the tenement districts she preferred (and not that far from middle-income towers at the time), but she powerfully framed high-rise tower-in-the-park communities of all kinds as perpetually corroding security and community life. Even early advocates of utopian style housing such as Catherine Bauer and Elizabeth Wood were, by the 1950s, criticizing declining design standards, social isolation, and the unhealthy role of public housing communities in urban renewal.[7]

The popular acceptance of Jacobs's design critique grew during the 1960s and 1970s amid many public housing projects' growing crime rates, declining maintenance, and spreading signs of social disorder. Very few observers were able to distinguish between the effects of planning and those of its socioeconomic context. Despite race riots and dramatic urban decline that destabilized thousands of conventional urban neighborhoods in the post-1960 period, the theme of public housing as a failed community ideal in time became a cottage industry in the work of leading architects, critics, and planners such as Oscar Newman, Peter Rowe, Richard Plunz, and Andrés Duany. Many designers and critics disavowed their loyalty to the modernist movement and its utopian goals; public housing, and particularly the high-rise tower in the park, became Exhibit A in the failure of modernist community planning and often, by extension, the social democratic welfare state.[8]

Since at least the 1960s, most planners and architects in the United States have viewed high-rise and low-rise public housing as essentially pathological and anticommunal, regardless of any value this form of housing may have as shelter or the fact that similar communities for the middle and upper classes have often been very successful. On the positive side, this rejection has encouraged design practitioners, who once subscribed religiously to the modernist canon and played such an important role in publicizing and promoting the tower-in-the-park ideal, to seek practical alternatives or creative renovation solutions. Their design experiments have, at times, resulted in more interesting financial and physical designs for public housing. In recent years, more controversially, the public housing critique has taken the form of the U.S. Department of Housing and Urban Development's HOPE VI program—an acronym now translated as Housing Opportunities for People Everywhere.

Here, the public policy goal has entailed replacing "severely distressed" public housing with community designs that respect the urban grid and surrounding context, even if this means very few public housing tenants get to return following extensive redevelopment into mixed-income communities. The policies known as "estate rescue" in Europe have addressed many similar issues, but with far less displacement and more extensive renovation of distressed housing projects.[9]

Criticism of public housing has progressed far beyond the planning and housing circles that gave birth to the program. Public housing has been, over the past few decades, one of the few domains of social policy where the ideas of thinkers from a variety of different political perspectives converge. Although critics on the opposing sides may not agree on causes, analysts from a surprising range of political ideals agree that public housing as built has almost no redeeming features.

Conservative partisans both in the United State and Europe have consistently viewed public housing as a dramatic failure of big government policies to create either a better community or more affordable housing. Whether epitomized by anticommunist crusaders in the McCarthy era, Thatcherite efforts to sell off Britain's council housing in the 1980s, or Howard Husock's 2003 dissection of *America's Trillion-Dollar Housing Mistake*, conservatives have viewed public housing as a tremendous waste of money that undermines the operation of a free market, unfairly competing with the private enterprise that could more effectively deliver affordable and better regulated housing to the urban masses. This critical perspective, sometimes cynically abetted by declining conditions connected to the withdrawal of funding introduced by conservative policies, has spawned a variety of myths, among them the widespread and erroneous notion that public housing residents are all criminals and welfare cheats; that the U.S. public sector stopped public housing provision in the 1970s as a result of programmatic failure; that all public housing projects have themselves become slums that must be destroyed; and that public housing can never be a tool of social and economic development. Nearly every myth in our collection has at one point or another been mixed into right-wing critiques of public housing.[10]

The academic left, which might have been expected to defend public housing because of its utopian goals and social democratic heritage, has not been much more generous. There have been a few upbeat accounts, focusing mostly on the early years when the utopian promise seemed within reach or on more recent attempts at public housing redevelopment; still, public housing plays an important role in urban history due chiefly to its frequently poor conditions and capacity to epitomize failed and unfair urban policy in the postwar era. For most American liberal scholars, including Arnold Hirsch (*Making the Second Ghetto*) and Joel Schwartz (*The New York Approach*), public housing was too intertwined in racist and frequently incompetent urban renewal policies to ever be successful in its own right as housing or community. The European left, in a similar manner, has criticized the isolation of immigrants in vast suburban housing projects with high unemployment. The left critique of public housing, particularly in the United States, has contributed to the myths that public housing can never be decently managed, that public housing by its nature traps its tenants in poverty, and that there is no conceivable role for public housing in economic or social redevelopment. The ambivalence liberals feel for public housing has contributed to the declining political support for the American program, and led to minimal backing from the left even for dramatic efforts to reform the program through public housing redevelopment. In Europe, where the left has more political power, the results of the critique have been more complex, and often more positive, in terms of redevelopment.[11]

Urban sociologists and some politically oriented planners have provided the most subtlety when it comes to critical perspectives, perhaps because they have been better able to separate out the various impacts of poverty and housing. Through their engaged fieldwork and sensitivity to context, they also recognize forms of community and support that go unnoticed by many middle- and upper-class observers and academics who may never venture into public housing, but still write about it frequently. At the same time, by their focus on the pathos, poverty, and crime in public housing, rather than on ordinary lives, some scholars have unwittingly contributed to myths that public housing is essentially defined by social disorder and crime.[12]

What the public thinks it knows about public housing is probably the most troubling. Reporters in the United States have developed a series of persistently demeaning and dehumanizing public housing memes and tropes. Mostly middle-class reporters find public housing as convenient shorthand for all urban poverty, government malfeasance, rampant criminality, and dependence. Overwhelmingly negative images and stories have been devoured for decades by middle- and upper-income readers. In fact, an almost Mad-Lib approach to urban reporting emerged in the twenty-first century, where simply inserting a project name and city, along with choice stereotypical images (urine-stained elevators, a broken window), generates a modern analog of *How the Other Half Lives* (to borrow from photojournalist Jacob Riis's 1890 publication). The same articles on public housing have been written a thousand times—although, tellingly, they have not been written about a thousand different places. At its core, public housing reportage suffers from a combination of two unfortunate factors: a disproportionate focus on a handful of highly troubled places (either nationally or within a given city) and a formulaic approach to diagnosing problems that evinces little capacity to probe underlying conditions. Edward Goetz characterized this as an "exaggerated discourse of disaster" because "media stories zeroed in on the most dysfunctional high-rise projects," emphasizing "social pathologies such as crime, violence, family breakdown, and drugs."[13]

Longtime *Chicago Tribune* columnist Mary Schmich pointed out that the word "notorious" became associated with Cabrini-Green so often that it was almost as if this were part of the project's official name.[14] Similarly, drawing on her lengthy dissertation that dissects the representations of Cabrini-Green's visual culture, Nicola Mann lamented that, "provocative headlines, dramatic photographs and sensational imagery frame Chicago's public housing residents as non-citizens, living in a place that isn't a community." According to Mann, most portrayals reduce "the complex political issues of economic stagnation and cuts in social spending into chaotic, ruinous narrative messages." In so doing, projects such as Cabrini "get mythologized in late twentieth-century popular visual culture as sites that deserve to be demolished."[15] Likewise, David Fleming emphasized in a provocative essay the ways that various representations of Cabrini-Green have worked to disempower residents.[16]

It is possible to trace the changing media portrayal of public housing through observing the rise of key words and terms used to describe it. Most benignly, a term such as "modern" appears with relatively high frequency in the pre–World War II period and again from the 1940s and throughout the 1950s before declining. It then peaks once more in the late 1980s and early 1990s under the guise of the need for "modernization" of public housing stock suffering from deferred maintenance. Most often, as this shift suggests, newspapers have charted the language of public housing's troubles and in the process, compounded them.

Taking seriously Schmich's comment about the ubiquity of the "notorious Cabrini-Green" moniker, it is possible to graph the presence of public housing notoriety in major newspapers and to assess where Cabrini's own problems falls within this depiction. Looking only at articles from the *Chicago Tribune*, by 1974 a Chicago school could be blamed for being "in the vicinity of the notorious Cabrini-Green housing project." In 1978, a secretary at the Department of Housing and Urban Development (HUD) optimistically opined that a "once-notorious symbol of all that is wrong with urban public housing can be saved by a special effort," but the Cabrini-centered notoriety returned with a vengeance in the 1980s and 1990s. In 1982, "notorious Cabrini-Green" is described as the place where poor women were forced to raise their children; by 1986, it is the "city's second-largest and, some contend, most notorious high-rise public housing development"; and the following year it is branded "the nation's most notorious public housing project." Press coverage of "notorious" Cabrini-Green peaked in 1992 following the senseless murder of first-grader Dantrell Davis, shot by a rooftop sniper while making the short journey from his Cabrini apartment to the elementary school located just across the street. By the late 1990s, just as the city's Plan for Transformation geared up for massive public housing demolition, the context of Cabrini's notoriety took a different turn: "There is probably no more startling visual representation of the turnaround in the city than the sight of the notorious public housing high-rises of Cabrini-Green backing up against new $300,000, Lincoln Park-style rowhouses."[17]

In this evolving narrative, Cabrini's notoriety, once self-contained, first affected neighboring institutions and then, rendered anomalous by encroaching gentrification, simply became a problem to be removed. Chicago's flagship newspaper frequently used the world "notorious" to describe other parts of the city's public housing, but these pieces tended to focus mostly on the other iconic symbol of distressed housing, the Robert Taylor Homes, or else cast more general disrepute upon its neighbors along the "Chicago Wall, the most notorious public housing in the nation."[18]

Looking across four major newspapers—the *Chicago Tribune*, the *Los Angeles Times*, the *New York Times*, and the *Washington Post*—the overall trajectory of "notorious public housing" is both clear and revealing (see Figure I.3). "Notorious" and "public housing" first emerge in tandem in newspaper accounts during the 1940s and 1950s, but in those years "notorious" is, not surprisingly, used to set up the contrast between modern public housing and the evils of the slums it replaced. By 1970 or so, the referent begins to shift, as "notorious" gains a new housing partner in crime. In 1981, a *New York Times* article explicitly shifted the reference, using "notorious" to describe a "public

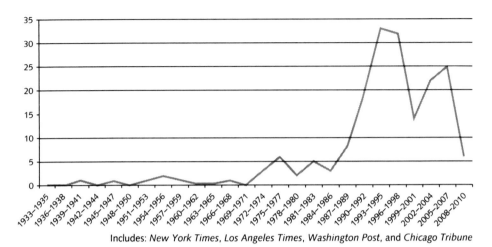

Includes: *New York Times*, *Los Angeles Times*, *Washington Post*, and *Chicago Tribune*

Figure I.3 Articles with "public housing" within fifty words of "notorious."
Sources: Proquest Historical Newspapers, Proquest Archives

housing slum" in San Francisco.[19] After that inflection point, the reportage of notoriety in the four papers increased during the 1980s; in the New York, Chicago, and Washington papers, it peaked between the 1990s and the early 2000s, as the HOPE VI program called attention to the demolition and redevelopment of various benighted projects. After 2007, with most of the nation's most vilified projects removed, use of the term "notorious" to describe public housing had begun to dissipate.

In all this, however, it is striking to note that if one graphs stories from the four newspapers in a disaggregated manner (Figure I.4), the trend lines are relatively similar; the overall graph (Figure I.3), however, is greatly skewed by the markedly higher number of negative articles in the Chicago paper. And, in turn, the Chicago articles are almost invariably about a few of that city's largest high-rise projects (all now demolished), with occasional mentions of failures in other cities, typically in New Orleans or St. Louis. In other words, the national picture of public housing negativity conveyed by four of the country's major papers may well be distorted by a few conspicuous failures in Chicago, coupled with the dramatic initial implosion of Pruitt-Igoe and the renewed spate of destruction and rebuilding occasioned by the HOPE VI program.

New York, a city that has far more public housing than Chicago, Los Angeles, and Washington, D.C. combined, seems to have had little in public hous-

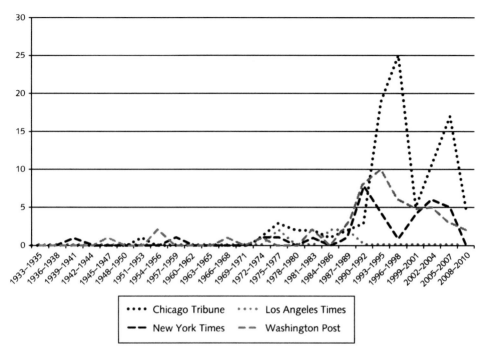

Figure I.4 Articles with "public housing" within fifty words of "notorious."
Sources: Proquest Historical Newspapers; Proquest Archives

ing that rose to the level of true notoriety, at least as described by the *New York Times*. With so many developments to consider, reporters tend to focus on management by the New York City Housing Authority (NYCHA)—and systemwide episodic operational shortcomings—rather than looking at one project or on project life per se. Moreover, some of that paper's most direct coverage about public housing is about problems in Chicago, St. Louis, and elsewhere, not a more localized referendum on NYCHA. The *Washington Post*, too, emphasizes the notoriety of public housing projects in cities far afield of the District of Columbia, especially Chicago and St. Louis, much more frequently than any local failures. More remarkably, in Los Angeles—where public housing is overwhelmingly delivered in a scattered form through portable housing vouchers or in low-rise developments—it has been more than twenty years since the last time the *Los Angeles Times* used the word "notorious" to describe public housing, whether in LA or anywhere else.

"Notorious public housing," by definition, refers to the presence of extreme cases, but similar evidence arises from other investigations of less tendentious language about public housing in the popular press. The same four city newspapers increasingly associated public housing with "violence" or "violent" during the 1970s and 1980s, with the use of those terms peaking in the mid-1990s and declining thereafter. Likewise, public housing increasingly became associated with being "rundown" during the 1980s, though this connection also dissipated after the early 1990s. Similarly, articles associating public housing with "isolation" (or "isolated" or "isolating") spiked in the mid-1990s and then rapidly declined.

Looking at a broader sample of newspaper coverage for the 1993–2010 period, the downward trend in the frequency of negative associations with public housing since the early 1990s is confirmed.[20] Associations between "public housing" and "crime/criminal" or "isolated/isolation/isolating" or "violence" each declined by approximately half between the early to middle 1990s and the end of the first decade of the 2000s (see Figures I.5–I.7). Taken together, then, there is some evidence that the overwhelming negativity about public housing in the popular press may finally be on the wane. Even so, public housing remains extremely stigmatized in the popular imagination.[21] Beyond living in one particular housing development, residents are often described as

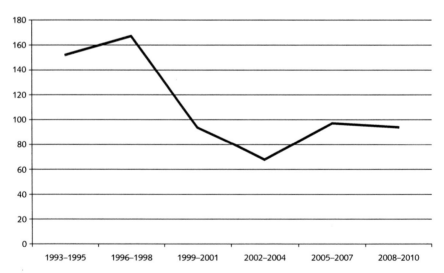

Figure I.5 "Public housing" within five words of "crime."
Source: LexisNexis

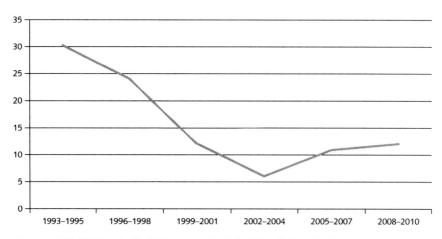

Figure I.6 "Public housing" within ten words of "isolation/isolated/isolating."
Source: LexisNexis

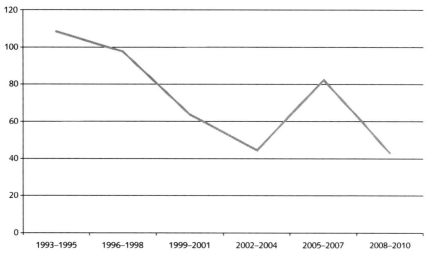

Figure I.7 "Public housing" within ten words of "violent" or "violence."
Source: LexisNexis

living in "the projects." In so doing, they are identified (and often self-identify) not simply with a specific neighborhood but with a type of place, one presumed to house a specific type of person. Worst of all, the term *projects* suggests not only a bounded place, like the original meaning of the word *ghetto*, but a category of place whose image to outsiders is perpetually degraded by the media

17

portraits of the disasters that lurk within, both actual and latent. NYCHA, for instance, scrupulously refers to its housing projects as *developments* in an often quixotic attempt to shed the mental image associated with the word *project*.

At its worst, stereotypes, class or political bias, and sloppy reporting shape much public housing coverage. At its best, reporting on public housing has conveyed to a large audience the particular issues of public housing projects and provided an empathetic portrait of the difficulties poor people face in securing housing and finding their place in society at large. Popular media can even be marshaled to highlight community empowerment themes in the most stigmatized of places, especially prominent in Ronit Bezalel's films about Cabrini-Green—both *Voices of Cabrini* (1999) and *70 Acres in Chicago: Cabrini-Green* (forthcoming), which explores the importance of festivals and community reunions.

The dominant "discourse of disaster" masks the reality that most public housing is neither high-rise nor burdened with the kind of "severe distress" that a National Commission identified with the worst 6 percent of the stock.[22] As Goetz put it, "The image of public housing communities wildly out of control, with a tenant base made up of violent criminals on the one hand and passive, cowering victims on the other, does not, in fact, describe the overwhelming majority of public housing in the nation. In most cities at most times, public housing provides a better alternative than private housing in poor neighborhoods." Even at the peak of public housing habitation, there were almost as many public housing units in single-family homes as in high-rises, and many of those high-rises have housed seniors quite well. In a country with more than three thousand local public housing authorities (80 percent of which operate fewer than five hundred units), the vast majority of localities have provided housing that "is very functional and provides an essential housing resource" for low-income residents.[23]

Beyond Myths

So what does one make of all this criticism? It is true that public housing nearly everywhere failed to meet the ambitious notions that were used to sell the program in the 1930s and 1940s. So many keen observers, many with solid research methods and honest intentions, can't all be wrong. Public housing has rarely been free of urban strife, nor are most projects necessarily the kinds of places that many middle- or upper-class individuals would want to either subsidize or inhabit. Even the best research, however, often shows a lack of nuance that parallels the naivety of the elite public housing proponents from seventy-five years earlier. Many well-intentioned critics are still in thrall to the founding myth of public housing. At some level, they still believe that the urban working classes could be transformed by providing more than shelter: a top-to-bottom process of social reorganization and physical redevelopment for a post-conflict urban order. HOPE VI–funded public housing redevelopment (which has usually involved both neo-traditional urban streetscapes and dramatically lower numbers of low-income residents living on the post-redevelopment site) has generated a new set of utopian predictions that link public housing destruction with the coming end of urban poverty and crime, despite the lack of evidence to support these strategies and outcomes.

Popular opinion rarely views public housing as simply one aspect of contemporary urban poverty—a condition that often has less to do with architecture's power or government's failure than with the fact that poverty and social exclusion are common occurrences around the globe. What public housing has actually delivered over time are complex forms of poor people's urban and rural housing and community that frequently partake in whatever social, administrative, and political challenges are found in their surrounding neighborhoods and cities. Sometimes projects work well, and sometimes they do not, even in the same city or right next door. Sometimes tenants build community, and sometimes they do not. The social situation of tenants, their age ranges, the quality of the buildings' construction, access to other resources, the state of the city and nation in which they are located, and even the generosity of social benefits each play as important a role in outcomes as the initial planning ideals.

Public housing's most dramatic failures, indelibly captured in photographs of Pruitt-Igoe's iconic implosion, invited scholars and pundits to craft for their audiences parable-like theoretical explanations that have become mythic. Even as the dramatic villains varied (modernist architects run amok, racist politicians emboldened by federal policy, or impractical do-gooders interfering with market forces), the narrative arc of well-intentioned plans undone by a small but influential cast of characters remained the same. Public housing, accordingly, appears to be exceptional compared to other public services (schools, hospitals, transit) that are also criticized but managed to remain valued throughout an era when public housing is being pulled down. Just as iconic high-rise towers stood apart from their neighborhoods, public housing history has rarely been woven into the larger findings, approaches, and trends of urban history— other than the familiar trope of inevitable decline.[24]

By contrast, the authors in this collection seek to integrate public housing history into the story of the larger urban experience by emphasizing context and contingency. Among the factors included in our essays are changes in policing, public administration, political trends, family structure, economics, demographics, and women's rights. The essays reframe conventional myths of public housing problems or failure by creating a richer political, social, and cultural narrative both in the United States and abroad. We want to know what worked, what didn't work, and why. We are also open to exploring unplanned outcomes, both good and bad. The essays in this book explore complex themes such as the effects of daily housing management and tenant selection on housing quality; public housing as a bellwether of white flight and suburban resistance to integration; the culture of struggle fostered by tenants and social workers; the need to distinguish between correlation and causation in public housing crime; and even the notion of public housing as a decent home valued by tenants. The end result is a way of looking at public housing that is distinct from the utopian and political tradition that has defined public housing history up to this point.

The problems of deindustrialization, for instance, had variable impacts on cities both here and abroad. New York, Hong Kong, and other strong market cities with activist governments and resilient economies have not only had better luck preserving public housing projects—even extraordinarily large ones—but have also succeeded in preserving and upgrading their citywide infrastructure as a whole. Cities in industrial decline or facing white flight, such as St. Louis, on the other hand, could certainly have preserved public housing had they made it a priority, but city leaders faced headwinds when marshaling sufficient resources to control social order in these new neighborhoods and, at the same time, maintain other urban services. It certainly didn't help cities like Baltimore, either, as their industry melted away. Tenants who had once formed part of the industrial army, who were supposed to be many of the tenants in the new projects, increasingly lost or never found the stability and income of employment's "honest eight." Moreover, once the Brooke Amendment (1969) linked residents' rents to their income, low incomes meant low rent receipts, making public housing maintenance that much more difficult. Long-term unemployment inevitably led to social disorder on a scale that tested government's basic capability not simply in public housing but also in neighborhoods across the city. Yet, there are examples of strong market cities, including Chicago, Paris, and London, that have had a quite mixed experience with public housing. Generalizations, our contributors find, turn out to have less salience than once thought.

20

Part I: Places

When analyzing public housing, it is a significant challenge to distinguish between public housing as a community and public housing as a series of buildings within an urban context. Because of the founding myth's power, the tendency of scholarship and reporting over the decades has been to treat public housing as a place removed from its social, economic, political, and neighborhood milieu. What we have been finding out, however, is that despite the goals of the early housing reformers to create islands of urban beauty and order, public housing is shaped primarily by its tenancy, management, and urban context.

The first chapter in the collection, Joseph Heathcott's "Myth #1: Public Housing Stands Alone," aims to reconnect public housing as a place to the cities in which it is located. This essay explores the ways in which the decline of public housing in St. Louis and elsewhere mirrored deteriorating metropolitan conditions more broadly. Rather than epitomizing the welfare state's allegedly poor social and physical design, as conventional wisdom holds, the failure of public housing developments like Pruitt-Igoe reflected the worsening state of many postwar cities in the American Rust Belt. St. Louis, for instance, lost hundreds of thousands of residents and most of its industrial and commercial base between the 1950s and 1980s. The collapse of public housing projects like Pruitt-Igoe had less to do with their inherent design qualities or tenancy than with the general collapse in city services and infrastructure as a result of deindustrialization. The hemorrhaging of population in the St. Louis urban center further complicated the ability of the St. Louis Housing Authority to maintain a tenant base that, from a financial or social perspective, could support and benefit from the high-cost, high-maintenance, high-rise public housing towers at Pruitt-Igoe.

The second chapter, "Myth #2: Modernist Architecture Failed Public Housing" by D. Bradford Hunt, takes on the distance between utopian notions and social reality directly. For many, architecture is to blame for public housing's downfall. Dreary modernism—especially in high-rise forms—sent a message of inferiority to public housing residents, deadened community life, and produced alien forms of living. But placing all the blame on modernist architects is unfair, according to Hunt. Architects worked within severe cost constraints due to bureaucratic imperatives and ambivalence about how well to build for the poor. Yet, the focus on architecture misses an even more important planning decision that affected numerous public housing communities around the country. In a desire to help families with children, public housing concentrated youth at historically unprecedented densities. In most communities—even in

21

baby-boom suburbs in the 1950s—adults outnumbered neighborhood youth. But in public housing, youths far outnumbered adults—by more than two to one in many projects across the country. Public housing's exceptional youth density had enormous consequences. Social order, as sociologists have explained, comes from adults policing shared community space in conjunction with authorities. Petty vandalism, youth violence, and other low-level problems require the supervision of public space by adults. But when youths far outnumber adults, social order becomes extraordinarily difficult. Hunt shows us that who lives in public housing—the design of the "unit mix"—is often more important than how public housing looks.

The third chapter in our collection, by Fritz Umbach and Alexander Gerould, also challenges a classic argument about public housing space and public security. "Myth #3: Public Housing Breeds Crime" can be traced in part to the exaggerated promises made in the early years about the potential impact of public housing on crime-ridden tenement neighborhoods. Public housing was touted as a remedy to inadequate sanitation and a cure-all for a variety of other urban ills; through the provision of quality housing and community goods, it was thought, the new neighborhoods would essentially eliminate crime. It did not take long to realize that public housing might not be the panacea for urban disorder that its original promoters envisioned. Unfortunately, the pendulum swung too far to the other side, and public housing residents were blamed for the high levels of crime in the projects. Umbach and Gerould, in their review of the different eras of public housing, found that public housing was once a safe environment, then a safe environment with a poor reputation (as a result of sloppy scholarship), and more lately, an unsafe environment that is finally receiving methodologically sophisticated crime studies. The authors demonstrate that public housing is not an essentially crime-ridden environment, even if in some cases it became that kind of environment over time.

The fourth chapter in the collection, "Myth #4: High-Rise Public Housing Is Unmanageable" by Nicholas Dagen Bloom, addresses more fallout from the early years of public housing myths. One of the central myths that helped promote public housing was the notion that new housing would reduce the costs to cities for municipal services. This new housing, according to erroneous claims, would eliminate problems such as tenement fires, disease, and general dilapidation in "slum" districts—urban regions that had imposed unwelcome and disproportionate costs upon municipalities. Because the new housing would be of such a higher quality than that which existed before, the tenants would no doubt be transformed into respectful and well-behaved citizenry. The reality on the ground in most public housing projects was less positive, and any significant savings over the decades remains quite debatable. The fireproof buildings of public housing projects may have endured, but the lower costs in services did not necessarily materialize. One city, New York, took a far less utopian view of public housing management. New York initially built large housing projects in order to achieve economies of scale and transform the city, but the city also created a dense network of housing custodians and managers on site who were put in place not only to clean the buildings but also to maintain control over tenants. This large staff still serves housing projects that house over four hundred thousand residents across the five boroughs. And NYCHA employees continue to keep a close eye on both physical property and tenant behavior through inspections, rent collection, and daily maintenance. New York's experience demonstrates that projects of a variety of scales, heights, and tenancy can be maintained, although there may be a high financial and social price to pay for this order.

Part II: Policy

In the United States, conventional wisdom holds that public housing fails to yield proper homes even for the poor. In much of Western Europe, social housing programs of the past variably targeted a wider spectrum of citizens; however, the European model has faced increasing criticism as more of it becomes targeted to the "residual" poor. To politicians of many stripes, public housing's long march away from utopian origins to urban disorder has turned support for such developments into a dangerous proposition that threatens their own careers and even their communities. Such a belief has become key to public housing's declining role in public policy in Western Europe and the United States. Recent public policy efforts have been aimed at inhibiting the construction of more affordable housing and eliminating what has already been constructed. In the United States, for instance, over the past twenty-five years, conventional public housing projects have declined in number, but other low-income housing policies have proliferated—including the creation of Section 8 vouchers (now part of the Housing Choice Vouchers Program) that tenants can use with private landlords; the construction of privately developed and privately managed project-based assistance; and the provision of additional subsidies through Low-Income Housing Tax Credits (LIHTC) (see Figure I.8). By looking at the wider context of public housing policies both in the United

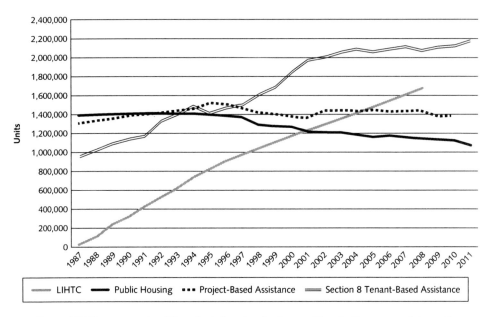

Figure I.8 The emergent public-private housing landscape: Twenty-five years of dramatic change.

States and elsewhere, the essays in this section raise probing questions about the essential nature of public housing policy as understood in the West.

One of the abiding myths of public housing history is that public housing came to an end in direct response to its problems. According to this myth, public housing was so inflexible that it could never be made to work; realizing this, politicians rightly ended the program in the 1970s. Yonah Freemark's chapter, "Myth #5: Public Housing Ended in Failure during the 1970s," disputes this myth and uncovers a more complex picture. In early 1973, the Nixon administration introduced an eighteen-month moratorium on new HUD expenditures, and by mid-1974, the federal commitment to new public housing—at least in the form that had existed since the 1930s—had been substantially eliminated. The literature suggests that this change in policy was motivated by a growing national consensus that the public housing program was too expensive and so poorly performing that it should be terminated. In fact, while opposition to "conventional" public housing founded on the program's perceived failures *did* exist in the early 1970s, these criticisms *did not* play the determining role in the administration's policy decisions. Rather, when pub-

24

lic housing was put on life support, it was undergoing a period of dramatic reinvention and growth that had expanded production, brought new financing techniques into the program, and garnered the support of bureaucrats from across the political spectrum, all indicating that prior to the moratorium there was no universal agreement about public housing's failure. A better explanation for the program's downfall was an ideological effort led by the Office of Management and Budget to reduce federal investments on "indirect" social programs such as federal low-income housing in favor of revenue sharing with states and localities and a guaranteed minimum income for poor households. In other words, public housing collapsed as much because of bureaucratic infighting as from any particular failure.

The rush to bury public policy mistakes of the past has led to programs of redevelopment that are addressed in Lawrence J. Vale's chapter, "Myth #6: Mixed-Income Redevelopment Is the Only Way to Fix Failed Public Housing." Since the early 1990s, the U.S. Congress has appropriated more than $6 billion under the HOPE VI program to facilitate the redevelopment of "severely distressed" public housing, and much of this has entailed the demolition of housing projects and their replacement with mixed-income communities. Although this has led to well over 250 redevelopment projects distributed across nearly every major city, there are four reasons why it is misguided to view mixed-income housing either as a panacea or as the only viable strategy for revitalizing distressed public housing. First, several cities have implemented successful redevelopment efforts *without* mixing incomes, both before the HOPE VI program began and under its auspices. Second, there is considerable variation from city to city in the ways that mixed-income housing has been interpreted and implemented, depending on housing market conditions and local political culture. Third, mixed-income development has been too loosely defined as a category. Finally, scholars and practitioners continue to debate the merits of mixed-income approaches: many of the assumed benefits of income mixing—such as role modeling—provide little positive impact on the lives of low-income people, whereas other aspects seem more promising, such as increased investment in neighborhoods and higher expectations for management.

The next chapter in Part II, Florian Urban's "Myth #7: Only Immigrants Still Live in European Public Housing," draws back the curtain on a widespread belief that public housing sank so low in Europe that only those with absolutely no choice would live in state-subsidized housing. The author discovered that while the marginalization of ethnic minorities is a serious problem in many European countries, the correlation of immigrants with public housing is rarely as clear-cut as in the suburbs of Paris. In Berlin, for example, the share of poor inhabitants with North African or Turkish ancestry was just about as high in nineteenth-century neighborhoods as in the public housing blocks of the 1960s—and in none do they constitute a majority. Urban's chapter focuses on Germany, where public housing is far more accepted among a middle-class nonimmigrant population than in the United States. In both Germany and France, the state authorities have always retained a responsibility for housing and on many occasions have renovated and upgraded their public housing estates.

Nancy Kwak's chapter, "Myth #8: Public Housing Is Only for Poor People," directly contradicts the fatalistic view of public housing in the United States and Europe. Singapore, like New York, cared less about the utopian vision than the economic benefits of state building. Kwak discusses the ways in which public housing can serve as a viable socioeconomic strategy for a developing nation such as Singapore. In that island nation, state provision jumpstarted the construction industry, raised living standards for the majority of citizens, and fostered greater political stability. Local leadership also created an innovative compulsory savings and homeownership program within the public housing system that helped increase domestic savings. By temporarily suspending market impact on housing price, Singaporean leaders removed most price volatility and ensured affordable shelter for the majority of its population. In this way, the Singaporean government successfully encouraged homeownership within the framework of a much more stable, state-managed public housing apparatus, even as it incentivized increased personal savings and reaped the political benefits of rising living standards. The city-state's massive public housing program was so successfully managed and executed that Singapore has since become a model for other nations—including, most prominently, China. Kwak finds that public housing can play a leading and largely positive role in urban and social development.

Part III: People

The residents of U.S. public housing have been treated shabbily in the literature for decades. The blatant fall from utopia may have conditioned the stereotype, but the switch from white to minority residency contributed enormously to the propagation of this negative vision in the media. Arguably, people of color are already at a disadvantage when it comes to media coverage, and a public housing setting adds a level of drama that is nearly irresistible. Sometimes tenants are lucky enough to be treated as victims of unfeeling administrators; other times, they are erroneously categorized as the shiftless and criminal undeserving poor. Certainly, there have been many unfeeling administrators over the years, and public housing has seen its share of criminal residents, but that's just a small part of the story. Less widely known are the stories of legions of public housing tenants who have fought for order in their communities or simply lived prosaic lives of quiet responsibility. The essays in this section address different dimensions of the fight for order. Public housing tenants may not always have exemplified the ideal that the housing reformers had in mind, but many took real action to maintain the dignity and order of these communities.

Fritz Umbach's chapter, "Myth #9: Public Housing Residents Hate the Police," tells a very different kind of story about public housing residents and crime. This essay maps the complex relationship that links tenants, management, and the police in NYCHA. Contrary to countless popular and scholarly depictions of hostility between nonwhite residents and the police as a fact of big city life, through the 1970s NYCHA tenants often embraced the officers of their separate police force, the Housing Authority Police Department, which existed from 1952 to 1992. At the same time, they applied pressure on officials to win tougher conditions of tenancy and law enforcement in their communities. Before the theory of community policing arrived in the 1980s, the practice was already alive and well in New York's public housing. From the 1950s through the 1970s, special housing authority cops (mostly black and Latino) walked their high-rise beats and worked closely with managers and NYCHA's largely minority residents to keep crime down. But this synergy did not survive the crisis years of the 1970s. Municipal labor politics and a burgeoning informal economy caused cops and residents to part ways, even as crime rates soared. NYCHA's sprawling red brick complexes were neither the dysfunctional wastelands imagined by social scientists nor the hulking ruins of failed social engineering invoked more recently by neoconservatives. Instead, "the PJs"—as residents often called their homes—served as largely unheralded sites of minority anticrime mobilization.

Public housing residents were also not the passive pawns of social policy and public housing, as Rhonda Y. Williams demonstrates in her chapter, "Myth #10: Public Housing Tenants Are Powerless." Williams shows how this myth fails to align with the experience of many residents in Baltimore. Simply because the tenants failed to save public housing should not be taken as an indicator of their complete powerlessness on the urban scene. This chapter tracks the ways in which public housing activism in Baltimore and other cities translated into wider political participation by women. If many see the difficulties of public housing tenancy, few recognize that it also served as an entryway into political participation for underrepresented social groups. Tenant activists—most of them women—responded to and shaped public housing conditions and legislation from the local to the federal level. In doing so, the activists often remade the parameters of Great Society antipoverty programs. Many of these public housing leaders, in turn, became part of a national movement of poor black women in the welfare and tenants' rights struggles of the late 1960s and 1970s.

Lisa Levenstein's chapter, "Myth #11: Tenants Did Not Invest in Public Housing," illustrates how black women in Philadelphia challenged the postwar city's racial and gender inequalities by seeking a variety of resources from government programs. These resources, including subsidized housing, provided them with badly needed leverage in their relations with employers and men—even as such public programs subjected their largely African American beneficiaries to intensive surveillance and public humiliation. Although poor women initially embraced the city's public housing complexes, where modern conveniences provided the trappings of a much-desired respectability, deteriorating conditions pushed the tenant activists in directions that often varied from the goals of national civil rights organizations. This analysis of public housing residents details how such women became active agents without formally participating in a traditional social movement; it counters stereotypes that have long plagued public debate about minority women, the stereotypical "welfare queen," in both public housing and poor neighborhoods generally.

True, public housing did not usher in utopia, as our contributors document. But that outcome makes the story more rather than less significant. The places, policies, and people in this collection—too-often filed together under the rough heading of "public housing and its problems"—defy the easy moral parables so beloved by the public, reporters, and many academics. Housing authorities both here and abroad have maintained many projects; housing policies and projects developed and changed for reasons other than a failure gene buried in public housing's DNA. Likewise, the residents of public housing often influenced public housing life in unexpected directions. The editors and contributors apologize in advance for replacing simple answers and stereotypes with complexity. Yet, such an important dimension of twentieth-century urban life, where millions still live, merits this detailed, evenhanded treatment.

I. Places

PUBLIC HOUSING
STANDS ALONE

Joseph Heathcott

One of the most durable myths about public housing in the United States is that it stands alone, operating in isolation from the city and neighborhoods that surround it. The very terms that we use to describe public housing— "housing project" or "the projects"—encapsulate this myth of distinctiveness and separation. After all, we seldom refer to a suburban neighborhood as a "housing project"; instead, we use terms like "subdivision" that suggest belonging to something greater. While this essay uses the term "project" to refer to particular public housing sites, it is with the understanding that it is a vernacular rather than technical term.

Certainly the architectural and spatial condition of public housing, from rigidly drawn boundaries to tower-and-slab construction, reinforces perceptions of separateness. The common identification of public housing as a landscape produced by the federal government, while inaccurate, isolates projects from the political life of neighborhoods and cities. The wide variety of rules, regulations, and criteria for living in public housing seem to separate it as a form of tenancy from most private rental markets. Perhaps most ironically, the response by housing authorities to the decline of projects in their portfolios— barbed wire fencing, consolidation of tenants into fewer buildings, deferred maintenance, and demolition—provide the most dramatic iconography of separateness.

The forensic efforts to account for the decline of public housing have largely reinforced the idea of projects as islands apart. Nowhere has this been more evident than in the cottage industry of criticism surrounding Pruitt-Igoe, a large housing project constructed in St. Louis, Missouri, in the mid-1950s. Even the titles of now-classic texts encapsulate the myth, from Lee Rainwater's *Behind Ghetto Walls: Black Families in a Federal Slum* to William Moore's *Vertical*

Ghetto: Everyday Life in an Urban Slum.[1] This chapter compares Pruitt-Igoe with projects in other cities in order to dismantle the myth that the fate of public housing projects are somehow separate from the fate of the cities and regions of which they are a part.

The Federal Role

While clearly a federal program, the U.S. government did not build, own, or maintain public housing. Nor did passage of the Housing Act of 1937 (also called the Wagner-Steagall Housing Act of 1937) guarantee the production of public housing everywhere in America. Rather, the principles of federalism required an intricate series of steps to coordinate the various levels of government. In the end, despite the centrally distributed funding allocations, expenditure requirements, and technical specifications, public housing emerged as an intensely local affair.

The Housing Act of 1937 established the United States Housing Authority (USHA), along with a series of regional public housing authorities (PHAs). The USHA and its successor agencies provided capital, technical service, and oversight to localities undertaking public housing development. First, however, it was up to the states to opt in to the program. States had to pass legislation that enabled cities to create state-chartered municipal corporations called "housing authorities," to exempt these entities from taxation, and to provide them with powers of eminent domain. The cities, for their part, also had to opt in, but they could do so only if their state had passed enabling legislation—cities were not to have a direct relationship with the federal government.[2]

Once state legislation existed, city lawmakers were required to pass ordinances of their own to request a state charter for an authority and to define the scope and limits of its operation. In most cases, a freestanding commission governed the housing authority, with appointments made by the mayor, city council, and governor or designee acting in concert. Typically the commission reflected the supporters of the local regime, with representatives from downtown business interests, civic organizations, religious groups, and professionals. In some cities, particularly in the Northeast and Midwest, housing commissions included representatives from African American communities and from organized labor—especially the building trades. The commission hired the executive director, who in turn hired and managed the staff. How involved the mayor or other power brokers were in the selection of housing authority directors differed from city to city. In Chicago and St. Louis, for example, mayors treated the local housing authority as a political spoil. In Cincinnati and New York, however, housing authorities exercised significant independence in staffing their ranks.

To undertake public housing development, local legislatures first had to pass ordinances to declare areas "blighted" before housing authorities could compel land purchases, clear slums, and build new projects. The selection of sites was always one of the primary prerogatives of the local regime and reflected the political, economic, and racial preferences of civic elites. Moreover, in cities such as Los Angeles and Houston, where labor unions were weak, Cold War–inspired attacks on public housing programs stalled the expansion of the program.[3] In cities with strong and politically connected unions—Chicago, New York, St. Louis, and Philadelphia among them—public housing production reached the maximum capacity authortized by the government.

Funds to develop projects came from congressional appropriations to the USHA, which were then channeled through the regional PHAs. These appropriations covered up to 90 percent of the cost to compensate property owners, clear the site, upgrade infrastructure, and construct the buildings. Most of these funds, however, did not come in the form of grants; rather, the federal government funded public housing through long-term (sixty-year), interest-free mortgage loans to the local housing authority. Local authorities retired these loan debts primarily through locally arranged bond issues, not direct federal taxpayer subsidy.[4]

Finally, while housing authorities received small annual contributions from the federal government to close the gap between income and expenditures, the bulk of operations and maintenance had to be funded through tenant rents. This system of federal contributions and tenant-financed operations proved to be a politically charged issue in the annual congressional appropriations process and turned out to be disastrous for cities like St. Louis, where public housing faced increasing vacancy rates *beginning in the 1960s*.

Designing and Locating Public Housing

American public housing advocates championed the European superblock form and modernist design approach that characterized nearly all projects built before 1968. Perhaps more than any other feature, the consolidation of numerous individual properties into large superblocks with well-defined perimeters enhanced the common view of public housing as a place apart.

In 1933, the National Industrial Recovery Act authorized the Public Works Administration (PWA) to develop housing targeted to families that could afford to pay higher rent but could not find decent housing. Working first through local limited dividend corporations and then through direct financing, the PWA realized over fifty projects, including the Carl Mackley Homes in Philadelphia, Harlem River Houses in New York, Lakeview Terrace in Cleveland, and Techwood Homes in Atlanta.[5] With their low-rise profiles, careful landscape designs, and numerous amenities, PWA projects constitute some of the best government-backed housing ever built. Still, the PWA program proved too costly and slow to have any effect on the nation's critical shortage of decent, affordable housing.

After 1937, the USHA projects grew more austere in their designs, reflecting sharp cuts in funding through periods of depression, war, and recession. Projects such as the Ida B. Wells Homes in Chicago, San Felipe Courts in Houston, Elyton Village in Birmingham, and Puerta de Tierra in San Juan arrayed relatively featureless buildings in barracks formations with minimal landscaping or amenities. Nevertheless, early residents routinely reported that the projects offered a substantial improvement in the quality of their living environment. Many experienced indoor plumbing, central heat, and on-site services for the first time.[6]

After World War II, many housing authorities in larger cities began to add high-rise tower blocks to their portfolio. While nearly three-quarters of all public housing units were distributed in low- and mid-rise buildings, the tower blocks garnered the most attention for their immense scale and stark transformation of the urban landscape. In Philadelphia, planners favored a mix of high-rise and low-rise buildings. By contrast, and with much national fanfare, St. Louis bundled all of its postwar federal allotment of fifty-eight hundred units into four massive high-rise projects.[7] Officials in Boston, Baltimore, Chicago, and New York built dozens of new projects within the vertical tower block form.

Regardless of the design of projects, the selection of sites reflected an intensely local set of determinations. Cities like St. Louis, for example, used public housing to deepen racial segregation and to prevent what city planner Harland Bartholomew described as "Negro deconcentration" from inner core neighborhoods.[8] Chicago officials saw public housing as a way to construct a great wall of exclusion that would amplify racial and class barriers along a north-south corridor of the city.[9] In Philadelphia, on the other hand, the priorities of officials shifted dramatically. Before World War II, housing advocates in Philadelphia succeeded in making slum clearance and decent affordable housing the key determinants of site selection. After the war, officials came to see public housing as a reservoir for sheltering families displaced from massive urban renewal sites; redevelopment, rather than public housing, emerged as their overarching priority.[10]

The St. Louis Program

As local officials sorted out their priorities for project development, the United States faced a mounting housing crisis. From the stock market crash of 1929 through the Great Depression and World War II, new housing starts plummeted to historic lows. After the war, with millions of GIs returning stateside and forming families, the need for new home construction became acute. Between 1932 and 1945, the USHA had managed to produce only two hundred thousand permanent units of public housing. But planners estimated that at least three million new units would be needed immediately. It was in this climate of crisis that Congress passed the U.S. Housing Act of 1949.[11]

The St. Louis public housing program took shape in this context of urban population growth coupled with decades of boom and bust in housing markets. This combination resulted in overcrowded tenement neighborhoods and deteriorating conditions in the daily life of the city. For Bartholomew, the city planner in St. Louis, the chief solution to the problem was large-scale slum clearance to rebuild the city at higher densities with improved housing.[12]

The Housing Act of 1937 came just in time for Bartholomew and his fellow housing advocates; it seemed to offer the precise framework they needed to begin urban reconstruction. However, a series of local and state court challenges delayed the implementation of public housing in St. Louis. The St. Louis Housing Authority (SLHA) would not break ground on the first two projects, Clinton-Peabody and Carr Square Village, until 1940. Further delays followed when the United States entered into World War II, which diverted funds from public housing. It would take five years from the passage of the Housing Act of 1937 for St. Louis to complete its first two projects. A third project, begun in 1942, had to be halted after site clearance but before construction due to lack of funds. The site remained empty for the next decade.

Meanwhile, throughout World War II and the early postwar years, the city boiled under a pressure cooker of housing scarcity. In one survey conducted just before the end of the war in April of 1945, whites and blacks both faced a rental market with about 0.5 percent vacancy; 321 vacancies existed out of sixty-four thousand rental units for whites, and 108 vacancies out of twenty-two thousand rental units for blacks. St. Louis, like most cities in the United States, faced dire circumstances as families doubled up and rooming houses proliferated.[13]

To address the crisis, Senator Robert Wagner introduced a housing bill to Congress in 1948. Both Harland Bartholomew and St. Louis mayor Joseph Darst testified before Congress on behalf of the bill. Once passed, however, the Housing Act of 1949 differed from its 1937 predecessor in that it was not, at its core, about public housing. Rather, the law sought to expand housing production in a variety of ways. Title I of the act inaugurated "urban redevelopment," where federal dollars wrote down the cost of slum clearance for new residential, civic, and commercial construction. Title II authorized an increase of $500 million for the FHA mortgage insurance program, largely to underwrite the rapid construction of private single-family homes on peripheral greenfield sites. Title III revived public housing with a commitment of 810,000 new units.

While each of the three titled programs ran largely independent of the others, over time they exerted a cumulative, often crossed-purpose impact on the American metropolis. The "suburban" Title II, with its higher initial investment and longer-term commitments, dwarfed the "urban" Titles I and III. Between 1945 and 1965, the FHA-backed home building industry constructed twenty-six million new homes. Public housing, meanwhile, constituted only 3 percent of new home construction in the same period. To date, the FHA has insured over thirty-four million mortgages, predominantly in new single-family home construction outside of central cities. Along with the GI Bill, the FHA mortgage insurance system dramatically expanded single-family home ownership and democratized private housing as an asset class.[14] It reshaped the American city, pulling millions of mostly white middle-class families to newly built tract housing in peripheral subdivisions.

Nevertheless, officials in cities around the United States welcomed the "urban provisions" of the Housing Act. Immediately after its passage, the SLHA resurrected plans for its third public housing development, now called Cochran Gardens. Unlike the first two projects, which took shape as two-story row houses in barracks formation, Cochran Gardens was the first to deploy high-rise towers, in a mix of four-, six-, and twelve-story buildings. Moreover, the SLHA continued the practice of segregated development. Carr

Square Village and Clinton-Peabody had been constructed for black and white occupancy respectively, Cochran Gardens for white occupancy.[15]

Armed with federal appropriations for fifty-eight hundred units, St. Louis officials made the dramatic announcement that they would bundle all of these into "four vast projects." The first of these would come to be known as Pruitt-Igoe. The Wendell O. Pruitt Homes, the city's fourth project, and the William Igoe Apartments, the city's fifth project, were sited adjacent to each other. Designed by Minoru Yamasaki, they took shape as a regiment of thirty-three nearly identical eleven-story tower blocks, with over twenty-seven hundred apartments on fifty-seven acres of land. Together, they were the largest of the nation's postwar housing projects to date, receiving significant attention in the press.[16]

At the same time, the SLHA continued the practice of racial segregation in site selection and occupancy of public housing. They conceived Pruitt for black families and Igoe for white families, introducing a radical separation of whites and blacks in a neighborhood that was racially mixed. However, even before tenants moved in, the certainty of segregation unraveled with the U.S. Supreme Court decision in Brown v. Board of Education of Topeka in 1954. As a result, white residents fled or dropped off the waiting lists, and Pruitt-Igoe was effectively rendered an all-black development.

The city's sixth project, the Vaughan-Taylor Homes, rose up next to Pruitt-Igoe in 1957 on the city's north side. While not officially segregated, the adjacence to Pruitt-Igoe meant that white families avoided Vaughan-Taylor, and it rapidly became an all-black project. Likewise, the seventh project, Darst-Webbe, located on the predominantly white south side, was effectively an all-white project when it was completed in 1962. Finally, the city's eighth and final conventional project, Blumeyer Homes, was located on the near north side— an area that in the late 1960s was transitioning rapidly to a predominantly black neighborhood.[17]

After the national termination of the conventional public housing program by the Nixon administration in 1969, the SLHA constructed several more small and mid-sized projects, mostly through the Turnkey Program organized by the Department of Housing and Urban Development (HUD); Turnkey is a proposal-based method of public housing rehabilitation and/or construction that awards federal funds to local PHAs; these PHAs, in turn, select private developers based on submitted proposals outlining their work plans. But the vast majority of SLHA tenants lived in the large conventional projects, which

37

by the early 1960s housed some eighteen thousand people in fifty-five hundred apartments. Even at this height of occupancy, however, cracks in the system began to show, as Pruitt and Igoe both began to post troubling vacancy rates. Was it evidence of a problem internal to the public housing program, or did it signal a deeper set of shifts in the urban condition?

The Flight of Capital and People

While the older industrial cities of the Northeast and Midwest underwent large-scale reconstruction through urban renewal and public housing in the 1960s, they also began to lose population as qualifying families moved to new suburban developments, and as American demographic growth shifted to the South and the West. Detroit, for example, lost 20 percent of its population between 1950 and 1970. The population of St. Louis fell by 27 percent over the same period as 60 percent of the white population fled the city, while the suburban population more than doubled. Philadelphia, Cleveland, Baltimore, and many other cities also lost substantial numbers of people in the decades after World War II.

The systematic dislocation of capital from central cities is a long-term process with roots in the early twentieth century. However, after World War II, industrial facilities began a rapid decampment from the urban core, spurred on by the rise of the trucking industry, new highway and road systems, stable fuel prices, and new flexible manufacturing technologies. This process resulted in staggering losses of well-paying industrial jobs that once sustained working-class families, along with a steep decline in the corporate tax base. As white middle-class families fled cities in search of better employment and housing opportunities, they took their wages and taxes with them. As a result, cities found themselves struggling to support an increasingly poor and elderly population with fewer and fewer resources.[18]

St. Louis experienced these dislocations more acutely than most cities. While the loss of manufacturing jobs and population from the urban core was not greater than that experienced in other industrial cities like Detroit or Philadelphia, the peculiar division between the City of St. Louis and St. Louis County meant that the city's urban core suffered more acutely from these losses. The City of St. Louis was a county in its own right (a condition established in 1876), hemmed in by St. Louis County and, therefore, prevented from expanding. It received no share of taxes from St. Louis County, where much of the new industrial and residential development occurred after the 1950s. Thus, unlike many cities, it could not use annexation to chase population loss or new industrial areas.[19]

Meanwhile, FHA-backed white flight from St. Louis and other cities opened up residential opportunities for black families in neighborhoods once off limits. At the same time, the push by African Americans and civil rights groups for fair and open housing challenged the racial covenants, steerage, and redlining that had long kept black urban dwellers trapped in segregated neighborhoods. These tensions culminated in Title VII of the 1968 Civil Rights Act. As black families spread out into the metropolis, they created new succession processes. By the 1960s, for example, black middle-class families could increasingly secure housing in formerly all-white St. Louis neighborhoods—and even in the suburbs of St. Louis County. Working-class African Americans, in turn, moved into the neighborhoods once occupied by the black middle class.[20]

This metropolitan-wide succession chain eventually created a shift in residential options for black families that filtered down to public housing. According to the Rand Corporation's 1973 report on St. Louis, the acute housing shortage that once propelled officials to construct projects had reversed—and it did so in St. Louis before most other cities, largely due to the relationship between political boundaries, population and manufacturing decline, and the structure of housing markets.[21] Consequently, the St. Louis Housing Authority began to see increasing vacancy rates in some of its projects well before other cities. Since the maintenance of projects had to come from tenant rents, vacancies spelled looming disaster for public housing in St. Louis. And the amount of annual contributions provided to housing authorities could no longer cover the gap.

Thus, beginning in St. Louis in the 1960s and spreading to other cities in the 1970s and 1980s, housing authorities were forced to defer maintenance, resulting in the acceleration of project decline. In cities such as Boston and New York, where population losses were relatively small, housing authorities could still cover most of their operating costs, albeit with some deferred maintenance, well into the 1980s and 1990s. However, in St. Louis, with its dramatic population loss, the vacancy rates rose so rapidly that the projects spiraled into severe physical dereliction. As federal commitments to public housing declined after 1968, cities around the country began to experience what St. Louis already knew well: the rapid deterioration of conventional public housing.[22]

Slouching toward Pruitt-Igoe

There have been many attempts over the past three decades to understand "what went wrong" with public housing. Much of U.S. housing policy today, from Section 8 to Low Income Tax Credits to HOPE VI, has emerged from efforts to isolate and identify the causes of public housing's decline. Nowhere was this effort more intense than around the Pruitt-Igoe public housing project. Beginning in the mid-1960s, scholars, journalists, and activists mounted a critique of public housing that drew largely on Pruitt-Igoe as a touchstone. Most of these critiques sought causes internal to Pruitt-Igoe and the public housing program.

Some observers saw in Pruitt-Igoe a story of good intentions gone awry, while others concluded that public housing was doomed from the outset by its own policy shortcomings.[23] Still others felt that Pruitt-Igoe declined because its modernist design precluded the direct surveillance necessary for preventing crime and promoting security.[24] Most critics found in Pruitt-Igoe a cautionary tale about the hubris of liberalism, the shortcomings of the welfare state, or the failure of modern architecture and planning.[25]

Debates over the causes of public housing decline have intensified over the years, as more scholars weigh in with improved data, deeper analyses, and sharpened arguments. Arnold Hirsch's landmark book *Making the Second Ghetto* (1983) placed public housing's troubles in the longer history of racial segregation and white hostility toward residential integration—a thesis reinforced by subsequent scholarship.[26] Leading housing policy experts have pointed to the legacy of shortsightedness built in to the original Wagner-Steagall law—for example, in requiring operation and maintenance costs to be covered by tenant rents, or in the burden of the annual appropriations process.[27] Others have documented the corrosive impact of drugs, crime, police surveillance, and violence on project residents and on public housing programs generally.[28]

All of these factors, varying by time and place, have played a role in the seemingly intractable problems related to public housing. But they cannot alone or even in combination explain the fate of the conventional public housing program. Indeed, most accounts have sought to identify causes of decline from within the specific policies, designs, populations, or environments of the projects. Several key internal themes emerge from this literature.

The most common internal theme is that Pruitt-Igoe declined because of its uncritical adoption of modernist tower block design by architects enthralled with the Corbusier vision.[29] Writers like Charles Jencks argued, without even the barest evidence, that the identical regiments of buildings created inhuman environments that fostered anger and anomie among residents. Other critics such as Oscar Newman focused on specific design choices employed at Pruitt-Igoe and other projects, such as skip-stop elevators, the lack of lavatories on ground floors, and broad galleries meant to create "streets in the sky." Newman argued, with some justification, that the high-rise configuration, skip-stop elevators and galleries exacerbated crime because they prevented easy surveillance, while the absence of bathrooms on the ground floors led children to pee in the stairwells.

However, architects differed widely in their embrace of international style modernism, and not all of them employed tower block design out of aesthetic conviction. Pruitt-Igoe architect Minoru Yamasaki, for example, did not favor the high-rise approach. His initial concept for the project included a mix of low-rise townhouses, medium-rise garden apartments, and a few high-rise towers.[30] Several factors intervened, however, none of which were intrinsically about design. Federal cost cutting during the Korean War and the subsequent recession of July 1953 through May 1954 reduced the amount of funds available for housing projects around the country; the solution at Pruitt-Igoe and elsewhere was to go vertical. This dovetailed with the interests of the local political regime, who had far more power to make design choices than the architects did. Bartholomew favored high-rises because they would provide the maximum number of units on the minimal amount of land. Mayor Joseph Darst embraced the high-rise design for St. Louis projects because their dramatic profiles gained his city and administration a great deal of attention and provided a visible symbol of progress.[31]

The design of high-rise public housing—however flawed some of its innovations might have been—was never inherently problematic; rather, it was made problematic by circumstances that had little to do with design as such. Indeed, architectural historian Katharine Bristol suggests that the deployment of Pruitt-Igoe as a symbol in the assault on modernism had much more to do with an Oedipal crisis in the architectural profession than with any kind of evidence-based account.[32] As early as 1973, critic Jane Holtz Kay dismissed the reigning idea that modern design caused the failure of Pruitt-Igoe. Writing against the grain, she argued that Pruitt-Igoe was being used as a scapegoat to legitimize new design approaches. "How easy it is," she quipped in *The Nation*, "to see failed architecture as King Kong and new architecture as Moses."[33] In his exhaustive study of the St. Louis public housing program, policy analyst

Eugene Meehan found "no consistent pattern linking building height and patterns of occupancy." Throughout the St. Louis pubic housing system, for example, he noted that "upper levels in the taller buildings had better occupancy rates than lower floors."[34] And the infamous galleries, pilloried by architectural critics such as Oscar Newman, actually worked as intended for at least the first ten years of the project, until rising crime rates rendered them unsafe.

Most problematic for the "decline by design" theme, however, is the simple fact that physical dereliction has never been limited to public housing. Modernist high-rise projects might very well have housed anomic and angry residents, but was that the result of design or of the broader urban conditions—poverty, segregation, crumbling schools, police brutality, and loss of employment and opportunity—that seemed to affect all inner city residents? The riots that erupted in Watts, Detroit, and Newark were by no means limited to housing projects: they were general revolts of inner city residents fed up with the conditions in which they lived. Public and private neighborhoods in North St. Louis deteriorated alongside one another, despite their radically different design histories. And they deteriorated for much the same reasons: deferred maintenance, abandonment, neglect, and loss of fiscal base caused by massive population loss.[35] Meanwhile, in New York City, many middle-class families lived in apartments very much like the housing projects that exist throughout the city. Apart from subtle landscaping differences, for example, it is difficult to tell middle-income Stuyvesant Town from the nearby Jacob Riis Houses or Campos Plaza. Indeed, many people around the world continue to live in high-rise apartments, pubic and private alike, with varying degrees of success.[36]

Another common internal theme is that Pruitt-Igoe declined because of crime, vandalism, and the character of tenants. Henry Schmandt and George Wendel argued that at Pruitt-Igoe, the tenant selection process saddled high-rise projects with families that supposedly lacked the "urban skills" necessary to live in such environments.[37] Again, Meehan disputed this notion and criticized many of the studies by sociologists that focused on tenants' lives in the projects rather than the structural conditions of public housing.[38] Moreover, police reports from the 1960s indicate that violent crime rates were no higher—and were often lower—in Pruitt-Igoe than in many of the low-rise neighborhoods on the city's north side. The crime rates at Pruitt-Igoe began to spike only in the late 1960s, when the SLHA started to move tenants out of high vacancy buildings, resulting in an increasingly abandoned project land-scape. In the end, the crime and vandalism plaguing public housing in the 1970s and 1980s was never all that distinct from the crime and vandalism that residents experienced in many older, low-rise neighborhoods.[39]

Finally, one of the most persistent internal themes holds that public housing declined because of weak policy and bad management. For many scholars, journalists, and pundits on the left and the right, public housing policy was always inherently flawed. For some, it undermined "self-initiative," corroded social relations, and distorted otherwise naturally occurring free markets. With no small amount of hyperbole, for example, Manhattan Institute scholar Howard Husock labeled public housing as "American's trillion-dollar policy mistake."[40] For others, public housing policy was a "programmed failure" due to its own internal contradictions.[41] Even Henry Cisneros, the secretary of Housing and Urban Development under President Bill Clinton, reproduced this narrative as a way to burnish his administration's record in overhauling public housing's "past failures" through the HOPE VI program.[42]

To be sure, the public housing program in America suffered from many policy deficiencies, from the formative practice of racial segregation in occupancy, to the time-consuming and inefficient annual appropriations process, to the requirement that operating and capital replacement costs be paid out of tenant rents. But the bigger policy failure had less to do with the public housing program per se, and more to do with the contradictory outcomes of the broader landscape of U.S. housing policy. That we do not refer to the massive FHA-backed suburbanization of America as a kind of public housing is merely a convention of language—after all, both were heavily subsidized, and both made considerable profits for large developers. And in any case, public housing projects can hardly be blamed for keeping poor people dependent on federal relief; that has much more to do with massive, even global shifts in the industrial economy and the staggering loss of good-paying jobs in the urban core.[43]

Public housing performance has differed from city to city, from project to project, and even from building to building within projects. In the case of Chicago, for example, historian Bradford Hunt has exposed a long history of mismanagement and poor decision making that exacerbated the local conditions of an already compromised federal program.[44] However, Nicholas Bloom's work on the case of New York City finds that, despite problems and missteps by the New York City Housing Authority over the years, the public housing program was relatively well managed, even in the face of the city's fiscal collapse.[45] And within the St. Louis program, Eugene Meehan found that "levels of occupancy in the twelve-story buildings at Cochran Gardens were far better than occupancy in the eight-story buildings at Vaughan," and that the more severe austerity practiced at Pruitt-Igoe resulted in the use of inferior hardware and other cost-cutting measures that contributed to the project's dramatic decline.[46] Further studies have shown that the older stock of public housing built by the Public Works Administration fared better than much of the stock built after the passage of the 1937 Housing Act.[47] And despite the dramatic decline at Pruitt-Igoe in the 1960s, there is no evidence of mismanagement by Housing Authority director Irving Dagen; on the contrary, Dagen brought a far more progressive approach to managing the public housing program than his successors. But even the best management could not have succeeded under the stark social and fiscal conditions that beset programs in St. Louis, Chicago, Detroit, Philadelphia, and other cities in the Rust Belt.

Even while architects, journalists, planners, and policy analysts honed the internal themes outlined above, a few scholars began to look beyond the projects for clues. Among the first to do so was architectural educator Roger Montgomery. As early as 1966, he dismissed the overdetermined power of architecture to solve the residential problems of poor people. In an exchange with sociologist Lee Rainwater, Montgomery argued that architects' capacity to improve housing conditions through design was limited.[48] In an important though much-overlooked essay, Montgomery shifted the analysis of Pruitt-Igoe's demise from design, management, and programming to the structure of the St. Louis housing market.[49]

Montgomery and his supporters noted that Pruitt-Igoe had been built for a city of 850,000 people facing a massive housing shortage. But even before it was completed, white middle-class and working-class families began their long flight from cities, opening up new housing opportunities for blacks through residential succession, and eventually through the application of fair housing laws. This loosening of housing markets undermined the very premise of public housing, which had been built on the expectation of inexorable urban growth and the specter of the overcrowded city. By 1970, that spectral city no longer existed. St. Louis had lost over two hundred thousand people, with plummeting real estate values and rising rates of vacancy and abandonment. Increased vacancy rates in housing projects led to a rapid spiral of decline: fewer tenants meant less rental income, which resulted in smaller operating and maintenance funds, which led to physical deterioration, which in turn pushed more tenants out. In the last days of Pruitt-Igoe, drug sellers and crime networks from other parts of St. Louis began to carve up the nearly empty project. Subsequent studies that positioned Pruitt-Igoe in the context of the local political economy support Montgomery's conclusions.[50]

The core problems that beset public housing in the twentieth century were always the same as those faced by cities more generally. Cities could not keep capital and people from flowing out of their boundaries. And cities could not unilaterally fix broken federal policies that worked at cross-purposes: on the one hand, slum clearance, urban renewal, and public housing were meant to improve cities, but the massive subsidies of suburban housing, expressways, and cheap fossil fuels gradually eroded the wealth base of cities—and, in St. Louis, dramatically reduced the number of people who relied on public housing for their principal shelter. Meanwhile, the deterioration of St. Louis city services such as schools, street repairs, fire protection, and trash collection made the difficult conditions of Pruitt-Igoe and its surrounding neighborhoods even worse.[51] What is clear from the relatively short career of project-based public housing is that its varied successes and failures resulted from an interwoven set of contingent circumstances, major and minor policy decisions, geographic locations, and political and economic conditions well beyond the control of any housing authority.

Conclusion

The fate of Pruitt-Igoe was a canary in the coal mine, but not in the way it is often portrayed. Rather than embodying the failure of modernist design, federal policy, or the social welfare state, the challenges faced at Pruitt-Igoe signaled massive seismic shifts under way in northeastern and midwestern cities through capital flight, disinvestment, suburbanization, and population decline. These shifts registered first at Pruitt-Igoe because the scale of population and job loss in St. Louis was so severe and rapid there, and the tools available to planners and officials to mitigate the disaster were so limited by the city's fixed boundaries. The same processes gripped Chicago and New York, for example, but at a slower rate, allowing for more adjustments over time.

Through all of these transformations, Pruitt-Igoe doggedly remained a symbol of failed government policies, and the blast image made its way into dozens of textbooks in planning, policy, social science, and architecture. It became the classic cautionary tale, the go-to symbol either for the failure of modern urban planning and design or for the shortcomings of the welfare state.[52]

In 1992, when HUD secretary Jack Kemp and President George Bush announced the initiative that would become HOPE VI, they made explicit reference to Pruitt-Igoe as an example of failed liberal policies of the past. The critical discourse surrounding Pruitt-Igoe, then, informed the winding down of conventional public housing as well as the programs created to replace it.

In the end, the architectural and spatial distinctiveness of public housing has long obscured the fundamental ways in which the projects are woven into the fabric of their cities. Pruitt-Igoe had been conceived and built for an overcrowded city, where future growth in population and industrial employment were assumed. Unfortunately, by the time the first tenants moved in to the project, that imagined city of the future was already beginning to unravel. In the most important ways, then, the fate of public housing in America has always been closely tied to the politics, economies, and cultures of the cities in which it exists. If we do not pay attention to these factors, we are bound to repeat the problems that beset public housing in the first place.

MODERNIST ARCHITECTURE FAILED PUBLIC HOUSING

D. Bradford Hunt

For many critics and the general public, the obvious explanation for public housing's problems lies with its architecture. Large-scale projects designed in a stripped-down modernist style created a dreary aesthetic that stigmatized public housing residents rather than uplift them. Buildings that looked like institutional barracks symbolized society's ambivalence, at best, toward its least fortunate members, and public housing inextricably linked architecture to social status. "Warehousing the poor" is an often-heard phrase that succinctly sums up the critique.[1] Architects and politicians are blamed, in essence, for designing projects to serve as long-term storage for racial minorities rather than as functioning, wholesome communities. If only officials had gotten the architecture right and not built cheap-looking, dysfunctional projects—and especially not high-rise buildings—then public housing outcomes would have been far different. This myth, which posits that modernist architecture is to blame for public housing failure, has never actually accounted for the complex interaction between design and social outcomes.[2]

This critique also has a long history. In 1957, housing activist Catherine Bauer bemoaned the postwar turn to dreary high-rise public housing and the wholesale slum clearance that preceded it. Four years later, Jane Jacobs attacked the assumptions of postwar city planning and articulated a defense of neighborhood diversity, contrasting the organic interactions on the streets of her Greenwich Village neighborhood with the anonymity of public housing projects. Oscar Newman's *Defensible Space* (1972) added social science heft to Jacobs's observations by analyzing the designs of building entrances and the allocation of common space in New York projects that resulted in different rates of disorder and crime. Later scholars continued the dissection of architectural modernism as a soulless experience, while satirists like Tom Wolfe skewered it as a self-inflicted disaster abetted by institutions under the spell of avant-garde architects.[3]

Blaming architectural design choices, however, is too simple an explanation for public housing's struggles in the United States.[4] In every major city, privately owned projects of marginal architectural attraction still house countless numbers of people—even poor families—at relatively high population densities and without unusual difficulties. Furthermore, in New York City, as Nicholas Bloom argues, high-rise public housing continues to serve as viable housing for the poor.[5] Pointing to modernist architecture, then, is not only insufficient but perhaps also misleading in any effort to understand public housing's struggles.

The focus on architecture distracts from other more relevant policy and planning choices that more directly shaped public housing outcomes. This chapter explores only one of those choices in depth: the concentration of youth at historically unprecedented densities.[6] High youth densities (measured as the ratio of youths to adults) destabilized many public housing communities, aggravated maintenance problems, decreased social order, and helped drive out working-class families. Nowhere was this more true than in Chicago, whose projects had extraordinary youth densities that contributed to dysfunction and led to the spectacular collapse of the Chicago Housing Authority (CHA).

The argument here is not that youth density is all-determining in a project's fate; nor is it that architectural design is irrelevant. As other chapters in this volume show, public housing's decline is multicausal and the result of numerous forces and policy choices. Counterproductive rent incentives, ineffective property management, insufficient federal subsidies, and racially discriminatory site selection hamstrung projects in Chicago and around the country. But this chapter focuses on youth density because it has been neglected in the literature on public housing and because it exacerbated the crucial task of maintaining social order in a large-scale, low-income development. The youth density argument also shifts emphasis away from the aesthetics of public housing and toward an understanding of the planning parameters essential to sustain a reasonably healthy public housing community.

Chicago's Public Housing

The literature on Chicago has centered on the egregious racism that pervaded the city's site selection process. As early as 1955, Martin Meyerson and Edward Banfield published a detailed account of the politics of site selection,

Figure 2.1 Robert Taylor Homes, 4,400 public housing apartments stretching north along State Street toward Chicago's downtown, 19 September 1996. Courtesy of Lawrence Okrent.

explaining how racist aldermen refused to allow the construction of projects outside of the black ghetto. In 1983, historian Arnold Hirsch elaborated on this past and articulated a "Second Ghetto" thesis that described how public action and private violence in the 1950s and 1960s created a domestic "containment policy" to prevent African Americans from residing in white neighborhoods. Public housing and urban renewal were tools that tore down the first black ghetto and built a second one—consisting of large-scale public and private projects—in its place. By the mid-1960s, Chicago's second ghetto was complete, including a four-mile stretch of projects along State Street, with seventy-eight hundred apartments of public housing, all of it in repetitious blocks of elevator buildings that housed African Americans exclusively (Figure 2.1).[7]

Major lawsuits challenged these racialized outcomes, though court action barely put a dent in the problem. In 1966, American Civil Liberties Union lawyers filed a class-action suit, charging the CHA and the U.S. Department of Housing and Urban Development (HUD) with racism in site selection and tenant selection practices. Known as the *Gautreaux* cases after lead plaintiff and tenant Dorothy Gautreaux, the tangled court rulings found the CHA guilty of discrimination and ordered it to build public housing in white areas. Little changed on the ground, however, as city officials dragged their feet; clearly, the courts proved a difficult arena in which to implement housing policy change.[8]

Nor could lawsuits turn around the increasingly dismal conditions in existing projects. In 1986, the *Chicago Tribune* ran a twelve-part series on public housing called "The Chicago Wall," a reference not only to the physically imposing high-rise buildings along State Street but also to the "psychological barriers" created by projects that stand "as a perverse monument to decades of misdirected public policy and race-conscious political decision making." More intimately, journalist Alex Kotlowitz profiled two young boys growing up in Chicago projects in his 1991 book *There Are No Children Here*, a heartrending story that drove home the human cost of lost childhoods.[9] Both exposés, however, cemented the idea in the minds of Chicagoans that the buildings themselves, with their grim aesthetics, were to blame.

Momentum grew for radical change. Visits by President Bill Clinton and HUD Secretary Henry Cisneros to the city's chaotic projects led to a belated federal takeover of the dysfunctional CHA in 1995.[10] Four years later, with the housing authority back on solid managerial footing, the city began an ambitious Plan for Transformation to tear down nearly all of the CHA's elevator

Figure 2.2 New Urbanism at the mixed-income Villages at Westhaven, which replaced the former Henry Horner Extension (background), 1998. Chicago Housing Authority.

buildings, disperse their residents into other (mainly poor) Chicago neighborhoods using housing vouchers, and rebuild or renovate only a portion of the public housing stock in order to avoid concentrations of poverty.[11] The plan resulted in a massive displacement of roughly twenty thousand families, nearly all of them African American, most of whom ended up in other poor neighborhoods.[12]

The lesson from public housing's past, policymakers concluded, was that high-rise architecture and concentrated poverty had been the cause of its collapse. The solution, then, involved the opposite of modernism: low-rise, "new urbanist" architecture that mimicked nineteenth-century vernacular designs. Further, plans called for mixing affluent, market-rate buyers with public housing tenants in rebuilt developments as a way to limit the proportion of poor families and socially restrain them.[13] In essence, the CHA's new design and mixed-income strategies were meant to make public housing nearly invisible. "The projects," with their ugly, hulking modernist structures, would be erased, and new "mixed-income communities" would blend in seamlessly with the urban fabric (Figure 2.2).

Designing Chicago's High-Rises

This new strategy was a far cry from the 1950s, when the CHA built its mammoth high-rise projects in a stripped-down style. Still, even then the CHA was never enthralled with architectural modernism. But it did have two pressing needs: First, the CHA wanted to build large amounts of housing as quickly as possible to relieve postwar housing shortages and to ameliorate the dismal conditions experienced by African Americans in the city's slums. Second, it had to build this housing with economy in mind, as federal officials—ever concerned about congressional support—worked to ensure that public housing cost less to construct than private housing (Figure 2.3).

The solution to both imperatives involved elevator buildings, following the lead of the New York City Housing Authority (NYCHA). Taller buildings could produce more housing without sacrificing green space. Elizabeth Wood, the CHA's progressive executive secretary, explained in 1945 that "elevator structures give us wide-open spaces, larger playgrounds, and a general effect of a park that will not be possible if the land were developed as three-story walk-ups."[14] Still, Wood was hesitant about the leap to new forms, calling them "experiments." She encouraged efforts to "humanize" elevator buildings by using "gallery" arrangements that offered outdoor corridors as entryways to apartments. Known as "sidewalks in the air," the gallery innovation is most clearly seen in Loomis Courts, a seven-story project singled out for praise by an architectural advisory board of the federal Public Housing Administration (PHA). Modernist plans had the added benefit of restraining costs by removing ornamentation and using space efficiently. From the perspective of public housing administrators, modernism was as much a budgetary choice as a stylistic one.[15]

Still, even as elevator projects were being developed, doubts about their efficacy grew in Washington and Chicago, and the concern had little to do with architectural styles. In 1950, a major policy bulletin from the PHA labeled high-rises the "least desirable" form of public housing because of "the grave and serious problems incident to the rearing of children in such [multistory] housing." Without elaboration, the bulletin argued that the problems were "too well known to warrant any comment," yet it cited no evidence for the claim.[16] Moreover, despite its own warnings, the PHA soon issued revised rules on density and cost that made it nearly impossible to build anything but elevator buildings on land deemed "high-cost." Such buildings would allow more units, thereby diluting fixed land costs in order to keep total development costs per

Figure 2.3 Sidewalks in the Air at Loomis Courts, 1952. Photograph by Harry Callahan for the Chicago Housing Authority. Chicago Housing Authority.

unit within politically acceptable bounds. In response, housing authorities in twenty-three cities across the country began planning fifty-three thousand apartments in elevator buildings by mid-1951.[17]

The CHA's Elizabeth Wood was among the first to publicly express reasoned doubts about elevator buildings and the difficulties of raising children in them. In a January 1952 *Architectural Forum* article, she argued:

> The row-house solution is simple and natural. The indoor-outdoor activity takes place close to where the mother is at work. The child can keep in touch

53

with her. . . . But in an apartment house project, where playgrounds are carefully arranged at some distance, vertical as well as horizontal, from the family supper table, there will be much less parent-child play.[18]

But *Architectural Forum* editor Douglas Haskell dismissed Wood's family-
centered thinking, contending that increased densities were the future of cities and that "a public not used to elevators or play corridors must learn to use
them, just as new car owners must be taught to drive."[19] Modernism and high-
rise forms held powerful sway over architects in the early postwar period.

Yet, the CHA's early experience with its mid-rise buildings confirmed Wood's
concerns about their suitability for families. Crucial building systems proved
vulnerable to large numbers of young people who played hard. Children were
particularly rough on elevator systems, as rampant games of "elevator tag"
led to frequent breakdowns (Figure 2.4). Trash chutes, mailboxes, doors, and
hall lights also suffered, as did overall tenant quality of life.[20]

Figure 2.4 Youth at the elevators of Stateway Gardens, mid-1960s. Chicago Housing Authority.

CHA administrators in 1955 viewed the problem as being rooted in design, with elevators as a central weakness. In response, they proposed developing the CHA's next wave of projects—which would include the Robert Taylor Homes and the William Green Homes (of Cabrini-Green)—as five-story walk-up buildings (Figure 2.5). But federal administrators rejected the walk-up plans as too expensive, as each apartment was projected to cost over $20,000 to build at a time when new single-family houses in the suburbs sold for around $15,000.[21] After four years of bureaucratic wrangling, Chicago caved in 1959 and reluctantly moved forward with elevator projects, constructing nine thousand apartments between 1959 and 1962, each at a cost of around $16,000, and nearly all in buildings over fourteen stories tall.[22] Chicago's tallest and largest projects, then, had been shaped largely by cost considerations, not by architectural modernism.

Figure 2.5 Five-story plan for public housing, with "row-on-row" design, 1957. The five-story design featured a bottom story of apartments, a middle tier of two-story "duplexes" (second and third floors), with a staircase internal to each apartment, and then another tier of two-story "duplexes" on top (fourth and fifth floors). Residents in the top duplexes would walk up four flights to enter their apartments. The design was never built. Chicago Housing Authority.

Youth Density

Throughout the debate in the 1950s over public housing's form, one assumption was never challenged: that Chicago's public housing would serve families exclusively, and, in most cases, *large* families with *many* children. From the earliest days of the program, one of public housing's main rationales had been to remove children from poor housing conditions so that their life chances might be altered for the better. The environmental determinism that pervaded the housing reform movement assumed that new housing—with its air, light, hot water, and space—would improve the lives of low-income households, especially for their children.[23]

By the 1950s, this mission had evolved in Chicago into a focus on large families with five or more children who had the most difficulty finding acceptable housing in the private market. Such families, a CHA monthly report in 1955 noted, "have been on CHA lists for five years or more."[24] In response, the authority programmed its late 1950s projects so that 72 percent of apartments contained three, four, and five bedrooms (at the Robert Taylor Homes, the figure was 80 percent). This was a significant increase over projects designed earlier in the decade, where only 32 percent of apartments had three or more bedrooms. Surprisingly, this major decision to dedicate public housing to large families received no scrutiny and no serious discussion.[25]

Yet, the choice had enormous implications. Building large apartments for large families meant that public housing communities, by design, would house unprecedented densities of youth. Chicago's projects opened in the late 1950s and early 1960s were overwhelmed by children, resulting in debilitating social disorder that helped drive out the working class and send projects spiraling downward.[26]

The typical Chicago neighborhood in 1960 had a mix of family types so that the average census tract had slightly more than one youth for every two adults, amounting to a youth density (expressed as a ratio) of 0.58. Significantly, only a handful of Chicago tracts had more youths than adults, and even baby-boom suburb Park Forest, a planned community for families, had a youth density of 0.97.[27]

But in Chicago's public housing, youth densities reached historically unprecedented levels. By 1965, after the completion of major projects, the CHA's overall youth density was 2.11, or over two youths for every one adult, effectively inverting the ratio for the rest of the city. Some projects had even higher youth densities: when the Robert Taylor Homes opened in 1963, it housed twenty thousand youths and seven thousand adults—an astonishing 2.86 youth-adult ratio in a community that, had it been its own municipality, would have been the tenth largest in Illinois. In no sizeable residential community in modern history had so many youths been supervised by so few adults.[28]

These extraordinary youth densities were driven primarily by the choice to build multibedroom apartments and less by social factors. While increasing numbers of single-parent families during the late 1960s played a small part in rising youth density, declining average household size in the early 1970s kept youth-adult ratios generally stable. Between 1965 and 1975, the CHA's overall youth density had risen only 6 percent, despite major upheavals in family structure.[29] Planning and policy decisions, not the social choices of public housing residents, resulted in the enormous concentration of youth.

High youth densities created an untenable social environment in high-rise projects soon after they opened. The timing of this social disorder is significant. Projects initially housed primarily working-class, two-parent families. But even with these advantages of class and family structure, adults could not manage the massive number of youths in their midst. Within a year of opening, residents of the Robert Taylor Homes organized a Law and Order Committee in response to chaotic conditions. In a December 1963 letter to the *Chicago Defender*, an anonymous tenant leader at Taylor claimed that youths had taken over public spaces: "The stairways and laundry rooms [are] being used for card playing, dice shooting, and sex parties by teenagers. . . . [Youths tie] up our elevators, throw bottles over the galleries, pick pockets, and steal groceries." Within two months of the letter's publication, an eleven-year-old boy fell from a broken eighth-floor railing, a ten-year-old boy died after being hit by a nine-pound drain cover thrown off a "sidewalk in the air," and a seventy-two-year-old resident was stabbed to death by a seventeen-year-old neighbor. Shaken mothers began picketing the CHA's management offices, demanding twenty-four-hour police protection, twenty-four-hour elevator attendants, and more responsive elevator repairs. In a display of public theater to draw attention to their plight, Taylor mothers placed a coffin in front of the CHA's management offices (Figure 2.6). The *Defender* called the protest "The Battle of the Robert Taylor Homes," but neither residents nor the newspapers identified the extreme number of youth as a key problem.[30]

Youth density is an overlooked factor contributing to a community's capacity for what sociologists call "collective efficacy," namely, the ability of residents to intervene and informally police their communities.[31] When that

Figure 2.6 Protest at CHA offices over conditions at the Robert Taylor Homes after the death of an eleven-year-old boy who fell from a broken balcony, 26 February 1964. Courtesy of the *Chicago Tribune*.

capacity is weakened—by poverty, lack of trust, barriers to community action, or excessive youth density—then communities struggle to resolve disputes, defend against disruptive outsiders, and minimize petty crimes like vandalism and theft. In public housing, residents faced many collective efficacy challenges. The large scale of projects made restricting outsiders difficult. Turnover reduced neighborly connections. Bureaucratic management practices undermined a sense of ownership. Deindustrialization eroded economic security. But enormous youth density also strained collective efficacy beyond repair.

It would be a mistake to see public housing tenants as passive in their efforts to foster collective efficacy. As with the 1963–1964 protests at the Robert Taylor Homes, residents living in numerous projects in the 1960s organized day care centers, Boy Scout troops, marching bands, sports teams, church groups, and other activities to channel youth energy (Figure 2.7). Mothers in some projects created their own elevator staffing system during "rush hours," generally when kids were going to and from school. They formed laundry co-ops to protect their laundry rooms. Social service agencies created Head Start centers and after-school programs for youth (Figure 2.8).[32] A tremendous amount of tenant energy was devoted to enhancing collective efficacy, but adults faced an uphill battle against enormous densities of youth.

For its part, the CHA was unwilling to confront the demographic disaster it had created in its projects. Demands by tenants for more security, more playground equipment, and new fieldhouses were fulfilled only partially or, in some cases, unmet entirely. Nor did other government agencies step up efforts to ameliorate the situation. The Chicago School Board willfully underestimated the number of children in public housing in order to limit school construction,

Figure 2.7 Youth cleanup crew, Robert Taylor Homes, Summer 1970. Chicago Housing Authority.

59

Figure 2.8 Rockwell Gardens Day Care Center, n.d. Chicago Housing Authority.

leading to massive overcrowding in existing schools in the 1960s. Pools built by the Chicago Park District were woefully inadequate to the size of the youth population. The police viewed projects as alternative zones immune to typical policing. Government at all levels lacked the capacity, creativity, or interest to address the social chaos of public housing.[33]

The inability of residents, managers, and the state to impose social order soon led to a downward spiral. Working-class families—whose income gave them the option to move—steadily left public housing between 1965 and 1974 and were replaced by the non-wage-earning poor. This had serious repercussions. The CHA's maintenance budget was funded largely by tenant rents, and those rents, in turn, were set at 25 percent of a family's income. As its tenants grew poorer, the CHA's rent receipts declined, giving it fewer resources to maintain projects. The slip in maintenance prompted those with options to leave, further impoverishing projects. The federal government belatedly created new subsidies to fill gaping budget holes, but funding never matched housing authority requests. By the late 1970s, Chicago's projects had descended into disrepair, becoming the city's housing of last resort.[34]

It is important to remember that many public housing youth were not delinquent or destructive, and many grew up to join the middle class. Public housing residents reject the stereotypes that label them as "underclass," and numerous accounts, ranging from scholarly to self-published, attest to the desire of residents to impose social order in the face of extraordinary odds.[35] Put another way, high youth densities did not determine *individual* outcomes, but it did create a *community* problem of social control. The residents didn't create this problem; public housing planners did by raising the bar for achieving collective efficacy to such daunting heights. The concept of youth density helps deflect attention away from tenants themselves and toward the policy choices that set the stage for decline.

The point is not to see youth density as a one-dimensional explanation for public housing's struggles. This would only repeat earlier fixations on modernist architecture as the main source of its woes. Instead, youth density is an overlooked explanation, one that combined with other policies to hobble public housing. Charging rent as a proportion of income pushed out upwardly mobile families and attracted the very poor. Construction cost limits imposed by federal officials pushed high-rise buildings despite concerns for families. Court rulings after 1967 made it difficult to evict problem residents. Housing authorities and HUD constantly fought over adequate subsidies. All of these policies contributed to the difficult in managing and maintaining a viable public housing stock. Still, youth density was a crucial element that undermined the social order essential to sustaining a viable community, especially in vulnerable high-rise buildings dependent upon fragile elevator systems.

Other Cities

Chicago was not alone in building projects with enormous youth density. St. Louis's Pruitt-Igoe Homes, completed in 1954, had a youth-adult ratio of 2.63 in 1968. After experiencing profound social disorder, St. Louis demolished the project in 1973. NYCHA's projects, on the other hand, had far lower youth densities. Its federally subsidized developments had an average youth density of 1.04 in 1968, with a peak density of 1.73 at the Woodrow Wilson Homes, a four-hundred-unit high-rise project.[36] NYCHA's youth density was

Table 2.1 Youth densities in selected cities, 1968*

Housing authority	Youth density
Chicago	1.92
New York	1.04
New Orleans	1.96
Newark	1.36
All U.S. family public housing**	1.94

Source: Chicago Housing Authority, "Annual Statistical Report, 1968," table 5; New York City Housing Authority, Project Data, Characteristics of Tenants as of January 1, 1968," in NYCHA Archives, LaGuardia Community College; Housing Authority of New Orleans, Annual Report, 1968, p. 12; Housing Authority of City of Newark, "Annual Report and Statistical Data Pertaining to Public Housing," 1968, table 24; U.S. Department of Housing and Urban Development, *1968 HUD Statistical Yearbook* (Washington, D.C.: Government Printing Office, 1968), table 31.

Note: Data from Family Projects only; excludes Seniors Projects.

* "Youth" defined as under age 21.

** "Reexamined families for continued occupancy," a sample of 179,604 families.

well below the national public housing average of 1.94, based on a large sample in 1968.[37] Table 2.1 shows youth density in selected cities that year.

These data need to be considered carefully. High youth density can indicate that a community faced a challenge in maintaining order, and that maintenance costs were likely higher than expected.[38] But youth density was *not* a precise predictor of disorder measures like crime.[39] Nor can youth density alone incorporate the numerous variables that entered into project quality of life. For example, former residents of public housing suggest that crime and disorder varied from building to building, depending on the collective efficacy of inhabitants and other variables like management competence, relations with police, and concentrations of poverty. More research is needed to better understand the role of youth density in the history of public housing projects that were (and remain) not only large but also small, not only tower blocks but also garden apartments, and not only for low-income but also working-class residents.

Conclusion

In some ways, a major problem facing public housing may be summed up by inverting the title of Alex Kotlowitz's book: *there were too many children here*. Undoubtedly, numerous variables influenced public housing residents' ability to exert collective efficacy, but the timing of social disorder in public housing is significant. Widespread problems emerged in Chicago's high-rise projects shortly after they opened in the 1950s and early 1960s, which is *before* poverty became entrenched, *before* jobs disappeared in black ghettos, *before* the CHA's finances collapsed, *before* deferred maintenance meant physical disorder, and *before* the drug scourge ravaged tenants. These structural forces later deepened problems in the 1970s, but social disorder was present in high-rises with large numbers of youth right from the start.

Blaming public housing failure on its architecture, then, misses the planning choices that created exceptional demographic burdens on projects. Administrators gave plenty of thought to cost, layout, and architecture but rarely examined the fundamental age structure of the communities being constructed. The lesson of public housing in the 1950s and 1960s is that community building is a delicate process, and attention to collective efficacy and social order is more important than total development cost. Architecture is one element that can encourage or impede collective efficacy, as Jane Jacobs and Oscar Newman have noted.[40] But architecture is hardly determining. Instead, social order is a finely tuned state, one not easily created or sustained. Only by understanding the complexity of social order in public housing and the planning parameters that foster it can planners, developers, and government officials ensure that future communities produce better results.

PUBLIC HOUSING BREEDS CRIME

Fritz Umbach and Alexander Gerould

"Everyone knows how quickly . . . housing projects in big cities turn into dangerous, demoralized slums."
—Howard Husock, 2003[1] .

Howard Husock, Harvard University's director of public policy case studies, was so confident that public housing's dangerous nature was common knowledge that he neglected even to provide citations for the sweeping generalization that opens his 2003 book, *America's Trillion-Dollar Housing Mistake: The Failure of American Housing Policy.* But a decade and half of robust scholarship has made clear that what "everyone knows" about crime and public housing is almost certainly inaccurate. At times, some public housing has undoubtedly proved to be more dangerous than other shelter for the poor. But that has not been the case consistently, and when it has been true, the origins of the disorder turn out to be very different from what is commonly believed.

Popular and academic discussions of public housing crime have focused on three broad questions. Does something about public housing generate more crime than private housing? Does public housing make surrounding neighborhoods more dangerous? And does dispersing public housing residents simply displace disorder? Answering these questions requires understanding that although criminal offenses may have precise *legal* definitions, the collection, analysis, and presentation of crime statistics is a *social* undertaking. Making sense of the numbers often means asking why, how, and for whom they were assembled.

Sorting out something approaching the truth about crime and public housing developments (PHDs) has been neither easy for analysts nor, as it turns out, much in demand. Empirical precision has often seemed beside the point

Figure 3.1 "Eliminate crime in the slums through housing." New York: Federal Art Project, 1936. Courtesy of the Library of Congress.

to an American public that has woven crime, PHDs, and racial minorities into an "unholy trinity." As criminologist Garth Davies observed in his 2006 book on the topic, "that public housing projects are rife with serious crime is . . . accepted as fact despite a discernible paucity of evidence."[2] So powerfully, indeed, has popular belief fused crime with PHDs that even the nationwide demolition of high-rise projects failed to quiet long-standing fears. In 2008, *Atlantic* magazine writer Hanna Rosin picked up where Husock left off, laying blame for spiking suburban violence on displaced residents of razed public housing. That Rosin neither offered much in the way of proof nor considered alternative explanations did not prevent her "American Murder Mystery" from being included in *Best American Crime Reporting 2009*.[3]

Portrayals of public housing complexes as "criminal paradises" stretch back to the late 1950s, when it became obvious that reformers' utopian visions of redeeming blighted urban tenements through modern architecture and state management had failed to deliver (Figure 3.1).[4] But this unsavory image emerged more from journalistic exposés than academic research, which was itself often sparse and incomplete. Only recently have scholars taken up the topic of crime and public housing with anything approaching statistical thoroughness.

Until the late 1990s, however, efforts to grasp the extent of public housing's influence on crime generally stumbled over two research challenges, reflecting both the limits of crime data and shortsighted understandings of "the projects." First, scholars hoping to establish a statistical relationship between PHDs and crime found there were no reliable numbers to crunch. Most police departments simply did not keep separate blotters for public housing (except in New York City, as discussed below). As late as 1998, federal Housing and Urban Development (HUD) researcher Harold Holzman was able to observe matter-of-factly that "valid statistics on the level of crime in public housing do not exist." Second, scholars tended to see the distinction between public housing and other forms of housing as one primarily of physical form. As a result, these studies attempted to correlate PHDs' designs with their crime rates or, more simplistically, to compare crime rates inside and outside public housing.[5] Such approaches, however, overlooked that PHDs are not simply brick-and-mortar constructions but also sociopolitical ones. As such, they came to be shunted into the most troubled neighborhoods; sheltered a demographic that victimization research identified as most likely to fall prey to crime; and, as communities, often suffered from more than their fair share of municipal neglect.[6] Ignoring such contexts meant that research often left open two questions: First, was the disorder criminologists found in PHDs actually generated there, or did the developments merely (and unwillingly) play host to criminal activity from elsewhere? And, second, if public housing did, in fact, elevate the risk of violence and other crimes, what share of the blame lay with their physical design, what share with their social makeup, and what share with managerial incompetence?

The importance of questions regarding PHDs' neighborhoods becomes more apparent in light of public housing's location nationally. Some 60 percent of units are to be found in the country's big cities. Establishing what impact the densely populated, highly segregated, and overwhelmingly poor neighborhoods surrounding most projects have on crime requires pinpointing where crime occurs. But most police departments tally up crime using large geographic units, such as precincts or districts. Better answers to some questions had to wait until the early 2000s, when affordable geographic information systems (GIS) technology became available, allowing crime mapping on small budgets.[7] By that time, however, the nation's public housing was deep into a life stage that scholars have called "housing of last resort" or "welfare housing," when many PHDs had descended into "severe distress"—to use policymakers' peculiar euphemism.[8] The sometimes-bleak conclusions about crime drawn from recent GIS data are often snapshots of particular complexes at arguably their most difficult points. And so, what follows proceeds chronologically, to highlight the importance of changing social, political, and technological contexts.

Oscar Newman and the Making of a High-Rise Myth

How is it that, decades before the arrival of real statistical knowledge about crime and public housing, the "projects" had already become synonymous with violence, not just among urbanites but also among professional urbanists? The first widely-read academic account of crime and public housing—and one that unintentionally fortified notions of such communities as deviant—appeared in Lee Rainwater's 1970 *Behind Ghetto Walls: Black Families in a Federal Slum*, a study of St. Louis's soon-to-be-razed Pruitt-Igoe. Rainwater numbered among a small army of mostly white, progressive social scientists who poured into poor, minority neighborhoods in the 1960s and observed residents' "adaptations" to poverty and racism. These idealists aimed to counter conservative talk of a "culture of poverty" by presenting ghetto norms as a coping strategy in response to deprivation rather than an inherited way of life that created it. But the practical impact of such work at the time, explained historian Robin Kelley, was that it "reinforced monolithic interpretations of black urban culture." Quickly forgotten, for example, was that Rainwater had researched not just any public housing development but perhaps the nation's most troubled. The National Institute of Mental Health (NIMH) had, in fact, hired him to evaluate last-ditch efforts to halt the uniquely massive decline of the 57-acre complex. But the crime-plagued Pruitt-Igoe of Rainwater's portrayal became a stand-in for all PHDs and a parable of failed antipoverty programs.[9]

Within weeks of the publication of *Behind Ghetto Walls,* St. Louis declared it would tear down Pruitt-Igoe. And just months after that too-oft-commented-upon demolition, architect Oscar Newman published *Defensible Space: Crime Prevention through Urban Design*, sealing public housing's criminal reputation.[10] After Newman, the high-rise towers of many cities' PHDs would loom as large in the public's mental landscape as they did in the urban landscape. Newman's work also marked the first sustained effort to use crime statistics to explore public housing's influence on crime. That Newman had numbers at all reflected the unusual fact that between 1952 and 1995, New York had not one but three police departments—one for its streets, one for its subways, and one for its public housing—and each one reported crime data separately.[11] But the existence of such separate statistics for Newman to use was not the same thing as a guarantee that he would do so with skill.

Newman spun for his readers, as he phrased it, "a tale of two projects." In Brooklyn, he had found the ideal setting for a natural experiment: two projects across the street from each other and practically identical in all regards. They housed a similar number of residents at roughly the same density and were under the same management. All that differed was their physical design—and crime rates. The low-slung Brownsville Houses experienced so few crimes that mothers left their doors open so as to keep an eye on children playing in hallways. But at the high-rise Van Dyke Houses, mothers kept their youngsters behind locked doors, fearful of the chaos that, Newman held, often erupted in the project's halls and stairwells. From this contrast, Newman drew lessons about physical environment and crime that seemed to him commonsensical. The tower-in-the-park design of many PHDs created public areas in and around the buildings where neither tenants nor management exerted much control, inviting stranger-on-stranger crimes in spaces with weak community surveillance. "High Rise = High Crime" read the headline to the *New York Times* article covering Newman's assault on an earlier generation's doctrinaire modernism, complete with a photograph of the young, rakishly bearded architect. Newman's thinking—which emphasized the role of informal community controls on crime—was more complex than the headline's distillation, but Newman did little to prevent such generic characterizations.[12] Ultimately, his take on public housing was decidedly that of an architect: people, policies, and history receded into the background, leaving only physical structures in view. As Newman concluded, "It is the apartment tower itself which is the real and final villain."[13]

Defensible Space reflected not simply Newman's professional training but also his institutional funding. In a sign of the changing research economy of the 1970s, Newman ignored the large-scale social forces—from rising costs to vanishing jobs—that were troubling public housing nationwide and turned instead to small-bore design tweaks focused on crime. As architectural historian Joy Knoblauch has noted of these years, "funding sources shifted from large federal programs to promote the health, education, and welfare of the population to franchise-state efforts to prevent crime, punish offenders, and manage the population through incentive structures."[14] President Lyndon Johnson's sensitivity to the political potency of the public's growing crime fears led to the Law Enforcement Assistance Administration (LEAA) and opened for the first time the spigot of federal dollars to local agencies for crime initiatives. In *Defensible Space* and other works, Newman—lacking a permanent institutional home—followed the new money, creating putative knowledge about public housing's criminogenic nature and occasionally peddling Band-Aids for the problem. In contrast, a call for a renewed and expensive War on Poverty would have won Newman, as a crime-policy entrepreneur, few grants. But federal funding of social science research into crime in general—and in public housing in particular—only deepened the public's exposure to both notions. And the simplicity of *Defensible Space*'s environmental determinism guaranteed that the book's assertions of public housing's crime-breeding qualities reached large audiences. *Defensible Space* ended up outselling all other architecture books that decade. But for the many urban public housing authorities whose brick-and-glass empires consisted largely of high-rises, Newman's choice of villain was particularly damaging.

Although Newman labored to give his conclusions the aura of slide-rule precision, *Defensible Space* suffered from a simple but profound defect. Newman's evidence pointed in one direction, but his claims pointed in another. The Brownsville and Van Dyke Houses were not as comparable as Newman suggested. The high-rise Van Dyke Houses were not simply higher, they also sheltered significantly larger families. And, apparently, this aspect of public housing life mattered immensely. The regression tables tucked away in *Defensible Space*'s final pages quietly contradict the book's conclusions by demonstrating that crime in the complexes was more closely correlated with family size (a rough proxy for child-to-adult ratios) than building height. Less adult supervision can elevate crime rates, as historian D. Bradford Hunt has documented using evidence from Chicago's public housing data.[15] Had Newman's been an "academic study," observed Knoblauch, his "methods of proof through data would have been inadequate and he would have received little attention." But *Defensible Space* was a hybrid of journalistic narrative and social science analysis, taking advantage of the former's lower methodological bar while simultaneously benefitting from the latter's greater authority.[16]

Defensible Space's tale of architecture as destiny had the additional advantage of sidestepping thorny national debates about poverty's causes and society's responsibility. If bad design were the real cause for disorder, then chicken-or-egg debates over ghetto norms and state solutions were irrelevant. Instead, cash-strapped cities should simply "design out crime" by hiring better architects. This perspective however neglected the increasingly troubled tenancy of many projects. The combination of loosened resident screening, growing white flight, and vanishing blue-collar jobs meant that by the late 1960s public housing sheltered a population far more desperate than it had a decade before. But Newman's popular writings—ignoring policy, poverty, and history—reinforced the notion that crime was a permanent fixture of public housing's iconic high-rises. Newman had access to statistics demonstrating that New York's public housing developments historically had lower rates of crime than did their surrounding neighborhoods, but he clung to the towers' design as his tale's culprit.[17] This insistence had real consequences. Newman's subsequent consultancy with the New York City Housing Authority (NYCHA) led to expensive and largely ineffective structural design changes to individual projects. Although the growing poverty of public housing's residents was perhaps beyond their control, policymakers and administrators ignored it in favor of an environmental determinism that distracted from other potentially effective crime control strategies—strategies grounded in policies that public housing authorities might have been able to control, at least in tight real estate markets. Recent scholarship on New York suggests that tighter screening policies, stronger eviction practices, and community policing might have made a meaningful difference. When even a small number of bad apples could duck eviction (at least until legal changes in the 1990s), it had an outsized impact on project disorder.[18]

Residents played such bit parts in Newman's drama of high-rise pathology that he neglected even to notify them when his firm— employing *Defensible Space*'s theories—imposed major changes on their homes.[19] It is worth noting, however, that the author's sidestepping of human factors in thinking about project crime was an elite dance. Significant numbers of PHD residents nationwide consistently reported in surveys (and often confirmed through their own activism) that they believed it was public housing's changing tenancy that had made project life more dangerous. And few reported believing questions of design mattered at all.[20]

Newman's verdict on high-rise towers looks even less reliable in light of more recent research. Aiming to tease out the relative impact of physical and social factors in PHD crime, Tamara Dumanovsky used the same data as Newman—NYCHA tenant demographics and Housing Police crime reports—but subjected them to the careful statistical modeling the architect had avoided. Reviewing more than a decade of data (1985–1996) from the nation's largest public housing system, Dumanovsky concluded in her 1999 study that the height of a complex's buildings had a very modest impact on violent crime. The poverty of a complex's tenants was by far the best predictor of how much violence occurred there.[21] Similarly, in 1996, Holzman sought to answer the same question nationwide. His large, stratified sampling found crime correlated more closely with the number of buildings and residents in a development than it did with building height.[22] The irony, then, of Newman's legacy is that New York—the one city that might have yielded a rich statistical understanding of public housing crime—actually ended up giving rise to perhaps the most pervasive and pernicious myth about it. Newman himself would eventually bring more nuance to his arguments, but the damage to public housing's image had been done.[23]

Newman's work remains popular in contemporary criminology—albeit more because of his theoretical contributions than his empirical ones. Much of *Defensible Space* can be seen as a direct precursor to an alphabet soup of acronyms in environmental criminology and police science: SCP (situational crime prevention), CPTED (crime prevention through environmental design) and POP (problem-oriented policing). Likewise, Newman's attention to a community's ability to exert informal social control is compatible with theories about neighborhood conditions and criminal activity that are popular across the political spectrum, from broken windows (favored by criminologists on the right) to collective efficacy (favored by those on the left).[24]

HUD Surveys and Unexpected Safety from Violence

At the time of its publication, *Defensible Space* captured the imagination not just of the public but also of public housing officials, and so launched a decade of research into PHD crime focused largely on physical design and funded mostly by HUD. Understandably, HUD officials hoped to rescue the most chaotic projects. Research money flowed to measure crime in the most troubled complexes in order to guide federal (and ultimately failed) rehabilitation efforts.[25] The unintended result, however, was that HUD paid for and distributed a picture of public housing lawlessness drawn not from representative projects but instead from distressed outliers—repeating the impact of Rainwater's Pruitt-Igoe study a decade earlier.

Even more misleading, because most cities lacked New York City's separate PHD crime statistics, HUD's researchers resorted instead to a substitute: victimization surveys. Such surveys were, in fact, the new criminological tool of the 1970s and an effort to compensate for underreporting of crime.[26] But surveying public housing residents (or a sample of them) only enabled researchers to compare crime rates in a particular project and its host city or the nation as a whole. Local officials typically saw to it that public housing projects were built in cities' most disadvantaged and crime-ridden neighborhoods. Did higher PHD crime rates reveal that something about public housing increased crime, or did those rates simply announce the not particularly surprising news that projects were located in more dangerous neighborhoods?

Surveys, in short, did not make it possible to consider public housing disorder within its larger "ecology"—criminologists' term for the constellation of social, physical, and spatial factors surrounding a research site. And so what passed in the 1970s for broad knowledge about public housing crime was really a collective portrait of some of the nation's worst projects presented without the necessary context. And *that* picture was certainly not pretty. The risk, for example, of getting robbed in Washington, D.C.'s Capper Dwellings was twice that of the Capitol generally and five times the national average. Matters were even worse in Baltimore. Residents of the Murphy Homes, for instance, experienced three times as many robberies as did other poor residents of the city, and sixteen times as many as Americans generally. And burglars targeted the Murphy Homes four and a half times more frequently than they did Baltimore's private residences.[27] But even within this sketch of crime in some of America's most difficult projects, there were important details that belied public housing's reputation and likely would have surprised readers of Rainwater and Newman.

Consider Baltimore's Murphy Homes. Sliced off from the city by a highway and encircled, thanks to urban renewal, by weed-filled lots during the 1970s, this modernist stew of low-rises and fourteen-story towers photogenically fit public housing's lurid image. But in 1976, when HUD researchers surveyed the residents, they discovered that the Murphy Homes were not, in fact, a particularly violent place for the poor to live as compared to Baltimore as a whole. Residents were actually no more likely to be assaulted than were other poor citizens. Nor were the Murphy Homes unusual. Tenants of DC's Capper Dwellings, for example, were actually somewhat less likely to be assaulted than the poor living in private housing. More remarkably, given the public housing of popular imagination, Capper Dwellings residents were *twice* as safe from assault than were poor Americans generally. Indeed, this pattern of PHD residents suffering from higher property crime rates but benefiting from equivalent or even lower violent crime rates (including robbery) than those experienced by the host city's poor held true across nearly all of HUD's research sites (and, in New York City, where HUD had not dispatched a team, both violent and property crime rates were lower in public housing). But no best-selling author trumpeted these unexpected findings, which emerged from a more rigorous statistical methodology than had underwritten *Defensible Space*. The HUD researchers themselves, acknowledging that their discoveries did not exactly square with conventional wisdom, insisted that what really mattered was public housing residents *feared* crime more than did other Americans.[28]

Curiously, this pattern of greater property crime but equal or lower violent crime was reversed in the 1980s and 1990s, when public housing residents started to experience more physical violence than property loss. Researchers in those decades often concluded that higher rates of violent crimes than property crimes merely reflected fixed economic and spatial facts of project life. Public housing residents, they asserted, simply possessed less that might tempt burglars, and superblock architecture, lacking retail stores and parked cars, occasioned fewer opportunities for theft. Such conclusions seemingly forgot the findings of the 1970s. Moreover, scholars associated with the "routine activity" school of criminology have recently challenged these economic and spatial interpretations of public housing's asymmetrical property and violent crime rates (see below).[29]

Scarce Funding, Conflicting Findings, and Methodological Challenges

Between the absolute failure of HUD's rehabilitation efforts in the 1970s and President Ronald Reagan's disinterest in urban affairs, federal funds for public housing crime research essentially vanished in the 1980s. As urban housing specialist Langley Keyes noted of the priority shift, any "serious investigation of crime reduction strategies was over. Research was out."[30] Academics tried to fill the void, but shoestring budgets meant their efforts lacked HUD's multicity scope. However, once freed from the necessity to provide practical guidance for troubled projects, scholars were able to choose more representative research sites. In 1982, for example, John Farley compared crime rates for ten St. Louis PHDs with their locations' *expected* crime rate "based on five predictors: distance from downtown, percentage black, percentage of population consisting of children under 18, median rent, and percentage of households with female head."[31] Farley, like other researchers outside of New York, did not have separate crime statistics for public housing and so had to impute them by using city blocks that were primarily filled with public housing. To Farley's surprise, St. Louis's projects experienced crime rates that were generally no higher than the expected crime rate for their neighborhood and sometimes significantly lower, leading him to wonder in his article's title, "Has Public Housing Gotten a Bum Rap?"

While Farley was interpreting research from St. Louis, Dennis Roncek was examining statistics from Cleveland. Roncek attempted to measure "spillover" effects of crime from Cleveland's eighteen public housing complexes into neighboring city blocks from 1971 to 1977, asking, in essence, Did public housing generate more crime than it could consume locally, and so endanger nearby neighborhoods? The question had particular import in the wake of growing resistance to public housing construction nationwide. With GIS technology still on the horizon, the use of city blocks—the smallest geographic unit for which reliable data could be tabulated—made sense as a starting point for finding an answer to such a difficult question. Roncek found that there were no statistically significant PHD spillover effects for property crime. Violent crime did spill over, but the effect shrank once the socioeconomic conditions of the surrounding blocks were considered. In fact, after Roncek controlled for such factors, even the presence of a one-thousand-unit project within a mile probably added no more than one-tenth of one violent crime annually. Roncek did find, in contrast to Farley, that blocks made up of public housing had higher rates of violent and property crimes than did nearby blocks without public housing.[32]

Roncek had hit upon an important methodological issue in assessing PHD crime—an issue that was often ignored by studies before his and has bedeviled similar research since. Statistical arguments frequently hinge on a study's use of a "control group." Ideally, the control group is just like the population being studied, except they have not been exposed to the experiment's conditions. By comparing outcomes between the control groups and "treatment groups," one can tease out the impact of a particular factor, from the efficacy of cancer treatments to the effects of welfare payments. Of course, the real world rarely gives social scientists the gift of experimental conditions, and they have learned to make do with control groups that share many, if not all, demographic variables with the treatment group, while adjusting for the rest. Public housing, however, may offer a case so extreme as to render it impervious to researchers' algorithmic maneuvering.

Appropriate control groups for public housing may be impossible to identify because public housing is not randomly distributed across space—rather it is concentrated in areas that often suffer from disorder and deterioration unrelated to whatever effects public housing may bring. The reasons are many. Municipal officials, eager to preserve or extend patterns of segregation, diverted public housing construction to some of urban America's most downtrodden districts. Likewise, wealthier neighborhoods were often able to resist such incursions. At the same time, it was typically only on the cities' fraying edges, or dying industrial pockets, that even well-meaning planners found the large swaths of real estate necessary for public housing's huge towers. Nor were public housing residents themselves randomly selected; whether because of deeper pockets or lighter skin, those with more options increasingly took them. And so the nation's most vulnerable people were often housed in its most vulnerable places, frequently isolated from even the declining employment and social services offered by the deindustrializing city.[33] According to criminologist Garth Davies, "The physical and social features of public housing [neighborhoods] differ so from those found in typical residential neighborhoods that contrasting areas with and without public housing . . . may be entirely inappropriate."[34]

It is not obvious how all of the jigsaw pieces of evidence from the 1970s might fit together to form a coherent picture of PHD crime. It is no surprise, however, that studies conducted at different times and places generated findings that varied in their details: crime fluctuated significantly across the decade, and PHD management practices varied greatly from city to city.[35] But like Sherlock Holmes's dog that did not bark in the night, what the researchers in the 1970s and early 1980s did *not* find may be the real story. Investigators did *not* discover that public housing was predictably a more violent place for the poor than was private housing. Nor did they find that public housing complexes particularly menaced surrounding neighborhoods. But the last research on PHD crime during this period appeared in 1982, and the next round of studies would not be published for more than a decade. The intervening years were hard ones for public housing. Deindustrializing urban economies created fewer opportunities for residents, and a flourishing new (and violent) informal economy centered on drugs emerged. Some projects faced both physical deterioration and depopulation as housing authorities, ravaged by funding cuts, sought to rid themselves of their most troubled buildings by withholding maintenance. Such neglect proved especially hospitable to crime—particularly narcotics trafficking, which brought money. With the money came guns and a violent scramble for markets.[36] When researchers did turn their attention again to public housing, the accumulated consequences of these changes made the projects look very different than they once had.

Federal Funding Returns and a Shifting Crime Mix

Federal funding for public housing crime research returned in the late 1980s amid the highly publicized arrival of crack cocaine and its devastating impact on urban communities.[37] For good reasons and bad, drugs occupied center stage in this era's PHD crime studies. In what became a creation myth of sorts for the new wave of research, Jack Kemp, HUD secretary during the elder George Bush's administration, reportedly witnessed drug deals firsthand while touring Baltimore's public housing projects in 1989. So "shocked" was Kemp that he ordered the nation's public housing directors "to report to him on the volume of drug trafficking occurring in the developments under their jurisdiction."[38] HUD money flowed to researchers to document drug dealing in public housing. And discover it they did—in spades.

There was just one catch. Drug deals are not like other crime—at least from the perspectives of sellers and buyers. The business is, generally, consensual and threatens no one's rights when money and product change hands. Moreover, everyone in the game has a keen interest in concealing their activities. In short, a drug sale frequently requires a cop's presence for it to exist as an offense "known to the police"—unlike, say, homicide, which is nearly always reported. And so researchers hoping to measure drug crime often have only the decidedly imperfect proxy index of drug arrests. Various studies in this period reported that public housing residents—from New Orleans to Los Angeles—were arrested for drug offenses far in excess of their share of the population. Had these studies uncovered extraordinarily elevated drug use in public housing?[39] Or had they just documented the consequence of more police in public housing? More arrests could indicate more cops just as easily as they revealed more drugs. Few doubted—and journalistic and ethnographic research confirmed—that trafficking had taken hold in public housing in a major fashion and often upended tenants' lives.[40] But whether or not drug distribution and use was more of a problem in PHDs than would have been true in a poor neighborhood without public housing was not empirically knowable. At a time when the Public Housing Drug Elimination Program was providing hundreds of millions in grants to cash-strapped housing authorities to combat drugs, few wanted to question the accuracy of figures upon which such money depended. Indeed, a disproportionate slice of antidrug money went to the projects. In 1992, the $1.5 billion federal dollars for all drug-related activities (enforcement, education, treatment, and prevention) amounted to an expenditure of about $7 per citizen, but totaled more than $47 per public housing resident with the additional investments.[41] As numerous scholars have pointed out, narcotics is one of the few places where the federal government, and politicians eager for votes, can inject themselves into America's otherwise highly local criminal justice system.[42] And so research, and the production of knowledge, followed federal drug money.

Moreover, some of the drug research suggested that crime in general was higher in public housing. One 1994 study commissioned by the National Institute of Justice (NIJ) compared violent and property offenses in PHDs in Los Angeles, Phoenix, and Washington, D.C., with nearby neighborhoods that were not home to projects. But as the researchers conceded, these neighborhoods were merely "comparison" areas rather than the "control groups" that statisticians might insist upon. Although the paired neighborhoods suffered from problems such as poverty and unemployment higher than citywide rates, such problems were "less grave in these nearby neighborhoods than in public housing." While the NIJ researchers did not control for these differences, their findings revealed levels of violent crime in LA and DC's public housing that were twice that of neighboring areas—a disparity so large that it probably would not have melted away entirely even after proper statistical controls.[43] The NIJ's raw figures for Phoenix, however, recorded that public housing complexes there suffered from just 20 percent more violent crimes than their "comparison" neighborhoods. This suggests that had the authors used multiple regressions, the difference between PHDs and nearby areas in Phoenix might well have been quite modest. (Such studies also make clear that public housing crime was far from monolithic; there were certainly high crime projects, but there were also low crime projects.)

Studies, however, continued to point in contradictory directions. Casting different methodological nets into different public housing developments, criminologists brought up different findings. The importance of controlling for socioeconomic conditions and historical forces, for example, was made clear in a study of Washington, DC., and Cleveland conducted by the Urban Institute the same year as the NIJ's study of Los Angeles, Phoenix, and DC. The researchers found that after considering rates of physical decay, social disorganization, and economic deprivation in comparison neighborhood and PHDs, public housing did not consistently elevate risks of violent crime.[44]

Despite the various studies' contradictory claims, it is still possible to divine broad trends. If the range of findings from the 1970s and early 1980s suggested public housing was either less violent or no more violent than similarly situated private housing, the findings from the 1990s suggested public housing was either about as or more dangerous. Moreover, it was not merely the *level* of crime that was changing in PHDs, it was the *mix* of crimes as well. For all of the methodological nitpicking that the NIJ's 1994 DC-Phoenix-LA study invites, the researchers were the first to observe the early signs of changes in project life that would become a near constant in later research. In contrast to what researchers had found in PHDs over the previous two decades, the NIJ team discovered that DC and LA's PHDs had *lower* rates of *property crimes* than either the city at large or their immediate neighborhoods—even as they suffered from more *violent crime*. (In Phoenix, public housing suffered from property crime at a rate four times that of the city at large, a figure more in keeping with HUD's 1970s research.)[45]

The Current Research Paradigm

Out of the inconsistencies and ambiguities of research, two significant steps forward came in the late 1990s, compliments of HUD money and changing technology. In 1994, HUD—eager to evaluate the impact of the hundreds of millions spent on the Public Housing Drug Elimination Program—contracted with the Research Triangle Institute (RTI) to "retrofit" the National Crime Victimization Survey for use in public housing. Public housing, HUD believed, posed distinct problems for such surveys. In response, the RTI researchers designed a methodology adapted to public housing's distinctive world. RTI produced a particularly powerful toolkit; not surprisingly, it was too expensive for use by individual public housing authorities. But before HUD decided that they had bought more than they wanted, the survey allowed Holzman to conclude (as noted earlier) that, contrary to Oscar Newman's assertions, public housing crime correlated far more closely with the number of residents in a complex than with building height.

While surveys proved to be a methodological cul-de-sac, the development of affordable GIS technology in the mid-1990s (combined with significant HUD money) did lead to both an explosion of PHD crime data and greater confidence in the findings. The emerging technology has also helped answer long-standing questions about the causal role public housing residents play—as both perpetrators and victims—in crime. Scholars have wondered, for example, whether public housing itself elevates crime, or if it simply stacks together individuals whose everyday lives, by dint of poverty and segregation, leave them more vulnerable to victimization regardless of where they live. The new GIS research suggests that the latter is probably more accurate than the former. HUD researchers, using crime data from two cities (identified for anonymity as City X and City Y), discovered that black women living in public housing suffered aggravated assaults more frequently than did black women living in private housing. Even for criminologists who traffic in such risk differentials, the heightened dangers confronting public housing residents were startling. After controlling for a host of demographic factors, black women living in City X's public housing were thirty percent more likely to fall prey to an aggravated assault than were those who did not; worse yet, black women living in City Y's public housing suffered assaults twice as often as did those in private housing. And while those numbers alone would have been significant and troubling, the real surprise in the study's findings—made possible by GIS—was not in the assaults' *frequency* but in their *location*. Indeed, when considered alongside other research, the geography of assaults in these two cities may point to new and important ways to think about PHD crime.[46]

In City X, seven out of ten of women living in PHDs who were assaulted suffered their ordeal on project grounds. But in City Y's public housing, where assault rates on females were even higher, the grounds of the projects themselves actually proved to "present little risk of serious personal violence for residents and visitors." Indeed, only 8 percent of assaults on City Y's female PHDs residents happened on project grounds; the vast majority took place somewhere else.[47] In short, although City Y's public housing was home to

79

women who were particularly likely to suffer an aggravated assault, that violence rarely transpired in a project. In contrast, despite the fact that City X's PHDs also concentrated women who were more likely to be victims, when such women were assaulted, it happened in the PHDs themselves. The relative size of the projects in cities X and Y, the researchers speculated, may explain these differences. Their thinking suggests that the small scale of City Y's public housing complexes—with many fewer units than City X's developments—allowed the project communities to subject residents and visitors alike to greater scrutiny, discouraging potential attacks in ways that City X's larger PHDs could not. Regardless of the deterrent value of particular PHD designs, however, the high assault rates for female residents in cities X and Y, coupled with the very different locations of those assaults, underscore that projects often concentrate a population that is already at particular risk of victimization outside of whatever ill effects public housing itself might contribute —whether such putative dangers spring from flawed architecture, incompetent management, or political neglect.

Researchers employing the same GIS technology also found that by the late 1990s, violent crime was significantly higher in public housing complexes than in their immediate neighborhoods. In a three-city analysis, Holzman concluded that (1) PHDs more dangerous than areas within 300 meters of projects, and (2) even those 300-meter buffer zones were, in turn, more dangerous than the city at large. Violent crime, it seemed, clustered in and around public housing—confirming long-standing stereotypes. Property crimes in public housing, however, told a different story. Holzman's research confirmed the curious mix of crimes identified by both the NIJ and Dumanovsky: *property crime was lower* in public housing than in adjacent neighborhoods and, perhaps even more surprising, was often lower than in the host city itself. Some analysts have concluded that property crime in PHDs is lower simply because public housing residents make unattractive targets for thieves. Such thinking has a certain logic: having less to steal lowers one's odds of being stolen from. Holzman, however, proposes an alternative explanation, arguing that criminology's "routine activity theory" helps us to see this mix of higher violent and lower property crime rates in public housing as two sides of the same coin. Moreover, combining Holzman's hypothesis with the historical shifts in public housing crime data may help shed significant light on the changing experience of public housing tenants during the past half century.

Holzman points out that PHD residents are more homebound than the typical city dweller. And that difference, Holzman argues, helps shape project crime. The more frequent presence of PHDs residents in their apartments makes them, on the one hand, "capable guardians" of their possessions (deterring theft); on the other hand, it means that they are more likely to be assaulted there (increasing violent crime rates). As Holzman notes, only a third of PHD households have wage income, while the remaining survive on public assistance, social security, pensions, and (at times) informal or illicit markets. Nearly half of all PHD households have children, and 30 percent are headed by the elderly. Collectively, then, higher rates of unemployment, infirmity, retirement, and child-rearing mean that comparatively more PHD residents are home at any given hour. And so, Holzman argues, "there is no shortage of potential guardians in public housing developments to discourage property crime."[48]

There is, however, the coin's other side. These "capable guardians" also face a greater chance of violent assault. Statistically speaking, to be a young African American woman in a low-income, urban household is to live with a greater risk of violence at the hands of a husband or boyfriend. And this demographic group disproportionately calls public housing home. According to Holzman, the same capable guardian "who, by her very presence, protects her home against thieves" is vulnerable "to physical assault by persons known to her" in her apartment.[49] In short, PHDs now gather a comparatively homebound population both more vulnerable to criminal violence and less likely to experience property crime.

Holzman's hypothesis goes a long way toward explaining the somewhat unexpected shift in public housing's crime mix over the past four decades. Recall that researchers in the 1970s found that public housing residents were more at risk of property crime rather than violent crime. But that pattern of offenses had reversed itself by the time criminologists finally returned to PHDs in the 1990s. As researchers at the NIJ discovered, by the middle of that decade, PHD residents faced more violent crime than property crime. Changing tenancy within public housing may well have caused this seismic shift in the mix of project crimes. As late as the 1970s, public housing nationally still contained a good many working adults whose jobs took them away from their apartments and whose paychecks allowed some off-project amusements. Those absences exposed homes to theft and placed residents in a variety of alternative environments where they might or might not suffer personal violence. But as wage earners increasingly abandoned public housing, their places were taken by those whose sources of income and affordable pleasures did not tug them from their project. Daily life unfolded closer to project grounds than had been true for earlier generations—cutting property crimes but also increasing PHD violence. And so the transformation of public housing's crime mix may well reflect the larger transformation of public housing's tenancy.

Does Public Housing Make Neighborhoods Dangerous?

Researchers have also turned the klieg light of GIS onto perhaps the longest-standing fear about public housing—that projects make neighborhoods dangerous. Such worries take several forms. Does public housing radiate violence outward? Or does it draw violence inward from surrounding areas?[50] As with other research questions, scholars studying different cities have produced findings that point in multiple directions. Davies, taking advantage of New York's uniquely rich PHD crime statistics, argues for what he calls "two-way diffusion" effects. With few exceptions, he observed that crime in Gotham's boroughs clusters in "hot spots." PHDs, however, seem to foster such hot spots. Hot spots appear near PHDs at twice their expected rate, and "extreme hot spots" three times so. But crime seeps in both directions: poor neighborhood conditions increase the number of assaults inside public housing, while drug markets centered in the developments push up homicide rates in surrounding areas.[51]

Research from other cities suggests that how, how much, and where project crime spills over into surrounding neighborhoods depends on local conditions and history. Sociologists Thomas McNulty and Steven Holloway assert that the impact of Atlanta's public housing on neighborhood crime rates is inextricably linked to the city's history of segregation. One consequence of that near-apartheid experience, they argue, has been that public housing is a "feature of the institutional fabric of Black Atlanta, from which White Atlanta is socially and physically insulated." And so when Atlanta's projects rub up against white neighborhoods, that proximity "has little effect on violent crime rates." But in nonwhite neighborhoods, nearness to public housing "is closely associated with violent crime." Segregation's legacy of social isolation shapes public housing's criminogenic impact across space.[52] Researchers in Los Angeles have found similar patterns. Elizabeth Griffiths and George Tita discovered that although LA's public housing is a disturbingly lethal place, that deadly violence sticks to where residents spend their time—on project grounds—and seldom spills out. Griffiths and Tita argue that residents' tightly circumscribed worlds help explain this geography of crime. The homicide statistics tell the story: murderers who do not live in public housing are three times more likely to take the life of someone living in a different neighborhood than are killers living in public housing. The researchers conclude that PHD offenders strike "close to home; they are not responsible for escalating violence in the larger community."[53]

Public Housing Crime in Historical Perspective

Many of these recent studies would seem to confirm stereotypes that have followed public housing residents for a half century. And in a sense, they do. But in other ways, the research can mislead. While the findings are genuinely disquieting, this recent scholarship is best understood within a larger historical context. These studies document public housing long after the program had decayed, in many places, into a shelter of last resort. Consequently, the research does a better job of capturing the accumulated costs of decades of neglect than it does in establishing an immutable relationship between public housing and crime. Moreover, because these studies do not always address how some projects sunk as low as they have, the research risks implying that some innate quality of public housing (or its residents) creates disorder. The problem stems partially from research conditions. In the absence of historical crime data, criminologists have tended to compare public and private housing areas at a single (and recent) point in time. Longitudinal studies of public housing violence have been rare. And so, in contrast to much criminological scholarship, where crime rates rise and fall (and structural causes can be pinpointed), public housing crime in the literature often just *is*.

New York City, however, provides an exception. There, the Housing Authority Police Department (1952–1995) kept separate, and reasonably accurate, crime statistics. These fortuitous circumstances allowed a charting of crime in NYCHA—the nation's largest public housing program—across time.[54] NYCHA's violent crime figures reveal that through the mid-1970s, New York's public housing was, on average, 60 percent safer than the city at large. Although violent crime rates rose in both NYCHA and the city during those decades, NYCHA's started lower and grew more slowly. Between 1967 and 1977, violent crime rates in NYCHA complexes tracked but did not intensify movements in New York's violent crime rate. Indeed, what might be dubbed the "safety dividend" of living in public housing grew in these years. In 1967, NYCHA's complexes were 42 percent safer than New York's streets; in 1974 they were 78 percent safer. Little wonder that NYCHA's projects enjoyed a reputation among the poor at the time as a refuge from Gotham's escalating violence. After 1977, however, the trend underwent a dizzying reversal, as every bump in the city's crime rates was accompanied by a greater jump in NYCHA's. When, for example, New York's violent crime rate floated up 13 percent between 1986 and 1988, NYCHA's leaped 40 percent. By the late 1980s, NYCHA's developments were more dangerous than their surrounding neighborhoods *and* the city at large (and remain so as of this writing). Changing tenant demographics, shifting policing and management practices, declining funding, rising informal markets, and the arrival of crack cocaine all help explain these patterns. But it is clear from NYCHA's experience that, contrary to popular belief, public housing can provide safe and stable neighborhoods—and did so for decades.[55]

Nor is NYCHA's history unique in the way it challenges the narratives of criminality that encrust public housing and, increasingly, shape public policy. No doubt, such images have suited some big-city projects in recent years. But as housing historian Edward Goetz points out, "the overwhelming majority" of public housing developments are not marked by criminality and "provide a better alternative than private-sector housing in poor neighborhoods."[56] Even in larger cities with high crime rates, the connection to public housing is not always clear. Sociologist Zaire Dinzey-Flores, for example, has observed that during the 1990s, police sectors in San Juan, Puerto Rico, containing public housing enjoyed lower crime rates than those without. According to Dinzey-Flores, these numbers undercut politicians' rationale for that city's highly publicized practice of militarized, predawn housing project sweeps as part of Puerto Rico's policy of *mano dura contra el crimen* ("strike hard against crime").[57]

Does Dismantling Public Housing Simply Displace Crime?

Just as criminologists started using GIS to answer timeworn questions about crime and public housing, the frequent target of this new statistical firepower—the large, inner-city project—was vanishing from view. Between 1990 and 2010, housing authorities sold or demolished more than 220,000 such units. As Goetz asked in a 2011 article title, "Where Have all the Towers Gone?"[58] In a reversal of public housing policy, nearly seven billion federal dollars have been spent on what is arguably the nation's most ambitious urban renewal scheme—HOPE VI. Aiming to "deconcentrate" poverty, the program tears down PHDs in varying states of distress—and occupied exclusively by the poor—and erects in their stead mixed-income developments with fewer impoverished residents. HOPE VI's environmental premise was as simple as its policy promise was grand. Once the towers disappeared, so too would the ills of the urban poor. Those former tenants excluded by the new developments' much higher rents or newly exacting screening standards, would (in theory) be given housing vouchers that would (again, in theory) allow them to fend for themselves on the private market, where (theoretically) individual landlords would shelter them better and at a lower cost than the state had done.[59]

Public housing's hulking, inner-city towers came down first, but soon even smaller cities with low-rise developments got in on the act. No doubt, HOPE VI's many critics are correct in fingering real estate interests hungry for profits and neoliberal politicians eager to remake the urban order as driving forces behind the program's wide embrace. But criminological thinking also played its role. Support for HOPE VI often came from a circle of increasingly pessimistic housing specialists. Many had been chastened by Chicago's failure in the 1990s to turn around its lawless complexes, even after spending hundreds of millions of dollars on elaborate community crime prevention efforts and aggressive policing. What this group of scholars came to share, observed Susan Popkin, was the "sense that a new, radical approach was the only way to improve the life chances for residents." Likewise, as Goetz documents, even in midsized cities like Tucson, Arizona, crime rates correlated closely with how frequently wrecking balls tore into a city's public housing. HOPE VI's results have been mixed at best, but the near extinction of the "projects"—those "towers in the park," so long and widely maligned—has changed the criminological research agenda.[60]

Two new questions—one posed by housing scholars and one forced upon them—have emerged. First, if to live in public housing is now frequently to live in a "bad" neighborhood that is truly injurious to children and families, would moving to better neighborhoods make for better lives (including decreased exposure to and participation in crime)? Answering this question was the explicit goal of the Moving to Opportunity experiment (MTO), a social experiment of unprecedented size and scope: $80 million spent, more than five thousand participants followed, and a decade's worth of longitudinal data collected from five cities. The second question—did HOPE VI relocatees raise crime rates when they moved to new their communities?—was the focus of a smaller but well-designed study.

MTO aimed to answer the first question through a study conducted under conditions approaching "experimental"—that elusive grail of social scientists. In doing so, MTO researchers hoped to avoid a methodological predicament that vexed previous studies of the court-ordered *Gautreaux* Project, which had assisted tenants of Chicago's hypersegregated projects move to suburbia. Although the life circumstances of *Gautreaux* participants seemed to improve in the suburbs, evaluations of the program could not answer a crucial policy-relevant question: If the PHD residents who opted to move out differed in meaningful ways—more ambitious, say—from those who stayed behind, might comparing the two groups tell us more about the power of individual traits than it did about the impact of one environment or the other? To avoid this problem, MTO used a lottery to randomly assign families (almost all female-headed and minority) to different research groups; each group would receive different types of help in moving, or not, from high poverty neighborhoods to lower poverty ones. The use of random assignments, the researchers believed, would generate comparable groups and so uncover the potential effects of neighborhood on how well families fared.[61]

MTO's results were more mixed than anyone had expected—and no more so than in the impact of environment on former public housing residents' experience of crime. That the program's benefits on that score were so ambiguous has a particular poignancy, since four out of five MTO participants identified escaping the lawlessness of their PHD as their overriding goal in moving to a new neighborhood. MTO's mixed findings spring from a puzzling gender split revealed by the experiment. Moving to lower poverty neighborhoods benefited adolescent girls in regard to a host of crime and risk-related aspects of their lives, but the move seemed only to make matters worse for boys. By leaving public housing for less poor neighborhoods, girls experienced a "profound drop in sexual pressures, predation, and related types of risk." Such gains in safety and sense of security had profound benefits for the mental health of relocating girls. Their levels of depression dropped by a fifth—a reduction researchers noted was "comparable to that achieved by some of the most successful drug treatments." But for boys, researchers concluded, "the picture is a sad one." Compared to those who remained in public housing, moving to a lower poverty neighborhood did not reduce their chance of being arrested for violent crime—and actually increased property crimes arrest rates. The researchers considered a number of explanations: increased police surveillance in the new neighborhoods, more (and more expensive) goods available for thieving, and differing parental gender expectations. The researchers tentatively speculated that complex interactions between parenting and neighborhood best explained these gender differences (and rejected increased police attention as a likely causal factor).[62] But given other studies reviewed here, the boys' increased arrest rates may simply reflect the fact that their new neighborhoods lacked the "capable guardians" of PHDs' comparatively more homebound population.

The second question was propelled not by academics but by Hanna Rosin's widely read and provocative *Atlantic* article, discussed briefly at the beginning of this chapter. Rosin painted a vivid picture of HOPE VI as a "grand anti-poverty experiment" that was backfiring. In Rosin's telling, former project tenants with a housing voucher in one hand and a Saturday Night Special in the other were "migrating" to the suburbs, bringing a crime spike in their wake. Despite holes in the article's arguments, its popularity obliged criminologists to explore this second question more explicitly. As displaced public housing residents moved to private market housing, did their problems—including violent crime—accompany them?

The scholarly response to Rosin's article was certain and swift. Within months, Shelterforce, a prominent affordable housing journal, published a rebuttal by Peter Dreier and Xavier de Souza Briggs and endorsed by two dozen housing experts. Dreier and Briggs asserted that Rosin had simply gotten her facts wrong. Few of the "migratory" poor arriving in suburbs did so with government help; the MTO experiment maligned in the article actually played no role in Memphis (the focus of her piece); and most former PHD residents moved to places that were not only near their original homes but also "already on the decline, with rising crime rates." HOPE VI could hardly have brought violence to once-bucolic suburbs. Rosin, likewise, failed to consider alternative explanations for suburban crime, leaving readers "inappropriately confident in her ghetto-migration hypothesis."[63]

In particular, Rosin overlooked that HOPE VI was only one of several forces remaking suburbia. Many of the poor *did* leave the worst ghettos in the 1990s, but it was market forces—gentrifying urban neighborhoods and robust job markets—that largely provided the push-and-pull dynamics. Government intervention played, at most, a small role. Additionally, most of the poor relocated to "first-ring suburbs"—older neighborhoods circling cities' ragged edges—that were often just barely better off than the areas they left. Indeed, the share of the poor living in suburbs quadrupled between 1970 and 2000. HOPE VI relocatees were a small rivulet in a larger demographic flow. Finally, Rosin offered no evidence that HOPE VI's beneficiaries contributed meaningfully to growing poverty in their new neighborhoods, let alone committed more than their share of crime there. But Dreier and Briggs themselves had no evidence that the relocatees were *not* increasing disorder. The answer to this question, however, would come shortly.[64]

In 2011, Susan Popkin, Michael Rich, Leah Hendey, Chris Hayes, and Joe Parilla undertook the most methodologically sophisticated study to date of relocated residents' impact on local crime. Their research tapped the rich veins of statistical evidence offered by the nation's two largest HOPE VI sites, Chicago (1999–2008) and Atlanta (2002–2009). The good crime news of recent years, however, complicated matters, making it difficult to determine whether or not PHD transplants elevated crime when crime itself was tumbling nearly everywhere. Rather than simply look at crime trajectories, the researchers constructed yardsticks of *predicted* crime declines against which to compare *actual* drops after HOPE VI relocations. The results suggested residents' fears (amply revealed in focus groups) of HOPE VI were largely, but not entirely, misplaced. In both cities, violent and property crime declined dramatically in neighborhoods where PHDs were demolished. The effects in neighborhoods receiving HOPE VI residents were a little more complex. As long as the number of former project residents in a new neighborhood remained low, there was no real increase in crime. But "once the number of relocated households reached a certain threshold, crime rates, on average, decreased less than they would have if there had been no former public housing in-movers." When relocated households made up more than six per one thousand households, the violent crime rate was 11 percent higher on average in Atlanta, and 13 percent in Chicago. When such neighborhood density exceeded fourteen, the average crime rate was 21 percent higher in both cities. So, although crime still dropped in such neighborhoods, it dropped less than if the neighborhood had not received HOPE VI residents. Although these modest increases belie Rosin's alarmist account, it was also clear from the data that HOPE VI voucher-assisted households who had previously lived in public housing brought more troubles with them than conventional Section 8 holders who had not lived in public housing. As Popkin et al. observed, "Traditional voucher holders have much smaller effects on crime rates than relocated [HOPE VI] households, and it takes a much higher density of traditional voucher holders before we see any effect at all."[65]

Such studies run the risk of casting public housing residents as innately criminogenic elements that, like radioactive ash, must be held below a certain threshold in the environment. To their credit, Popkin et al. use their findings to bolster an argument for "responsible relocation," with a particular emphasis on supportive services. But the political and social choices that created the conditions for former public housing residents' criminal participation can easily vanish from view given the framing of such research.

Conclusion

If questions about the relationship between public housing developments and crime rates have been of such concern to researchers, why were good answers so long in coming? And why did those answers often seem to be frustratingly mixed, if not outright contradictory, when they did arrive? No doubt, a public that had already made up its mind about public housing—whether that opinion was favorable, as during the New Deal, or hostile, as during the Reagan Revolution— did not clamor for complete and complex answers. And even specialists can overlook methodological lapses when findings align with useful paradigms. The 1930s experts who championed the crime-fighting potential of "hygienic" structures and open spaces were as imprecise as those who, four decades later, linked modernist architecture to criminal invasion.[66] As Michel Foucault reminds us, historical moments generate the authoritative specialists and putative knowledge broader social agendas require.[67] But even doggedly independent researchers with large budgets and open eyes might have found it difficult to assess the moving target that public housing presented. As a program, public housing has long been both varied and changing. What was true for St. Louis was not true for Baltimore, and what was true for New York in 1965 was not true there in 1980. Different methodologies applied in different cities at different times generated—unsurprisingly—different findings. But the simple and frequently invoked idea that "public housing increases crime" is demonstrably false as both an analytic conclusion and a causal model, even as it has proved remarkably powerful as a cultural narrative. The variations in public housing's context, physical form, and management policies require answers with more explanatory suppleness. Nearly two generations of research on public housing and crime leaves us with this fairly unsatisfying generalization: some public housing seems to have increased crime rates under certain conditions, while other projects, under different conditions, are actually safer than private housing.

Taking a historical approach to research about public housing crime highlights the importance of context for understanding both the nature of public housing itself and how knowledge about it gets produced. Simplistic comparisons of crime rates between PHDs and their surrounding neighborhoods generated research questions that ignored the larger social and historical forces that located public housing in the most vulnerable neighborhoods. This made it nearly impossible for researchers to identify the "comparison areas" required by statistical analysis. Likewise, the research environment of the 1970s narrowed scholars' analytic vision from larger social forces to the criminogenic impact of architectural details. The lure of federal dollars a decade later pushed discussions (and finger-pointing) away from design and toward drugs, despite a dearth of reliable crime numbers.

The emergence over time of more discerning analytical tools has made it possible to disaggregate the data and so achieve greater specificity about crime at the neighborhood level. Pinpointing crime with quantitative data, however, underscores the importance of attention to the larger social context. Public housing's shifting tenancy changed both how *much* crime occurred and the relative *mix* of property and violent offenses. The architectural determinism of "high rise = high crime" proved overly simplistic under more rigorous analysis, as the number and demographic characteristics of residents proved to be much more important for crime than the type of structure in which they lived. As more and more deeply disadvantaged people found themselves concentrated in public housing and left without meaningful support, the chances that their PHD would be marred by violence grew as well.

But it was not just the research questions about public housing crime that proved vexingly complex; the large-scale policy solutions of recent years have not unfolded as originally envisioned. Despite social scientists' straightforward predictions and politicians' easy platitudes, the safety benefits of breaking up the concentrated poverty of PHDs have proved to be highly contingent and sometimes contradictory. In practice, deconcentration has benefited girls more than boys; worked less well with PHD residents than Section 8 holders; and occasionally elevated crime. As this and so many other examples confirm, questions about crime and public housing offer no easy answers for stakeholders—researchers, policymakers, and public housing residents alike.

HIGH-RISE PUBLIC HOUSING IS UNMANAGEABLE

Nicholas Dagen Bloom

Most Americans believe that high-rise public housing, by its very nature, is unmanageable. If this premise were true, then New York City's public housing system should have collapsed decades ago for the simple reason that *the system is dominated by large, high-rise public housing developments.* More than half of NYCHA's towers (58 percent) are seven stories or higher, with some structures, such as the four massive towers of Polo Grounds Towers (1968), reaching 30 stories. The myth that high-rise public housing is unmanageable looks solid when applied to cities such as St. Louis or Chicago, but it fails to account for the long-term experience in New York City, home to 15 percent of the nation's traditional public housing units.[1]

Between 1934 and 1965, the New York City Housing Authority (NYCHA) built sixty-nine developments (of 154 total it constructed during that time), *each* with at least one thousand apartments in the modernist "tower in the park" formation (Figure 4.1).[2] Even "smaller" NYCHA developments from this time usually included high-rise superblocks with hundreds of units per development. In many cases, these developments were built adjacent to each other, creating public housing concentrations rivaling any in the world. Surely some of those developments should have failed as spectacularly as Pruitt-Igoe in St. Louis or Cabrini-Green in Chicago. But they didn't.

Even Hurricane Sandy, which hit New York City on October 29, 2012, and was the worst storm in the region's modern history, was not able to wipe New York's public housing from the map. After an incomplete resident evacuation in flood-prone areas and a lot of bad press concerning tenant well-being post-storm, NYCHA employees and emergency contractors rapidly restored all the systems, or at least put in place long-term temporary fixes such as mobile

Figure 4.1 East River Houses (1941, 1,158 units, 2,435 residents) includes a mix of six-, ten-, and eleven-story buildings. East River Houses became a model for NYCHA design and site planning in the postwar period, often at even greater building heights. The development was still fully occupied and maintained in 2014. Photograph by author.

boilers, even in the hardest hit areas of the Rockaways in Queens and Coney Island in southwest Brooklyn. All of the approximately eighty thousand public housing residents in the affected buildings had power and heat within one month; by contrast, some residents in conventional housing in the Rockaways ended up waiting months for basic services. In 2014, FEMA announced its first major grant, for Coney Island Houses, of $108 million dollars for rebuilding building systems and flood proofing; the scale and aim of the grant was announced as a precedent for fifteen other developments in flood zones. The difference between the experience in New Orleans (post-Katrina in 2005), when a storm was used as an opportunity to close and demolish most of the city's public housing developments, could not be more stark.[3]

As of 2014, New York has twenty-six hundred public housing towers (178,557 units) that provide shelter for four hundred thousand mostly poor residents (with an average family income of approximately $23,000). Many activists, and even some NYCHA officials, believe the actual total population of these developments, including unregistered occupants, may be closer to six hundred thousand. Nearly 11,700 full-time employees tend to NYCHA apartments, buildings, and grounds. The average rent of $434 per month is significantly less than one would pay for market rent in most American cities, much less New York City. The vacancy rate for NYCHA apartments is only .6 percent, and the waiting lists for conventional public housing include over two hundred thousand families. Only 11 percent of residents are on welfare; 47 percent are working families (at least one member employed or pensioned), and the remainder, including growing numbers of seniors who head up most NYCHA families, are reliant on Social Security, pensions, or disability insurance. Violent crime in public housing remains significantly higher than in the city as a whole, and vandalism is extensive, but NYCHA developments have experienced significant and sustained crime reduction since the 1990s. Even more impressive, the surrounding neighborhoods have seen still greater drops in crime—a remarkable trend considering the big high-rise developments that loom over them.[4]

This successful maintenance, when acknowledged at all, is usually attributed to factors other than NYCHA management. Indeed, contextual factors that distinguish New York from other cities certainly complicate any one-to-one comparison between New York's public housing and that in other cities: (1) the historically tight housing market means that a public housing apartment is worth getting and keeping; (2) New York City's better financial health has provided extra policing and social services; (3) the city's diverse economy provides jobs for many residents that are unavailable in other cities; (4) New York—both as a city and in public housing—has been and is today more diverse socially and ethnically than many other cities where public housing came to be viewed as primarily a program for poor African Americans; (5) politicians citywide, most of whom have a development in their districts, tend to support greater upkeep and security rather than calling for public housing destruction as was common in other cities; (6) most housing developments in New York have better access to mass transit, and therefore to employment, than those in other U.S. cities; and (7) apartment living is the norm in New York City so residence in high-rise public housing may carry less of a stigma than in a predominantly low-rise city. Acknowledging contextual influences does not, however, explain away the dramatic differences in public housing outcomes between New York and other cities.

Contextual factors, for instance, have not and do not today render New York public housing environments free from poverty, crime, and social disorder. While perhaps less stigmatized than other cities, most New Yorkers can distinguish between "projects" and other apartment buildings. Vandalism is common; many residents throw trash from windows daily and break front door locks; visitors or residents frequently urinate in elevators—and have done so for decades. These developments house a disproportionate percentage of the city's poorest residents, including many single-parent families, and many developments continue to experience above-average rates of crime (albeit in a city where crime on average is very low). Compared to Chicago, NYCHA as a whole has had lower youth density, but there have been and are today a number of developments with high youth densities and accompanying issues. Woodrow Wilson Houses (1961), for instance, has many large apartments, and in 1966 hit a high of 63.5 percent minors: a figure on par with troubled developments in other cities. In 2013, Wilson Houses still housed a disproportionate percentage of youth: 42 percent of the population was under 21 (528 out of 1,260 registered residents). This high youth population creates extra security and vandalism issues, but the development is still decent and maintained over half a century after it opened.[5]

Nor has the New York location always been an asset. NYCHA developments, while found in every borough (Figure 4.2), are mostly concentrated in some of the city's poorest, low-income neighborhoods such as Brownsville, Bushwick, the South Bronx, and East Harlem. Gentrification may be advancing today in some of these districts, but for many decades these neighborhoods experienced major social disorder as a result of deindustrialization, white flight, and disinvestment. They remain mostly troubled neighborhoods today with lower incomes, largely mediocre school performance, and higher crime than the rest of the city. Tens of thousands of formerly homeless residents, whom managers believe are often more disruptive and typically have less income for rent, were also given priority for NYCHA apartments in the 1980s (and are again receiving priority in 2014). The New York context matters, but it is obviously not determinative nor an entirely positive influence.

This article focuses on two key elements in the management of high-rise public housing towers: daily maintenance and resident selection. These are not the only elements in the NYCHA story (see *Public Housing That*

Figure 4.2 Astoria Houses (1951, 1,102 units, 3,135 people) includes a mix of six- and seven-story buildings on the Queens waterfront. Astoria Houses is one of NYCHA's typical, large, elevator apartment complexes of the type often found outside Manhattan and Brooklyn. It was still fully occupied in 2014. Photograph by author.

Worked: New York in the Twentieth Century and Fritz Umbach's Myth #9 detailing the important role of housing police in maintaining order), but it is certainly the case, as was demonstrated negatively in other cities, that maintenance and tenant management are critical elements in high-rise public housing survival. Despite episodes of administrative bungling, aging infrastructure, declining federal support, and a vast amount of critical press over its more than seventy-five-year history, NYCHA has developed a custodial system at developments that still works. If anything, NYCHA's biggest challenge today is that it has maintained its developments so much better than other cities that the system now demands massive capital, now in short supply, for renovating building systems that have reached the end of their projected lifespan.

95

The research for this chapter is derived from historical documents, recent reports, news coverage, and on-site visits I made to a variety of NYCHA housing developments. My visits included extensive interviews with managers, supervisors, and other employees who, because of my reputation as a fair observer, were frank and open about the challenges they face in managing these large developments. We also walked the grounds, visiting randomly selected buildings, rode elevators, walked down stair halls, and chatted with caretakers as we went. I have also visited many of these developments unaccompanied and discussed conditions extensively with two prominent NYCHA resident leaders, Carol Wilkins and Ethel Velez. The following developments were visited in March 2013: Bushwick Houses, Van Dyke Houses, Brownsville Houses, Whitman Houses, Ingersoll Houses, Kingsborough Houses, Johnson Houses, Woodrow Wilson Houses, and Ravenswood Houses. These developments are mostly in the major concentrations of public housing in New York (Harlem and East New York) and are typical in terms of size and height. Together, these nine developments officially house nearly twenty-six thousand New Yorkers, but the actual number of residents is likely much higher than that.

Custodial Labor History

What separates New York from many other cities is that administrators have viewed their system as apartment buildings where poor people happen to live, not as "poor people apartments." What is remarkable is that this attitude persists nearly eight decades later in NYCHA developments. Early on, NYCHA set specific staffing numbers and has largely maintained them today, at levels commensurate with or exceeding those found in middle-class buildings. Administrators, for instance, placed thirty-six permanent staff members in the Kingsborough Houses in 1941 to manage 1,100 units.[6] During the postwar era that birthed most of NYCHA's large developments (1945–1965) this heavily staffed system expanded in tandem. In 1952, for instance, officials reported that they maintained a systemwide ratio of staff to residents of one employee per twenty families (approximately eighty residents). The distribution on site was described in more detail in 1957: "Our basic method of staffing is one housing caretaker (porter) for each high-rise building (14 stories or over) . . . and one housing caretaker for three 6 story buildings." While the details have changed over the decades, the general notion of assigning large numbers of workers directly on developments remains. Table 4.1 shows staffing levels at the developments I visited in March 2013.[7]

Table 4.1 Typical NYCHA staff levels

NYCHA development name	Unit total/# of bldgs.	Pop. total	Height: stories	Total staff (official)	Caretakers (% of official total staff)	Maintenance staff on site
Brownsville (1948)	1,337/27	3,447	3/6	37	26 (70%)	5
Bushwick (1960)	1,220/8	3,023	13/20	39	16 (41%)	5
Ingersoll (1944)	1,823/20	2,445	6/11	45	26 (58%)	6
Johnson (1948)	1,299/10	2,277	6/14	36	21 (58%)	5
Kingsborough (1941)	1,154/16	2,393	6/25	34	19 (56%)	2 (5 approved)
Ravenswood (1951)	2,167/31	4,541	6/7	64	28 (43%)	9
Van Dyke I (1955)	1,603/22	4,207	3/14	50	24 (48%)	6
Whitman (1944)	1,652/15	2,336	6/13	47	24 (51%)	7
Woodrow Wilson (1961) (consolidated with E. River, etc.)	399/3	1,273	20	N/A	6	N/A

Source: Actual total staff often varies from total official approved lines as a result of retirements, delays in hiring (related to budget cuts), union rules, civil service tests, etc. Most variations from total approved were minor (1 or 2), but at Van Dyke 42/50 and Kingsborough 29/34, the difference was notable. Most unfilled positions mentioned to me during my visits were above caretaker level—such as housing assistant or maintenance—that require Civil Service exams and come with higher pay. The total number of maintenance workers budgeted citywide, for instance is 800, but 130 of those positions are currently unfilled as a result of both general human resources issues and budget shortfall. Caretaker numbers above did not include supervisor caretakers, caretaker grounds, etc. Selected data from NYCHA developments visited in 2013 as part of the author's research.

The next step was to professionalize the force of workers and managers. Civil service requirements for NYCHA employees, initiated in the 1930s, have played a major role in reducing patronage that corrupted staffs in many other cities. By 1941, 84 percent of NYCHA's 719 employees had been selected through civil service exams, and this requirement persists today for all staff above caretakers, including maintenance workers, supervisors, housing assistants, and all managers. Caretakers are not required to pass civil service exams, but most eventually do so that they can move to a higher level in the organization. Civil service requirements cannot prevent all patronage, but they certainly make patronage more difficult.[8]

The final step was to create a logical and regular division of labor. Abundant staff on site, of course, did not guarantee anything; there are examples of housing authorities (Chicago's, for example) with large staffs that failed to maintain developments at all. But staff always had regular routines at NYCHA: the porter/caretaker, on a daily basis, swept all the stairways and mopped the elevators; weekly, he or she mopped the stairwells. Many of the superintendents and managers in the early developments also brought methods of management from the military. One longtime employee remembered one manager in particular who "would line up all the caretakers in the morning. . . . And he would march them down the development and they would drop off at their buildings."[9]

The challenges of maintenance for this staff were often as serious in New York as in other cities. Fort Greene Houses (1944, 3,501 units, and now referred to as Whitman-Ingersoll), for instance, has endured despite experiencing social and vandalism issues for over half a century. In contrast to the high-quality developments of the 1930s, such as Williamsburg and Harlem River Houses, which boasted high-quality materials and excellent masonry work, cost cutting and wartime exigencies during the construction of Fort Greene necessitated the use of lower quality materials and labor. These economies made maintenance more difficult; behavioral issues quickly compounded the construction problems. In 1945, for instance, residents faced unsanitary conditions "created by the children's misuse of the elevators and public halls, showing an absence of parental guidance and supervision."[10] Social problems continued after the war. By 1957, Fort Greene had "two gangs of men assigned solely to the task of replacing glass" because "one of the forms of amusement for the children in the area seems to be throwing stones at these large panes of glass." Fort Greene by this time not only had broken glass, but also cracking walls, broken light fixtures, and unhinged doors. NYCHA administrators, rather than allow for continued decline, decided to renovate the complex in 1957 including replacing all of the plumbing, repaving the paths, substituting wood doors with stainless steel, renovating benches, and replacing broken glass.[11] This early intervention, followed up by additional renovation in the years to come, indicates how even the weakest of NYCHA's developments received extra attention.

Fort Greene may have been one of the more troubled developments of the era, but in the 1950s NYCHA initiated a decades-long battle to maintain even its best-constructed developments. Reformers brought in to lead NYCHA in the late 1950s, to curtail Robert Moses's hold on the authority, found that "the program as a whole consists of well built, well maintained, well managed modern structures,"[12] but they also identified worrisome trends. In 1957, for instance, one external review found that 20 percent of housing developments were "suffering from 'heavy vandalism and serious disorder'" and another 29.5 percent were "experiencing 'constant vandalism of a petty nature.'"[13] New York public housing was not a paradise, even if the comparatively upwardly mobile population of the time (Sonia Sotomayor, Joel Klein, and others) went on to high-profile careers after living in the developments.

In order to respond to these problems, administrators in the 1950s and 1960s changed design standards. New buildings featured more glazed brick or block rather than painted interior halls. The long-term value of these glazed surfaces is evident even today at high-rise developments such as Bushwick Houses (1960) where the glazed block entries and apartment corridors can be cleaned to a higher level than the painted surfaces at a development such as Fort Greene. Elevator speeds in developments under construction in the 1950s and 1960s also increased in order to reduce the amount of time that children would spend waiting for elevators; long wait times equaled greater opportunities for vandalism, as seen in cities such as Chicago. The fast elevators at the thirty-story Polo Grounds (1968), for instance, are testament to this change of direction. Each of the four towers has six elevators, which are evenly divided between the first and sixteenth floors and the seventeenth and thirtieth floors, and are as good or better than anything comparable in the private-sector housing market.

Historian Samuel Zipp also makes a convincing case that redesign of apartments in the 1950s and 1960s in new developments allowed for greater family privacy and played an important role in keeping NYCHA apartments competitive in the New York market.[14] Apartment interiors now had "bright color, practical tile floors, modern kitchens and separate dinettes, larger windows, and the simple amenities of closet doors, showers, and toilet covers." Some of these basic elements, such as closet doors, had been left out for economic reasons in early developments such as Queensbridge Houses (1940) in order to boost the number of units per development.[15] The many large apartments at Woodrow Wilson Houses (1961) in East Harlem, for instance, were larger than the units in early developments and included eat-in-kitchens, a rarity in New York City as a whole. Apartment upgrades, both to new and many older developments, yielded positive long-term effects. In a 1966 study, 70 percent of the residents in Claremont Village (1962), for instance, rated their apartments highly. Almost 80 percent believed that their new public housing development was better than the neighborhood where they lived before.[16]

Apartment standards may have improved by the 1960s, but the demands on NYCHA staff grew greater every decade, even as the authority updated its methods and materials. At Johnson Houses (1948) a longtime manager recalled in an oral history interview that in the 1960s "the field staff was excellent. The caretakers who are sort of the forgotten soldiers of this fight . . . would go from week to week. They start out on a Monday and start cleaning up the place, straightening out the place, and by Thursday or Friday, the development looks good and really nice. Then of course we got bombed on the weekends, even though we had a crew coming in, but a limited number, on Saturday and Sunday. . . . So that [on] Monday morning the work had to begin again almost from scratch."[17] All that effort may have been frustrating for workers, but it saved the buildings. Johnson Houses in 2013, for instance, remains a well-maintained development with twenty-one caretakers and thirty-six total staff. The hallways are bright (no broken corridor windows), the floors clean, elevators relatively new, and the roof, parapet, and top-floor apartments of all the fourteen-story buildings were recently renovated. The development also received high marks on its HUD PHAS review, which includes random, detailed apartment and building inspections—an achievement that is difficult to attain in such a large and complex system. What is even more remarkable is that this development is situated in the middle of an interproject gang war that has led to many shootings, and some murders, over the past few years.

One of the developments singled out in the 1960s as unsatisfactory because of vandalism and crime, Van Dyke Houses (1955) in Brownsville is representative of the lengths the housing authority has taken to keep some its most troubled developments habitable. Van Dyke Houses is composed of 1,603 units in twenty-two buildings (13 fourteen-story towers and 9 three-story low-rise structures) on 22.35 acres for approximately four thousand residents. Van Dyke was, in fact, one of the prime examples of high-rise design errors featured by Oscar Newman in his book *Defensible Space* (1972). Newman faulted Van Dyke for its height, the orientation of its entrances away from the street, and long, double-loaded interior hallways that created a more anonymous condition. Newman acknowledged that NYCHA staff performed better daily maintenance than other housing authorities, and even his photographs of NYCHA projects illustrating design flaws were notably tidy, but he was right that serious crime and other problems, some of them related to design, could very well have rendered the development uninhabitable in the same manner as Pruitt-Igoe in St. Louis. A highly troubled neighborhood and thousands of other public housing apartments in tower blocks also surrounded, and threatened the peace, of the development.

The managers at NYCHA at first committed supplemental funds to Van Dyke on a temporary basis, but this did not seem to be enough: "janitorial standards have deteriorated since removal of [the] supplementary task force program which ended November 30, 1970. Buildings suffer from abnormally high tenant abuse, no tenant cooperation. Janitorial timecards reflect a high absenteeism rate." Even "the use of a carpenter full-time does not keep pace with the damaged doors and hardware." Hundreds of windows were being broken every month and residents frequently flooded the halls by turning on the standpipes. Residents, for their part, claimed that "simple services such as hot water, heat, decent lighting in halls . . . seem very hard to come by."[18] The authority responded to the continuing issues by adding permanent staff to Van Dyke in the early 1970s. NYCHA hired nineteen additional caretakers and one additional foreman of caretakers. According to the authority, "The added staff is concentrating on washing and waxing of the buildings . . . and cleaning up the grounds. In addition a painter has been assigned full time" and "two glaziers have been added to the staff to handle the heavy replacement of glass lights [panes]." The authority also hired a full-time elevator mechanic and helper in the Brownsville developments and extra teams of repair workers. In 1975, Van Dyke finally received a satisfactory mark, as "the alarming trend towards an irreversible decline has been halted."[19] This turnaround happened at the very time that many high-rise public housing developments around the country reached their nadir.

More than three decades later, and despite ongoing crime, littering, and tenant vandalism, Van Dyke is still providing housing for 4,330 residents.

The development has forty-two full-time workers (of fifty budgeted), including five maintenance workers, four housing assistants, and twenty-four caretakers. Each caretaker looks after one high-rise or three low-rises. As at other NYCHA developments, caretakers "police" the grounds every day, sweeping all hallways, cleaning out trash, and emptying compactors; on a weekly basis, they mop floors and stair halls top to bottom. A brick-repointing project was recently launched, and elevators in the high-rises are relatively new. Six full-time maintenance workers address thirty to fifty work tickets a day and manage to keep up with requests filed with the Central Call Center (CCC), although there is a backlog in skilled trade requests such as plastering. The high-rises I visited were passably clean with limited graffiti, had working (if clearly hard used) elevators, and litter-free halls. The vast open spaces at Van Dyke are less impressive than other developments that have had renovations. The longtime manager admitted that the high-rises were not easy to manage, but he also reported that in his experience Van Dyke, and nearby Brownsville Houses, are now significantly safer than in the 1980s and 1990s.

Many troubled developments like Van Dyke were targeted in the 1970s for extra janitorial service, and, according to NYCHA administrators in that era, there were "dramatic improvements in the appearance of building quarters, floors, and lobbies due to the use of improved materials, better techniques, and modern equipment as well as the utilization of plain old elbow grease."[20] It was not simply a matter of regular clearing either, but frequently expensive repairs. In 1972 alone, for instance, NYCHA reported that systemwide "more than 188,000 panes" of glass were replaced at a cost of more than $1.2 million. On an annual basis, the authority was spending $3 million just to remove graffiti.[21] In order to reduce future vandalism costs, the authority installed "vandal resistant fixtures" systemwide. Management also began "using more Plexiglas as well and tempered glass and steel in high breakage areas," and simply reduced the amount of glass in entrances, lobbies, and stairwells. These new materials improved durability, but they also gave developments a more institutional ambiance that created a greater distinction between public housing environments and privately managed housing.[22]

This adaptation process has been a constant at NYCHA in its race to maintain the standard of living on development grounds. The transformation of landscapes, for instance, provides a concise case study of these changes. Limited budgets, anti-social behavior on the grounds, and the authority's focus on building interiors during the 1960s and 1970s eventually took a toll on once verdant lawns and plantings. Managers paved over many grassy areas and ripped out many older plantings. Steel benches and sodium vapor lighting gave the grounds of many developments a more institutional appearance. Mature trees survived, but many of the development grounds began to look more like large parking areas than the green spaces they were supposed to be. On the positive side, and different from the situation in many cities where administrators failed to provide adequate recreational facilities, growing youth populations motivated administrators in the 1950s to change many green lawns to a mix of passive and active recreation zones that included playgrounds, spray fountains, and basketball courts.

Since the mid-1990s, and in contrast to so many other cities, the landscapes of nearly all NYCHA developments have been renovated with an eye toward decreasing the likelihood of vandalism and increasing the usefulness of the space through design changes. Grassy areas have been rehabbed in many cases, benches added or restored in configurations designed to maximize sociability and casual surveillance of entrances, additional basketball courts and jungle gyms constructed, and attractive steel fencing has replaced flimsy chain link along nicely paved walkways. Many NYCHA developments also have community garden plots that are popular with residents. Much of the landscape redesign developed in consultation with resident from the developments. Some of these renovated landscapes are, however, already starting to show signs of wear as budget cuts, vandalism, and heavy use take their toll. Most community centers have also been renovated over the past two decades, and many new centers built since the 1990s, some designed by leading architects, bring color and life to development grounds.[23] Johnson Houses' new community center, for instance, dramatically transformed one entire area of the development with an indoor basketball court, a child care center, and other community amenities.

NYCHA has also devoted enormous resources to elevator maintenance and renovation since the 1970s. Without functioning elevators, high-rise systems cannot function at all. Many cities proved unable to keep their elevators in serviceable condition even in the early years of development life. Chicago in the early 1980s had one-third of its elevators out on a daily basis. By the 1970s, by contrast, NYCHA employed 350 mechanics solely devoted to the maintenance of the approximately three thousand elevators in the developments. Their work had become so essential to maintaining the system that a labor action in 1973, which pulled repairmen from the front lines, led within a few days to at least twelve thousand residents without elevator service: four hundred of the three thousand elevators had already stalled out.[24] By 1988, NYCHA's elevator staff had grown to 390 full-time repairmen.

NYCHA elevators still experience considerable wear and tear, some of it in the normal course of events (over a billion rides per year by hundreds of thousands of residents), but a significant amount number of outages are the result of vandalism. For instance, teenagers "surfed" the tops of elevators for fun in the 1970s; even today, elevators are frequently vandalized or mistreated out of either antisocial attitudes or frustration at slow speeds. Over two-thirds of all elevators have been replaced in the last decade, and remote sensing of elevators now enables more efficient monitoring of their condition. A major push by the authority to add elevator repair personnel and upgrade elevator service, after embarrassing revelations about repair service in 2009,

Table 4.2 Reported service quality, NYCHA

Performance statistics	Actual				
	FY08	FY09	FY10	FY11	FY12
*Average time to resolve nonemergency service requests (days)	6.8	5.1	NA	29.0	30.0
*Average time to resolve emergency service requests (hours)	8.3	NA	NA	18.3	7.5
Average time to resolve heat service requests (hours)	8.7	7.4	NA	12.9	11.9
*Average time to resolve elevator outages (hours)	10.4	11.4	13.1	5.2	3.8
Annual HUD Assessment Rating	NA	83.0	79.0	NA	NA
*Major felony crimes in public housing developments	4,686	4,275	4,090	4,406	4,771
Elevator service uptime	98.2%	98.1%	97.9%	99.2%	99.4%
*Average outage per elevator per month in days	1.15	1.12	1.15	1.08	1.01
Percent of elevator outages due to vandalism	29.8%	29.7%	29.9%	31.8%	34.8%
*Number of alleged elevator injuries reported to DOB per year	30.0	33.0	30.0	24.0	13.0
Number of elevator related fatalities	0	1	0	0	0

Source: Selected NYCHA operations data from the Mayor's Office of Operations (2012). CPR: Agency Performing Reports. City of New York.

*Critical indicator "NA" – means not available in this report

Table 4.3 NYCHA development maintenance routines

NYCHA caretaker tasks		
Daily	Weekly	Long term/seasonal
Mop elevators and lobby	Mop all floors	Strip and seal floors
Check door locks	Mop all stair halls	Grounds tasks (leaves, snow)
Send maintenance requests		
"Police" grounds (collect trash dropped from windows, and debris left outside)		Special assignments from caretaker supervisors
Compact trash and remove		
Remove graffiti		
Sweep all hallways and stair halls		
Remove bulk trash left in stair halls		

Note: NYCHA daily, weekly, and long-term caretaking tasks citywide at most developments.

has apparently met with operational success (Table 4.2). As of 2013, the authority employed a staff of 459 elevator repairmen for its 3,324 elevators (and this division is budgeted for 524 employees), a ratio better than most privately run buildings in the city and a significant boost from just a few years ago. On my visits over the years to NYCHA developments I have frequently occasioned on elevator repairmen in some phase of their work. The amount of funding poured into elevators may, however, be undermining other areas of maintenance.[25]

My impression on visits, both formal and informal over the years, is that the authority still maintains a hierarchical organization with clearly defined responsibilities. This system is partly responsible for the higher standards maintained as compared to public housing in other cities. The large number of employees in one job title, that of caretaker, is particularly crucial to NYCHA's survival. Their daily tasks are described in Table 4.3, and nearly every manager I spoke with stressed the crucial importance of daily custodial functions in maintaining the livability of NYCHA developments, no matter the location.

Significant daily vandalism and littering could, within just a few days, make development grounds entirely unlivable.

Many of the NYCHA caretakers are recruited from resident seasonal workers on NYCHA grounds. The authority has an incentive to upgrade the income of its residents (it can raise their rents) and the caretaker role is relatively well paid (starting at $26,000) and unionized. It is also a physically taxing and frustrating job because of the hard treatment meted out by residents and visitors in many buildings. Approximately 38 percent of NYCHA employees, many of them caretakers, still live in NYCHA apartments. There is no civil service requirement for caretaker (nor is a high school diploma required); caretakers mostly learn on the job, yet they are encouraged and subsidized by the union to gain skills that will lead them to higher-level jobs. I met many supervisors and managers on my visits who began as seasonal help or caretakers but worked their way up within NYCHA ranks. In essence, the system not only maintains the buildings but also functions as a successful antipoverty program. Other cities are just experimenting with this system today, but NYCHA has maintained it for decades with relative success. Managers believe that having residents as employees enhances the connection between residents and NYCHA. Some managers did note anecdotally that they tend to have additional problems in work habits, competency, and technical ability with some employees recruited from resident populations.

NYCHA better maintained its public housing than other cities, but the longevity of this housing presents its own challenges as buildings age, rent returns stagnate, and operating subsidies decrease. Criticism has been growing from many residents who, accustomed to higher levels of service in the past, experience delays in apartment repairs including walls, ceilings, bathrooms, kitchens, and windows. In 2005, for instance, *the percentage of apartments with one or more observable maintenance defect was just 3.2 percent* according to an independent city analysis. This was a remarkable accomplishment in light of the age of the buildings and various social issues system wide. In 2008, however, that figure had jumped to 8.5 percent. Between 2008 and 2011, conditions declined further. In 2008, for instance, only 5.5 percent of NYCHA units had 5 or more deficiencies (a very serious situation), but by 2011 that same figure had risen to 8.8 percent of units.[26] The number of units with three or more deficiencies in 2011 was 34.8 percent, a rate 10 percent higher than other rent regulated rentals citywide. Even taking into account differences in sampling methods and standards over time, a decline in maintenance is evident since 2000; a change confirmed by many resident leaders, community activists, and federal reviews.[27]

Declining standards are the result of a number of factors, beyond the aging infrastructure of the system as a whole. Above all, NYCHA experienced reductions in maintenance and other skilled trade staff as a result of federal and city budget cuts since 2001. NYCHA employs a total of 670 skilled maintenance workers systemwide in 2013, yet, if actually fully funded by HUD, would have 800 maintenance workers on development grounds (this figure does not include other skilled trades and contract private-sector staff who complete more comprehensive repairs). As some employees told me, sometimes you can "do more with less," but sometimes "less is less." Despite workers clearing approximately two million systemwide repair work orders per year, a backlog of 333,000 nonemergency repair calls had developed by early 2013, with some residents given work tickets for repairs years in the offing because of skilled trade shortages. Managers, understandably, focused remaining human resources on emergency calls. Repair teams in FY2012 may have taken, on average, thirty days to resolve a nonemergency request, often involving a skilled trade for work such as plastering or painting, but only 7.5 hours to resolve an emergency service request.[28]

Organizational issues likely compounded the staff cutbacks. A centralized call center system, borrowed from the private-sector model, seems to have added confusion and created delays in fulfilling repairs. In this system, tenant calls are evaluated based upon seriousness and sent to either development-based maintenance workers or floating "skilled trades" teams rather than addressed directly by development-based staff as was usual in the past. Some workers believed that rather than smoothing the process of making repairs, the call center added errors and redundant visits. Declining labor relations between NYCHA management and its unionized staff, because of cutbacks in overtime and staffing levels, may also have contributed to the backlog.

With growing public awareness of these problems, and a boost in funding from city officials, administrators have introduced major initiatives to improve conditions. NYCHA has reorganized procurement and repair protocols and initiated a task force to deal with the backlog of orders generated by the declining buildings and call center activity. Skilled trades, in an innovative program expanded in 2011–2012, now complete thousands of repairs, including all outstanding work tickets, in a single development in a matter of weeks. Maintenance staff are also being added or at least rehired; and it appears that a certain amount of repairmen/contractors were hired outside union rules in order to expedite repairs.[29] By December of 2013, NYCHA had reduced the apartment backlog to just 48,000 through expedited repairs, extra staff, flexible hours, and more efficient follow-up. Fall 2013 PHAS reviews by HUD independent reviewers, showing a 20 percent improvement in apartment scores, confirmed this progress. NYCHA has also created a comprehensive website, NYCHA Metrics, showing recent performance levels in most of the Authority's operations; the figures provided, not yet verified by an independent study, indicate continued progress in meeting both emergency and non-emergency repair demands in 2014.[30]

Despite the catch-up in repairs, and a new focus on elevators, major capital issues still need to be addressed in thousands of these aging structures. In fact, the large number of resident maintenance requests is related, in part, to the declining state of major systems such as exterior walls, plumbing, and windows that create multiple, and often recurring, problems inside apartments. Since the 1990s, over $7 billion has been spent on capital renovation, including brick repointing, elevator replacement and overhaul, window replacement, new heating systems, new roofs, and new appliances. The red-brick uniformity of NYCHA design may not be to everyone's liking aesthetically, but the repetition has enabled relatively cost-effective contracting and renovation of brickwork, roofs, elevators, and windows. Fort Greene Houses, for instance, was coming off a decade-long round of renovation in 2013 when I visited, with total costs of approximately $250 million. Among the many renovations in the apartment houses were newly installed stairs, new floors, new elevators, and complete apartment reconfigurations that finally remedied longstanding quality issues.

Yet ever more aging NYCHA developments need updating as the mass of housing constructed in the postwar era reaches its projected life span. In 2011, for instance, 255 developments were thirty years old or more, and eighty-four developments were between forty to forty-nine years old. Most NYCHA developments were designed with a projected fifty-year life span. Federally financed capital funds (much reduced since the 1990s), new annual subsidies secured for formerly city and state developments (known as federalization), additional city funds, and the recent federal stimulus have addressed only some deferred maintenance. A 2013 study estimated that over a twenty-year period, NYCHA would have to spend $17 billion to renovate its entire apartment stock and building systems. With a steady decline in federal capital and operating subsidies over the past decade, resulting from successful Republican opposition to social programs, other solutions are being sought to renewing NYCHA such as city bond sales, rent increases, staff reductions, and even leasing of open land on NYCHA properties for new developments.[31]

Residents, and resident leaders, have been widely featured in recent years on the pages of *The Daily News*, *New York Post* and *The New York Times* complaining about various, and growing, problems they have with NYCHA administrators and quality of life. Survey results, however, reveal a more complicated picture of NYCHA existing outside the political realm. An extensive survey by Baruch College in 2010 that questioned one thousand residents in housing developments and six hundred Section 8 voucher holders (in privately run housing) found that voucher holders do have a better view of their buildings, apartments, and neighborhood conditions than project-based public housing residents. But the survey as a whole did not demonstrate the overwhelming superiority of the voucher programs in creating a high-quality urban existence; nor do the results provide a justification for drastic redevelopment of public housing in New York. For instance, "approximately 66 percent of residents in conventional public housing are satisfied with their apartments and their neighborhood compared with 80 percent of voucher holders" and "70 percent of public housing residents rate their apartment positively as a place to live; and more than 80 percent of voucher holders rate their housing unit favorably." In light of the dramatic difference in typology, conditions, and management between public housing and most Section 8 apartments, this difference is not that striking. The survey also found that most public housing "respondents consider[ed] their apartments to be a good value." One of the brightest spots in the survey was NYCHA staff: "85% of residents [are] satisfied with how NYCHA staff treats them when performing repairs." Resident leaders I have spoken with, such as Ethel Velez at Johnson Houses, generally say nice things about their local caretakers, but also believe that they and other NYCHA staff are spread thinner than in the past. Residents so value NYCHA apartments that they, and activists who support them, have beaten back any serious discussion of widespread demolition or redevelopment of the type pursued in other cities.[32]

These surprisingly positive reviews from critical New Yorkers, rarely published in the press, are clearly the result of the extensive human system in place. Where maintenance staffing levels are high, management strong, and renovation recent, as at Ravenswood, Johnson, or Rangel Houses, the quality of upkeep of everything from entryways to playgrounds is indistinguishable from a well-managed private-sector apartment complex (and probably better than many apartment buildings in poor neighborhoods). Similar efforts are made at socially troubled developments such as Bushwick and Van Dyke Houses, but maintaining a high standard is more challenging as a result of vandalism and deferred maintenance.[33] As in any institution, context, funding, and the work ethic are variable, but without the thousands of hard-working employees, the high-rises would have become unlivable decades ago. That New York defies conventional wisdom when it comes to high-rise public housing is indicated by the fact that activists, and most city officials, are actively seeking ways to preserve this housing system rather than demolish it.

Social Management

As the father of public housing, Senator Robert Wagner, so nicely put it in 1937, public housing "after all, is a renting proposition, not a complete gift."[34] New York's history reveals that liberal policy initiatives sometimes need a conservative hand in practice. Public housing was, in fact, designed to be partly self-supporting and self-managed rather than an institutional environment. Early tenant families were required to be married, employed, and were selected on an unblemished record of decorum. Rents needed to be paid and residents needed to manage the bulk of their own affairs. The design of public housing developments to emphasize private apartment living reflects the notion that the family, rather than institutional controls, was the most important building block of community.[35]

New York, like other authorities in the 1930s, thus sought to attract and keep working-class residents who would both pay rent and control their children. Early NYCHA administrators in the 1930s were outspoken in their belief that it would be "harmful to the whole movement of housing if we collect such low rents that the taxpayer will be called upon to make further contributions." They were also worried that favoring low-income residents would "put a premium on sheer lowness of income. It acts as a positive deterrent to all attempts to increase the family income." Administrators were equally concerned that concentrating and isolating poor families would deprive them of the "beneficial effect of contact with families who are self-supporting."[36] The administrators were prescient, because such an idea is now dominant in affordable housing circles; nevertheless, the Housing Authority was forced in the 1930s by federal officials to accept more welfare residents. NYCHA developed and expanded its city- and state-financed system of public housing, built to higher standards, in part to establish higher income populations in public housing that administrators knew could pay sufficient rents to support maintenance.

More notably, NYCHA in the 1950s put in place a series of behavioral and other standards (known as the Twenty-One Factors) that, for more than a decade, kept welfare tenancy much lower than it was in other cities. These standards included factors such as drug addiction, unwed motherhood, irregular work, and other factors that essentially barred many applicants from gaining access to NYCHA apartments. What distinguished New York from other cities was the length of time that standards like these persisted and were maintained *at the entry point of public housing*, rather than emphasizing punitive rules on existing residents. Administrators were able to use the market pressure in the New York citywide, which generated many more applicants than units, to maintain this selectivity; most other cities were not so lucky and often struggled to find qualified applicants.

In spite of pressure to focus public housing on the most needy in New York, particularly in the urban renewal era when so many site residents were displaced, NYCHA continued to use traditional moral judgments to select residents, evicted effectively for misconduct and nonpayment, and had near-perfect rent collection up until the late 1960s. These socially conservative standards remained even as the housing authority switched from a primarily white to an entirely minority tenancy of African Americans, Puerto Ricans, and ethnic newcomers in all of its developments.[37] Historian D. Bradford Hunt has also identified the higher percentage of smaller apartments created in NYCHA buildings as an important factor in preventing large, multiproblem family from dominating the towers in New York City. NYCHA administrators showed no great concern for the needs of large families, but it is not clear whether this was for behavioral or financial reasons.[38]

Rapid white flight from NYCHA developments by the late 1950s transformed the system from a white working-class system to a minority dominated working-class system, with a mix of white, Puerto Rican, and African American residents. The fact that the housing authority had initially been successful in integrating public housing developments in the postwar period did not stop the white exodus from public housing. In 1962, whites were still 42.7 percent of the entire tenant population. By 1969, however, the white population was only 27.9 percent of tenant population, the black population stood at 46.2 percent, and the Puerto Rican population had reached 25.9 percent. This growing minority resident population was at first judged by the same strict standards faced by the whites prior to the late 1960s.[39] This was the era when upwardly mobile minority families, such as that of Justice Sonia Sotomayor, found public housing developments to be a temporary but essential refuge in a highly restricted and expensive housing market.

It became too controversial for NYCHA, despite the comparative social order in New York's public housing, to maintain these policies in the late 1960s. Welfare activists and politicians forced NYCHA to change its tenant selection policies in 1968. Welfare residents in public housing in New York went from 11.7 percent citywide in 1962[40] to 34 percent in 1973. In 1972 alone, NYCHA made 50 percent of its open rentals to welfare families. New residents dramatically increased the welfare percentages, but even some old residents could be counted in the growing welfare population at NYCHA as expanding benefits dovetailed citywide with deindustrialization and recession.[41]

Even though the rate of welfare recipients in New York public housing was roughly half the rate of Chicago at this time (welfare rates there skyrocketed in the 1970s to above 70 percent of all tenant families),[42] some individual NYCHA developments suffered from rates of welfare concentration above 40 percent. Social issues mounted in developments; drug trafficking, robbery, and violent crime became widespread. Remaining white residents, and many minority families, moved out of developments, including many city-funded ones, for private housing in the city or the suburbs. During this time, the housing authority added only a few new units as it attempted to maintain control over its existing and increasingly troubled communities. Complicating matters further, tens of thousands of homeless persons gained NYCHA apartments in the 1980s, a key element in the reduction of homelessness on New York's streets, but one that added to the fiscal challenges by adding many residents with very low incomes or prospects of higher income which could be used toward rents. NYCHA became more and more dependent on federal subsidies to make up for the difference between the actual costs of upkeep and the maximum amount that residents could pay. Even today, rents cover less than half the cost of operating a typical NYCHA unit.

As the reality set in that the changes in tenant standards had dangerously shifted finances and behavior among residents, NYCHA administrators in the 1970s raised income limits, turned a blind eye to higher income residents generally, and created the Tier System. The Tier system gave higher income residents priority for open apartments in many developments as a way to restrain poverty concentration. In the 1990s, because of a continuing but slow uptick in welfare concentration both in the system as a whole and in certain developments, administrators created the Working Family preference that gave one of two open apartments to a working family. Eviction processes were also reinstated that did not ultimately force many people out, but sent a strong message that nonpayment of rent and antisocial behavior would meet a strong institutional response. Rent collection has often been a matter of going door-to-door to collect late payments, and annual apartment inspections remain a management tool today.[43]

Through these means, welfare reform (that ended benefits), and a tight housing market, NYCHA maintained and even rebuilt working family tenancy. Average family income at NYCHA as of 2013 is $23,000; eighty-eight thousand total NYCHA residents hold jobs, with the largest numbers in health care and social assistance (31 percent). This reality (Table 4.4) contrasts strongly with the persistently high rates of welfare tenancy in public housing in a city such as Chicago; a factor that contributed to both financial problems and aggressive redevelopment schemes under HOPE VI.[44] NYCHA has in recent years raised rents on its higher income residents in order to help close deficits created by declining federal subsidies, and it is set to raise them more in the coming years, thus staving off more draconian service cuts that even larger deficits would have created.

The fact that NYCHA residents have some income should not lead one to mistake the system as barring poor residents. Not only are about 11 percent of tenant families receiving public assistance, and many receive the new welfare (Social Security Disability), but also the average family income of $23,000 is well below the adjusted (for cost of living) New York City poverty line of $26,138 for a family of four. Fully 60 percent of households earn less than 30 percent of the Area Median Income. Single parents, many subsisting on retirement benefits, also head the majority of families with children in NYCHA buildings. This complex demographic reality (Figure 4.3) likely reflects the high divorce and low marriage rates in minority communities in New York City.[45]

The social challenges at NYCHA developments with low-income families demand a strong management hand. The housing assistants (usually two to four per development) at each NYCHA development have, as one of their jobs, the thankless task of trying to collect rent arrears. As indicated by the chart below (Table 4.5), delinquent rent levels are now relatively high at many

Table 4.4 Reported NYCHA statistics

Performance statistics	FY08	FY09	FY10	FY11	FY12
*Number of apartments (000)	178	179	178	179	179
*Occupancy rate (%)	99.1%	99.3%	99.5%	99.4%	99.2%
*Average turnaround days for vacant apartments	46.2	43.9	36.5	35.2	40.0
Average time to prepare vacant apartments (days)	27.0	30.2	39.4	30.9	31.8
*Public housing apartments that are occupied or available for occupation	175,453	176,428	177,068	177,711	178,062
*Rent collection (%)	100.2%	99.0%	98.7%	99.0%	99.2%
Management cost per dwelling unit ($)	$788	$795	$826	$858	$885
*Section 8 occupied units (certificate and vouchers)	88,554	95,501	100,570	95,896	93,789
–Working families residing in public housing (cumulative) (%)	45.2%	46.2%	47.2%	46.7%	48.0%
–Applicants placed in public housing	5,220	5,744	5,554	5,650	6,012
Working families placed in public housing (%)	64.1%	64.1%	68.5%	69.2%	67.0%
Disabled persons placed in public housing (%)	27.1%	26.4%	24.1%	22.4%	23.9%
Families on Section 8 waiting list (000)	136	128	125	NA	124
Utilization rate for Section 8 vouchers (%)	86.8%	94.0%	101.0%	98.3%	95.3%
Applicants placed through Section 8 vouchers	11,847	12,313	7,523	NA	421
*Percentage of active capital projects in construction phase on schedule	62.8%	79.6%	87.4%	71.6%	91.1%
*Percentage of active projects on schedule	22.1%	39.2%	38.7%	27.5%	29.1%

Source: Selected NYCHA data from Mayor's Office of Operations (2012). CPR: Agency Performing Reports. City of New York.

*Critical indicator   "NA" — means not available in this report

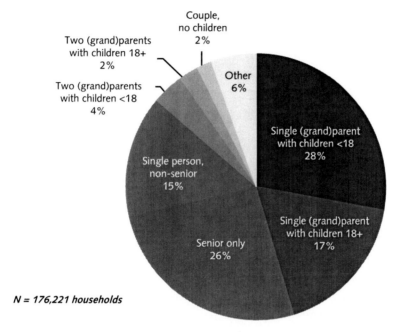

Figure 4.3 NYCHA family structure citywide as reported by the New York City Housing Authority (2012).
Source: New York City Housing Authority.

NYCHA developments and reflect both chronic nonpayment and the impact of the recent recession on working families of color. My findings on the ground correspond with newly released citywide rent delinquency figures for NYCHA that show a citywide average hovering, month to month, around and sometimes below 80 percent. Managers explained to me that the increasing rate of rent delinquency correlated strongly with the recent recession as many working families lost employment.[46] NYCHA employees also reported to me that rent is not a priority for a many families; they will pay other bills, such as cable or cell phones, before paying their rent.

Housing Assistants, as they have for eight decades, still chase late rents. When even one rental payment is missed, housing assistants will immediately visit apartments, make calls, and schedule appointments to try and collect rent. If there is a second missed payment, NYCHA begins legal action. It is well known that NYCHA is a major and constant presence in the housing courts in New York City because of the size and complexity of the caseload. Housing assistants may spend up to two days per week in court and now have

Table 4.5 Resident management

NYCHA development name	Unit total	Pop. total	Rent delinquency/ 2012 estimate	Evictions 2012/ Estimate # (% of units)	Moveouts 2012/ Estimate # (% of units)	Housing assistants
Brownsville (1948)	1,337	3,447	15%	18 (.01)	60 (4%)	3
Bushwick (1960)	1,220	3,023	16%	15 (.01)	69 (6%)	3
Ingersoll (1944)	1,823	2,445	19%	12 (.006)	80 (4%)	4
Johnson (1948)	1,299	2,277	11%	5 (.003)	80 (6%)	3
Kingsborough (1941)	1,154	2,393	15%	17 (.01)	N/A	3
Ravenswood (1951)	2,167	4,541	12%	20 (.009)	117 (5%)	4
Van Dyke I (1955)	1,603	4,207	18%	18 (.01)	64 (4%)	4
Whitman (1944)	1,652	2,336	14%	7 (.004)	75 (5%)	4

Source: Selected data from NYCHA developments visited in 2013 as part of the author's research.

regular scheduled days in various housing courts. At Ravenswood Houses, for instance, there might be ten to twenty cases heard per week in court. As indicated in the chart above, however, the actual physical evictions (dispossession of apartment) in public housing are low, and are far exceeded by regular move outs (including transfers) in all the developments I visited. An unknown number of the move outs, however, may be resident families, behind on their rents, moving before the shame of formal dispossession.

Legal proceedings are used to keep pressure on residents, but many NYCHA residents are aware that the courts are reluctant to evict residents. Residents may also see in their developments many others who have avoided payment for long periods with little visible penalty. Residents will try to use maintenance issues, which are more common today than in the past, as an excuse to not pay their rents (even if they have missed their repair appointments or vandalized their own apartments). Many managers explained that while there is often a change in who does not pay, there are chronic nonpayers who have learned to work the system. The legal dance between NYCHA and particular residents may go on for years. Some NYCHA managers focus on repairs for these residents, create a long-term plan for repayment of back rent, and charity or public assistance may also make up for some back rents, but in the end managers must write off a percentage of delinquent rents every year. NYCHA housing assistants must also contend with fraud, including illegal subletting, unreported income, working out of state, or even residents owning homes elsewhere. Computerization has helped the tracking of these cases and there have been recent fraud prosecutions, but it is well known that "off the books" income is common in public housing both in New York and in other cities.

The entire system, everything from knocking on doors to dispossession, seems to exist to keep pressure on the vast majority of residents who *do* pay regularly; the system can be considered reasonably successful given the difficult and often complex economic and social issues of many residents. Threat of legal action is real and time consuming for those barely getting by, and it is clearly avoided by approximately 80 percent of the resident population. Most NYCHA residents are neither victims nor villains, just lower-income New Yorkers who pay a rent they can afford.

Conclusion

NYCHA's history proves without a doubt that public housing form matters a great deal less than most people believe. NYCHA, for instance, has maintained everything from two- to thirty-one story towers, mostly in vast superblocks. NYCHA managers acknowledge that high-rises are more challenging (heavy use of equipment, expensive renovations, and greater anonymity), but they were also unanimous that such developments, with the right combination of elbow grease, tenancy, and financing, can be well maintained for a majority poor population. These findings indicate that blaming a specific typology of public housing for management and tenant failure (high-rise superblocks), as has been done in many other cities, makes little sense. Moreover, many cities with notoriously bad public housing—such as pre-Katrina New Orleans— have mismanaged a portfolio of developments, at great cost to the federal government, that were overwhelmingly low-rise.

Sound housing management, much like one finds in market buildings, has simply been applied to the greatest degree possible in New York to high-rise public housing communities full of poor or working-class people. The comparative success of NYCHA in maintaining its system has meant that planned redevelopment includes renovation of existing buildings (with the residents remaining in place) and additional market/affordable rate structures on development grounds, rather than the demolition and replacement of existing public housing as has been taking place so extensively in other cities.

To say that NYCHA has proved a point is not to claim that the system was ideal in conception, that the NYCHA system today is perfect in practice (there are significant quantitative and qualitative differences across the many developments), or that within a few years NYCHA will be the same as it is today. If the city government, for instance, does not step in to fill declining federal support, it is likely that the entire management system will collapse. Nor is it the point of this article or the *Public Housing That Worked* book to debate the wisdom of putting low-income residents in high-rise public housing. The constant raining down of trash from high windows, often underutilized open spaces, and elevator vandalism has demanded extra costs and superhuman maintenance that might have been better utilized elsewhere or mitigated with better design. At the same time, providing decent housing for hundreds of thousands of poor people for decades in America's most expensive city is no small achievement.

II. Policy

PUBLIC HOUSING ENDED IN FAILURE DURING THE 1970S

Yonah Freemark

In early 1973, the Nixon administration put in place a moratorium on most subsidized housing assistance, essentially eliminating funding for the construction of public housing and for other forms of subsidized housing. This sudden cutoff in aid, announced by Department of Housing and Urban Development (HUD) secretary George Romney, marked an ostensible transition away from the use of federal funds to pay for new housing construction for low-income families. In defending the action, President Richard Nixon argued that the government had become the "biggest slumlord in history." With time, Nixon's statement congealed into today's widespread sense that liberal governmental policies were running out of steam. According to this myth, public housing ended in failure during the 1970s due to its inability to innovate in response to its failures—the projects' institutional architecture, "ghettoized" residents, poor management, and physical isolation from surrounding neighborhoods.[1]

Yet, by the time the moratorium was announced, the subsidized housing program had already been transformed by a series of innovations that, while far from perfect, were nonetheless responsive to previous criticisms. Though "conventional" public housing—apartments that the federal government funded and that local authorities planned, built, and managed—accounted for a shrinking portion of the overall housing program, the failures of early complexes were being addressed by reforms to the public housing program and by an increased role for private actors in subsidized housing development. Moreover, despite Nixon's rhetoric, support for public housing persisted—even within the ranks of his own administration—and, indeed, more units were funded in the late 1970s during the Carter administration.

By discussing the efforts to transform subsidized housing policies in the 1960s and by highlighting the Nixon administration's deep internal tensions on the issue, this chapter argues that Nixon's moratorium was not the inevitable response to public housing failures. Rather, it represented an ideologically driven move in an ongoing struggle over federal government involvement in subsidized housing development. The hold on funding resulted from the confluence of two conservative[2] Nixon administration policies: (1) its effort to enact severe budget cuts on domestic programs, either by proposing and enacting reduced funding, or by refusing to spend congressionally appropriated funds; and (2) its effort to decentralize urban development funds to local and state governments through block grants while shifting federal social spending to an income-support, rather than government-program, model.[3] Nixon's second term provided him the opportunity to move forward on each of these fronts, and public housing was a casualty.

Public Housing Evolves in the 1960s

The "conventional" model of public housing construction—federal funds distributed to local housing authorities for the purposes of providing apartments to low-income families—was initiated in the 1930s and developed into a major program after passage of the 1949 Housing Act. Conservative opposition to the program was considerable. Even after funds began to flow—often to private contractors completing the actual construction—powerful real estate lobbies decried public housing as "communistic," and the program was subject to resistance in cities across the country.[4] In 1951, President Dwight Eisenhower reduced funding for new construction significantly. A mid-1950s presidential advisory committee argued that Washington should work to "steadily lessen the need for direct subsidies," and optimistically predicted selling off public dwellings "when no longer needed for low-income families."[5]

During the 1950s and 1960s, critics of the government's approach to urban renewal, including public housing and highway construction, denounced big city projects as out of scale with their surroundings. The projects that resulted from the federal Urban Renewal Program, stemming from the Housing Acts of 1949 and 1954, featured modernist architecture inspired by Le Corbusier's "tower-in-the-park" planning. Built on "megablocks" that required demolition and resident displacement, they were isolated from the street grid and monofunctional (housing only), rejecting the mixed-use urbanity of the communities they had replaced. And tenants who earned more than low-income salaries were forced out of their apartments, keeping project households almost entirely impoverished. Moreover, the planning process ignored citizen participation in favor of so-called expert opinion on the question of how to rehabilitate city centers.[6]

Public housing advocates resisted critics' arguments and kept the program alive, though they accepted the need to incorporate some aspects of these criticisms. Leonard Freedman suggests that their original conviction that the program should fund only publicly owned and operated housing (to prevent abetting slumlords) moderated as they tired of defending the program and recognized that there were multiple ways to help the poor find housing. The utopian vision for public housing—one that underpinned the initial movement for government construction in the face of a market failure to provide decent homes for the poor—no longer seemed realistic; the concept had not resolved the social problems it was supposed to address. Simultaneously, private-sector factions that had initially opposed the program began to recognize its financial benefits. They realized that "the projects" could produce considerable profits from contracted construction.[7]

These countervailing forces put the meaning of public housing into question. Was it the government's role to fund, build, and manage apartments for people who could not find reasonable homes elsewhere? Could some of those steps be performed by state-level or even nonpublic entities? Indeed, the political discourse was changing. In 1959, Congress altered subsidized housing policy by creating the Section 202 program to offer priority loans for private developers constructing housing for the elderly. Subsequently, the federal government began subsidizing privately developed moderate-income housing through Section 221(d)(3).

Once in office, President Lyndon Johnson called for the expansion of the public housing program, while continuing to search for new ways to involve the private sector in subsidized housing, much of it for moderate-income households. "We are striving . . . to get private business to take on some of this development," Johnson argued.[8] The 1965 Housing Act included the Rent Supplement Program, which provided aid for low-income (public-housing level) households to help them rent moderate-income priced housing. Federal funding provided under Section 23 of the act allowed housing authorities to rent private dwellings to low-income residents at affordable rates. This provision was one of several innovations intended to quickly increase the "public housing" stock. In 1967, under the guidance of Secretary Robert C. Weaver, HUD developed an administrative procedure known as the Turnkey Program, which allowed housing authorities to acquire privately built new or existing housing projects as public housing.[9]

Unsatisfied with the progress of new housing construction, the Johnson administration convened three independent commissions to assess, among other issues, the nation's need for affordable housing. Each commission recommended substantial investments in home construction for low- and moderate-income Americans. The President's Committee on Urban Housing recommended new loans, tax credits, and direct grants, with the end goal of producing six million affordable units; most would be new construction. This would be a huge increase over the one million low-income units subsidized *in total* by federal aid through 1968. The committee recommended "attracting the fullest private participation," because "private enterprise has demonstrated that it can build subsidized housing with speed, efficiency and economies." Other groups, particularly civil rights advocates, argued for similar increases in federal housing aid.[10]

President Johnson was concerned that urban problems were stirring up the civil disorders of the 1960s. He assumed these housing recommendations as his own and pushed Congress to pass the 1968 Housing Act. The law expanded and replaced Section 221(d)(3) with Section 236, which offered significantly reduced interest rates for the construction of moderate-income rental housing, and Section 235, which added benefits for moderate-income family homeownership. Both supplemented direct public construction of new affordable housing by promoting subsidies for private corporations to do the same. Alexander von Hoffman described the 1968 act as an effort to "call upon the genius of private enterprise" in response to the perceived failures of the low-income program, particularly its inability to respond quickly enough to the need. This response was provoked in part by a willingness among liberals to support public-private partnerships to supply this program.[11] But in terms of quantity produced, private involvement did not mean a move away from public housing. In fact, proponents of the 1968 bill saw investments in programs like Sections 235 and 236 as a complement to, not a replacement for, public housing; more public housing units were added in each year between 1969 and 1972 than in any previous year.

Other reforms were equally influential in altering the federal approach to urban redevelopment by reforming the way public housing was implemented. In terms of design, the government advocated that housing authorities build public housing on scattered sites, rather than in concentrated megablocks, and the 1968 act banned almost all high-rise construction. Retail was allowed in buildings beginning in 1961, and some families whose incomes increased above the low-income bar were allowed to stay in their apartments. Moreover, in certain cities, public housing was incorporated into neighborhood renewal plans that sought adjacent buildings with a mix of incomes as an important element of the design.[12]

By 1968, the traditional model of federal funding and local housing authority development had faded. Meanwhile, a revamped public housing program was running strong. Private-sector actors were increasingly encouraged to be involved in construction and management, and the design flaws that characterized early public housing complexes were addressed through a new, less top-down, planning and architectural approach. The 1968 Housing Act, implemented over the next five years, represented the most productive period of public housing construction in the nation's history (and a major period of moderate-income unit production). Between 1968 and 1975, the number of federally subsidized public housing units almost doubled, increasing from 687,000 to 1.15 million. The character of this housing also changed. In the peak production years of 1969 and 1970, of public housing structures completed (151,000 units), only 36 percent of units were "conventionally" built; the rest were completed or acquired using the Turnkey Program. An additional fifty-eight thousand low-income units were leased through Section 23.[13]

Urban renewal, and the subsidized housing program, had been redefined—though the results of such reforms were not wholly successful. With the switch to an increasingly private mode of construction, profit seeking became a matter of concern, often resulting in lowered construction standards. Private and nonprofit managers frequently had less experience than their public-sector counterparts, and maintenance—both of building quality and tenant satisfaction—suffered. Nevertheless, most of the previous criticisms of public housing no longer applied to the reformed program.

The Nixon Administration's Support for Devolution

When he assumed the presidency in early 1969, Richard Nixon did not articulate criticisms of public housing, despite his conservative credentials. Rick Perlstein notes that on domestic issues, Nixon seemed ready to extend Johnson's Great Society. Nixon had promised to end the Vietnam War—an opportunity for increasing spending elsewhere. Observers such as the head of the

National Association of Real Estate Boards suggested that Nixon's promotion of a balanced budget would not adversely affect housing programs.[14] Nixon's choice of George Romney as HUD secretary supported the notion that his administration would continue funding of public housing. As governor of Michigan, Romney had battled in favor of integrated housing and believed in the antipoverty initiatives promoted by the previous presidential administration. He entered office at HUD with the understanding that there were significant ways in which the federal government could play a role in improving lives through housing. Even so, he espoused the more traditionally Republican rhetoric of states' rights and the importance of the American work ethic.[15]

From the start, Nixon administration officials endorsed the conservative goal of decentralization. In particular, they initially identified Model Cities, a 1966 antipoverty program that offered grants to neighborhood groups to encourage local control over the planning process, as an exemplary way to reduce the influence of Washington on local decision making. Two weeks after Nixon's inauguration, a White House staff paper proposed that the administration "adopt the Model Cities program as its central strategy for dealing with the problems of the cities." Model Cities, Romney hoped, would concentrate and coordinate funds from all levels of government; encourage local initiative; decentralize decision making; develop local and state governmental capacity; and "increase the involvement of the private sector." But some were skeptical. A memo to Romney from Floyd Hyde, HUD's assistant secretary for community development, suggested that the program might be effective, but indicated that it might also make sense to encourage more state involvement or reverse the charge toward Washington.[16]

In early 1969, Secretary Romney assembled a task force of conservative academics, chaired by Edward Banfield, to reflect on the program's viability. The group concluded that "most federal aid should go to the cities by way of revenue sharing rather than by categorical grants-in-aid." In other words, general grants free for cities to use as they wished, rather than conditional funding, should be emphasized; this was a step further than Model Cities. The end of the war in Vietnam, they expected, would provide a sudden infusion of funds for local projects, and the Nixon administration could transfer those dollars through revenue sharing rather than federally specified expenditures.[17] This ideological shift affected public housing, along with other affordable housing programs and the federal Urban Renewal Program, since they were dominated by funding from and decision making in Washington.

Transferring money and power down the line to state and local governments defined Nixon's New Federalism. Romney endorsed Nixon's vision for the transformation of the federal government's role in American life. Unlike in the Johnson administration, where it had been generally ignored, state action would be actively encouraged. Romney believed the Banfield Report recommendations would help in "making federalism work."[18] Revenue sharing had been explored under Johnson, but it was never accepted. Nixon endorsed it during his campaign and planned to eventually offer states and localities $16 billion annually in flexible funds (of which $6 billion was to be "new" money). Money would be provided through both "general" and "special" funding. "General" sharing would allocate a portion of federal tax-derived revenues to states and localities according to a formula. These governments would then be able to use the money for whatever programs they desired. "Special" revenue sharing would require recipients to spend money in specific areas such as education, workforce, transportation, and community development.[19] Nixon's goal was to reduce federal authority on spending that affected local government directly. Richard Nathan, former assistant director at the Office of Management and Budget (OMB), noted that decentralized functions were those "where [local] government itself manages an activity . . . services for which conditions and needs vary among communities."[20]

Nixon's efforts to encourage revenue sharing were controversial. Congressional Democrats reacted angrily to the idea that Washington would hand funds to state and local governments without requiring anything of them, and they questioned whether states would use the money effectively. Moreover, they were concerned that the change would reduce funding for cities. Nonetheless, HUD began devising a formula-based block grant program to replace Model Cities, the federal Urban Renewal Program, and other categorical grants. Virtually as soon as plans were introduced, however, it became clear that they would, as critics feared, be funded at lower levels than predecessor programs. A HUD analysis showed that only thirteen cities would receive more funding under revenue sharing than under Model Cities.[21] If HUD's future spending were to follow the revenue sharing model, it likely would involve more limited funding, and certainly less direction from the federal government.

In a March 1971 meeting with the vice president and other top advisers, Nixon discussed the possibility of including public housing as one element of the revenue sharing program.[22] Support for the concept was growing in Congress, but progress was slow, in part because Democrats questioned whether

to support a GOP initiative. However, the nation's states and cities found themselves in the midst of a growing fiscal crisis, and this was enough to convince
legislators of the need to advance a partial version of the bill. On October 20,
1972—more than three years after President Nixon announced the idea—a
general revenue sharing bill was signed into law. While it did not include provisions on housing, the federal government had endorsed the idea of devolution, and the case for direct Washington control of a program like subsidized
housing had been forcefully questioned. But a "special" revenue bill had yet
to be approved by Congress.[23]

During the first years of Nixon's administration, spending on affordable
housing programs grew; HUD outlays expanded from about $1.5 billion in FY
1969 to $3.3 billion in FY 1971.[24] Even so, the White House—and especially
the OMB (until 1970 it was called the Bureau of the Budget)—worked to limit
future spending. Two principal issues emerged. It became clear that the Vietnam War was *not* about to conclude, and that the expected "peace dividend"
would not materialize. In addition, significant inflation existed in the early
1970s. The combination of war and inflation restricted the amount deficit-
minded conservatives were willing to commit to domestic affairs. Under Robert P. Mayo, OMB began lobbying for a reduction in HUD spending in
March 1969. Despite HUD's argument that its budget would require a minimum increase of $150 million to fund the new affordable housing proposed
by the 1968 Housing Act, the agency's overall outlay ceiling was limited substantially. The Urban Renewal Program was sacrificed particularly severely,
with no increase in spending unless HUD could offset it "by other means—
such as selling assets." Later in the year, in planning the FY 1970 and 1971
budgets, Mayo argued that "the inflationary outlook" was so bad that it was
"imperative that we adopt a very restricted fiscal policy."[25] The Nixon administration wanted a balanced budget. One way to would produce this would be
to sacrifice HUD.

Romney protested, instructing his department to defend the Urban Renewal
Program, which OMB had trimmed from its $1.25 billion request to $1 billion. The secretary noted that, in the absence of revenue sharing, the Urban
Renewal Program was "the single most important tool for achieving the physical rehabilitation of our cities." Responding to a tightened budget for public
housing later in the administration, Romney warned that "the need for such
housing is a critical national issue." He was so attached to the program that

he was willing to endorse a tax increase to pay for his agency's budget, but that was heresy in the Nixon administration.[26]

As if hoping to frame his appeal in the terms of President Nixon's political calculations, Romney said that funding Urban Renewal at a reasonable level "would avoid an intensification of the criticism . . . that the Administration is insensitive to the needs of the cities."[27] Romney's pleas, however, fell on deaf ears. By fall 1970, OMB suggested a 40 percent cutback to Model Cities, which Hyde argued had "never been viewed objectively by this Administration," despite the fact that it appeared to fulfill the Republican goal of supporting local initiative.[28] Charles Orlebeke, a Romney assistant, argued that the administration had, by that point, determined that the "program [was] simply not working well enough to justify a continuing high level of budget support," even as HUD publicly supported it. According to Orlebeke, Romney's opinion was that "Model Cities is essentially a sound program" and that it should continue to be funded. But the U.S. Conference of Mayors complained that there was a "shocking lack of commitment by the Administration to meet even the very minimum requirements of our vital urban areas."[29] Romney was losing control over his agency's programs.

Despite his protests, Romney followed the government's line. In early 1970, he announced to the cabinet that he was willing to "cut flesh and bone" to "curb inflation and avoid excessive unemployment." In fact, when the Senate passed a bill to expand Urban Renewal's take to $1.7 billion from Nixon's $1 billion proposal, HUD undersecretary Richard C. Van Dusen suggested that the president allow the bill to become law but then "refuse to spend the excess funds."[30] Officials at HUD had begun thinking not only about how to limit their own agency's spending but also about how to circumvent congressional authority. The writing was on the wall: The conservatives in power saw public expenditure on federal housing and urban programs as something that needed to be cut.

Decreases in proposed HUD spending were not primarily a comment on the effectiveness of the department's programs, including subsidized housing. In fact, despite some evidence that the reformed housing production programs were suffering from implementation problems, many of the agency's administrators continued to endorse them in internal communications. Instead, these reductions reflected two keys points: (1) the administration's desire to reduce domestic spending in order to curb inflation, and (2) a simultaneous effort to promote revenue sharing, which was supposed to replace locally oriented policies like public housing.

The Conservative Critique

Affordable housing programs were questioned more directly from a different, but related, front: the ideological issue of how the government should aid the poor. With revenue sharing, the Nixon administration had indicated its interest in shifting control over government spending away from the federal capital, toward states and cities. Now it was planning a shift from government altogether, moving funding out of programs and toward direct income supports. In December 1969, President Nixon argued:

> Our basic policies for improvement of the living conditions of the poor are based on this proposition: that the best judge of each family's priorities is the family itself; that the best way to ameliorate the hardships of poverty is to provide the family with additional income—to be spent as that family sees fit. . . . The task of Government is not to make decisions for you or for anyone. The task of Government is to enable you to make decisions for yourself.[31]

In 1969, the Nixon administration proposed a new entitlement, the Family Assistance Plan (FAP), which would have replaced welfare (Aid to Families with Dependent Children) with a broader, sliding-scale income-support plan. The policy would provide supplemental income to working-class families and guarantee minimum aid to families with children. The administration argued that policies directed toward the poor should be less paternalistic (replacing Great Society programs), divided up by need (such as housing or food), with cash aid. But FAP would have imposed a work requirement.[32]

How did HUD's programs conform to the ideological perspective that led to the FAP proposal? In 1969, OMB questioned the focus of the agency's affordable housing policy. HUD had previously concentrated on a production-based approach. But funds were increasingly being directed into subsidizing operations of public housing complexes; in other words, HUD was aiding low-income households with their rents, a form of income support that potentially overlapped with FAP.[33] At the heart of the problem was the fact that local housing authorities were no longer able to cover the cost of operations with rental revenues due to the increasing poverty of tenants and their inability to pay reasonable rents. Housing authorities cut back on maintenance because of unpaid bills. In response, Senator Edward Brooke's (R-MA) 1969 Housing Act amendment guaranteed that public housing residents would only have to pay rent equivalent to 25 percent of their family income. A second amendment, passed later, provided authorities with funds to subsidize operations.[34]

OMB officials argued that such subsidies for public housing residents, but not for all poor households, were irrational. On the one hand, federally sponsored construction might be acceptable, but only if local authorities agreed to cover the cost of any operating deficits; on the other, there might not be a need for construction at all. Cities could give "the same housing allowance for public housing welfare cases as for private housing. . . . Public housing can no longer afford the luxury of acting like a welfare program."[35] This argument indicated that the White House was either considering the development of a new entitlement that would guarantee housing aid based on income, or sensed that FAP would offer enough aid to obviate the need for housing assistance.

Despite—or perhaps because of—Romney's irritation over OMB's willingness to slash HUD's budget, the agency began formulating an alternative to the department's existing programs. HUD official Eugene Gulledge, the former president of the National Association of Home Builders, suggested in August 1970 that public housing was "extravagant" and serving too few needy households. In its place, he proposed providing poor families allowances to buy or rent new or existing housing. By September, Romney had drafted a proposal that would radically redefine HUD's role in the subsidized housing market, referring to his effort as a "drastic reorganization" that would represent the "first step toward the development of programs which fit in with the revenue sharing approach."[36]

The conservative intellectual discourse supported a federal rethink of housing aid. In 1970, HUD attorney Irving Welfeld argued that "the question of housing production must be divorced from the question of housing assistance to low-income families." Instead, the government should encourage homeownership for middle-income families and subsidize rental payments for low-income families.[37] Proposals to redirect the federal housing's emphasis away from construction and toward private stock dovetailed with HUD's initial study of housing allowances, authorized in the 1970 Housing Act through the Federal Experimental Housing Allowance Program (EHAP). EHAP tested the reaction to such housing subsidies among eighteen thousand households in about a dozen cities at a cost of more than $150 million paid to families through vouchers. But experimentation was limited and did not begin until 1973. Furthermore,

HUD never examined the vouchers' impact in cities with no other housing subsidy programs in effect, calling into question any conclusions that might be made from the study.[38]

In 1970, Romney did not accept the argument that public housing be entirely eliminated. He suggested that there remained a class of individuals for whom even the filtered-down existing housing stock would be too expensive or too poor in quality. He thus proposed that HUD provide some new public housing, though 60 percent of those dwellings would be leased through Section 23. This approach had several benefits—allowing more units to be available more quickly and "achiev[ing] dispersion of minority groups throughout majority areas."[39] Missing from Romney's proposal was the provision of direct aid to families to help them pay rent.

Toward a Moratorium

Romney's alternative vision for HUD was ignored by OMB, which cut the agency's proposed budget. The secretary appealed the OMB budget to the president, arguing it would result in "a dramatic slowdown in assisted housing production" and "a political debacle" if Model Cities were terminated and Urban Renewal were cut in half. The result would be "derailment of HUD's carefully considered strategy to move from the old grab bag of categorical programs" to revenue sharing.[40] Moreover, Romney claimed that OMB's strategy amounted to eliminating proven housing policy models before identifying better alternatives. Referencing his previous work as head of American Motors, Romney said that "no manufacturer would be foolish enough to discontinue production of existing models until his new model had been thoroughly engineered, designed, road-tested, and put into production." The competition—the Democratic Party—would lash out and convince the public that their alternative was better. That year, Romney's pleas were heard: The agency's budget was in large part preserved.

The fight over public housing operating subsidies continued into late 1971, when the White House pushed a change in funding that would radically decrease the amount of funding available for facility maintenance.[41] In July 1972, OMB again reduced HUD's proposed budget and, three months later, asked the agency to submit to additional reductions.[42] In September, Romney pleaded with the new OMB head, Caspar Weinberger, suggesting that the president's effort to "apply creative solutions to national problems" could not be "achieved through program cancellations or curtailments." HUD remained committed to the public housing, 235, 236, and Rent Supplement programs for FY 1974 funding—but the administration was not.[43]

In a conversation recorded on White House audio tapes, Nixon told his advisers that "Romney and his guys have run the federal participation in housing right into the ground." "It's just cheaper," he argued, "to hand people the money" to rent vacant housing.[44] In October, as FAP was mired in a skeptical Congress, OMB questioned some of the premises of "special" revenue sharing, suggesting it was duplicative of the taxing capabilities of cities and states. Meanwhile, officials at the White House asked HUD staff "about the effect on total housing production of elimination of the subsidized programs" and raised the possibility of eliminating revenue support altogether.[45]

The government had some evidence that the Johnson-era housing policies were not performing up to expectations. A 1971 HUD study showed that many of the new programs, particularly those for moderate-income housing, were too expensive, poorly administered, and had produced buildings of inferior construction quality. Section 235—the homeownership program—had been used fraudulently by builders. Nonprofit sponsors of Section 236 rental projects were often inept, and the program suffered from high housing costs. However, these problems were *not* influencing White House decision making; as late as July 1972, according to a conversation recorded at Camp David, Nixon had no knowledge about the aforementioned implementation issues, yet he remained fully committed to the ideological goal of reducing the housing budget.[46] The projects sponsored by state housing finance agencies had few of these problems, and the public housing and Section 23 programs, most of which were run by municipal agencies, had been implemented with relatively few problems.[47] So HUD, and its secretary, continued program implementation.

But Romney was increasingly isolated, suffering from the White House's centralization of policymaking in the West Wing.[48] A series of planned meetings with the president to discuss OMB's demands that HUD cut employees never occurred; Romney felt he was in the dark. On August 10, 1972, he submitted a letter of resignation. He wrote, "I have concluded more can be accomplished in the future if the Department is headed by someone whose counsel and advice you want."[49] White House audio tapes document that in a meeting with Nixon the next day, John Ehrlichman, assistant to the president for Domestic Affairs, said, "I think he's [Romney] just playing a little game, serving us all up on the idea that we're going to cave" unless he received additional employees. Subsequently, Nixon met with Romney, who complained impassionedly, "I have no effective voice in the policy areas or the operational areas relating to my own department." Nixon convinced him to remain, delaying his resignation to the end of the term in an effort to avoid campaign distractions.[50]

Nixon's administration shifted to the right after the president received a massive mandate in November 1972, taking more than 60 percent of the vote. Late that month, OMB privately determined that HUD would impose a moratorium on new investment in spending on housing—public housing, but also the programs meant to encourage private involvement, including rent supplements and Sections 235 and 236. This moratorium would begin on January 1, 1973, and was to last eighteen months, by which point Congress was supposed to have passed a new housing act conforming to the president's desires. OMB rehashed its criticism of the use of operating subsidies for public housing. Weinberger had previously stated that he was "quite disturbed" by the prospect of building public housing that would need operating subsidies.[51] The policy objective was to "discontinue Federal support for programs and activities which do not serve national (as opposed to local) interests."[52]

Romney, now a lame duck, reacted angrily. "My frustration is at the apparent message to me that all the good we have accomplished is to be undone," he wrote Weinberger. He questioned how private industry would respond and contrasted the policy of providing assistance through "massive tax subsidies for the middle income and wealthy . . . while the poor are cut adrift." Romney presented his thoughts at the White House in December 1972, noting that the administration was "discriminat[ing] against central cities" in a "hard-headed, cold-hearted indifference to the poor and racial minorities."[53] Three days before New Year's, Romney focused on the moratorium's "abruptness, harshness and injustice." He argued that HUD's reduction in funding for housing subsidies could be offset by eliminating the mortgage interest and property tax deductions provided in the federal tax code.[54]

In early January, it fell on Romney to make the public announcement about the moratorium. Federal commitments to new public housing, as well as moderate-income subsidies and urban renewal grants, ceased immediately.[55] Nixon stated in March 1973 that "fears of doom" about urban centers were "no longer justified," and that housing policies should adjust correspondingly. Though he could not yet provide a clear answer as to how housing aid would evolve, he denounced the previous "old and wasteful" policy, noting that "no single, rigid scheme, imposed by the Federal Government from Washington, is capable of meeting the changing and varied needs" of states and localities. He would be reintroducing housing legislation to Congress that would offer $2.3 billion in block grants to communities as additional revenue sharing. Clearly, Nixon wanted the federal government out of the game.[56]

New Approaches

Although there were rumors the government was considering suspending housing aid in December 1972, the announcement of the moratorium came as a major surprise, even at HUD. Opposition was instantaneous. Democrats in Congress, unable to assemble the adequate political support in the previous years to complete new housing legislation, nevertheless assailed the government. They were frustrated by the government's new policy of impounding congressionally appropriated funding, which extended beyond urban housing, also affecting policies such as rural electrification; George McGovern accused Nixon of asserting "one-man rule." Even before the suspension of aid had been announced, a national coalition including the National Tenants' Organization and the League of Women Voters suggested that the "human and economic results of such an action can only be described as catastrophic." A lawyer representing several housing groups said that "the cities in the U.S. will resemble the cities in Vietnam: a very bombed-out look."[57]

Under the leadership of James T. Lynn, HUD defended the moratorium. An internal report titled *Housing in the Seventies* proposed a new strategy for the administration. At the heart of the document was the claim that the existing subsidized government housing programs, particularly public housing, were too expensive, serving too few people, and producing a poor environment for residents. It also indicted Section 236 (though not public housing) as poorly managed and prone to foreclosure, a claim later refuted by scholar R. Allen Hays. These conclusions were made despite findings in the report of conflicting numbers: while subsidized housing was costing Washington about $5 billion a year, twice as much was going to middle- and upper-income householders through deductions and other taxes forgone by homeowners. The latter, however, were not identified for elimination. HUD argued that a cash assistance program for poor families could serve more people at a lower cost than a construction-oriented program like public housing.[58]

In September, Nixon announced his proposed new housing program. He condemned public housing complexes, arguing that "too many are monstrous, depressing places" and suggested that "the federal government has become the biggest slumlord in history." The shock of the failure of St. Louis's Pruitt-Igoe public housing complex, which had been demolished in 1972 after mass abandonment and vandalism, weighed heavily on his address. These criticisms, though, applied largely to the pre-1960s public housing program; Nixon, in effect, made no effort to recognize the reforms and transformations that had occurred in the intervening decade. To present his moratorium as the unavoidable response to the failures of public housing, Nixon elided the innovations in federal involvement implemented under President Johnson as well as Secretary Romney's proposals to rethink subsidized housing.

Fully endorsing the conservative approach, Nixon suggested instead that the government's involvement in the construction of new housing was "attacking the symptom" rather than "the cause": the lack of adequate family incomes. Thus, he said, the future of American subsidized housing would be in direct cash assistance. He began campaigning for Congress to pass a new housing act along these lines. In addition, Nixon lifted the moratorium on Section 23 (leasing of housing units) because it could be "administered in a way which carries out some of the principles of direct cash assistance."[59] In other words, subsidized housing construction remained unacceptable, but a housing program that paralleled the cash-based aid the Nixon administration hoped to use as the basic form of social welfare provision was allowed.

Though Democrats showed they were willing to rethink the federal government's housing policy in the 1960s, many opposed the administration's proposed changes in policy. Former HUD secretary Robert Weaver, for example, argued in congressional testimony that he had "long advocated a mix of production and better use of existing housing," but he emphasized that vacancy rate should play an important role in determining whether new housing was necessary. He suggested that the administration's willingness to abandon any sort of production goal and simply allow money to be spent however localities wanted was against the national interest. Moreover, he noted that providing people direct housing aid rather than funding new construction could further the deterioration of neighborhoods by encouraging abandonment of existing housing.[60]

Conclusion

Any argument that there was a consensus for eliminating the nation's public housing program in 1974 based on a failure of previous projects can be refuted by examining the debate in Congress over the passage of a new urban development bill. Increasingly empowered by the Watergate proceedings, the Senate ignored the president's appeals to completely revise the nation's housing subsidy system. In legislation passed overwhelmingly in March, Democrats offered a concession to Nixon—block grants to localities—but provided significant subsidy for new public housing units and maintained funding for Section 236. According to *Congressional Quarterly Weekly Report*, the influential Democratic senator from Alabama, John Sparkman, argued that "only production of new housing . . . would help guarantee enough decent housing for all Americans." The bill included a provision that would expand the powers of local housing authorities to build new units under Section 23 (not just lease existing ones), spreading the reach of public housing further.[61] Clearly, Nixon's argument about the failures of public housing was not accepted by substantial segments of the political class.

The House, whose leaders wanted legislation that would steer clear of Nixon's veto pen, passed a bill that canceled the Section 236 program in June 1974. Nonetheless, it included some aid for new public housing and an expanded and revised Section 23. In an attempt to "salvage his presidency," according to Hays, Nixon rescinded the moratorium and agreed to a House-Senate compromise on August 6, two days before resigning in the aftermath of the Watergate scandal. The new bill provided massive funds for four hundred thousand newly constructed housing units under Section 8 (which reformed Section 23), in addition to a rent supplement program for existing private housing, the latter becoming the mainstay of HUD aid in the 1980s. Instead of construction subsidies, Section 8 offered low-interest long-term mortgage repayment, as Section 236 had. This bill was signed into law by President Gerald Ford on August 23, 1974.[62]

The new law provided only thirty thousand new units of conventional public housing over the next six years, a major decline from past appropriations. But the Section 8 project-based assistance program provided for the construction of low-income housing complexes very similar to public housing projects of the past—just with a different financing approach. Therefore, while public housing construction slowed considerably in the 1970s, the federal government funded more than eight hundred thousand new or substantially renovated low-income housing units through Section 8 between 1974 and 1983. Though the program offered aid to private and nonprofit developers, many of these apartments were built by the same local housing authorities that had developed conventional public housing.[63]

Eugene Meehan wrote that "the principal thrust of the [housing] program was redirected to support the profit-making element in the private sector," thereby "condemning" publicly owned housing.[64] Yet, the 1974 Housing Act in fact extended many of the reforms begun during the Kennedy and Johnson years, continuing to involve the public sector, but with an increasingly private perspective. It did not eliminate the role of local housing authorities in the construction of homes for the least well-off; it changed the financing device with which they completed such work. While the Nixon administration attempted to stop the American low-income housing production program through budget cuts and the introduction of cash aid, legislators effectively sidestepped that effort by reframing much of the program under Section 8, while keeping public housing alive.[65]

This partial pushback enables us to reexamine the myth that treats the moratorium on subsidized housing as the logical result of its perceived failures—a narrative that the rhetoric of Nixon's 1973 statement encouraged. Instead, I have argued that federal policy had been innovating to address many of the program's flaws since the 1960s. Moreover, political support for federal programs that supported new apartment construction for low-income families—even by local housing authorities—remained strong despite the Nixon administration's attempt to undermine them. Additionally, Romney's active efforts to prevent the elimination of funding for such programs show that federal programs had loud supporters even within the administration. The evidence suggests that the Nixon administration's motivation for the moratorium was rooted in conservative ideology about the need to reduce federal expenditures; the need to return decision making and funding to the states and cities; and the need to allocate funding to the poor through cash aid, not social programs.

MIXED-INCOME REDEVELOPMENT IS THE ONLY WAY TO FIX FAILED PUBLIC HOUSING

Lawrence J. Vale

Public housing in the United States began as a mechanism to house an upwardly mobile segment of the working poor, evolved into a program that housed chiefly the least economically advantaged and the poorest welfare-dependent households and, since the 1990s, has been slowly replacing many failed low-income projects with new mixed-income communities.[1] Mixed-income redevelopment, frequently touted as an approach that benefits everyone and often assumed to be an almost self-evident good thing, has nonetheless been subjected to ongoing skepticism, expressed through the academic literature, the popular press, and the views of affected tenants. Supporters contend that it yields safe and attractive neighborhoods that serve all incomes, including some former public housing residents from the site, while permitting other former public housing residents to gain from dispersal to other mixed-income neighborhoods with the assistance of subsidized housing vouchers. Detractors counter that mixed-income redevelopment usually entails a loss of much-needed "hard units" of public housing, and unjustly displaces too many low-income households to other poor neighborhoods where they lack their former social networks. Especially since "mixed-income" housing has no commonly shared definition and since many alleged benefits of income mixing remain undemonstrated in practice, it is hardly surprising that mystification and mythification have proliferated.[2]

At least since the New Deal, housing policymakers in the United States have attempted to redesign and reengineer distressed urban neighborhoods to foster particular social and economic aims, often verging on the utopian. Then, as now, they sought to achieve the triple objective of revitalizing an area, providing higher-quality housing, and uplifting low-income tenants. All too often, these grand intentions overestimated the capacity of housing projects to effect such total transformations.[3] The earliest incarnations of American public housing—the pre–World War II efforts of the Public Works Administration (PWA) and the United States Housing Authority (USHA)—frequently attempted to reduce areas of concentrated poverty through slum clearance. Under USHA guidelines, any new public housing had to be accompanied by an "equivalent elimination" of slum areas. Private-sector real estate interests insisted on this to prevent an enhanced supply of government-subsidized affordable housing from unfairly competing with their own efforts. Public housing advocates of the 1930s and 1940s decried slums as the source of disease, dispiritedness, and delinquency and viewed modern public housing as the antidote to both unsanitary conditions and behavioral problems. They argued that constructing public housing would be in the best interest of the poor, but—like many advocates of mixed-income developments today—did not always examine the actual range of outcomes that often countered their assumptions.[4]

From the 1930s through the 1950s, city officials optimistically viewed public housing as part of a broader effort to spur investment in depressed urban areas and to curb poor behavior in low-income communities by replacing slum dwellers with a more carefully screened and upwardly mobile brand of tenant. These residents of early public housing surely had a range of incomes, though the range was set in a deliberately narrow way. If they were too poor, they would be judged too risky to admit; if they were too rich, they would be declared ineligible for continued occupancy and asked to move onward and upward. High levels of formal and informal social control accompanied the extensive social networks of early public housing. Management enforced the rules, and tenants frequently responded by taking personal responsibility for the outdoor common areas adjacent to their apartments. If residents wanted to look for role models, early public housing was full of households that used hard work and savings to move on quickly—often even to homeownership. Again, no one called this mixed-income housing then; it was just a collection of families seeking to better their circumstances. In these early years of public housing, the public sector could still take the lead in facilitating a mix of incomes that could yield safe and desirable planned communities. The intent here is not to wax nostalgic about an era of public housing that was segregated, brutally exclusive, and overwhelmingly paternalistic. It is merely to point out that there was a time in the United States when public housing authorities themselves tried to achieve all of the objectives now claimed as goals by advocates of mixed-income developments.

As public housing shifted into its welfare phase during the 1960s, 1970s and 1980s, policymakers increasingly came to blame the "concentration of poverty" as the source of all problems.[5] As tenant incomes declined, public housing communities suffered from some combination of inadequate financial structure, excessive deferred maintenance, poor design, indifferent management, and protracted racial tensions. These were all accompanied by a gradual shift in the tenant population away from the carefully vetted collectives of the first twenty years, when public housing was regarded as a reward, to a system where public housing became the last stop short of homelessness (or the first stop back) for the least advantaged of U.S. households. Housing authorities responded to the increased desperation of those who applied for units by admitting them regardless of the problems they might bring. They did so consciously, even conscientiously.

Starting in the 1970s, local housing officials began to experiment with deliberately created mixed-income communities as an alternative to public housing that contained only those with extremely low incomes, and this trend has accelerated. Since the early 1990s, U.S. Congress has appropriated more than $6 billion under HOPE VI (currently translated as Housing Opportunities for People Everywhere), a program of the U.S. Department of Housing and Urban Development (HUD) designed to facilitate more than 250 efforts to redevelop "severely distressed" public housing. Much of this redevelopment, spread across nearly every major American city, has entailed the demolition of housing projects and their replacement with mixed-income communities. Proponents have eagerly proffered evidence to suggest declining crime and disorder, higher neighborhood maintenance, reduction of social stigma, escalation of housing values, enhanced neighborhood attractiveness, improved local services, and increased local investment by the private sector.[6] Critics counter that income mixing has been a thinly veiled attempt by a neoliberal state to commit public funds to support gentrification, while displacing the poor and disrupting social networks.[7] As the disputes continue, most public housing redevelopment has become almost synonymous with income mixing.[8] Lost in the shuffle of incomes, however, is the possibility that public housing salvation by income mixing may be more myth than reality.

There are three principal reasons why it seems misguided to view mixed-income housing as either a panacea, or as the only viable strategy for revitalizing distressed public housing. First, mixed-income development has been too loosely defined as a category, and unhelpfully allowed to encompass a huge range of scenarios—everything from market-rate developments with a small remaining number of public housing units, to developments that remain chiefly public housing, to those that include few or no market-rate units and instead mix public housing with other subsidized housing produced with Low Income Housing Tax Credits. In other words, even if there are positive effects that follow from the introduction of mixed-income housing, important unresolved questions remain: Which kind of mixed-income housing is needed to generate such gains, and which kinds of residents actually benefit from the changes?

Second, scholars and practitioners continue to debate the merits of mixed-income approaches, having found that many of the assumed benefits of income mixing for low-income residents, such as role modeling, provide little positive impact on their lives. By contrast, other aspects seem more promising: enhanced security, increased investment in neighborhoods, and higher expectations for management.[9] Given that some rationales seem to be much more persuasive than others, and that benefits are not evenly shared, how can mixed-income housing best be justified?

Finally, several cities have implemented successful public housing redevelopment efforts *without* mixing incomes or by keeping their entire engineered mix wholly confined to various levels of low-income households. Such initiatives have been implemented both before the HOPE VI program began, and under its auspices. Recognizing this kind of alternative, is all the cost and effort associated with mixed-income public housing really necessary?

Mixed Incomes, Mixed Definitions

Mixed-income public housing is an ill-defined subset of the equally ill-defined but much larger phenomenon of mixed-income neighborhoods. Such neighborhoods can either be seen as produced by deliberate social policy (as in the case of HOPE VI public housing redevelopment) or as emerging in a more organic fashion.[10] The policy shift toward deliberately created mixed-income neighborhoods emerged out of a sense that neighborhoods of "concentrated poverty" had been dangerous failures;[11] it did not emerge as a policy response to some clear empirical evidence about the positive value of income mixing.[12] The latter, for the most part, has simply been assumed rather than tested, constrained by the fact that the broader phenomenon of mixed-income neighborhoods has been defined so loosely and inconsistently.

At base, such neighborhoods are difficult to situate both in time and in space. First, neighborhoods may exhibit income heterogeneity for only a short period of time, a period of transition between a place that is predominantly low-income and a gentrified locale that is dominated by high incomes, or a transition moving in the other direction.[13] Second, neighborhoods often have manipulable or contestable boundaries, and the degree of income mixing may vary markedly depending on how and where such boundaries are drawn. Should the mixed-income nature of a mixed-income public housing development be measured on its own, for instance, or should assessment of the degree of income mix also take account of the socioeconomics of surrounding blocks? If the latter count as part of "the neighborhood," this may skew the nature of the income mix either upward or downward in quite substantial ways.

This jurisdictional matter also cuts to the heart of the question of how one classifies "concentrated poverty." For example, a public housing development with most residents living below the poverty line will presumably have a far smaller percentage of impoverished residents if it is redeveloped into a mixed-income community composed of one-third public housing, one-third shallow-subsidized "affordable" housing, and one-third market-rate housing. It also matters considerably whether the surrounding neighborhood is low poverty or high poverty, since some high-poverty public housing located in affluent areas might already be considered less affected by "concentrated poverty" if this poverty is measured to include that larger area of neighborhood affluence. Conversely, if the neighborhood boundaries are drawn more tightly to encompass only the housing development footprint itself, the resultant mixed-income development (even if two-thirds of its residents are not in public housing) may still exhibit a poverty rate of 33 percent, a figure considered "high poverty" by most social policy analysts. Because of slippery definitions that are easily subjected to manipulation for political purposes, it is possible to define a public housing project—such as Chicago's Cabrini-Green—as an isolated enclave of "concentrated poverty" only if the surrounding affluence is not counted as part of the neighborhood being assessed. Policymakers can claim that they have benevolently supported most Cabrini residents by relocating them away from such poverty, but, if the neighborhood boundaries are framed differently, it is equally true to say that they have been forced out of a larger low-poverty neighborhood and into one that is very likely to have a much higher poverty rate.

Next, at least in an American context, the definition of "mixed income" also must encompass considerations of race and ethnicity. Mixed-income neighborhoods that vary by class but are more homogeneous in terms of race or ethnicity may well have a different social dynamic than those where substantial income differentials are correlated with distinct racial or ethnic groupings. Also, since different races and ethnicities exhibit different income profiles, the very definition of income mix can vary in relation to these sorts of factors. Clearly, there can never be some single standard for a mix.

Similarly, a mixed-income housing development or neighborhood may also operate differently as a social and political unit if it contains mixes of housing tenure. Inclusion of homeownership opportunities, especially if accompanied by separate institutional associations that exclude renters, may yield communities that operate differently from those that are rental only. Homeownership often signals a longer-term investment in a place than does market-rate rental housing, though subsidized low-income renters may also take a long-term stake in their home neighborhood, and some owners are interested only in short-term investment opportunities. Finally, deliberately produced mixed-income neighborhoods can vary widely by building type, by type of management, by location (from urban to suburban), and by housing market (from "tight" markets where renters have few alternatives to higher-vacancy places where competition is less fierce); all these important factors also detract from the value of the term, rendering it as little more than an ambiguous catch-all.

At its core, though, the definitional morass of mixed-income housing stems from the failure to distinguish among narrow mixes—mixes that cut across a broad continuum of incomes, and mixes that are starkly polarized between high-income and low-income contingents. Moreover, there is no consistency in how income groups are defined; those who are "high income" in one mixed-income context could even be considered "low-income" in another.[14] As Alex Schwartz observed in 2010, "Virtually no research exists on the actual financial performance of mixed-income housing," since financial reporting systems used by the operators of mixed-income housing fail to separate out the distinct contributions of each income group.[15] Narrow-mix options have famously included Vincent Lane's Mixed-Income New Communities Strategy (MINCS) deployed at Chicago's Lake Parc Place in the early 1990s, which filled half of the apartments with very low-income public housing households and the other half with employed households earning 50–80 percent of the area median income. By pairing public housing residents with those whose earnings put them the upper end of what counts as "low income," Lake Parc Place managed an income mix where all incomes were nonetheless some variant of "low."[16] Similarly, some HOPE VI initiatives, such as San Francisco's North Beach Place, have successfully crafted mixed-income strategies that replaced all existing low-income public housing units on site, while adding in another tier of shallow subsidy housing, funded by Low Income Housing Tax Credits. At North Beach, policymakers managed to combine public and private investment to create a "mixed-income" community that nonetheless served an exclusively low-income clientele.

By contrast, the much-touted development of Boston's Harbor Point during the 1980s (i.e., pre-HOPE VI) replaced 100 percent public housing with a predominantly market-rate community,[17] a practice frequently echoed in HOPE VI mixed-income developments. Most HOPE VI communities defined as "mixed income" have had at least three tiers of income groups: a market-rate tier, a tier still composed of tenants receiving public housing subsidies (or similar project-based vouchers), and a middle tier of more moderately subsidized households.[18] In practice, however, there is no commonly deployed terminology that separates out these very different concepts of "mixed income," and there has been little systematic effort to measure the outcomes from each type.

Mixed Incomes, Mixed Outcomes

Just as the term "mixed income" has stubbornly resisted consistent definition, so too the expected advantages from adopting this approach have remained woefully unclear, often subject to blind assumptions and wishful thinking rather than empirical assessment. It remains crucial to gain clarity about what mixed-income housing *is,* but it is equally pressing to understand what it *does,* since the results of this approach to policy need to be measured. To date, empirical investigation of mixed-income communities, at least in the United States, suggests that their outcomes are at least as mixed as their incomes.[19]

Social policy analyst Mark Joseph and his colleagues have provided a particularly astute dissection of the diverse motives behind mixed-income development.[20] Their research encompasses ethnographic work on several new mixed-income communities created to replace public housing in Chicago but also includes a broader analytical framework—one that looks across the findings of many researchers to explain and assess the diverse rationales that undergird the phenomenon of mixed-income housing. Until policymakers and developers can answer Joseph's apt question about whether mixed-income housing is intended "to revitalize the local area and provide additional housing options for urban dwellers, to provide low-income residents with higher-quality housing, to help lift low-income families out of poverty, or some combination of the three,"[21] it will be impossible to assess its effectiveness—

especially if it turns out that some of these goals are mutually exclusive. By separating out several ways that mixed-income developments potentially could benefit the urban poor, Joseph usefully connects these assumptions to what is known from the literature and thereby allows those involved in housing redevelopment efforts to have a better way to situate claims and measure success.[22]

As Joseph's framework reveals, proponents justify mixed-income developments (however variously the mix is defined) as facilitating four distinct kinds of gain. The presence of higher-income residents is said to provide: (1) increased social capital for low-income residents, (2) direct or indirect role-modeling of social norms for work and behavior, (3) informal social control leading to safer and more orderly communities for everyone, and (4) gains for the broader community through enhanced engagement of political and market forces. Analysis of a wide variety of mixed-income communities, including those studied by Joseph and by others, casts doubt on the first two forms of presumed success. These rationales, emphasizing social capital and role-modeling, seem to be the most frequently claimed benefits, but empirical social science researchers have rarely found much supporting evidence when analyzing the social practices of actual communities. By contrast, researchers have found more support for rationales that emphasize enhanced security and greater neighborhood investment.[23] These last two rationales are certainly important factors for judging the desirability of a community, but they are less centrally or exclusively the kind of benefit that inures primarily to those with the lowest incomes.

More pointedly, James DeFilippis and Jim Fraser observe that all four of the most frequently voiced rationales for mixed-income policies are "largely based on the (hegemonic) mantra that low-income people themselves are the problem, and that a benevolent gentry needs to colonize their home space in order to create the conditions necessary to help the poor 'bootstrap' themselves into a better socioeconomic position." Framed this way, "poor people . . . come to be simply 'a problem' that we need to spread out—and the language of 'fair share' or 'regional equity' that is often heard sounds remarkably similar to how people involved in environmental justice movements talk about things like waste transfer stations or incinerators." DeFilippis and Fraser ask a pertinent question: "Why do we want mixed-income housing and neighborhoods?" Their point is not to denigrate the potential value of mixed-income places; they just question who should benefit from them, and how benefits to low-income households can be maximized. They ask how mixed-income communities can be better governed, and how power inequities that continue to penalize on the basis of race, class, and gender distinctions can be minimized. Implicitly, they also ask which "we" should be empowered to choose the rationales for establishing the mix.[24]

Closely related to the assessments of mixed-income communities created as part of the HOPE VI program, others have questioned whether the dispersal or "vouchering out" of low-income residents from public housing and into the world of private landlords has helped them achieve the same sorts of goals ascribed to intentionally designed mixed-income communities.[25] Here, too, the realities have not often met the hopes of proponents who expected substantial socioeconomic gains. HOPE VI dispersal programs have rarely followed relocated residents in any systematic, long-term way, but more fully studied programs, such as the Moving to Opportunity (MTO) demonstration, have proved to be no more than a mixed success, at best. Although dispersal programs consistently reveal important gains in perceived safety in comparison to former neighborhoods of concentrated poverty, there is little evidence of comparable gains in terms of social networks, employment, or economic security. As Edward Goetz and Karen Chapple summarize, "There seems to be little in the record of MTO or forced displacement to suggest that relocated low-income families will fulfill the expectations of the dispersal model and form relationships with their (presumably higher-income) neighbors, thereby building 'bridging' social capital critical to finding employment activities." More generally, "dispersal efforts have not had any demonstrable positive effect on employment, earnings, or income of individuals." Similarly, their survey of the literature on voucher-based dispersal resulting from HOPE VI finds "limited benefits" to families. Although they typically move to places where they feel safer, most move to other poor neighborhoods rather than to low-poverty destinations, and "there are conspicuously no benefits in employment, income, or [reduced] welfare dependency. Furthermore, many of the families suffer significant interruptions in their social networks." In short, the overwhelming negativity of the research emphasis on the contagion effects of concentrated poverty may well have undervalued the vital and compensatory role of locally rooted networks of support.[26]

Given that research findings consistently provide no more than limited support for most of the cherished assumptions about the value of mixed-income housing, this raises questions about the advisability of large public investment in mixed-income developments. This is a particular concern for mixed-income communities implemented through the HOPE VI program, since these tend to reduce the already scarce supply of units serving those with the lowest incomes. If the presence of higher-income residents does not consistently provide the assumed benefits for low-income residents in terms of enhanced social capital, behavioral improvement, or economic advancement, then one may ask whether these important social goals could be better met by means other than mixed-income developments. Likewise, it is not clear whether the modest support in the literature for the third goal—enhanced informal social control—really depends on having a mixed-income community to achieve it. Finally, this raises questions about whether the remaining social goal—the fourth justification centered on neighborhood political and economic gains— might be met equally well by other policies.

Fixing without Mixing

If mixtures of incomes are good because they leverage resources and enforce higher standards, it is worth pressing harder to identify exactly which kinds of mixes are necessary to achieve the desired objectives. Narrow-mix experiments like Chicago's Lake Parc Place may actually provide *more* of the presumed social benefits of mixed-income housing than a wide-mix HOPE VI development.[27] In the latter, the gaps between very low-income, transit-dependent, long-term public housing tenants with children versus childless, auto-equipped, transient households with market-rate apartments or owned homes may simply be too vast for any form of social capital to bridge. The situation may be even more difficult if there are linguistic barriers or racial tensions as well.[28]

If providing greater informal social control and stimulating higher quality goods and services are the main benefits that mixed-income developments can proffer, it is worth examining more closely just what institutional mechanisms are needed to achieve these benefits. The first goal would mainly seem to be a management and tenant selection challenge. Whatever else the construction of a HOPE VI mixed-income community may be, it is an excuse to rethink the terms of housing management and an occasion to re-select the members of a community.[29] The return to more careful tenant screening today reflects a partial revival of the hard-headed realism of strict entry selection practiced during the 1930s and 1940s. The efforts to reassert such social control today are made much more difficult because HOPE VI redevelopment sites are not a social tabula rasa; every move to import a higher socioeconomic group is met with mistrust from at least some among the less upwardly mobile previous residents who understandably fear displacement.

It is sometimes possible to achieve many of the social goals that are wishfully ascribed to mixed-income public housing without actually allocating any units to market-rate tenants or homeowners. Most discussion of the Chicago Housing Authority's immensely ambitious Plan for Transformation boldly features CHA-led efforts to construct new mixed-income communities on and adjacent to the sites of some of the city's most notorious developments. Yet, well over a decade into the plan's implementation, only about three thousand public housing households had been accommodated in such places. By contrast, the city has quietly rehabilitated about five thousand public housing apartments for families and about nine thousand for seniors, all without any mixing of incomes—and all without any evaluation.[30] Before assuming that only income mixing can fix distressed public housing, closer examination of many other national efforts to improve public housing management and design ought to be considered as alternatives.

Fixing without Mixing, Boston Style

At Boston's Commonwealth Development—redeveloped a decade before the HOPE VI program existed—the Boston Housing Authority, the Commonwealth Tenants Association, a private developer, and a private management company worked together to replace a severely distressed 648-unit housing project with a well-designed, safe, and supportive community (Figure 6.1). They did so while screening out "troublemakers" but nonetheless rehousing the majority of former residents. The housing authority continued to use a citywide public housing waiting list, and preserved virtually all of the redeveloped apartments for very low-income and extremely low-income renters.[31]

The tens of millions of dollars spent in the early 1980s to transform Commonwealth is a story of a strong core of residents, activated with the assistance of a hired community organizer, and backed by a vibrant network of neighborhood, city, and state organizations. The housing authority, developer, and management company worked with residents to negotiate the physical and social goals for the redevelopment, building a level of mutual trust among parties that had previously been perpetual adversaries. Residents, working with skilled architects, landscape architects, and urban designers—as well as with the housing authority redevelopment team and sympathetic legal assistance advisers—agreed on the priorities for the physical redevelopment, and helped

Figure 6.1 Commonwealth Development, Boston, as of 2013. Photograph by author.

craft a 223-page management plan that covered a wide variety of community rules and procedures. Remarkably, this plan even gave the tenants the right to fire the private management company with 30 days' notice.

Nearly thirty years after the redevelopment was completed, it is arguably still the best public housing in the city. Commonwealth's success has taken at least seven different forms: the team 1) implemented the redevelopment smoothly, 2) designed a high-quality place, 3) improved the capacity of the tenant organization, 4) enhanced maintenance and management performance, 5) dramatically boosted security, 6) made progress on socioeconomic indicators, and 7) created a community that yields high rates of resident satisfaction.[32] Writing more generally about housing redevelopment success, Joseph observes: "It may be that the combination of strong management and more active informal control by residents is the most effective means of maintaining social order."[33] At Commonwealth, this is just what happened, except that everyone there is a very low-income public housing resident.

If, in the end, one measure of success in American public housing is the rate at which its residents become economically able to leave it, Common-

wealth's success is more limited. If, on the other hand, success in public housing redevelopment is measured by the enhancement of an attractive, safe, and
stable community, where even many of those who can afford to leave will
choose to stay, then the effort at Commonwealth warrants the highest praise.
Moreover, because Commonwealth's success in these terms was achieved
through tenant activism, responsive design, and effective management—
without resorting to the income mixing so often touted as necessary to revitalize public housing—it raises important questions about current policy trends.

Despite the seeming promise of interventions such as the Commonwealth
redevelopment, Edward Goetz correctly laments that "the possibility of public
housing with excellent property management, good schools nearby, high
quality public services, engaged and informed public-sector supervision of
housing authorities, and private-sector investment providing jobs and retail
opportunities for residents" seems to be "off the table, altogether" as a policy
direction. Still, as Goetz points out, "There is very little inherent in the public
housing model that precludes these outcomes; it is how our public and private
institutions respond to public housing that has produced the negative outcomes
we have seen in American public housing."[34]

The Commonwealth example suggests that distressed public housing can
sometimes be reclaimed for its residents and for its neighborhood without income mixing. Yet this model seems to have dropped off policymakers' radar
screen, presumably because it does not leverage the same sort of additional
private investment that mixed-income developments do and because it fails
to reach moderate-income households that are also legitimately struggling to
find affordable housing in high-priced cities. Instead, our collective embrace
of the mythic mixed-income model reflects the prevailing view that enhancing private investment is what matters most in public housing redevelopment.
In other words, income-mixing may enhance the statistical profile of a given
neighborhood, and it may be the trigger to investment that improves the appearance of the built environment, but it may not be the catalyst that improves
the lives of low-income individuals and families, since many of these more
mobile poor may find themselves forced out of a place that is new and attractive, but also newly and unattractively unaffordable.

If we cared about maximizing the utility of the public housing system for
very low-income households, we might look at the income mix in developments in a different way. Right now, the deeply political implicit question that
is asked when calculating an income mix is, How can the number of very

low-income households that need to be accommodated be kept to a minimum so that redevelopment will remain financially appealing to private developers and investors? Combining all of the multiple goals for mixed-income housing, a more equitable approach would be to ask instead, What is the maximum number of equitably screened very low-income households that can be accommodated in a mixed-income development while still ensuring a safe and stable community? Sometimes, as is the case at Commonwealth, that number may reach 100 percent.

Conclusion

Analysis of the literature on mixed-income developments reveals different motives for its backing and casts significant doubt on key assumptions about its presumed benefits. This literature provides more support for the ability of mixed-income developments to enhance social control and help leverage neighborhood political and economic gains. However, some of those advantages could presumably be achieved for low-income households through well-managed housing, careful tenant selection, and good design—without income mixing. The inconclusive endorsement for mixed-income housing proffered by Mark Joseph and other scholars suggests the need for further ethnographic research on these communities, including an analysis of the importance of homeownership, the pattern of engagement with public schools, and the advantages of different kinds of income mixing.

Most important, it is worth systematically comparing those mixed-income HOPE VI communities that have achieved their deconcentration of poverty by development-based dilution of poverty (keeping the original number of public housing units on site but mixing in some additional units of affordable or market-rate units) versus those that have pursued mixed-income strategies by means of neighborhood-based dispersion (reducing the percentage of low-income housing units on the original site while scattering replacement housing into other communities). In rapidly gentrifying areas, the mixed-income approach can either join the trend and shift the remaining deeply subsidized housing elsewhere or, alternatively, it can serve as the last chance to preserve some affordable housing in an area where low-income households are being priced out of the market. If the goal is to assess the benefits and costs of mixed-income approaches to low-income residents, higher-income residents, and neighborhood dynamics, then all of these need to be carefully considered together.[35]

The many mixed-income developments built outside the HOPE VI system—assuming that they do not displace existing low-income housing and households—do not face quite the same equity hurdle. Even so, given the immense challenges facing low-income households seeking affordable housing in U.S. cities, we should still hold all mixed-income developments to high standards. If advocates of such developments do indeed want to pursue a triple goal of area revitalization, better housing quality, and support for low-income households, it may well be that only those narrow-mix models that attempt to maximize—rather than minimize—participation by low-income households have a chance of reaching all three goals simultaneously. Comparative neighborhood research could empirically show which kinds of income-mixing matters most for which kinds of outcomes. At the very least, policymakers should scrutinize the assumptions that are used to justify mixed-income developments and researchers should develop more comprehensive methods to assess empirically whether the assumed outcomes are actually being realized. Only then will the mythic promises of mixed-income housing be given a true test.

ONLY IMMIGRANTS STILL LIVE IN EUROPEAN PUBLIC HOUSING

Florian Urban

Few images are as persistent as that of the public housing estate as a tower block ghetto for marginalized and impoverished immigrants. The media has perpetuated the myth that only immigrants still live in European public housing. And yet nothing could be further from the truth in most European cities. In contrast to the United States, countries such as Germany, Austria, Sweden, and the Netherlands have been continuously investing in their public housing stock. At the same time, public housing in these countries is commonly accepted among the middle classes and by no means an exclusionary refuge for the neediest.

This is not to say that there are no challenges. The towers in Amsterdam's Bijlmermeer, in Stockholm-Vällingby, or in Cologne-Chorweiler have a significant share of poor immigrants, and the marginalization of citizens with foreign ancestry is a serious problem in many European countries. If one looks at the whole of Europe, however, there seems to be little correlation between disadvantaged minorities and public housing. This is not only because the countries of the former Eastern bloc, which tend to have a large amount of state-built tower-and-slab designs, generally have a very low immigrant population. It is also that the traditional destinations of the postwar immigration wave—Great Britain, the Netherlands, Sweden, and Germany—have relatively few public housing estates that show characteristics of ghettoization (and those that do have received disproportionate media attention).

This chapter will focus on Berlin, a city with a significant immigrant population and one that boasts some of Europe's largest public housing estates. However, the largest concentration of first- and second-generation immigrants can be found in nineteenth-century tenements near the city center rather than in the public housing blocks on the periphery. The following chapter will show

how this distribution resulted from particular sociocultural circumstances and how Berlin's peripheral public housing estates, despite many challenges, did not become tools of spatial exclusion.

Berlin's most famous public housing estates—Marzahn (Figure 7.1) and Märkisches Viertel (Figure 7.2)—are not ghettos in the sense of the now-demolished Robert Taylor Homes in Chicago or the Pruitt-Igoe development in St Louis. First, in both parts of Germany—to a greater extent in the East, but noticeable also in the West—state-subsidized and controlled housing became an accepted form of dwelling even among the middle classes. Second, the parameters of ethnically based exclusion—however painful for those who suffer from it—are different in Germany than in the United States.

Figure 7.1 Märkisches Viertel, West Berlin (built 1963–1975), section designed by Oswald Mathias Ungers. Photograph by author.

Figure 7.2 Märkisches Viertel, West Berlin (built 1963–1975), section designed by Shadrach Woods. Photograph by author.

This chapter will present the historic development of public housing in Germany and analyze how it intersected with patterns of ethnic division. It will then look at the different approaches that the German government has taken since the 1990s and compare these to housing policy initiatives in neighboring European countries.

The bulk of Berlin's public housing estates were built between the mid-1960s and mid-1980s. Thus, they date from the era of Cold War division and include both those built under the socialist-planned economy in the East and by the capitalist welfare state in the West. While there are formal distinctions—among other things East German tower block estates tend to be larger and more standardized—the differences are not obvious to the layperson and became blurred in the course of two decades of renovation and structural modification. In any case, Berlin is a unique example of how, under similar sociocultural conditions, two different regimes generated formally similar buildings that nonetheless had a very different significance in their respective contexts.

Public housing in Germany, as in most European countries, consists of policy and architecture. Both are often collapsed in popular imagination, but not necessarily connected. At the policy level, the instruments varied at different points in time, and both the West German *gemeinnütziger Wohnungsbau* (nonprofit housing) and the East German state-operated housing differed in many ways from, for instance, the French *habitations à loyer modéré* (moderate-rent dwellings) or the British council housing. Public housing, in the context of this chapter, is therefore defined very generally as affordable rental housing that is subsidized and maintained by public or publicly regulated institutions, which retain the right of tenant allocation and guarantee a certain degree of protection against eviction.[1] At the architectural level, public housing is mostly connected with the *Großsiedlungen* ("large estates" of mostly tower blocks), which cropped up on the peripheries of German cities beginning in the 1960s and were built according to the principles of Le Corbusier's urbanism. They represent only one particular type that stands next to the smaller low-rises of the 1950s or the postmodern perimeter blocks of the 1980s. But the tower block estates are by far the most conspicuous physical presence, the housing type that is most debated in the media and, at least with regard to East Germany, also the most widespread form. Hence, these will receive the most attention in this chapter.

An Accepted Form of Dwelling

Berlin's public housing estates, like those all over Europe, are the product of a great hope. Along with rapid modernization in the mid-twentieth century, there was a widespread conviction that the dreadful housing conditions of the early industrial era could be overcome, and the divide between the life standards of the rich and the poor narrowed. A strong state was believed to be capable of carrying out this epochal task: providing modern amenities for everybody and ending substandard living and overcrowding.

These ideas spawned the much-celebrated *Siedlungen* (housing estates) of the 1920s, with their innovative design and technology. In Berlin, for example, these include the Hufeisen-Siedlung (Horseshoe Development, designed by Martin Wagner and Bruno Taut, 1925–1931), the Siedlung Schillerpark (designed by Bruno Taut, 1924–1930) and the Weiße Stadt (White City, designed by Martin Wagner and Otto Salvisberg, 1929–1931), which in 2009 were declared UNESCO world heritage sites. They were too few to have a wider impact on society at the time, but they clearly set the stage for a new type of architecture that a few decades later was constructed at a broader scale. In the 1950s and 1960s, when the West German economy grew at breathtaking rates, large amounts of state-subsidized apartments first went up in the West. East Germany did some planning at the same time, though construction on the largest estates did not begin until the 1970s. By that time, public housing had become an integral part of many Germans' daily life.

The ideological conditions of modernization and increasing state intervention were similar to circumstances in the United States, but they developed against a different cultural background. In Europe, state authorities were traditionally perceived as benevolent. Even die-hard market liberals acknowledged the necessity for state regulation in matters of basic life. Voices in favor of a lean state were virtually nonexistent until late in the century.

Germany's interventionist housing policy was forged under a particular set of conditions. At the end of the Second World War, most large cities were heavily damaged or destroyed, and approximately twelve million ethnic German refugees had fled from the territories that Germany had to cede to Poland and the Soviet Union, as well as from countries such as Czechoslovakia and Hungary. More than eight million ended up in West Germany, where they were soon joined by another wave of refugees from East Germany. Millions had to live in camps or emergency shelters throughout the 1950s and 1960s. In this context, all social groups perceived the housing shortage as one of the region's most pressing problems. In the bombed cities, both rich and poor suffered from dire conditions; a refugee's fate was not class-specific. The Pomeranian and East Prussian aristocracy had lost their homes in the same way as the Silesian coal miners. Members of both the conservative Christian Democratic Party and the leftist Social Democratic Party, therefore, supported the attempts to regulate the market and pour state funds into housing.

Their efforts were eased by the fact that in the whole of Germany a free housing market had been nonexistent for decades. Already during the economically unstable Weimar Republic, state authorities had imposed numerous restrictions in favor of tenants. The Nazi regime in 1933 had reinforced these regulations, effectively replacing the free rental market with a system of apartment distribution through municipal authorities.[2] Also in the early postwar years, a free housing market was absent in both the socialist East and the capitalist West. Only as of 1951, when West Germany passed its *Wohnraum-*

bewirtschaftungsgesetz (Law on the Management of Dwelling Space), did houses and apartments cease to be distributed exclusively by state authorities, although numerous regulations remained in place. In East Germany, a parallel openness in markets did not occur until after the German reunification in 1990.

The greater acceptance of state intervention was also related to the fact that Germany had developed a particular form of tenant culture. Unlike England, the Netherlands, or the United States, Germany has had a centuries-old tradition of apartment living. In dense metropolises such as Hamburg or Berlin, even the upper-middle classes lived in flats within multistory structures. There was, therefore, no cultural bias against sharing an entrance with strangers.

Tenancy was also favored by the simple fact that between 1900 and 1951, German legislation outlawed ownership of individual apartments.[3] In an era when homeownership spread rapidly in Anglo-Saxon countries, German city-dwellers could rarely own their living space. With the exception of the very wealthy, who possessed entire buildings, urbanites tended to be tenants. Even today, 85 percent of Berliners rent their apartments—in London the rate is less than 50 percent.[4] In the whole of Germany, the homeownership rate of only 45 percent of all households is one of the lowest in Europe, compared to approximately 70 percent in the United Kingdom.[5] The fact that influential middle-class groups were tenants not only advanced a staunch acceptance of tenancy as a way of life but also helped promote particularly tenant-friendly legislation, which has determined the course of German housing to date. Tenants frequently stay for decades in the same apartment, and unless the owner of a building wants to move in, it is next to impossible to end a contract against the tenant's will.

Public Housing in East and West Germany

During the four decades of the German Democratic Republic (GDR; 1949–1990), almost any dwelling could be considered public housing; with the exception of owner-occupied single-family homes, all buildings were administered, maintained, and rented out by state institutions. In the West and later in reunified Germany, public housing was a temporary status granted to particular dwelling units that had been erected with public subsidies. This status expired after a certain time period—usually twenty to forty years until the subsidies were amortized—and the units could then be rented or sold on the free market. This temporariness distinguishes German public housing from that in other European countries such as Sweden or Austria, where it is permanent. The arrangement in Germany has also led to a substantial diminution of public housing units in past decades, as most support programs have been discontinued. However, given Germany's tenant-friendly legislation, many units for which the official status has expired have retained some of the characteristics of public housing: they are affordable and tenants are protected against eviction.

When West German Conservatives and Social Democrats forged a coalition in the 1950s to funnel state funds into the production of housing, they claimed that their efforts would benefit the entire population. In practice, however, public housing was first directed to the middle classes who could afford rents that were higher than in older buildings.[6] In the early years, approximately 70 percent of the population was considered eligible for public housing. This reflected the desolate state of the war-ravaged country, but at the same time, it signaled a situation in which receipt of state benefits was no embarrassment for anyone. Although the economic situation improved over the course of the 1950s, the institutional culture of public housing had been firmly established and would remain in place for decades to come.[7]

West Germany's big housing drive was carried out in the 1950s and 1960s under various conservative national governments, but it was supported by the Social Democratic Party. During that time, 3.9 million public housing flats were built in a country of approximately fifty-five million inhabitants.[8]

In the early postwar years, flats were predominantly built in the inner city, often in areas that had been bombed. They formed comparably small developments of unadorned three-to-four-story blocks, assembled in continuous rows, with loosely scattered green spaces in between. Examples include the Ernst-Reuter-Siedlung in West Berlin's Wedding district (420 apartments designed by Felix Hinssen, 1953–1955) or the Heinrich-Heine-Viertel in East Berlin's Mitte district (four thousand apartments designed by Werner Dutschke, Josef Kaiser, and others, 1958–1961).

Since the 1960s, the new paradigm *Urbanität durch Dichte* ("urbanity through density") spawned the *Großsiedlungen*.[9] They were public housing estates composed of six- to twenty-story high-rises, situated on the urban periphery, and organized by the principles of the Athens Charter (functional separation, separation of traffic flows, and predominance of light and air). Such large tower block developments were erected all over West Germany and included Neue Vahr in Bremen (1957–1962, designed by Ernst May for twenty-five thousand inhabitants); the Cologne-Chorweiler (begun in 1957, designed by Gottfried Böhm and others for twenty thousand inhabitants); Hamburg-Steilshoop (begun in 1960, for nineteen thousand inhabitants); Hamburg-Mümmelmannsberg (1970–1980, for nineteen thousand inhabitants); Frankfurt-Nordweststadt (1963–1968, designed by Walter Schwagenscheidt and Tassilo Sittmann for twenty-five thousand inhabitants); Frankfurt-Limesstadt (1962–1973, designed by Hans Bernhard Reichow for ten thousand inhabitants); and Munich-Neuperlach (1963–1978, designed by Bernt Lauter and others for fifty thousand inhabitants). All large estates were fitted out with ample car infrastructure, but were reasonably well connected to the city center through public transit.

East Germany carried out a comprehensive restructuring of its construction industry from 1955 onward. From that time, buildings were predominantly erected from prefabricated concrete slabs. To date, these buildings are referred to as *Plattenbau* (slab building) or simply *die Platte* (the slab). At the same time, the first large estates were planned. The new town of Hoyerswerda was begun in 1957 to house the workers of a newly founded chemical plant; eventually, apartments for fifty thousand people were built. Construction on Halle-Neustadt, the largest slab estate in East Germany, was planned for one hundred thousand inhabitants in the 1950s and begun in 1964.

The bulk of East Germany's housing estates nevertheless did not go up until at least a decade later. Walter Ulbricht, East Germany's head of government from 1949 to 1971, had limited economic resources and preferred to concentrate architectural investment in the city center. His successor, Erich Honecker, by contrast, strongly promoted housing. Under his auspices, Honecker's East German parliament passed the *Wohnungsbauprogramm* (Housing Program) in 1973. It promised the construction of approximately three million new dwelling units for a country of just seventeen million inhabitants. In the remaining years of the GDR, the government built approximately two million of these, most of them on large estates using prefab technology.[10] The program had a massive and lasting impact.

THE STRUGGLE OVER WEST BERLIN'S TOWER BLOCKS

In West Berlin, the housing policy of "urbanity through density" yielded three great settlements: Falkenhagener Feld on the northwestern periphery (1962–1975, planned by Hans Stefan for ten thousand inhabitants); Gropiusstadt in the south (1962–1975, originally planned by Walter Gropius, modified by

Figure 7.3 Slab buildings in East Berlin's Marzahn district (built 1980s). Originally, the buildings displayed an unadorned concrete façade. The bright white panels and the blue and yellow ornaments were added when the buildings were renovated in the 1990s. Photograph by author.

Wils Ebert, for fifty thousand inhabitants); and the Märkisches Viertel (Figure 7.3) in the north (1963–1975, planned by Hans Müller and Georg Heinrichs for thirty thousand inhabitants).

Of these three, the Märkisches Viertel received most attention. During the 1966 building fair *Berliner Bauwochen,* forty thousand Berliners admired pictures of shiny towers, while the press enthusiastically celebrated what they called an innovative approach to end the shortcomings of the past.[11] Public opinion nevertheless swung against it only two years later, when in the wake of the 1968 student protests a rebellious young generation questioned the principles of expert planning and top-down decision making. Labels such as "inhuman ghettos" referred to infrastructural shortcomings as well as the disruption of old neighborhood structures through large-scale tenement demolitions.[12]

The initial outcry was just as harsh as in the United States, Britain, and France.[13] Subsequent investment, however, mitigated the protests. Over the following decades, the municipally owned housing companies improved insulation and finishing and the local government invested in public services. The city completed the promised infrastructure—parks, shops, schools, and nurseries—and public transit connections improved. By the 1980s, the storm had waned, and the estates received considerably better press.[14] The tenants as well as the general public pragmatically accepted the tower blocks as an unspectacular but at the same time comparably cheap form of dwelling.

SLABS IN EAST BERLIN

East Berlin's most famous public housing estates were built on the eastern fringe of the city. In 1990, they housed approximately 350,000 of the half-city's 1.1 million inhabitants. The first, Marzahn, was started in 1978 in an area formerly covered with fields and garden plots; the land was declared East Berlin's ninth city district in 1979. Two new districts followed: Hellersdorf in 1981 and Hohenschönhausen in 1983. Prefab blocks were continuously built until the German reunification in 1990.

Like those in the West, the first residents of East Berlin's tower blocks received them with enthusiasm, since many had vivid and unpleasant recollections of life in overcrowded tenements. At the time, a prefab block was the only type of housing that offered central heating, warm running water, and elevators. These amenities did not become generally available until the early 1970s, when the first tenement renovations reconciled the former opposition between old buildings and modern living. Despite the generally positive response, criticism of monotonous design and unimaginative planning began to be voiced at an early stage and increased over the years. But the majority of the new residents were only too willing to put up with such deficiencies in return for a self-contained flat where they did not have to carry coals and heat their bathwater over the kitchen stove.

Social inequality was comparably low in the German Democratic Republic. The apartment distribution policy reinforced a social mixture where medical doctors and factory workers shared the same buildings. Those with party connections or influential friends sometimes secured preferential locations or slightly bigger flats than the average, but, with the exception of a handful of top leaders, all East Germans shared rather similar living conditions. Against this background, *die Platte* was widely accepted as a home for the ordinary citizen.[15]

ETHNIC BERLIN

The postwar boom, which afforded Germans a higher degree of housing equality than ever before, nonetheless generated a new set of disparities. Since World War II, the country had been, for the most part, ethnically homogeneous; it soon became a destination for immigrants.

Like other European countries, West Germany experienced a large influx of foreign nationals in the 1960s. Between 1955, when the first bilateral agreement was passed, and 1973, when official recruitment was stopped, the West German government actively attracted labor from Italy, Spain, Greece, Turkey, Morocco, Portugal, Tunisia, and Yugoslavia. During that time, approximately 2.9 million foreigners entered West Germany, mostly to work in factories or at menial jobs. They were referred to as *Gastarbeiter* ("guest workers"), which emphasized that not only the majority population but also many of the workers themselves considered their tenure in Germany as temporary. This changed in the 1970s, after many had established themselves and migrants were increasingly understood as permanent residents.

West Berlin became home to 120,000 Turkish nationals, most of whom originated from the underdeveloped areas of Anatolia. Germany's island city counted approximately 12 percent non-Germans in the 1980s, one of the largest foreign communities in the country.[16] The provisional status of the "guest workers" and their weak economic situation, as well as racism and xenophobia, often confined them to the least-desired residential areas, which at the time were the tenement neighborhoods in the inner city. These included the districts of Neukölln, Wedding, Tiergarten, Schöneberg, and above all Kreuzberg, whose eastern half near the subway stations Kottbusser Tor and Schlesisches Tor came to be known as "Little Istanbul." Many of these areas had been slated for demolition as part of the city's 1963 First Urban Renewal Program. The temporary presence of guest workers in the crumbling tenements fit the official plans, which assigned these buildings a life span of only a few years. But just like the "guests," the buildings also lingered and became an integral part of a reconfigured urban geography. For the most part, these are not considered public housing units, although rents have been comparably cheap and tenancy is protected under the general German rent laws.

The situation in the German Democratic Republic was quite different. The insular socialist regime barely tolerated migration. By 1990, East Germany had a non-German population of only about one percent, compared to more than 8.4 percent in the West.[17] Apart from a few students, most foreign residents in the East were so-called *Vertragsarbeiter* ("contract workers"). They were sent by communist countries such as Vietnam, Ethiopia, or Angola, officially to support international exchange but unofficially to fill unattractive manual jobs. Reflecting the regime's implicitly racist structures, these migrants were separated from their German colleagues and confined to strictly controlled group homes, though not to particular areas. Given their small number, they had little influence on East German society as a whole. At the time of the German reunification in 1990, approximately ninety-one thousand contract workers lived in East Germany; ten years later, only thirteen thousand remained, most of them Vietnamese.[18] There were never any immigrant neighborhoods in East Germany, and the housing estates on the periphery as well as the tenements in the inner city remained almost entirely "German."

In West Germany, on the other hand, immigrants exercised substantial influence. As in many European countries, city planners and politicians largely ignored them during the 1960s and early 1970s. This changed in the mid-1970s, however, once the slackening economy affected both Germans and foreigners, as German-born children of "guest workers" challenged traditional conceptions of an ethnically based German identity. West Berlin, the country's most liberal and most experimental city, soon embraced an image of a multicultural metropolis. Kreuzberg, which boasted Germany's largest concentration of kebab stands, became an attraction for both Berliners and tourists. In a society where many could afford regular holiday trips to southern Europe for the first time, Berliners began to cherish Mediterranean cuisine and global music, and West Berlin's tourist brochures featured Turkish culture prominently. The moniker "Little Istanbul"—applied to an area in which Turks made up less than 27 percent of the population—reflects the ambivalence of a country that had not yet come to terms with its new ethnic diversity. Everywhere the new lure of the exotic remained uncomfortably mixed, with resentment against the unknown "other."[19]

At the beginning of the twenty-first century, Berlin's ethnic geography has become more diverse. Turkish nationals are still the largest group among the 14 percent of Berliners who have a non-German passport.[20] They are followed by Poles, Russians, Italians, Greeks, and several others. In addition, there is a large community of nationalized citizens, as well as several thousand *Aussiedler*, ethnic Germans from Eastern Europe (mostly Russia). Both groups hold German passports but are often perceived as foreigners by their German neighbors. Kreuzberg and the adjacent Neukölln district have become hip neighborhoods with fashionable clubs and bars. The rent level is now higher than in the traditional bourgeois districts of Charlottenburg or Wilmersdorf, which puts additional pressure on the poorer immigrants.[21] Protection of existing contracts, however, has so far prevented a comprehensive redistribution of the population.

Public Housing in the Neoliberal Era

Since the 1980s, Germany has followed a contradictory policy with regard to public housing. At a time when countries all over the world have cut back state-provided services, Germany has also been steadily reducing its housing programs. In 1988, the West German government abolished the eighty-year-old legal privileges for *gemeinnützigen Wohnungsbau* (nonprofit housing).[22] Shortly thereafter, the German Democratic Republic collapsed and East Germany's state-owned homes were transferred to newly created companies, which were mostly owned by towns and cities but privately managed as limited liability corporations. At the same time, however, the state continued to pour generous subsidies into the housing stock. Municipal companies, not only in the East, received ample funds to renovate buildings that frequently had started to crumble less than two decades after their completion. During the 1990s, nearly all *Großsiedlungen* in Berlin were renovated. Those in the East received additional insulation, updated plumbing, and often added balconies. Bleak spaces between the buildings were refurbished and in some cases built up with shops and service buildings. Since that time, East German slabs have boasted bright colors with geometrical ornaments in a retro-1970s style. In 2007, the federal government transferred responsibility for housing partially to the *Länder* (regions), which are compensated for this task with ample subsidies (€600 million per year in 2011).[23]

At the same time, Germany's municipally owned flats began to fall victim to a political move that was originally unrelated to housing. German towns and cities, which were suffering from high debt burdens, discovered that sales of apartments could be used as a quick fix to relieve their financial misery. Between 2000 and 2006, Berlin sold one hundred thousand dwelling units to international private investors, thus deliberately divesting itself of a powerful tool to influence the local housing market.[24] A system working with long-term success was thus sacrificed for short-term profit.

The privatization policy introduced a sharp increase in rent levels, as the new owners tended to exploit all options for profit offered by the law. It also resulted in a further polarization between attractive flats, which received the bulk of investment by their new owners, and less attractive ones, which were deliberately neglected.[25]

To some extent, the privatization resonated with policies in other countries.[26] But in contrast, for example, to Britain, the parameters were reversed. Slightly simplified, one can say that, in Britain, state-owned flats were sold because the owning institutions maintained them poorly and hopes were that private owners would do better. In Germany, on the other hand, maintenance by state institutions was largely acceptable, but buildings were privatized for political reasons, after which maintenance deteriorated in the cheaper apartments.

Other foundations of the German welfare state have not yet been abolished. State authorities continue to assume a general responsibility for the housing situation, regulate the rental market on a variety of levels, and cater to the most vulnerable through welfare and housing allowances. The increase in rent levels as well as the widening gap between rich and poor nevertheless shows a gradual erosion of societal cohesion and a waning support for social justice. It seems that the goal of greater equity has lost its lure precisely for those middle-class groups who owe their current high living standards to the social policies of the past.

Berlin's *Großsiedlungen*, however, have largely been spared the effects of privatization. Presumably, investors seeking a quick profit from resale found Marzahn or the Märkisches Viertel less attractive. Many buildings there remain owned by municipal companies, and rents have stayed comparably low.[27] For a small two-bedroom flat of 65 square meters in a renovated Marzahn slab, a tenant has to pay about €400; in a similar tower block flat in the Märkisches Viertel, the rent would be about €500 (2011 figures).[28] These numbers have to be judged against the local minimum wage in the construction industry (€11.05 per hour for an unskilled worker in 2012, or about €1,800 per month before taxes).[29] While some who could afford it have left for inner-city flats or single-family homes in the suburbs, most long-term residents remained.

Integrated Tower Blocks

Berlin's tower block estates are modest neighborhoods, but generally well-integrated socioeconomically and not significantly worse off than the rest of the city. At the peak of the economic crisis in the early 2000s, only 14.5 percent of the Märkisches Viertel inhabitants were on social welfare, well higher than the Berlin average of 8.1 percent but not overwhelmingly different,[30] and the unemployment rate was at 17 percent, compared to the Berlin average of 13 percent.[31] Immigrant presence never became as strong as in the tenement neighborhoods in the inner city. In 2006, only 9.3 percent of the residents in the Märkisches Viertel held a non-German passport (2.5 percent Turks), well below the Berlin average of 13.8 percent (3.6 percent Turks), and markedly different from the ratio of 39.5 percent in Kreuzberg's "Little Istanbul" (26.5 percent Turks).[32]

The low share of foreigners in the Märkisches Viertel is reflected in other West Berlin tower block districts such as Gropiusstadt (14.3 percent foreigners, including 5.5 percent Turks).[33] There is no sign of the development of ethnic enclaves.

East Berlin's housing estates are similarly well integrated but have changed significantly since the end of the socialist regime. The slabs in Marzahn, Hellersdorf, or Hohenschönhausen were once loved for providing modern amenities; now they have turned from a comparably privileged to a comparably underprivileged environment, given the general rise in living standards. The days of the proverbial mixture of university-educated workers and unskilled laborers are gone. Those who have stayed are mostly elderly, and those who move in increasingly belong to the lower classes. The areas are nevertheless not exclusively inhabited by the marginalized. In 2004, the unemployment rate reached 18.5 percent in Marzahn, 16.5 percent in Hellersdorf, and 15.2 percent in Hohenschönhausen—certainly very high, but not so far above the Berlin average of 13 percent.[34] Most inhabitants, both employed and unemployed, are Germans: the rate of foreigners was only 3.4 percent.[35]

The massive investment by the Berlin government in renovating these buildings enabled them to remain socioeconomically integrated. With their low ceilings and small flats, they could not compete with stately tenement flats or single-family homes, but the technical improvements prevented many long-term residents from leaving. The typical inhabitant of East Berlin's tower block is now elderly and not wealthy, and the large majority are of (East) German rather than immigrant origin.

It has to be stressed, though, that the absence of ethnic enclaves has not necessarily led to more equal opportunities for second- and third-generation immigrants. Unemployment rates are still disproportionally high.[36] The number of politicians, business leaders, or cultural celebrities of Turkish or Middle Eastern origin remains tiny. Many of the liberal hipsters who appreciate Kreuzberg's multicultural shops and eateries at the same time fear the bogeyman of

Muslim fundamentalism and take extreme measures to keep their children from entering public schools dominated by immigrants. Meanwhile, politicians frequently conjure the necessity of cultural integration and the promotion of "Western values." At the same time, Berliners only loosely connect these discussions to the debates over public housing, which by and large is conceived as a social rather than an ethnic challenge.

The position of first-, second-, or third-generation immigrants in European societies is thus very different from that of ethnic minorities in the United States. Like Latinos or African Americans, European immigrants also suffer from racism and prejudices, carry layered identities, and hover between conflicting impulses of integration and retreat to their own groups. In many respects, they face more obstacles to social advancement than American minorities, since European societies are more homogeneous, and widespread ideas about an ethnically based national identity still account for numerous glass ceilings. In terms of housing, however, their situation is likely to be more influenced by their financial means than by their ethnicity.

Public Housing in other European Countries

Berlin's public housing policies are to some extent reflected in other European countries. Everywhere state involvement has been receding, and at the same time hardly anywhere has the state completely renounced regulation of the housing market. Individual countries have nevertheless adopted very different approaches. With regard to the aforementioned definition of public housing (affordability, right of tenant allocation by public institutions, link with public policy, and security of tenure), the percentage of public housing units in relation to the whole housing stock therefore ranges from 1 to 30 percent (Figure 7.4).

Perhaps most striking, Eastern European countries have been the ones that most thoroughly embraced neoliberalism. In the former Eastern bloc—where state accountability for housing had been all-encompassing under socialism and two generations had grown up sheltered from high rents, insecurity, and homelessness—post-socialist regimes were rapidly abandoned, exposing many residents to predatory capitalism. In the 1990s, when millions were offered the opportunity to buy their apartments at very low cost, the older generation could still profit from early forms of privatization. The younger generation, however, had to rely on the uncertainties of a barely regulated market.

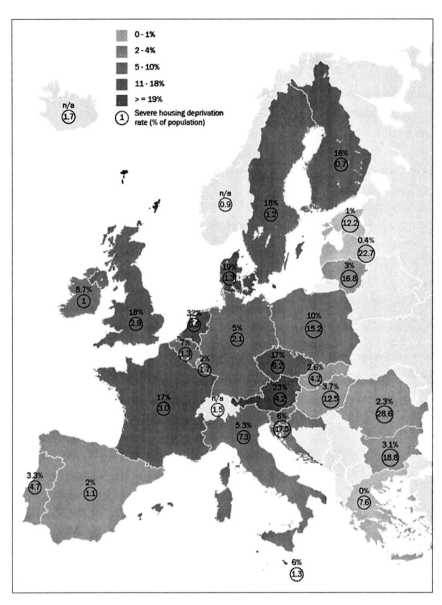

Figure 7.4 Percentage of public housing units compared to the total housing stock in different European countries, and correlation with severe housing deprivation. The numbers are comparable only to a certain extent, since the specificities of public housing are different in each country. For the purpose of this chart, public housing is defined as affordable rental housing that is subsidized and maintained by public or publicly regulated institutions, which retain the right of tenant allocation and guarantee a certain degree of protection against eviction. "Severe housing deprivation" refers to indicators such as overcrowding, lack of sanitary facilities, or structural deficiencies. Chart by author; definition and data from Alice Pittini and Elsa Laino, *Housing Europe Review 2012,* Brussels: CECODHAS Housing Europe, 2011, pp. 19 and 23.

The percentage of public housing is therefore very low in Eastern Europe. It ranges from less than one percent in Estonia and Latvia to about 3 percent in Lithuania, Slovakia, Hungary, Romania, and Bulgaria to about 10 percent in Poland. A notable exception is the Czech Republic, which deliberately chose not to privatize its large housing estates.[37]

The correlation between a low percentage of public housing and a high percentage of severe housing deprivation is obvious. In Western European countries, less than 3 percent are considered to suffer from substandard housing conditions such as overcrowding or leaking roofs, whereas the highest rates can be found in Eastern Europe (Romania at 29 percent, Latvia at 23 percent, and Bulgaria at 19 percent).[38] The de facto abolition of public housing in the former Eastern bloc about two decades ago is likely to have contributed to this housing distress. Many tenants-turned-owners are hard-pressed to maintain their buildings, and many young people cannot afford to move out of their parents' homes.

This contrasts with higher rates of public housing in Western Europe—32 percent in the Netherlands, 23 percent in Austria, 16 to 18 percent in Britain, Denmark, Sweden, and Finland, and 5 percent in Germany.[39] Austria has successfully resisted the privatization fashion and continuously invested in its public housing stock.[40] Vienna is famous for its innovative public housing estates built in the 1920s under the "Red Vienna" government. Unlike Berlin, where the Horseshoe or Schillerpark developments from the same era have been largely privatized in recent years, the Austrian capital still operates architectural icons such as the Karl-Marx-Hof (designed by Karl Ehn, 1930) (Figure 7.5) or George-Washington-Hof (designed by Karl Krist and Robert Oerley, 1927) under the aegis of the municipal company Wiener Wohnen. The approximately 220,000 residential units in Vienna's *Gemeindebauten* (council buildings) house about half a million people, more than one-fourth of the population.[41] They are highly desired dwellings, with no hints of ghettoization.

The Netherlands, where public housing comprises 32 percent of the total building stock and 75 percent of all rental units, is another country where regulated rental units continue to be the backbone of a successful national housing policy.[42] Dutch public housing is largely provided by private, nonprofit organizations. The restructuring of housing policies since the beginning of the neoliberal era was limited to the 1994 *bruteringsoperatie* ("balancing-out"), in which direct subsidies were abolished and the housing companies received greater financial freedom from the national government. The rents nonetheless

Figure 7.5 Karl-Marx-Hof (design: Karl Ehn, 1930), one of Vienna's most famous *Gemeinde-bauten* (council buildings). More than one-fourth of the Austrian capital's 1.7 million inhabitants live in public housing. Photograph by author.

remained regulated, and the national government continued to supervise housing companies and provide access to guaranteed capital market loans.[43] In contrast to Germany, where the construction of new public housing had largely stopped by the turn of the twenty-first century, Dutch housing associations continue to produce new units—about seventy-two thousand in 2005 alone.[44] In light of a system that effectively serves the majority of Dutch renters, the spectacular case of southeast Amsterdam's poverty-ridden Bijlmermeer public housing project (begun in 1966 and partially demolished in the 2000s) ought to be viewed as a clear anomaly.

Architecture, Policy, and Social Cohesion

In the European context, the equation of public housing with crumbling tower blocks where disadvantaged groups eke out a miserable living is profoundly flawed. This is not to say that European cities are all well integrated. But the spatial geographies are very different than in the United States.

Three fundamental aspects of public housing are uncontested in most European countries, at least until very recently. First, there is no stigma attached to being a tenant or living in a multistory building. This applies particularly to Germany, where cities are traditionally built up densely with apartment buildings, and where postwar suburbanization and the rise of the motorcar never managed to obliterate the predominance of the city center. Early-twentieth-century legislation made Germany a society of tenants, a condition that is supported by the middle classes and guarded by a high degree of rent protection. Other European countries have higher homeownership rates, but tenancy still tends to be an accepted way of life.

Second, state intervention on the housing market, always a main bone of contention in the American debate, is to a large extent accepted in most European countries. A long tradition of uncontested state powers made municipal authorities the obvious actors to tackle the exacerbating housing situation in the early twentieth century. Despite the fact that the German Empire as well as the Federal Republic of Germany were capitalist countries, there was no free rental market throughout much of the twentieth century. Large portions of both the working and middle classes lived comfortably in apartments that were controlled by, and increasingly also built and administered by, municipal authorities. Being the rule rather than the exception, no German schoolchild at the time would have been bullied by his or her classmates for living "in the projects."

And third, urban changes are slow because of rent protection and a cultural bias against frequent moves. This has so far prevented the growth of ethnic neighborhoods in the American sense, places where an overwhelming majority belongs to the same group. Even Berlin's "Little Istanbul" in the Kreuzberg district, which is widely portrayed as an ethnic enclave, is less than one-third Turkish. In this context, one can hardly speak of ghettoization on the basis of architecture or housing policy.

Notwithstanding the serious challenges facing many German estates, public housing as an institution has been highly successful in Germany in achieving its original goals. Since the 1970s, overcrowding and deep housing deprivation have largely disappeared, and the overwhelming majority enjoys acceptable living conditions and modern amenities. Demographic stability and an unprecedented level of wealth provided a strong foundation, but success has mainly been a consequence of national policy.

At the same time, public housing to some extent has fallen victim to its own success. The significant improvement in dwelling conditions for the majority has led to diminished political support; those who had improved their situation no longer regarded housing as an extremely pressing problem. The fact that from 2000 onward many German municipalities shortsightedly traded long-term influence for short-lived financial relief may well constitute the most consequential side effect of these shifted priorities.

The comparison of Germany with other European countries nonetheless shows that there is ample scope for local policy, and that demands for greater flexibility can be met by many possible responses that do not entail a surrender to the free market. Most important, however, the European cases demonstrate that public housing need not enhance marginalization and deprivation but, on the contrary, can be a successful response to the challenges of social instability and polarization.

PUBLIC HOUSING IS ONLY FOR POOR PEOPLE

Nancy Kwak

Perhaps the most commonly held misconception about public housing is that it is synonymous with strategies to house the poorest. Historically, however, this claim has not been true even in the United States, given that managers of most early public housing projects declined to house the unemployed and the least economically advantaged residents. And, when one looks outside the United States, the myth that public housing is only for poor people explodes completely. A more international look at housing experiments can infuse new perspectives into tired debates about American public housing, perhaps revivify our understanding of public housing's possibilities in the United States, and provoke us to reexamine our definitions of "public" and "private."

Overseas examples have demonstrated the critical role public housing can play in propelling economic development for countries in the first stages of industrialization: erstwhile colonial leaders in cities like Hong Kong, for instance, promoted mass state provision in order to address needs not met by the private market, to stabilize potential political unrest in a Cold War context, to clear slums occupying central real estate, or to jump-start export-oriented development by lowering the cost of labor.[1] Whether for good or ill, public housing played a key role in state-led development, dominating local housing options (46.2 percent of all Hong Kong housing in 2006) and providing an effective means for the state "to manage private sector growth and . . . to support stability in private markets."[2] In Hong Kong, public housing may have begun as emergency shelter for the poor, but it quickly became much more, with a Ten-Year Housing Program offering new government-sponsored options for lower-middle income households through the Home Ownership Scheme (1976) and the Private Sector Participation Scheme (1978). Local leadership in Singapore, meanwhile, instituted an innovative compulsory savings and homeownership program within the public housing system that helped increase domestic savings while eliminating the much decried "hidden subsidy" of American middle-class housing assistance. By regulating housing speculation, the Lion City's leaders ensured affordable shelter for the majority of its population. In this way, the Singaporean government successfully encouraged homeownership within the framework of a state-managed public housing apparatus, even as it incentivized increased personal savings and reaped the political benefits of higher living standards. As scholars Manuel Castells, Lee Goh, and Reginald Kwok observed in 1990, "In one of the most striking paradoxes of urban policy in the world, the two market economies with the highest rates of economic growth in the last twenty-five years [were] also those with the largest public housing programs in the capitalist world."[3]

Singapore's mass public housing program facilitated economic development and promoted gradual upgrading in mass living standards, with sometimes laudable and other times deeply problematic social and political outcomes. Most of the analysis in this chapter will center on mass public housing in Singapore because of the city-state's phenomenal rates of construction and unique, state-facilitated homeownership *within* public housing (as opposed to the Hong Kong system, for instance, which encouraged the graduation of public housing residents into private homeownership through such mechanisms as a Home Purchase Loan Scheme, whereby the Hong Kong Housing Authority provided public housing tenants with interest-free loans for down payments on private housing). Still, comparisons with other cities will be added when useful.

Increased Private Savings through Public Housing

Many housing programs around the world, including those launched during the Great Depression in the United States, began with the primary goals of bolstering the construction industry and increasing private savings. Singapore's Parliamentary Secretary and Ministry of National Development were no different from their American counterparts in thinking about housing as a stimulant for savings in the late 1950s and 1960s. This connection was made plain very early in the life of the transitional (1959–1963), Malaysian (1963–1965), and then independent (1965–) governments. According to the Parliamentary Secretary in 1964, "The most important device vital to the success of a national housing programme is a government-directed or supported institutional apparatus to mobilize savings specifically for building and construction purposes."[4] Most often, governments in both industrializing and industrialized nations favored some form of owner-occupied housing as a way to galvanize private savings and release "unproductive capital," since "people will save for housing even when they might not save for anything else," to quote the United Nations Economic Commission for Asia and the Far East (ECAFE, 1947–1974, predecessor to the Economic and Social Commission for Asia and the Pacific, 1974–).[5] Unlike the United States, however, owner-occupied housing in Singapore did not entail government insurance programs for private lenders or a government-sponsored secondary mortgage market; rather, owner-occupied housing flourished *within* an ever-expanding public housing program.

How and why did homeownership become part of a larger public housing campaign? From the very beginning, the newly elected People's Action Party (PAP, 1959–) and its charismatic leader, Lee Kuan Yew, made explicit the desire to avoid any hidden subsidy along the lines of the American housing system. While realtors and the home-building industry played a large role in securing government aid for their private ventures in the United States, and while the U.S. federal government had strong Cold War motives for quietly backing a "private" housing system, Lee faced the exact opposite incentives in the early years of his tenure as prime minister. Specifically, he faced three challenges: first, Lee needed to clearly differentiate his regime from the colonial British one that preceded him; second, his party's political control was tenuous and repeatedly challenged by leftist trade unions and communists; third, he had to negotiate regional ethnic tensions as the leader of a Chinese-dominated state with Malaysia, Indonesia, and the Philippines as neighbors. As such, Lee and the PAP had a strong motivation for avoiding any appearance of corruption, favoritism, or erratic management as publicized in such notorious cases as the Tiong Bahru housing estates (operated by the Housing Development Board's predecessor colonial agency, the Singapore Improvement Trust [SIT], and an ultimate symbol of unjust public housing distribution). The U.S. system of central and local government assistance for urban renewal, roadways, tax exemptions, and the like—some within public, others within private housing programs—had little political resonance with a government needing to prove its transparency and its pragmatic, fair approach to housing distribution. It was no surprise, then, that Housing Development Board (HDB) chief architect Teh Cheang Wan concluded in 1961, "The extent and scope of aid given by the American Government [to housing] . . . is interesting. However, so long as the principle of 'no hidden subsidy' is to be followed in Singapore, existing financial arrangements here will have to continue."[6]

In the 1960s, Singapore was hardly alone in instituting direct government provision and planned dispersal of residents in overcrowded primate cities out to satellite towns. Pakistan planned refugee satellite towns outside of Karachi, Ceylon's Central Planning Commission began making recommendations for slum clearance and satellite town development, and the People's Homesite and Housing Corporation in the Philippines (1945–1975) relocated thousands of slum families and built resettlement housing projects in greater Manila in roughly the same era. Nor was Singapore unique in its policy of gradually upgrading housing for the majority rather than rapidly improving housing standards for a few at a time; the PAP essentially replicated the "Hong Kong approach to public housing, in which a shelter of minimum standard [was] provided for immediate use with built-in provision for improvement and expansion when additional resources become available."[7] To be clear, this was not core housing along the lines of later World Bank programs, where small central units were equipped with basic services and land was left around the core to encourage owner-constructed expansion. Rather, the PAP—like Hong Kong— favored rudimentary, small apartments in large public housing complexes that would be replaced by larger, more luxurious accommodations as the nation developed.

The PAP's real innovation lay not so much in its organization of New Towns, nor in its basic (at times, even crude) architecture or system of upgraded housing, then, but rather in its financing plan and persistent categorization of subsidized housing as "public housing." Lee and fellow PAP leaders devised an innovative scheme to mobilize private savings that could then be used to finance massive new public construction. Instead of U.S.-style "hidden subsidies," Lee, Housing Minister Lim Kim San, and Finance Minister Goh Keng Swee enacted policies that curbed land speculation through the exercise (or threatened exercise) of eminent domain as permitted under the 1955 Land Acquisition Ordinance, the 1966 Land Acquisition Act, and the 1973 Land Acquisition (Amendment) Act, while also keeping interest rates low on loans for new construction by borrowing against the Central Provident Fund (CPF, 1955–), a statutory board implementing a compulsory savings program first begun under the British as a colonial-era retirement and disability program.

This compulsory savings system proved critical in financing construction after independence, increasing steadily from 5 percent contributions by both employer and employee in 1955, to a high of 25 percent each for a total of 50 percent of wage or salary going toward savings in 1984. The vast majority of

CPF funds (about 95 percent by 1990) went to government securities that were then used to pay for public investments, including new housing construction.[8] Goh explained the fundamental principles of this housing program in a 1967 speech, aptly titled "Cities as Modernizers": in addition to the aforementioned beliefs that housing should not be developed purely for profit, but should still "give reasonable return to capital invested" (that is, it should not be subsidized beyond the "initial grant of capital on soft terms"), and that the public housing program should be directed at the masses and not an especially fortunate or unfortunate minority, new homes should also be mass-produced with permanent industrial building materials and modern utilities, albeit on austere terms. "Ten thousand apartments in high-rise blocks would consume 25,000 tons of steel, 120,000 tons of cement, 370,000 tons of stone, 240,000 cubic yards of sand, 8.7 million clay bricks, 9 million cement bricks, 1.75 million square feet of tiles as well as US$1 million worth of pipes and plumbing, . . . US$500,000 worth of electric cables and switches, . . . [and] US$1.52 million for other items including earthworks, lifts, and TV antennae," Goh noted.[9] The HDB was building twice that number of apartments annually in the late 1960s, and by the end of the 1970s could boast the completion of 270,000 units in a single decade.[10] Public housing, by Goh's calculations, provided a major impetus to the domestic production of building materials and therefore could serve as a vehicle for rapid industrialization and modernization, all of which was made possible by the mobilization of mass savings. Goh made no secret of the political advantages, either: "Basically, what Southeast Asian countries need most [are] stable government[s]. . . . The provision of large-scale public housing in the capital cities would increase the stability of the government to a considerable extent."[11]

After 1968, an important modification in CPF rules allowed Singaporeans to put part of their savings toward the purchase of a public housing flat in addition to its ongoing functions as a health and retirement system; this modification greatly accelerated participation in the Home Ownership for the People Scheme, which was launched in 1964. The government further incentivized participation in this homeownership plan through lowered assessments, while mandating increases in select rates of CPF contributions and increasing the range of contributors from less than half a million individuals in 1967 to well over two million by 1987, all of which mobilized ever-growing domestic savings as part of a broader counter-recession strategy.[12] After 1974, CPF savings could also be used to pay for middle- and upper-income housing through the newly minted if short-lived Housing and Urban Development Corporation (HUDC, 1974–1982). Not surprisingly, these policies had immediate positive effects on homeownership rates.

In addition to the unquestionably novel form of housing finance mechanisms being put into place, members of Parliament Inche Abdul Aziz Karim and N. Govindasamy rushed to naturalize the demand for homeownership on ideological terms, arguing the use of CPF balances was commendable not only for practical contributions to nation-building but also because (1) "home ownership fulfills the desire of every person to own a home," (2) "the scheme itself is in accordance with socialist principles," and (3) it permitted more people to finally "give effect to their desire to become homeowners."[13]

Public Housing as a Facilitator of Modern Housing Consumption

Perhaps Singaporeans did crave stability of tenure, but the homeownership the PAP offered was a distinctly modern ideal packaged with inevitable changes in lifestyle, family organization, labor distribution, and consumption. As such, homeownership within a new public housing system was not so much the fulfillment of long-cherished desires so much as it was a practical financial decision for working-class families with limited alternatives. From the point of view of the state, public housing could also serve as a coercive form of political management, with the state empowered to clear slums and break apart communities in the name of improved access to decent shelter.

For a developmental state, public housing served as a highly effective—if problematic—way of acclimatizing and teaching diverse populations to behave "appropriately" in a modern capitalist society. Put a different way, public housing provided a useful training ground for the state to manage, supervise, and otherwise educate rural or former slum dwellers to inhabit modern housing, to grow and accommodate properly sized households, and to acquire or aspire to suitable household consumer items. Much as British colonists had employed Octavia Hill Women Housing Managers in Singapore to inspect and enforce housing regulations in SIT units and to manage "recalcitrant" tenants, so also did the "public" aspect of social housing permit state intrusions and behavior management—often with the same result of antagonizing residents along the way.[14]

The HDB made no secret of its desire to change how people lived. HDB workers organized the first of what would be a series of exhibitions at Selegie

Road in December of 1960 to explain the functions of the new board (which replaced SIT), and this initial display proved highly illuminating. At a total cost of nearly $18,000, each department created presentations with photographs, layouts, and other paraphernalia to give some eighty thousand local visitors "a better appreciation of the difficulties which face the Board and of the efforts which are being made to encourage neighbourliness and build up peaceful and harmonious communities in the Board's housing estates."[15] In image headings and banners, the HDB's various departments made explicit their goals: the Estates Department wanted Singaporeans to live in "a happy new home," with "the tenant reading a newspaper, his wife sewing and his children playing [with] toys on the floor." The male tenant and his family could avail themselves of many amenities (playgrounds, sports facilities, car park, community centers, markets, and clinics); a display detailing unacceptable behaviors also indicated that the new HDB flats would be hygienic and controlled. Photographs portrayed such no-nos as children urinating in an elevator or writing on a wall, tenants throwing refuse out of a window, pulling up plants, rearing poultry, hawking on the estate grounds, throwing away large boxes in the garbage chute, knocking nails into a wall, or attaching multiple connections to one lighting socket. The Resettlement Department, meanwhile, informed attendees of the many improvements brought about by resettlement and clearance. The Planning Department emphasized the need for more housing and the remedies outlined in the Master Plan, the need to decentralize, and the proper planning of new towns and new or enlarged urban centers.[16]

Such exhibitions of HDB goals abounded and served a twofold purpose: urbanizing and modernizing individual behavior within HDB housing, while also propagandizing the efforts of a caretaker state to local and international audiences alike. In some of these showcases, public health messages were coupled with live demonstrations of HDB workers modeling how to sit, eat, and sleep in actual public housing units. In the entrance of one display, for instance, visitors viewed detailed charts explaining how one might identify and combat malaria before entering an actual HDB housing estate to view furnished rooms with compact, multiuse furniture and models playing a game of cards in one of the rooms. All exhibits included large placards discretely placed, announcing the price of each piece of furniture seen in what essentially was a diorama.[17] According to HDB architect Alan Fook Cheong Choe, these sorts of exhibitions were prioritized because HDB staff realized they needed to demonstrate to future residents how they might actually occupy the much smaller, foreign interiors of HDB flats: "They don't know how to organize the furniture, make the place more livable. . . . [So we needed to] build prototypes, build up true-to-scale units, [and teach future residents] how it can be furnished comfortably, economically, and meet their needs. That was the purpose. It was not to sell to people. It was more about resettlement. . . . They're forced to go there, so you still have to win them over."[18]

In one of many efforts at modernization, HDB leadership actively, deliberately changed Singaporean conceptions of "family" to fit developmental goals. Much like the SIT, the board defined "family" along kinship lines, but by 1967, the board had become much more specific about dictating what types of families it would accept into its units, and it amended its requirements to include definitions of "a *proper* nucleus of a family": acceptable relationships might consist of the applicant's spouse, parents or parents-in-law, children, siblings, grandchildren, and any blood relation between the ages of 21 and 60. While these kinship requirements were fairly all encompassing, income limits set stringent caps of $500 per family member per month with a total not to exceed $800 for the entire family.[19] These state definitions of "family" served the practical purpose of ruling out exploitative sublease agreements, but the small size of the housing units coupled with squeamishness about gender mixing revealed the multiple rationales for such guidelines.[20] The ideal size and composition of the family would come increasingly under government purview over the course of the 1960s, shrinking the once-expansive multigenerational housing system of kampong and informal settlements to form discrete cells for the nuclear family, such that the 64 percent of Singaporeans living in such family units in 1957 increased to over 80 percent by 1990.[21] In reducing the number of people living together in one household, another equally critical change occurred: women were released from some of their former social service responsibilities and able (and indeed, actively encouraged) to enter the workforce—in particular, the PAP's closely nurtured manufacturing industries—which they did in escalating numbers, from 21.6 percent female labor force participation in 1957 to 29.5 percent in 1970, 44.3 percent in 1980, and over 50 percent by 1990.[22] The PAP coupled this sort of housing "persuasion" with explicit family planning programs, including the "Stop at Two" campaign of the 1960s and a truly revolutionary movement led by the prime minister's wife to give women "equal pay for equal work" and equal retirement ages for women and men.[23]

All of these efforts to regulate and transform resident behavior led to a re-thinking of ideal tenure type on the part of the HDB. Choe explained: "It all started at the architectural level. We felt that although we had a very disci-plined people living in public housing . . . they [were] renter properties [and] vandalism and disrespect of environment was quite a feature. Many residents didn't care about the building; they just dirtied the building because they [didn't] own it. That prompted the government to think about [a] homeownership scheme."[24] Whether to regulate tenant behavior, decrease maintenance costs, increase national savings rates, or promote a benevolent image of the PAP, the new homeownership program *within* public housing increased popular "buy in" to the state and its programs in the decades that followed.

Growing Wealth and Public Housing "Upgrades"

How exactly did the HDB structure homeownership within a public hous-ing program? The Home Ownership for the People Scheme began by opening up housing investment to lower-middle income households with individual in-comes capped at $800 per month.[25] In fixing prices well below open market values and amortizing payments over fifteen years, the government brought the cost of the initial sale of two- and three-bedroom units at Queenstown well within reach; in fact, the secretary of the HDB claimed prices were so low that "a family is faced with the choice of either purchasing a home or a car."[26] The population responded slowly to such economic incentives at first, with the HDB selling a mere 2,967 flats in the first year of the program. That num-ber of purchased flats skyrocketed to 40,013 from 1966 to 1970, however, af-ter the government permitted the use of CPF funds toward purchase in 1968; the number continued to rise exponentially thereafter. The HDB sold 123,213 more units from 1971 to 1975; 205,502 from 1981 to 1986; and 308,454 from 1991 to 1996.[27] By 2008, more than 80 percent of Singaporeans lived in HDB flats, and over 90 percent of those residents owned their own units. Urbaniza-tion rates in Singapore also easily surpassed those of its neighbors, with slum clearance literally paving the way for comprehensive urban redevelopment. The HDB cleared 63,000 squatters from 1960 to 1974 alone, making possible record-breaking construction rates of new public housing flats.[28] Meanwhile, gross domestic product also climbed steadily under the careful management of the Economic Development Board (1961–), reaching a phenomenal annual growth rate of 10 percent in the 1970s, while unemployment dropped as low as 3.5 percent in the same years.[29] By 2005, Singapore surpassed the United States in GDP at purchasing power parity per capita.[30]

Economic development thus proceeded in tandem with rising CPF-fueled ownership of HDB units, resulting in a comparatively affluent class of public housing dwellers. Lim Kim San reflected on some of the paradoxes of this system in 1998, noting that HDB flats had moved "from being a basic necessity . . . [to] a source of wealth—all this while the Government has continued to subsidize the cost of the flats."[31] Growing affluence did not mean the state lost its control over housing units, however. Since the HDB flat was "so heavily subsidized by the Government, it would not be correct if there were no restraints," Lim added. "Of course these [could] be irksome. All restraints are. But in the final analysis, the question is one of balance between the individual who owns the flat and the rest of society who helped to pay for it." This modified understanding of homeownership and homeownership rights alongside measured, ongoing "public" control (state control) of housing grew very naturally from a public housing system that had from its inception political as well as economic and social motives; homeownership played a critical role in structuring political legitimacy for the PAP.[32]

According to sociologist Chua Beng-Huat, there was one other factor that helped explain the upward mobility of HDB residents. Very simply, the HDB structured that mobility in incremental steps within its housing options, creating a wide array of prices based on age and size of unit. By committing to universal provision but differentiating that subsidy according to "the consumption abilities of the different housing classes," the government created "incentive[s] for families to upgrade their housing consumption as their economic circumstances change[d] for the better, which in turn [led] to filtering down of older housing stock to the lower-income groups."[33] Within the first decade of construction, the HDB had already launched an upgrading program that accelerated in the 1980s with the launch of a multimillion-dollar program dedicated to removing older, now-defunct, one-room emergency flats in favor of larger self-contained units. By the 1990s, that upgrading process became a formalized part of the government's plans for asset enhancement, with residents required to vote on whether or not to participate in the program (75 percent had to agree), and if passed, required to share the cost of upgrading with the national government and town councils at a rate of 8–21 percent of the total sum.[34]

The government also oversaw an incremental approach to local management in public housing estates. By the 1990s, the HDB had designed new institutions addressing demands for less centralized management; as the People's Association observed in 1990, "A large centralized estate management system [could] result, among other things, in [a] lack of opportunities for public housing residents to participate in the management of their own estates and to establish a sense of belonging and identity."[35] In response, the HDB organized local community leadership through parapolitical organizations like Town Councils (Town Councils Act, 1988), People's Associations, and Citizens' Consultative Committees. According to First Deputy Prime Minister Goh Chok Tong and Prime Minister Lee, it was never the original intention for the HDB to become a management corporation for the vast majority of Singaporeans, nor did it have the capability of making life "meaningful and worthwhile," or of "enabl[ing] individual towns to develop their own character and identity."[36] In reality, however, the HDB continued to be "the manager of Singapore's everyday life" through these sorts of partially enabling agencies.[37]

Nor did HDB efforts remain strictly within the realm of public housing. This model of incremental improvement extended to include semiprivate housing, as in the case of the aforementioned HUDC units from 1974–1982, which the HDB built as an initial foray into condominium development on higher priced central real estate. This semiprivate middle-class housing catered to those segments of the population whose income disqualified them from HDB units but who could not afford homeownership in the unsubsidized private market, largely in the form of apartments and townhouses. In yet another move to shift homeowners incrementally up the housing scale, the HDB privatized these same HUDC units in the 1990s in order to "enable their current owners to improve the value of their property and to move from public housing to private housing without having to make a physical move."[38] Meanwhile, the national government helped facilitate executive condominium consumption by wealthy local and foreign residents in the same decade, appointing private developers to build such suites at a price point of 15–20 percent less than comparable private units. These condominiums offered greater architectural variety, presented a "sharp visual contrast" to the uniformity of slab block HDB construction, and "provide[d] residents with a country-club lifestyle and more gracious living" replete with swimming pools, manicured gardens, and marble floors.[39]

III. People

PUBLIC HOUSING RESIDENTS HATE THE POLICE

Fritz Umbach

Ivory Alford paused, hunting for the right phrase. She was trying to capture for her grandson, Nicholas, how she and her neighbors in her South Bronx public housing development had viewed the police at the explosive close of the 1960s. Recalling the Housing Police who had patrolled the projects in those years, she settled on a simile to express her emotions, still forceful after four decades, about law enforcement in a neighborhood that had once epitomized bleak urban realities. "The officers," she pronounced, leaning in for emphasis, "were like family."[1]

This nostalgia may surprise many today, particularly against the backdrop of countless popular and scholarly depictions of hostility between nonwhite residents and the police as a fact of big city life—and public housing in particular. But memories such as Ivory Alford's resonate broadly with those who still recall the New York City Housing Authority Police Department (HAPD), an autonomous police force that, between 1952 and 1995, served the roughly one out of ten New Yorkers who made public housing their home.

The tenants' sense that the Housing Police were the "last neighborhood cops" developed from the conditions under which the force unavoidably operated: the need for foot patrol; the distinctive demographics of its personnel; a decentralized organization; and structural ties to the New York City Housing Authority (NYCHA) management. These unusual characteristics created opportunities for tenants to influence both community order and law enforcement practices in ways that surprised the few outsiders who paid any attention to the new force, which operated largely out of sight of the vast majority of New Yorkers. Because of the reciprocal nature of their interactions with the officers who served them, NYCHA tenants only partially shared in the contempt for the police that many city dwellers began to express in the 1960s.

189

Figure 9.1 Housing Officer Cynthia Brown with children, April 1974. Courtesy of the New York City Housing Authority.

Thus, at a time when minorities in northern cities identified police brutality as a threat more grave to their communities than unemployment, inadequate housing, or unequal education, NYCHA's growing population of black and Latino tenants repeatedly declared their approval for the officers patrolling the city's low-income developments. The relationship between NYCHA residents and their police was indeed exceptional (Figure 9.1). As residents frequently described it, "Housing" was "our police force." Ask older NYCHA residents and former Housing officers to explain this seeming exception to received urban truths and you will likely get an earful about the HAPD's thirty-year experiment with crime-fighting strategies that would later be called "community policing."[2]

As NYCHA's glass-and-brick empire expanded after World War II and its complexes progressively broke with the street grid, public housing became isolated from the services provided by the NYPD—particularly as that department increasingly shifted to what it termed a "radio motor patrol" style of policing.[3] Recognizing that the protection provided by the NYPD was "not particularly suited to project needs," in 1952 the Housing Authority reluctantly formed its own Property Protection and Security Division. This new police force, however, would increasingly differ not only from the NYPD but also from other departments nationwide as a consequence of both NYCHA's policy decisions and project designs. Elsewhere in the country, excessive reliance upon squad cars meant, as historian Lawrence Friedman notes, "a ton or more of steel separated the motorized officer from the community." By creating its own police force, NYCHA avoided this "ton of steel" divide as well as a grab bag of urban law enforcement problems that had accompanied the drive to "professionalize" policing. Housing's path was dictated not by national trends in police practice but by the unique law enforcement requirements of NYCHA's distinctive complexes. The Housing Police were free to evolve in their own direction.[4]

As police departments increasingly pulled officers out of neighborhoods in order to fill squad cars, many urban communities in mid-century America experienced the loss of patrolmen walking stable beats. But NYCHA's architecture spared its residents that fate, replacing it with what became known as "vertical patrols." Designed to prevent crime, rather than merely arriving after one had been committed, housing officers' regular beats included walking down busy stairwells and through long hallways, in the thick of the daily domestic worlds of NYCHA's residents. Psychologist Morton Bard concluded in a 1970 study of NYCHA residents' interactions with HAPD that the department was a "paradox in urban law enforcement." Although NYCHA's buildings had some of the highest population densities in the nation, they also represented the last place in America where "the citizen is still in direct and regular association with the police officer."[5]

The HAPD was also, to a degree unprecedented nationally, a black and Latino police force. In 1965, when the Housing Police was the fourth largest force in New York State and the twenty-fourth largest in the country, 45 percent of Housing officers were minorities. Merely ten years later, that figure surged past 60 percent—all at a time when roughly nine out of ten New York Police Department officers were white.[6] When New York's roughly six hundred thousand public housing residents, over half of them minority by 1960, interacted with the Housing Police, they had a good chance of doing so with a black or Latino officer.[7] Tenants' perception that the Housing Police force was uniquely theirs stemmed from more than racial affinity, however.[8] Many Housing officers both served and lived in public housing. Although NYCHA did not keep records documenting this phenomenon, Assistant Chief of Department Joseph Keeney— who ran the Office of the Chief in the 1970s—estimates that until at least 1980 one in five HAPD officers was also a NYCHA resident, with the number growing through the 1960s and peaking sometime in the 1970s.[9]

Until the mid-1970s, project tenants and housing officers relied on each other to enforce community norms. Many residents recall a braiding together of informal social controls and formal police presence. Maria Vasquez recalls of the HAPD in Manhattan's Amsterdam Houses (1,084 units): "They did their jobs, but they knew the kids . . . they knew what apartments they came from. So if they did something wrong, they take you by your coat, take you to your parents."[10] Such recollections of officers who knew where to track down an errant teen's mother are common among older NYCHA residents, in part because of a unique feature of the Housing Police in these years: record rooms. When the supervisors of the growing Housing Police detailed officers to a new development, they simply commandeered an apartment or basement space as an additional small office for the use of patrolmen (and they *were* all men until 1973). So it was in the record rooms of their assigned project, and not at a distant police station, that patrolmen filed their incident reports, collected their paychecks (until 1965), interviewed their suspects, kept their firearms, and reported to and from their daily tours.[11] Record rooms ensured that nearly every manifestation of police presence or exercise of police authority, other than formal booking and incarceration, occurred locally. The proximity of record rooms could imbue NYCHA's lively hallways and airy courtyards with a remarkable sense of security.

That the policing of the city's public housing occurred within the compass of each NYCHA complex was a distinction with important consequences. As Raymond Henson—a building manager at the James Weldon Johnson Houses (1,310 units) in East Harlem in the late 1950s and early 1960s—remembers, managers conferred daily with the officers who "turned out" from the record rooms, exchanging details about tenant concerns and neighborhood conditions. Such discussions, Henson recalled, were as likely to be about "broken bulbs" in a hallway as an "apartment that had been broken into."[12] According to Henson, this daily contact allowed managers to hold "officers accountable" for problems in the complex. Former Housing officers concur. "The managers knew the families and they knew the cops," explained one retired HAPD lieutenant who joined the force in 1965. "So if there were complaints, you heard about them right away even if you didn't want to."[13] The daily interaction that evolved among Housing officers, building managers, and project residents also enabled the HAPD, as one retired officer put it in the colorful parlance of the city's police, to "nip shit in the bud before it got the fuck out of hand." The officer (and eventual detective) described his eight years as a patrolman in the Sound View houses (1,259 units) in the Bronx during the late 1960s and early 1970s: "If I saw someone from the roof selling fireworks, well you just knew that was gonna be a problem on the Fourth of July so you went and talked to their parents. . . . Or you see a husband and wife disputing on the street, so you stopped by their place later."[14]

As both NYCHA tenants and HAPD officers tell it, however, the linchpin in the maintenance of the daily order they constructed together during these years was the Housing Authority's system of fines for violations of NYCHA regulations. With the creation of the Housing Police in 1952, the power of such fines to shape daily life in NYCHA increased, as officers walking their beats wrote up tenants for violations of Housing Authority rules—from shaking mops out of windows to shattering lightbulbs in hallways—and conveyed that information to building managers. By 1959, HAPD officers were reporting an average of two hundred breaches of authority rules a month in the seventy projects they covered.[15] As East Harlem social worker Ellie Lurie described the system of fines in 1955, managers saw the charges not so much as a source of revenue—they rarely even covered the cost of processing—but as a means to "pinpoint" for residents the social conventions contributing to "decent project living." Moreover, the fines served "to bring the family into the manager's office for a conference." The authority left managers free to calibrate the "service charge" to the seriousness of the infraction and the circumstances of the family. Such broad discretion no doubt shaded into bureaucratic capriciousness on occasion. Former police commissioner Arthur Wallander, hired by NYCHA to study its housing force, faulted the authority in a 1957 report for a "lack of uniformity in imposing fines," noting that charges for the same offense ran "from 50¢ to $15.00."[16] Some residents clearly would have agreed with Wallander. Lurie noted that tenants in the East Harlem developments where she worked "resented the arbitrariness" with which managers enforced fines. But she also concluded that the majority of residents, as one mother reported to her, thought the fines "forced people to raise themselves up and better themselves."[17]

Less punitive than the criminal code but possessing more bite than a neighbor's reproach, fines helped define and enforce community standards in the city's public housing until the early 1980s. Consider the memories of Peter Grymes, the son of southern migrants to New York City; he grew up largely in the Bronx's Castle Hill Houses in the late 1950s and early 1960s and became a Housing officer in 1968. Written up and summoned with his parents to the manager's office several times for "loitering," Grymes nonetheless credits fines with nudging residents to make "an effort to be responsible" and allowing Housing officers to signal "we mean business here" without having to make arrests.[18] Terri Sheeps, a Castle Hill resident since 1967 and a tenant leader for more than two decades, also believes the fines sustained neighborhood standards of behavior because they made clear to residents that "we had a responsibility not only to our families but to our community." Residents' belief in the power of fines to reinforce order was so great that when budget cutbacks, policy changes, and court challenges of the 1970s made NYCHA reluctant to impose "service charges," tenants' organizations citywide demanded that NYCHA enforce the rules as vigorously as it had in the past.[19] NYCHA's willingness to maintain standards by imposing fines, tenant leader Gonzalez recalled, had demonstrated to residents that management took seriously their desires for "dignity in our homes."[20]

This system of clear rules and swift (if occasionally arbitrary) fines characterized New York's public housing for more than a quarter-century after the HAPD's founding. By the mid-1960s, that system had come increasingly to distinguish NYCHA's complexes from surrounding neighborhoods and, indeed, most of the nation. While the HAPD would continue to try to manage project orderliness by enforcing NYCHA's regulations until the 1980s, outside of public housing a sweeping legal transformation between 1965 and 1972 made the task of regulating street life more difficult for ordinary police by invalidating the statutes they had previously depended on. At much the same time that courts began challenging order-maintenance laws, police critics began to question the wisdom of controlling panhandling, loitering, and other behaviors when rising crime rates suggested the real threats to public safety lay elsewhere. According to this argument, officers busily rounding up youthful vandals and disheveled vagabonds weren't available to pursue the violent criminals who increasingly stalked both the city's streets and—polls revealed—the public's fears.[21] The city's overall arrest statistics tell the story: in 1964, more than four out of ten "collars" made by NYPD officers fell into the lowest grade of severity, but by 1970 such arrests had fallen to less than one-fifth of the total, as patrolmen increasingly turned a blind eye to minor crimes on the city's streets.[22] The same, however, was not true for NYCHA's complexes.

Because the Housing Authority had become a distinct region within the city's legal terrain, New York's public housing developments followed a different course. Rules for daily conduct and a system of fines, established in a more paternalistic era, remained both on the books and enforced (albeit with wide variation and declining vigor). Through the 1970s and in some places into the 1980s, Housing officers continued to write up and apprehend tenants for comparatively minor infractions of NYCHA's regulations. In 1976, for example, HAPD officers made 1,157 apprehensions for "bike riding," 1,998 for "playing in a prohibited area," and another 6,386 for loitering, noise, and even housekeeping violations. Indeed, that year HAPD officers made 13 percent more apprehensions for violations of NYCHA's rules (9,991) compared to arrests under penal law (8,129).[23] In ways that had become rare elsewhere in the city and the nation, public housing's officers policed not just major crimes but minor disorder as well.

It would not have been surprising if HAPD officers, authorized to enforce NYCHA rules for remarkably small incivilities, had abused their broad discretion; police elsewhere had long done so, turning many African American and Latino neighborhoods in northern cities into tinderboxes of resentment by the late 1950s.[24] Instead, the HAPD's policy choices and daily practices largely spared New York's public housing the bitter alienation between residents and the police that increasingly characterized city life beyond NYCHA's complexes. Indeed, in ways large and small, minority communities signaled their preference for the brand of law enforcement they witnessed in NYCHA's projects.

Of course, NYCHA in these years was no Shangri La of tranquil police-community relations. Nation of Islam members, for example, led a mob that briefly stormed a Brooklyn HAPD record room in 1962, insisting only their presence could insure justice for a fifteen-year-old detained inside. A decade later in East Harlem, two white Housing patrolmen were pelted by bottles hurled by an unruly crowd in the aftermath of a fatal shooting the night before by an HAPD officer.[25] Nor did all Housing officers embody racial progressivism. In 1976, Robert Barbieri, a HAPD sergeant, served prison time along with three neighbors for repeatedly vandalizing a house in their all-white Staten Island neighborhood in an effort to dissuade a black Venezuelan-born psychologist and his Princeton-educated wife from moving into the home that they had rented with an option to buy.[26] But NYCHA documents, press coverage, and tenant recollections demonstrate that such incidents were few and far between. New York's African American and Latino communities generally drew a sharp distinction between the city and NYCHA police forces. As one African American recruit explained in 1973, "I wouldn't want to work for the City Police Department. . . . Only [Housing] deals with the community."[27]

In contrast to New York City at large, where the sources of power could seem remote and inscrutable, the very structure of NYCHA reduced municipal bureaucracy to an approachable size, allowing some residents individually and collectively to enforce responsible policing. NYCHA's grounds may have sometimes been patchy and the tenants nearly always poor, but its building managers and Housing patrolmen, working out of local offices, were known by name to the residents who felt free to express grievances. In 1970, Ruby Hogans of the Pink Houses (1,500 units) in Brooklyn, reported an officer for handling her son a mite too roughly, but declined to file a charge because the officer in question was a "new member of the force" who had now "been made aware that people [in Pink Houses] are interested in the welfare of their children."[28] Hogans withdrew her complaint, content that through her actions the novice officer had learned the unspoken conventions—developed through countless daily interactions between officers and tenants—that governed policing in her complex.

In demanding changes in police behavior, NYCHA's tenants not only raised their individual voices but also exerted the collective power that had developed in their communities—power that arose during the era of expanded rights and neighborhood activism ushered in by the War on Poverty. Historian Rhonda Y. Williams demonstrated in her extensive study of Baltimore's public housing that, "in providing living space and setting forth rules governing working-people's tenancy," the government "set a standard for decent housing and government responsiveness for tenants as renters [and] citizens." Structures built into public housing intended by NYCHA and other housing authorities to build community—such as tenants' associations and patrols—quickly became vehicles for more politicized forms of engagement with the state.[29] In New York, public housing tenants could mobilize relatively quickly on behalf of their communities in ways that the citizens of the city's other poor neighborhoods could not. During the 1960s and 1970s, through lobbying of elected officials, demonstrations, and rent strikes (both threatened and actual), NYCHA residents demanded, and frequently secured, what they saw as their fair share of protection from the city's law enforcement agencies. They achieved not only expansions in the Housing Police ranks but also alterations in HAPD practices.[30] This record of collective action by NYCHA residents rarely figures in popular accounts of New York's public housing complexes, which are more often portrayed by present-day observers as little more than depressing warehouses for their "demoralized" and "disorganized" tenants.[31]

In struggling to preserve the safety of their communities, the largely Puerto Rican and African American tenants filtering into postwar public housing by the 1960s often enlarged their engagement with the state and deepened their expectations of citizenship. They drew upon the collectivist traditions of their own cultures, in particular a heritage of community mothering well suited to the new public housing developments of East Harlem that were thick with children by the late 1950s.[32] Even Lurie, a committed social worker at the time, found these networks of women in the city's public housing hard to identify at first, although their effects were plainly visible.[33] In 1957, as a representative of the East Harlem Project, Lurie went in search of neighborhood groups and leaders that her organization could help mobilize, with the assistance of private foundation funds, into a "voice for decisions which involved their own futures." Only after two years of meetings with NYCHA residents in East Harlem did she encounter the most "formidable" association in the neighborhood: *Los Vigilantes*, an anticrime organization of mothers "well known" to their fellow tenants in the Lexington Houses (448 units). "In reflecting as to why this group had not been discovered earlier," Lurie pointed to a male building representative ("domineering and easily threatened," she observed) who had insisted that no other associations existed in the complex and blocked her inquiries. Only by outflanking him and making her own connections had Lurie discovered the "real" source of energy that had begun organizing the building's tenants.[34]

As Lurie discovered, this group of six Puerto Rican women enjoyed prominent status in the building because of their roles as neighborhood caretakers, reflecting a seasoned tradition of "othermothers" and "activist mothering" that scholars have traced in African American and Latino communities.[35] First, the women's "high incidence of children" (twenty-seven) brought *Los Vigilantes* credibility in the building. Second, the hours they logged in their particularly visible meeting place—the benches outside the building's laundry room—made staying involved with *Los Vigilantes* as inevitable for the building's women as doing the week's wash. Finally, the group had an "interest in promoting social change" among the broader "bench society" of mothers in the building. However modest their organization's "office," their accomplishments were significant: stimulating a mass protest of residents that persuaded the Housing Authority to install window bars on the first floor after a ground-floor tenant was brutally attacked; organizing the building's "different fathers so that they would take turns at various times day or night, depending on their shifts, to help patrol the building" for several months after a rape of a child; working with the HAPD to "discourage the illegal use of [their complex's] street by vehicles"; and winning from management the right to plant flowers around the complex—a practice NYCHA would later adopt systemwide.[36]

Tenant organizations mushroomed throughout the city's low-income housing in the 1960s, fostered by NYCHA's efforts and dollars. As historian Nicholas Bloom details in his study of the authority, after 1958 NYCHA increasingly worked to build community in the projects, hoping to stave off vandalism and disorder through tenant commitment. Official residents' organizations, the authority calculated, could help it meet its management challenge. By 1965, all but twenty-eight of NYCHA's 134 developments had tenant associations. The results, however, didn't always match the authority's expectations.[37] To begin with, NYCHA discovered that funding tenant groups didn't necessarily result in improved order. Tenant organizations, it turned out, were as likely to divide the authority's residents as they were to bring them together. NYCHA—having created an official base for tenant power, however narrow, and having offered money, however little—now regularly found itself obliged to serve as a neutral arbitrator in what proved to be frequent clashes between black and Latino tenant factions over the new benefits. NYCHA, indeed, resorted on several occasions to hiring outside firms to oversee disputed tenant elections in an effort to bolster the integrity of the voting process and the credibility of the leadership that emerged.[38]

In addition, NYCHA wasn't the only government agency hoping to enlist disadvantaged people in plans for their own uplift. President Lyndon Johnson's War on Poverty sought to persuade the poor of the virtues of bettering themselves by using their own political muscle—if only within the existing system—rather than relying on the allegedly enfeebling charity of the federal government or philanthropic institutions.[39] By 1968, over one thousand "community action" groups opened offices in predominantly black and Latino neighborhoods across the country, four-fifths of them funded by the Office of Economic Opportunity (OEO), the agency administrating the bulk of the new Great Society programs.[40] From 1964 to 1975, the authority's complexes buzzed with the activities not only of NYCHA-backed groups but also a throng of community action organizations brought into existence by the OEO. To such organizations, NCYHA's readily rented community facilities and clearly defined neighborhoods made the developments particularly attractive places to set up shop. Indeed, NYCHA officials publicly offered up the authority's complexes as "social laboratories" for "involving the poor in planning and administrating the programs they require," noting that "with the community facilities and the tenant body at hand, it is comparatively easy to test emerging hypotheses in community living." By 1965, forty-nine of the authority's one hundred community centers were operated by OEO or other volunteer associations.[41]

Whatever notions NYCHA and the OEO had regarding improving the lives of residents, tenants associations and community action groups tended to have ideas of their own, and these strong opinions often put them at odds with their government sponsors. Despite the variety of tenant organizations and their rapid growth through the 1960s and 1970s, they generally shared three goals that frequently conflicted with those of the housing authority's personnel: expanded and more responsive HAPD service, stepped-up enforcement of Housing rules, and the eviction of troublemakers. The new spirit of collective action in NYCHA complexes, in other words, meant the Authority often found itself being held accountable by its own tenants for failing to use its institutional power to curb disorder in New York's low-income housing.

This pattern was at work, for example, at an October 1966 Cooper Park Houses meeting on the subject of "rent parties." Even though the building manager, responding to tenant demands, had already promised to evict the disruptive family hosting the "rent parties," and despite the fact that the HAPD brass had agreed to step up that weekend's patrols, the gathered residents and community leaders were looking for more durable changes. Linsy Hart, the tenant association president, and Mrs. Mildred Tudy, the former president who had recently been hired as an organizer for a local OEO community action group, took the assembled NYCHA officials to task. These two women— mothers and veteran civil rights activists—complained that the building manager was rarely forceful enough with the many Cooper Park families who violated Housing rules.[42] Tudy and Hart insisted that NYCHA officials should be "more severe in these cases." They put the Authority "on notice" that Hart's tenant association and Tudy's Community Progress Center would be watching to see that tenancy regulations were "firmly enforced" at Cooper Park. To these activists, preventive policing and community security required both fines and evictions—and they used their leadership positions to prod the authority to action.[43]

Such popular pressure, focused on neighborhood safety rather than individual rights or other causes historically championed by the political left, often remained invisible even to sympathetic outsiders. The radical social theorists and activists Richard Cloward and Frances Fox Piven concluded at the time that NYCHA had successfully deployed tenants' organizations to channel residents' discontent "away from actions troublesome to the Authority" and into "middle-class" endeavors such as "project beautification." Moreover, the maintenance of public order in NYCHA, the two academics argued, reflected the efforts and interests not of the tenants themselves but rather of the Authority, which wielded "policing practices" to "contain the poor" and "reinforce their powerlessness."[44]

Cloward and Piven's analysis would have surprised Mildred Tudy, whose insistence that NYCHA enforce its rules against her unruly neighbors fit squarely with her concept of political action on behalf of her community. Indeed, Tudy, looking back decades later, described her central goal in a lifetime of activism in African American struggles as fighting for "'basic needs': the opportunity to be healthy and independent in one's environment." Demanding that the authority impose standards of behavior in Cooper Park was no exception to her politics. Rather, Tudy's sense of her community's positive right to the "basic need" of neighborhood safety meant individuals' claims to their NYCHA lease should be conditional on responsible behavior. This fusing of group rights, conventional volunteerism, and more radical demands shaped Tudy's participation in neighborhood campaigns that, over the course of forty years, included efforts to expand black employment and education opportunities, fight lead poisoning in poor communities, overcome racist violence, and protect what Tudy saw as poor people's rights to government assistance.[45]

And Tudy was hardly alone. NYCHA's new tenant associations often pressured managers for evictions. Until 1971, management could evict families for the criminal offenses of any of their members, but removing tenants was always a last resort for public housing managers who generally, as one noted, preferred stability and low turnover to evictions, as long as families paid their rent.[46] Evictions for "non-desirability" occurred infrequently—even in the late 1950s, when NYCHA's institutional power over tenants was at its peak. In 1958, 110 families were either evicted or asked to move out of federally funded complexes by the NYCHA: 7 for "noncooperation," 15 for "breach of regulations," and 88 for "objectionable conduct." The 487 individuals involved represented merely 1.2 percent of all residents in the federal program. But the rarity of evictions does not seem to have lessened residents' confidence in their power as a deterrent against misbehavior. As tenant leader Terri Sheeps reported, "eviction was absolutely key" to the fragile order the police, tenants, and management had forged in the Castle Hill Houses where she lived in the 1960s. Other tenant association leaders shared this belief and often demanded that NYCHA evict particular families for serious violations. Tenant leader Sarah Martin, for example, remembered residents throughout the city in the 1960s organizing to send petitions to building managers requesting action against unruly residents. NYCHA's files from these years even contain numerous telegrams from tenant groups sent to the Housing Authority's chairman identifying families they no longer wished to have as neighbors.[47]

From the late 1950s until the end of the 1970s, tenants' most urgent and insistent political goal was the hiring of more Housing Police. At nearly every meeting with authority staff, in a flurry of letters to elected officials, and— starting in 1966—with increasingly strident demonstrations, residents demanded that NYCHA increase police coverage in their complexes. Indeed, between 1963 and 1980, New York's public housing residents engaged in at least thirty-nine significant protests of varying kinds—demonstrations, rent strikes, sit-ins, and vigils—calling on NYCHA to provide more officers.[48] Such activism by NYCHA residents neatly inverts Cloward and Piven's notion that the housing authority aimed to disrupt tenants' political aspirations by enforcing orderliness in its complexes. Instead, the records show that neighborhood order was frequently the purpose of NYCHA residents' political struggles and that tenants believed they could achieve greater order by increasing the presence of Housing patrolmen.

The tenants' most dramatic strategy in this campaign was the rent strike, a tactic borrowed from civil rights agitators in cities around the country. In New York, Mobilization for Youth (MFY) and other Lower East Side organizations launched a rent strike campaign against private landlords in 1964 designed to "disrupt the slum system." Within weeks, however, the Lower East Side Rent Strike Committee had disintegrated. Accounts differ as to why this particular insurgency dissolved, but the failure of New York's first wave of rent strikes was not the end of the story. MFY's supporters and detractors alike have tended to omit from their rent-strike tales the occurrence of a second wave of strikes in 1968— this time undertaken by public housing residents on the Lower East Side and in Harlem and the Bronx, and all focused on getting more Housing officers into NYCHA's complexes.[49] This second, largely forgotten mobilization lasted far longer, gathered more support, and in many ways required greater courage of the tenants than the first strike had in 1964. State law provided seventy-six violations for which tenants could legally withhold rent from a landlord—from rodent infestation to plumbing defects—but insufficient security was not on the list.[50] Public housing residents who withheld rent in a bid for more patrolmen enjoyed no such legal protections. Even so, a mother protesting with her children for more police for their Harlem housing development boasted to the *Amsterdam News*'s famed reporter Simon Obi Anekwe, the rent strike was, "one of the most beautiful things that ever happened here."[51]

This "beautiful thing" also reflected a compromise of sorts between the radical ambitions of MFY's staff and the practical needs of the poor whom they hoped to organize. Although MFY activists had assumed they could ignite the city's oppressed in an uprising against callous municipal bureaucracies, the masses had instead inundated them with routine service requests—usually for access to those very agencies. One historian found, for example, that close to half of MFY's casework in the summer of 1966 involved applications for public housing. Eager to push beyond the seemingly limited impact of social work in the mold of old-line settlement houses, MFY had to adapt its favored strategy of "direct action" to the residents' expressed hopes of greater order through more police.[52] It was an unlikely tactical compromise. MFY had, in fact, long cultivated a reputation for being antipolice, publicizing its practice of stationing lawyers at precinct houses to curb police excesses.[53] But MFY soon learned that "maximum feasible participation" of NYCHA tenants, who generally supported the Housing officers patrolling their complexes, required a different strategy: not a war against cops, but a strike for more of them.

Launched in February of 1968, MFY's rent strike for more Housing Police was a multi-neighborhood affair. MFY-led strikers in the Jacob Riis and Lillian Wald houses (1,190 and 1,860 units respectively) on the Lower East Side and the Paterson Houses (1,791 units) in the Bronx coordinated their effort with tenants in five additional complexes in Harlem: Manhattanville, Grant, Douglas, St. Nicholas, and Drew houses. Lawyers from or affiliated with MFY defended a majority of the tenants. MFY helped the residents deposit payments into escrow and then filed a lawsuit on behalf of tenants in the Lillian Wald Houses against the Housing Authority on the grounds that the complex lacked adequate police. The court ruled against MFY in that case (*NYCHA v. Medlin)* in June, but the strike continued for eight more months, punctuated by attention-getting vigils and demonstrations to keep the pressure on the authority. Only in January of the following year—when NYCHA commenced eviction proceedings—did the rent defiance end, having held together roughly four times as long as MFY's much-discussed 1964 rent strike. NYCHA, however, quickly accepted back rent and restored the strikers' tenancy.[54] But both the strategy itself and the demand for more officers spread as other groups eager to lay claim to the popular movement for greater law enforcement in public housing took up the residents' cause.

Consider, for example, the Young Lords Organization (YLO), a former Chicago Puerto Rican street gang eagerly reinventing itself in the late 1960s as a political movement in the style of the Black Panthers. YLO's bold rhetoric and combative stance had caught the attention of Puerto Rican activists in New York. Organizing residents in Spanish Harlem, Young Lords leaders announced—in further emulation of the Black Panthers—a Thirteen-Point Program of political objectives in October of 1969. The manifesto's twelfth item had called for "revolutionary war" against the "the businessman, the politician, and the police," warning "ALL PIGS" that "BORICUA IS AWAKE!"[55] Young Lord organizers working in NYCHA complexes, however, discovered they had to break with ideological purity; *Nuyoricans* in East Harlem's public housing wanted more Housing Police officers, not a racialized war against them. And so 1970 found the Young Lords organizing NYCHA residents in a rent strike for an increased police presence in their communities. The Young Lords settled on the George Washington Carver Houses (1,246 units) for their campaign. Fifty-three percent of Carver's residents were Puerto Rican, making it the most Latino of the many NYCHA developments that blanketed much of East Harlem with a nearly unbroken landscape of modernist high-rise towers. In December, the Young Lords announced their threatened strike at Carver with a disciplined sit-in at the manager's office by 150 tenants, who chanted in unison their willingness to withhold rent until the authority provided them with more Housing Police officers.[56]

The willingness of NYCHA residents to risk their tenancy by withholding rent is certainly a tribute to the HAPD, as well as clear evidence of community support for "our cops." Measuring the effectiveness of particular strikes, threatened and actual, is trickier. The promised rent strikes, for example, often failed to materialize because the Housing Authority frequently—if temporarily—reassigned police officers from elsewhere to pacify the protesting residents. After a single day of protest and a threatened rent strike at the Whitman Houses, for example, NYCHA committed additional officers immediately, prompting the tenant leaders to declare they were "holding off on the rent strike for now."[57] More broadly, on a systemwide level, the Authority significantly expanded the Housing Police in these years. NYCHA boosted the HAPD's ranks by more than 17 percent in 1968, again in 1969, and by more than 7 percent in 1970—despite no more than minor increases in the tenant population. While City Hall had agreed in 1969 to base its subsidies of newly hired Housing officers on the number of new NYCHA units, the growth in the HAPD far outpaced that calculus. The 60 percent expansion that the Housing Police enjoyed during the most active years of tenant militancy (1968–1970) was roughly double the increase the force experienced during the previous six years of tenant quiescence—suggesting that the residents' political pressure had real impact.[58]

Beyond the numbers, internal NYCHA documents reveal the extent to which the new tenant insurgency shaped the authority's thinking. By the late 1960s, NYCHA officials recognized the need to contend with residents' political leverage not just at individual projects but throughout the authority. When NYCHA's top officials, for example, convened for a closed meeting about "Project Security Problems" in 1968, they acknowledged that citywide, the now "well organized tenants . . . are able to make their complaints known more readily than the general public."[59] Moreover, housing authority administrators took advantage of tenant militancy in their efforts to draw more money from the city's coffers. NYCHA's chairman, for example, concluded his 1968 plea to Mayor Lindsay for an increased housing subsidy by invoking the tenants as a political force to be reckoned with. "Unless . . . we voluntarily meet the demand . . . for enlarging our police force," he wrote, "pressure from our tenants and their representatives will become so great that compulsory legislation may well be adopted."[60]

Against the backdrop of the dramatic civil rights battles that unfolded nationwide in the 1950s and 1960, the tenant activism that emerged out of the authority's complexes—whether holding NYCHA accountable for enforcing community order or demanding that the city provide what residents saw as their fair share of policing services—can seem trivial. It was not. Even as cities elsewhere saw their public housing implode into national symbols of failure, public housing in New York survived America's "urban crisis" in large measure because of the NYCHA tenants who drew upon their collective strengths to help preserve the security of their communities. In demanding that the Housing Police and NYCHA work on their behalf, the city's public housing residents made their homes, and their daily lives, political—even if the goals of their activism deviated from the era's more visible channels of protest and prominent ideologies of resistance.

The success of this tenant activism was built in part on years of relationships fostered by the unique structure of policing in NYCHA. These relationships did not happen by chance. With vertical patrols rather than squad cars, on-site record rooms rather than distant precinct houses, and officers who might be neighbors rather than suburbanites, tenants had every reason to consider Housing officers "our cops" rather than a hostile presence. The mutual understanding and structures for communication generated by years of such interactions, while not perfect, helped carry NYCHA, its residents, and its police through two decades of urban change and turbulence. Together, in the daily world of the sprawling complexes, the authority's officers and tenants forged and practiced a distinctive form of community policing long before think tanks and foundations had even worked out a theory.

PUBLIC HOUSING TENANTS ARE POWERLESS

Rhonda Y. Williams

From the inception of public housing, racial segregation, economic marginalization, urban politics, and housing policies shaped the daily lives and activism of low-income tenants in Baltimore and across the United States. The myth in public housing history, and even contemporary media images of public housing residents, is that public housing tenants are powerless in the face of these trends and policies. Their poverty is taken as a sign of their inability to act in the face of more powerful institutions and patterns. Yet the fight for resident empowerment in Baltimore in the 1960s through participation in the policymaking process reflected poor people's demand for justice in an activism-rich decade. Tenant organizers felt that living in subsidized housing did not mean they had to be quietly satisfied or forfeit their voice, even though many tenants clearly feared that contesting management might result in retaliation. For them, public housing residency did not mean they were powerless and, to that end, cadres of tenants refused to accept inadequate or unsafe living conditions without question.

With the passage of the National Housing Act of 1937 that established the United States Housing Authority, the city of Baltimore formed its local Housing Authority and began clearing "slums" and constructing racially segregated public housing complexes—developments that intentionally preserved the city's Jim Crow landscape by turning racially mixed neighborhoods homogenous and undermining integration. The first public housing apartment complex, Poe Homes, opened on Baltimore's west side in 1940 for black residents only. Four additional apartment complexes, which housed black and white residents separately, opened between 1940 and 1941. McCulloh Homes opened on Baltimore's west side and Douglass Homes on the east side, both for black tenants only, and Latrobe and Perkins homes opened on the east side for white tenants only.

These apartment complexes, situated alongside emergency defense housing constructed as a result of World War II, expanded the city's subsidized housing supply. Postwar housing policies, such as the Housing Act of 1949, resulted in the construction of extensions of already existing low-rent black complexes, including additions in the planned black community of Cherry Hill that featured the first permanent black public housing complex built on vacant land. Finally and critically, the Housing Authority constructed additional public housing in racially segregated or transitioning neighborhoods where low-rent public housing already existed. This wave of low-rise construction, which occurred through slum clearance and "Negro removal," facilitated downtown urban redevelopment, reinforced Baltimore's Jim Crow racial geography, and enhanced economic apartheid. It also inaugurated the city's high-rise public housing program. Lafayette Courts was the first high-rise to open in 1955 in the vicinity of Douglass Homes and Latrobe Homes, followed by Flag House Courts near Perkins Homes. Lexington Terrace opened near Poe Homes in 1958 and Murphy Homes followed five years later near McCulloh Homes. Three of the four high-rise complexes—Flag House Courts not among them—were initially built for black tenants, and even in the wake of desegregation mandates primarily housed black residents.[1]

Whether in the initial low-rise or the subsequent high-rise complexes, working-class residents who experienced marginalization along race and class lines sought out new public housing in order to improve their daily surroundings and quality of life. Moving into housing that was not only government subsidized but also government controlled, black and white tenants formed resident organizations and initiated tenant-based projects. They lauded their new modern spaces, complete with indoor plumbing, and the new social status it afforded in neighborhoods suffering from well-worn housing, crumbling and outdated infrastructure, and blocks riddled with poor sanitation and disease. When pioneer public housing tenants' visions of a better life and living conditions were threatened, whether in the initial low-rent, wartime, or postwar public housing complexes, cadres of white and increasingly primarily black residents lifted their voices to the rafters, put their feet to the concrete floors, organized campaigns, and confronted housing officials whom they deemed unresponsive and recalcitrant. They expected decent housing. After all, the federal government—the self-avowed purveyor of American democracy and freedom—was their landlord. Even in the face of discriminatory government policies, tenants fought back and demanded better. Low-income women, in particular, who found themselves in public housing for a variety of reasons led many of the critical battles that secured small and substantive wins, including representative voice, and demanded greater respect and dignity for poor people.

By the mid-1950s and 1960s, when the last wave of traditional public housing opened in Maryland's Charm City, social struggle had become a familiar feature of urban communities across the country. The Upper South city of Baltimore did not escape urban activist discontent, black liberation protests, or their politicizing impact on black and white residents. Nor did its public housing communities. The streets (even the elevated concrete ones behind wire fences), courtyards, and public and private gathering spaces—whether at Housing Authority or public welfare offices, individual public housing complexes, or community centers—became stages for broadcasting mounting concerns and challenging maltreatment and marginalization based on race, class, gender, and place of residence.

Across the nation, public housing tenants—particularly black women who, with their families, were often deemed as unworthy breeders of social ills and urban pathology—mobilized to fight for representation, voice, and the power to make programmatic and policy decisions affecting their lives and communities. This included challenging unaffordable rent levels and retaliatory evictions, pushing for fair grievance policies, and demanding a say in how local housing officials spent federal Department of Housing and Urban Development (HUD) modernization money. In numerous cases, their activism within public housing exposed their participation in local black liberation campaigns that often spoke to and overlapped with antipoverty, welfare rights, and tenants' rights crusades. Public housing and their cities, then, gave rise to "awakening giants" engaged in struggles for political power, rights, respect, and dignity. Some of these struggles were successful; others were not.[2]

"An Awakening Giant"

Within a couple of decades of moving into Lafayette Courts in Baltimore, Maryland, on December 10, 1955, Shirley Wise had married and separated from her children's father, held several jobs, attended Cortez Peters Business School, and become a beautician. Possessing a sense of community belonging, she became active in the PTA and Lafayette Courts Mothers' Club. But Shirley Wise avoided controversy and "leadership" roles. While she was happy to serve as vice president or treasurer, she did not want to be head honcho. "In those days . . . I did not want to be the leader" or the person "who had to do, to make sure everything happened."[3]

Between 1955 and 1970, Shirley Wise shed her timidity as she learned more about rights: her civil rights, her legal rights, and her rights as a tenant. By the early 1970s, the petite Wise had made an unpaid career of advocating for the poor in her housing complex and citywide. Before her political awakening, Shirley Wise often said, "Let somebody else take care of that. I was one of those people. Like I say, social commitments, that's me. Anything that was really rocking the boat, I wasn't into that until I found out I had the legal right to do that—to rock the boat." Shirley Wise's transformation—her heightened consciousness of power relations, inequality, and rights—mirrored that of other poor black women living in cities. As black freedom movements and antipoverty programs grew in northern cities, "rights," "struggle," "power," "control," "respect," and "dignity" became popular words and goals. Referring to the local housing and political bureaucracy, Shirley Wise maintained that public housing "provided a place for me to raise my children. It [also] provided me with a serious education that I couldn't have got in no school. I had good teachers—some of the best congressmen out there."[4]

In the 1960s, greater awareness of economic inequalities and poor people's rights ushered in intense disruptions and demands in cities. In Baltimore, militant black and white groups helped radicalize the urban terrain. To be sure, "traditional" civil rights protests occurred, like the boycotting of Jim Crow restaurants, stores, hotels, and taverns in the city and along the fiftymile stretch of Interstate 40. However, in the mid-1960s, grassroots efforts also took another activist route—one that sought subsistence rights, empowerment, and economic equality. By the time black freedom activists, white student radicals, and federal antipoverty workers converged on cities, concentrated black poverty had produced communities and situations ripe for organizing working-class people.

Out of East Baltimore's public housing complexes emerged black women like Shirley Wise, whose activism ultimately altered poor people's relationship to government. Politicized by their living conditions and activist discontent after World War II, low-income black women grew more confrontational in the 1960s, a time when "people got to talking to people, [to] know more about their rights," according to Julia Matthews, a Douglass Homes tenant activist. Shirley Wise similarly argued that a "new generation of public housing residents came along who said, . . . we have rights too," and they worked to "effect some kind of change."[5] Viewed as "objects of charity" and policed by the state because they received government aid, poor black women mounted housing and social welfare campaigns. Joining generations of low-income, working-class activist women, these women mobilized in communities. Some drew on a familial historical legacy; others built on the knowledge gained from their community participation efforts. They became involved in parents' school groups, mothers' clubs, recreational activities, and other civic activities. They continued the age-old demand for safe neighborhoods and subsistence. But they also did something different: this new generation of activist women pushed for respect, a right to representation, and power as not only citizens but as human beings deserving of basic rights.

Alongside family, historical, and community influences, the presence of militant grassroots activists and antipoverty workers helped politicize low-income black women in these new decades of struggle. Some public housing tenants met local officials, antipoverty workers, and black freedom fighters, or at least knew of their presence. Goldie Baker identified two of the city's most popular organizers, U-JOIN's Walter H. Lively and CORE's Walter P. Carter, as mentors alongside her grandmother and mother, who were activists for poor people's rights and Progressive party members during the McCarthy era.[6] She recalled the diehard commitment on the part of Lively and Carter to working-class black people's advancement: "They were really hard on white people, but they would keep black and white people accountable of the rights of poor people. . . . They were in the struggle and they were going to fight for their rights."[7]

The relationship among organizers and low-income black women was synergistic. Just as organizers inspired black women, black women inspired organizers. For instance, even though Goldie Baker labeled Lively and Carter as mentors, she initially met them because they sought her out. They wanted her advice on how to deal with the welfare department and welfare rights issues. They learned from her even as she learned from them. A Community Action Agency (CAA) neighborhood counselor at Lafayette Courts, Clyde Hatcher joined the Congress of Racial Equality (CORE) and the civil rights movement partly at the insistence of "a lady I knew [who] lived around the corner." She urged him to attend CORE's 1966 national convention, where he heard an impassioned speech by Fannie Lou Hamer. "I mean she talked about how she had [been] picking cotton in the fields and she was trying to organize and how they came down and intimidated her. She was a dynamic person." A short time later, Hatcher became a CORE member. As a neighborhood counselor, Hatcher interacted with many committed black women activists, some of whom were more radical than he was. One such woman was Goldie Baker, whom Hatcher described as a "legend" and "one of the most dynamic leaders I have ever seen."[8]

The War on Poverty also politicized cohorts of public housing residents and the cities they lived in. Men and women antipoverty workers, like Clyde Hatcher, came prepared to coordinate services and rally the poor to action, the most militant aim of a program that otherwise bought into the argument that poor people needed to be altered to succeed. That rhetorical mandate to rally the poor legitimized poor people's community action and provided them with an infrastructure to contest local city agencies.

Within the first couple of years of the Community Action Program in Baltimore and throughout the 1960s, power struggles emerged. U-JOIN criticized the Baltimore program for its lack of poor people on the Community Action Commission (CAC) board and organized residents in private and public housing in East Baltimore to speak out at numerous city hearings. Eventually the CAC expanded its eleven-member board, appointing four people from poverty areas.[9] Even then, neither poor people, nor the CAC board generally, had unhampered decision-making authority.[10]

Poor people and their advocates consistently charged that because the agency was top heavy, it could not address their economic and social problems. In December 1966, poor people led by Murphy Homes tenant Mattie Parker held an Action Area Convention attended by sixty-three delegates—two-thirds of them women—from twenty-one poverty centers in the city. Several Lafayette Courts and Douglass Homes tenants served on the steering committee, and other public housing tenants, like Daisy Snipes of Perkins Homes (also a welfare rights activist), attended as delegates. Overall, the woman-led and majority-female delegation complained about "poor police protection and discourteous treatment, bad housing, rats, unemployment, money going to the Vietnam War instead of helping them, crime, low welfare payments, management of housing projects, and help for youth of today." This panoply of issues reflected the breadth of low-income women's concerns.[11]

The neighborhood action offices, which had their own staffs, worked more closely with residents on the ground. Although political tussling remained a consistent feature of the local program, and neighborhood action centers were not "fighting organizations," according to Goldie Baker, some antipoverty workers really did try to help poor people "organize the community." She recalled that public housing CAAs

> put enough literature and material out . . . to bring us together and let [the residents] know what it means to be united. . . . They didn't get in the forefront of the fight, but they were educational. And as far as resources, you could find out different information on your rights, constitutions, you know, things you [were] entitled to. . . . And bringing people together . . . telling them how to stand up, be strong, and organize. I think that was their basic goal.[12]

Tenant activists made use of these resources as they struggled for economic stability and resident empowerment.

As public housing tenants talked and learned more about their rights, they also targeted the Housing Authority, questioned management, and sought a participatory role in the decision-making process in their complexes and eventually agency-wide. Lafayette and Douglass tenants Bonnie Ellis and Mildred Lee, respectively, led such a campaign. Mildred Lee moved into Douglass Homes in 1955. A widow, Lee worked as a domestic to make ends meet. She had a history of civic activism and leadership responsibilities. She was a member of the fraternal Elks and Reindeer Association, the Nazarites, and United Baptist Church." Both Lee, who envisioned Douglass as her permanent home, and Ellis, who struggled to raise her family in Lafayette Courts, were invested in keeping Lafayette-Douglass (the two complexes were jointly administered) safe, and that meant ensuring that management responded to tenants' needs. In the late 1960s, Lafayette-Douglass tenants formed the Resident Action Committee (RAC) with help from CAA and Legal Aid volunteers. Ellis, RAC's chair, and Lee requested administrative separation of the two complexes. This request represented tenants' attempts to secure an official voice and input in the housing policymaking arena.

In public housing, residents' growing poverty had resulted in a concomitant decline in the operating budget, which depended on rent collections. In 1963, housing officials, who had hoped to realize "substantial financial savings," combined the staff of Douglass Homes and Lafayette Courts.[13] Within five years, however, the cost-cutting measure proved neither efficient nor desirable to tenants. Tenants argued that one staff could not efficiently manage and maintain more than one thousand units nor address the entire tenant population's needs. Julia Matthews, who after twenty-five years of residency became Douglass Homes' tenant council president in 1971, argued that tenants felt Douglass was neglected: "This place was coming down. They was doing more for Lafayette. . . . Well, [we thought, if] we separate and have our own staff, it would be better." RAC and tenant leaders also argued that the residents of Douglass and Lafayette had different needs. Over one-third of Douglass's households were elderly people, while in the newer high-rise complex of Lafayette Courts, 89 percent were families. Ellis and Lee told officials that Douglass's elderly residents found it difficult to walk several blocks to Lafayette Courts to pay their rent, and they wanted their own community facilities for meetings and recreation. Tenant leaders maintained as well that Lafayette needed a "seasoned manager" to deal with the problems of highrise complexes like safety, elevator maintenance, and servicing families and children. In 1968, after six months of tenant-management meetings and negotiations, the administration of Lafayette-Douglass was separated.[14]

Challenging the housing agency's administrative purview, tenant leaders also fought for input in personnel decisions by demanding the right to choose their managers. In Douglass and Lafayette, tenant-management relations were so strained that even housing officials considered it "a matter of extreme concern to this Agency." Managers' condescending attitudes spurred fear and discontent and stymied tenants' complaints. Goldie Baker of Lafayette and Ann Thornton of Perkins Homes (and, later, Rosetta Schofield of Murphy Homes) criticized Joel Newton, who served as a manager in all three complexes. Newton, Clyde Hatcher remembered, "was the man that [tenants] used to hate."[15] Never late with her rent, Ann Thornton recalled Newton's hostility when she requested a payment extension. At the time she was working, but her paycheck was short because she missed a week and did not have sick leave. She recalled: "Oh, he got to hollering at me. . . . I said, Hey slow down. . . . Don't holler at me no more. Am I hollering at you? You treat me like you want to be treated and we going to get along fine." According to Thornton, that was when Newton uttered: "Well, just one of them welfare . . . " She immediately cut him off, told him that she worked, and that, no matter, he had no "business classifying nobody. . . . You understand what I'm saying? See, people classify you and if you don't nip it in the bud and stop 'em, they'll continue."[16]

213

Managerial mistreatment exposed how some housing officials viewed tenants as "worse than, less than a dog." In one instance, Baker simply wanted housing maintenance to remove the ancient icebox in her apartment so she could make more space for a refrigerator—one of a few remaining possessions from her days as a homeowner. The refrigerator sat in the middle of her floor and took up vital space in the small three-bedroom apartment. When she went over to maintenance to put in her request, she experienced unexpected condescension:

> I didn't know the residents, tenants had to go through all that kind of stuff they had been going through. . . . I had rights, you know. I was one of them . . . sassy niggers who had some right. They ain't know where I come from. They ain't know who I was listening to all them years. So I said, you know, "I don't know who you think you talking to." . . . And then I went over to the manager's office to report them. . . . So anyway, Joel Newton, he talked to me and asked me was I crazy. Get out of his office. Honey, that's when I went to see the commissioner. And I told him, I don't know who he [Newton] think he's talking to. I am not nobody's slave. I *am not* no*body's slave,* and he *ain't* talking to no slave. Slavery's over. . . . I said, he don't have no respect for me, he don't need to be over there.[17]

Given their experiences with the managers, a cadre of outspoken Lafayette and Douglass tenants sought the right to be treated decently in their homes and communities. Tenants asked for input in managerial selection because the manager represented, as RAC secretary and CAA tenant worker Margaret E. Johnson maintained, a "king in his kingdom." He set the "tone" for the complex and "controlled daily decisions like the flexibility of rent payment procedures." Echoing the laments of black tenant dissidents in the 1940s, Lafayette and Douglass tenants wanted to secure managers they believed would help them, "not talk down to them" because they were poor black people.

The RAC supplied officials with the names of candidates, but central administration told tenants that personnel decisions lay with housing administration. Dissatisfied RAC representatives, accompanied by CAA and VISTA workers, went to the February 6, 1968, housing commissioners' meeting. Margaret E. Johnson conveyed tenants' desires to select the new manager; she also told commissioners that Bonnie Ellis believed that management had retaliated against her after she ignored warnings to suspend organizing meetings. In what became a three-hour hearing, commissioners devised a compromise that incorporated tenants. Arguing that "the success of a housing project is a direct result of the tenant council," board members encouraged the establishment of a joint panel to develop criteria for the selection and evaluation of the manager. While commissioners incorporated tenants, the plan fell short of the RAC's demand to pick the manager. Tenant representatives, however, accepted the compromise even as they realized that management retained decision-making power. To this end, Johnson remarked that she hoped housing officials would not select managers whom tenants "violently opposed."[18]

The RAC's campaign marked Baltimore residents' entry into the policymaking arena. Their complaints and actions revealed their attempts to alter the institutions dispensing services, and that meant carving out a concrete, officially acknowledged space for tenant involvement. Tenants secured recognition and the power to negotiate policy. But local officials ultimately did not relinquish authority when acquiescing to residents' demands. The institutions, by incorporating tenants' voices, may have become more democratic, but the systems of inequality that kept poor women impoverished and reliant on public housing remained firmly in place. Even so, these women had achieved a primary goal—the right to affect the systems that structured their daily lives. And they also made clear, and public, tenants' expanding displeasure with public housing's living conditions.

These stories also illustrate the power that managers had, and some did wield, against tenants who protested a mite too forcefully about poor housing conditions. The repercussions could be detrimental, affecting the comfort and very survival of poor families who already found themselves relying on government subsidies to make ends meet. In 1967 in Durham, North Carolina, the Housing Authority evicted tenant leader Joyce Thorpe and her three children without a hearing and for no apparent reason, except that she was organizing tenants. Her case went to the U.S. Supreme Court and would forever change housing policy: retaliatory evictions were outlawed. Eviction and grievance procedures were established. While the fear of losing one's residence still endured, activist women like Julia Matthews remained resolute. Matthews argued that tenant participation, community responsibility, black empowerment, and advancement went hand in hand: "I have always been active in the community. What they say, charity starts at home. . . . This is my neighborhood. This is my tenant organization. All of us, get yourself together, have more say, input. . . . They've been too quiet. For how long we been slaves?"[19]

Politicized by their personal histories, daily circumstances, black freedom movements, and the efforts of antipoverty workers, black women activists also benefited from federal housing officials' incorporation of the maximum feasible participation concept. In 1967, HUD staff members focused on addressing two urgent problems—deteriorating housing and residents' burgeoning discontent. Soon thereafter, HUD established the modernization program, which sought to upgrade the physical condition of public housing.[20] The program also aimed to improve tenant-management relations by requiring tenant involvement in developing local modernization plans, altering management policies, and expanding services. In a 1968 HUD circular titled "Social Goals for Public Housing," the federal government suggested that municipal housing authorities "undertake a mutual commitment to cooperative action and trust with tenant organizations."[21]

This federal program, like CAP, provided residents, some of whom had confronted management already, with the necessary weapons to challenge municipal policies. The requirement of tenant participation and consultation in the modernization program helped transform the character of many tenant groups, which were clubs concerned with "activities and group interests of the tenants . . . not with management of the project."[22] In Minneapolis, the first city to receive modernization money, HUD delayed the program until the local housing agency satisfactorily showed that tenants had participated "in drawing the proposals." Shirley Wise, the self-described "Malcolm X of public housing" in Baltimore, maintained that the modernization program became a key residential "organizing tool." Wise recollected: "I know people, now as they look back, they're sorry that HUD" required that "a resident group sign off on the modernization plan. . . . Because that gave [residents] their true rights to sit at the table with the decision-makers and effect some changes in their community."[23]

Federal dictates, however, did not necessarily translate into local agency cooperation with tenant activists. Some public housing authorities refused to share power with tenants and "told HUD to 'keep the money.'" Subterfuge also occurred. In 1970 in Nashville, according to Mattie Buchanan, president of the Nashville Tenants Organization, the Housing Authority disregarded tenants' participatory claims and still sought the grant—so local intransigence to federal mandates did occur.[24]

Nevertheless, the new federal regulations gave black women public housing activists the authority to elevate their rights and to claim a voice in central administration matters. Drawing on their organizing experiences with RAC and alliances with federal workers, activists in Baltimore mounted a campaign to push for decision-making power in agency matters and demanded citywide tenant representation. Led by Margaret E. Johnson of Lafayette, the nine-member delegation requested a meeting with Robert C. Embry, Jr., the newly appointed executive director of the Housing Authority, in 1968.

Residents from Lafayette, Flag House, and Perkins—accompanied by representatives from Legal Aid and CAA—met with Embry on August 16, 1968, and with the board of commissioners on August 17. The delegation demanded that housing officials withdraw the $3 million modernization budget for 1968–1969, since tenants were not consulted—a stipulation of the new program. Margaret E. Johnson also told Embry that the delegation wanted a "recognized channel for [citywide] representation." Although Embry acknowledged the validity of tenants' demands, he refused to withdraw the modernization budget, saying it was too close to approval and that Washington had expressed "no concern . . . that Baltimore was lagging in tenant participation." However, he did promise future participation—but only for tenants. Embry disapproved of the presence of Legal Aid lawyers and CAA workers and did "not intend to be harassed by persons who are not tenants."[25] Tenants' demands and Embry's promise resulted in the formation of the citywide Resident Advisory Board (RAB).

Black female tenants' fight for tenant participation and power in Baltimore between 1967 and 1968 made them part of a vanguard of community activists in the civil rights and black power eras. Through the actions of many female tenant activists, Baltimore became one of the first cities to establish a formal citywide advisory board. Poor black women's early 1960s activism in East Baltimore had laid the groundwork for their citywide success. On October 3, 1968, Van Story Branch recognized the critical role of the RAC. Branch stated that the new RAB was "an opportunity to have total involvement for our residents." However, Branch added: "This did not begin today. It began about a year ago when Mrs. Ellis and Mrs. Lee from Lafayette and Douglass Homes requested the separation of Lafayette and Douglass and the right to help in the selection of their managers."[26] The extension of poor black women's traditional roles to the community garnered representation for all public housing tenants, black and white, women and men.

Baltimore's RAB was one of the first in the country. New York, while having representation in individual complexes, did not establish a citywide tenant council until 1970. That same year, Pittsburgh also formed a citywide group, and the Chicago Housing Tenants Organization, which sought "resident control," became embroiled in a fight with the Chicago Housing Authority to gain recognition as well as address its demands for participation in policymaking and management decisions. In 1971 a *Journal of Housing* article featured Baltimore's story, claiming the city was "one of a number of communities that report that greater tenant participation in management under the modernization program has also led to greater tenant responsibility for and understanding of the problems involved in operating public housing projects."[27] By 1972, Baltimore's RAB served as a liaison between the Housing Authority and 12,598 tenant families in twenty public housing complexes and 945 families in leased or renovated housing.[28]

Throughout the nation, poor black women emerged as leaders in public housing tenant struggles—some of which resulted in the establishment of similar representative groups—in their local communities in the 1960s and 1970s. In 1968, the same year that Baltimore tenants questioned their local agency's modernization budget, Philadelphia Housing Authority officials had refused to negotiate with their tenants. Represented by Legal Services lawyers and led by black resident activist Rose Wylie, Philadelphia public housing tenants successfully barred the agency's access to modernization money. In March 1969, Philadelphia housing officials finally entered into a "memorandum of understanding with the project organizations, recognizing the right of the tenant groups to help determine and to be regularly consulted on the modernization programs."[29] In Baltimore, Goldie Baker worked with a group of tenants who called themselves Residents in Action. Baker described the group, which had forty to fifty participants and pushed for improvements in Lafayette Courts and other complexes, as "an action group that was fighting." Residents in Action had, for instance, threatened a rent strike if the Housing Authority did not supply residents with new refrigerators. In 1969 in St. Louis, public housing tenants resorted to a citywide rent strike to address rent, repair, and maintenance issues. That action resulted in the withholding of more than $300,000 in rent. Led by tenant activists, including the "more militant strike leader" Jean King, the action had numerous results, including the selection of an entirely new board of commissioners and housing manager and the establishment of a tenant affairs board.[30] According to one private manager of middle-class and luxury apartments in Boston, women were the "big organizers," "the biggest complainers," and "some of them drive you nuts with their constant bitching."[31]

As poor black women struggled to democratize systems of social welfare and alter the housing service delivery system, they eased the pangs of daily living and garnered new rights for tenants in public housing. Just as important, by occupying critical leadership roles in their communities, many poor black women managed to alter public poverty policy on the local and national levels. No longer were they simply clients who received services from housing and welfare bureaucracies and engaged in cooperative social service activities within their own communities. They also were consumers and constituents who fought successfully to influence the institutions that served them. And as active constituents, they engaged in social actions that earned poor people an official voice in welfare institutions and resulted in concrete policy changes on the local and federal levels.[32]

Tenants across the city pushed for a greater voice in the operation of their communities and the policy decisions affecting them. Like Lafayette Douglass's RAC, the Murphy council eventually sought to gain greater control of housing operations by choosing its own manager. However, there was a difference. While Lafayette Courts' tenants complained that they were tired of managers treating them in nasty ways, Murphy tenants sought to replace their manager in part because he was white. The Murphy struggle illuminates a particular constellation of political empowerment in public housing. Not merely the result of "actual" oppressive treatment, Murphy tenants acted on the oppressive history linked to whiteness. The campaign in Murphy reflected much more overtly racial cultural politics, particularly as the rhetoric of black power began to envelop the nation and black nationalist groups moved into the Murphy Homes neighborhood.

These links among race, representation, and power became apparent in Murphy tenants' direct encounters with the grassroots black nationalist group Soul School. The Soul School on Fremont Avenue served as a meeting place and cultural center. Black junior and senior high school students gathered there to organize a citywide Black Student Union. And police kept surveillance on Soul School leaders, particularly Benjamin McMillan (also known as Olugbala), a former CORE member. Members of the group exuded militancy.[33]

On June 11, 1969, Gladys Spell and the youth committee of the Murphy improvement council invited Soul School members to a tenant council meeting as part of their two-day Black Seminar series. The tenant council wanted Soul School members to display and talk about their African carvings and paintings. The recreation room at the George Street School, where they held meetings, was filled to the brim—and that included their white manager, Walden Gorsuch, who left Perkins Homes in 1965 to head the Murphy management team. Spell recounted the event:

> But instead of bringing it and talking about that, first they said when they went up . . . our office was integrated then. Honey, McMillan and them, they insulted everybody with a white face that was there that night. And told me, "I wouldn't even be here if I had known you were going to have the blue-eyed devils sitting in here. . . . I thought it was just going to be the tenant council members. I thought it was just going to be a black audience. I had no idea." *[Laughs]* Oh, they carried on. . . . The black people in the management were there. But he begged their pardon, said he wasn't after insulting nobody black, but he was after getting rid of them blue-eyed devils. "They don't mean you no good. You should kill them right now. . . ." We didn't have to kill them. They got up and walked.[34]

Soul School members clearly wanted to oblige black tenants; white people had no space in their vision of black power politics. The white managers and staff represented the oppressors, and their presence conjured up a long history, as well as the contemporary practice, of black subjugation—not a glorious past of African rule and innovation. They were "blue-eyed devils"—a popular phrase evoked in Nation of Islam (NOI) parlance and often used by Malcolm X before his separation from the NOI in the early 1960s. Gladys Spell maintained that she felt so awful that she apologized to management the next day, "because I felt really bad over that because you know some whites lost their lives in the civil rights struggle because they believed in right. . . . But [Soul School members] didn't look at it that way."[35]

Gladys Spell presented this incident as a turning point for some residents in the Murphy Homes Improvement Council. Shortly thereafter, according to Spell, residents started circulating a petition requesting a black manager and excluded white management from the meetings. Black nationalism had influenced some tenants, who believed that racial solidarity and self-determination led to black power and community control. Rosetta Schofield recalled the campaign for black management: "One of the guys, I remember in particular . . . was coming around knocking on the door, because he was then working here. And he said we need a change, and we need all black management, because the whites don't understand the blacks." Schofield asked the petitioner, "Who will take the white people's place?" And he answered, "We don't know, but we want black power. We want all black. We want black power. We want black power." Schofield responded, "Well it doesn't matter to me. 'Cause all I want is to have a place to stay, pay my rent. And I respect them, and in return they respect me. There you go."[36]

The black nationalist critique of white supremacy, particularly white participation in black affairs, shaped the responses of some of Murphy Homes' tenants and influenced broader political activities throughout Baltimore. Before the March 1968 rebellions in Baltimore, black activists "covering all shades of beliefs," including Homer Favor of Morgan College's Institute of Urban Affairs, Walter Lively, and Olugbala of the Soul School, participated in a conference to consider forming a united black front.[37] Unlike her characterization of CAA, which experienced financial difficulties by the 1970s and closed down one-third of its neighborhood centers, Goldie Baker described the Black United Front as "a fighting group" in the forefront of the black struggle.[38]

Murphy Homes represented a microcosm of these larger political debates on the black political scene. Just as all tenants did not connect with the black power insurgency, some black political and religious leaders disagreed with the militant separatist wings. While Baker worked with black power advocates, she labeled herself as a human being interested in liberation: "If you fighting for my rights and all the poor people's rights, I'll join you."[39] Maxine Stephenson, who worked with the Murphy Homes council, argued that equality and freedom did not mean separatism. Stephenson, who also had spoken out against the urban rebellions, stated that Dr. Martin Luther King, Jr., "wanted equal rights for everybody. He didn't say kick the *whites* over that side and we jump on this side."[40]

In Murphy Homes, cultural and political nationalism won. Activists' efforts exposed a simplistic belief: that a black manager would look out for their best interests. The knowledge of troubled black tenant-management relations in the 1940s, or even in the 1960s across town, seemed lost on those who decided that "black" was automatically better and unproblematic. The tenant campaign was successful, according to Gladys Spell. Murphy Homes received its first black manager in the early 1970s. Ironically, that manager was Joel Newton, about whom black tenants and activists had complained in the late 1960s. Having a black manager neither enhanced tenants' positions nor countered the demise of Murphy Homes, which, along with its low-rise and high-rise counterparts across the city, continued to decline in the wake of budget and security issues and a neglected urban landscape.

Black female tenants engaged in struggle in "customized wars" within their communities.[41] They took advantage of the spaces open to them, whether through the Community Action Program, Legal Services, VISTA, HUD, or grassroots civil rights and black power organizations—all in an attempt to improve their lives, fulfill their roles as caretakers of their homes and communities, and achieve the rights of citizenship. They infused their activism with the empowering messages of equality, rights, and self-determination, which undergirded the more generally held black struggles for freedom. And they demanded a form of tenant power to address quality-of-life issues, like poor maintenance and increasing vandalism. Tenants' search for rights, whether through the RAC, RAB, or tenant councils, not only encompassed a sense of what residents believed were their rights as Americans but also revealed a more expansive notion of community participation.

TENANTS DID NOT INVEST IN PUBLIC HOUSING

Lisa Levenstein

During the 1940s and 1950s, African American women claimed ownership of public housing by investing in their homes and neighborhoods. Envisioning public housing providing them with a refuge that they had long desired, they tried to turn their apartments into places they could call home. Many women put great effort into creating attractive living arrangements for their families and tried to maintain their gardens and public spaces. They cared for their children, established relationships with neighbors, and invested in their communities. By the 1960s, however, most women and their families had become disillusioned with public housing. The staff's rigid rules limited tenants' autonomy and discouraged them from creating personal attachments to their surroundings. Living in cheaply constructed, increasingly run-down apartments, often segregated in poverty-stricken neighborhoods, tenants found it extremely difficult to create comfortable and safe homes. Therein lies the tragedy and missed opportunity of postwar public housing. Rather than nurturing tenants' investments and aspirations, it became a public institution that increasingly restricted their abilities to substantially improve their lives.

In 1954, Mildred and Joseph Spencer moved with their four children into brand new public housing at Raymond Rosen Homes in North Philadelphia. Mrs. Spencer had stood in line for hours to submit an application to the Philadelphia Housing Authority (PHA) and had managed to obtain one of the coveted apartments for six-person families. Like almost all of the public housing constructed in postwar Philadelphia, Raymond Rosen was racially segregated. Serving African American tenants in a predominantly black neighborhood, it combined high-rise towers with row homes, and the Spencers considered themselves fortunate to receive one of the low-rise dwellings. The Spencers and their neighbors appreciated the dramatic improvement in their standard of living that they experienced upon moving into public housing. They tried to put their mark on Raymond Rosen by decorating their homes, forging relationships with neighbors, and caring for public spaces. Many of the women who lived in the low-rises took particular pleasure in their yards and competed with one another over who had the "prettiest" garden.[1] These commitments by tenants were critical to the success of Raymond Rosen. Public housing in Philadelphia thrived when tenants felt invested in their surroundings.

Over the course of the postwar period, government policies and practices began to undermine tenants' commitments to their new homes. Fearing that tenants would ruin public housing if they were not tightly controlled, the management staff discouraged them from personalizing their apartments and intrusively supervised many elements of their daily lives. Federal authorities demanded low-cost construction, which resulted in barebones living spaces, growing numbers of high-rises, and a dearth of facilities for children's recreation. With local officials not investing in the maintenance work and upgrades needed to keep public housing clean and efficient, tenants found it increasingly difficult to take pride in their homes. The PHA often located public housing for African American families in or near black neighborhoods that were deteriorating and dangerous, ultimately making it nearly impossible for tenants to maintain clean and safe surroundings. By the 1960s, tenants who had once felt deeply invested in public housing began to view it as a place of last resort.

African American women stood at the front lines of these transformations in public housing. Like African American men, they saw great promise in public housing because of the way racial discrimination limited their economic opportunities and confined them to the worst housing in the city. Yet women, and especially single mothers, faced unique burdens in their search for decent housing because many private landlords refused to rent to them, particularly if they had several children. Public housing replicated aspects of this sex discrimination by barring unmarried mothers. However, during the 1950s, widows and growing numbers of separated and divorced women secured admittance. Since women were typically the ones who held primary responsibility for housekeeping, child care, and community building, they played a key role in fostering the success of public housing and had the most to lose from its decline.

Public housing became an increasingly important presence in Philadelphia's working-class neighborhoods during the 1940s and 1950s. Between 1940 and 1942, the PHA constructed Tasker, Richard Allen, and James Weldon Johnson Homes, and in 1947, the authority took over the federal government's emergency wartime housing: Abbotsford, Passyunk, Bartram Village, and Oxford Village. More public housing followed the 1949 Housing Act, which called for the construction of 135,000 new units annually across the country for six years. Between 1952 and 1956, the PHA opened Arch, Wilson Park, Norris, Raymond Rosen, Schuylkill Falls, Liddonfield, Mill Creek, Queen Lane, Spring Garden, and Harrison Plaza (see Table 11.1). As in other cities, considerable public debate accompanied this rapid construction of public housing. Proposals to locate new public housing in working-class white neighborhoods became particularly contentious as residents feared that their property values and quality of life would plummet if African Americans moved in.[2]

Nevertheless, public housing's affordable rents and modern conveniences inspired thousands of working-class Philadelphians to seek apartments. By 1949, the PHA had a waiting list of over ten thousand families, and the list

Table 11.1 Philadelphia public housing, 1940–1956

	Units	Year of occupancy	Percentage black 1956	1964	Race predominant in neighborhood
Hill Creek	258*	1938	0.7	0	White
Johnson Homes	589	1940	99.0	100.0	Nonwhite
Richard Allen	1,324	1942	100.0	99.3	Nonwhite
Tasker	1,007	1941	23.0	38.0	White
Abbottsford	700	1942	9.4	19.3	White
Bartram Village	500	1942	9.9	23.0	White
Oxford Village	200	1942	0.7	N.A.	White
Passyunk	994	1942	4.6	18.0	White
Arch	77	1952	74.0	98.0	Nonwhite
Wilson Park	746	1954	9.6	21.0	White
Norris	326	1954	100.0	97.0	Nonwhite
Raymond Rosen	1,122	1954	99.9	100.0	Nonwhite
Schuylkill Falls	714	1955	11.5	28.0	White

Sources: Committee on Public Housing Policy, "Basic Policies for Low-Income Families in Public Housing in Philadelphia" (Philadelphia: Philadelphia Housing Association, 1957), 34; "Developments of the Philadelphia Housing Authority: March 1964," Box 283, Folder 4953, Philadelphia Housing Association/ Housing Association of the Delaware Valley, 1909–1975, Urban Archives, Temple University; John F. Bauman, *Public Housing, Race, and Renewal: Urban Planning in Philadelphia, 1920–1974* (Philadelphia: Temple University Press, 1987), 172–73.

*Later enlarged to 340 units.

would have been even longer if more people thought they had a chance of getting in.[3] African Americans—and single mothers of color in particular—were overrepresented among the applicants because they were largely confined to the worst housing in the city.[4] Yet, as in other places, they did not gain access to public housing in proportion to their applications. In 1956, African Americans constituted nearly 90 percent of the applicants for public housing in Philadelphia, but only 51 percent of its tenants.[5] Single women faced additional burdens because authorities gave preference to two-parent families, accepted only a limited number of separated women with small families, and sought to exclude unmarried mothers from public housing altogether.[6]

During the 1950s, civil rights activists successfully campaigned to persuade authorities to grant African Americans admission to public housing in proportion to their applications and to cease segregating public housing according to race. Consequently, African Americans increasingly became a dominant presence in public housing that had been previously reserved for whites.[7] However, postwar civil rights activists did not address the gender-based restrictions on single mothers, which remained in place until 1968. Some single mothers advocated for themselves by repeatedly applying to public housing and forcing local authorities to grapple with their predicaments. Through such pressure, growing numbers of separated and divorced women secured admission, joining widows and women who had ended relationships with men while living in public housing. As a result, by the early 1960s, single mothers occupied nearly half of all of the units in Philadelphia's public housing.[8]

The high numbers of applicants signaled the tremendous promise of new public housing. In the 1940s, the PHA employed innovative architects and encouraged them to improve the standards of urban design. During these years, the city's public housing consisted mainly of low-rise buildings arranged in a "communitarian" fashion, facing a grassy court or common area where residents could gather. African Americans took particular pride in their 589-unit James Weldon Johnson Homes, which had 58 two- and three-story red brick buildings located around pleasant courts and walkways. Gabled roofs, landscaped walks, and white canopies over doorways made Johnson Homes uniquely warm and attractive. Although the 1,324-unit Richard Allen Homes for African Americans was larger and had a less original layout, its 53 three- and four-story red and yellow brick buildings formed pleasant quadrangles with small courtyards, and it had a conveniently located community center and library (Figure 11.1).[9]

Inside new public housing, tenants appreciated quarters that were more spacious and modern than their previous living situations. One of the first tenants at Richard Allen, Agnes Hawryluk, had previously lived with her two children in a one-room apartment with no sanitary facilities or running water. Her apartment at Richard Allen felt luxurious in comparison. Downstairs it had a living room and a kitchen with a gas stove, electric refrigerator, and built-in cabinets. The upstairs had two bedrooms, a bathroom with a sink, bathtub, and toilet, and a laundry tub for washing clothes.[10] Mrs. Hawryluk had paid $14 each month for rent and utilities for her one-room apartment. At Richard Allen she paid $14.50 for her much nicer accommodations.[11] Because of strict federal budgets, public housing had no "frills." Apartments lacked dining rooms, closet doors, baseboards, and splashboards for the sinks. Floors were made of concrete, closets had steel shelves, and banisters were made of

Figure 11.1 Richard Allen Homes. Courtesy of the Library of Congress.

227

iron pipe. Still, because so many tenants who moved into new public housing had previously lived in the slums, they appreciated the significant improvement in their standard of living.[12]

Within public housing, tenants tried to create safe havens for themselves and their families where they could feel comfortable and take pride in their surroundings. Since women typically took responsibility for household labor and community building, they played an essential role in this process. Many women sought to personalize their apartments to make them feel homey and inviting. On shoestring budgets, they tried to obtain a few pieces of decent furniture and added personal touches such as knickknacks and pictures.[13] Those who had the means engaged in ambitious decorating projects, putting up curtains, buying rugs, and covering shelves with decorative paper. Edna Cooper explained, "All my life, I've been dreaming of a pretty little kitchen in red and white. I used to look at magazine pictures that showed the kitchen all white and shiny and plan how I'd make mine—someday." Mrs. Cooper had not been able to realize her dream "in the place we used to live. The kitchen was dark and musty, with nothing but an old gas range and a dilapidated wooden ice box that wouldn't keep anything cold." Mrs. Cooper claimed ownership of her new apartment in public housing by decorating the kitchen entirely in red and white. She put up homemade curtains, covered her shelves with paper, and carpeted her floor.[14]

Women with more limited means still sought to create respectable and comfortable homes for their families. Mrs. Felton Reddy took great pride in the working bathtub in her new apartment. "We had our own bath in the old place," she explained, "but no hot water. . . . Since we had to heat all our bath water on the gas range we couldn't take many baths; it cost too much." Mrs. Reddy told the *Philadelphia Evening Bulletin* that she bathed her five children daily in her new apartment at Richard Allen and sometimes gave them baths twice a day in warm weather.[15] Her bathing routine served as a key marker of respectability that signaled her commitment to raising her children properly in public housing.

Women viewed the cultivation of community relationships as an essential part of their efforts to turn public housing into real homes. As in other neighborhoods, many of them formed close relationships with other mothers who lived nearby, shopping together and exchanging food, clothing, and child care. In 1955, shortly after moving into Raymond Rosen, Dorothy Medley described the bonds she had formed: "The neighbors here are all wonderful, after you have been here for a couple of months you feel as if you have known them all of your life."[16] Some women participated in Mothers' Clubs and encouraged their children to join Boys and Girls Clubs and Scout troops as well as sports and other recreational activities. The Department of Recreation ran playground activities in public housing, and the Free Library of Philadelphia operated two branch libraries, three extension libraries, and one bookmobile. With many mothers urging their families to make use of these facilities, in 1955 alone, tenants made 10,097 visits to the library at Richard Allen and 15,756 to the one at James Weldon Johnson.[17]

The energy and optimism that characterized public housing's early years of operation proved difficult for tenants to sustain. Over the course of the 1950s and early 1960s, morale began to plummet as public housing became increasingly run-down, dangerous, and conflict-ridden. This transformation in public housing occurred at the very same time that the tenant population began to change, with more African Americans, women, and the poor gaining admission. Although authorities often blamed these new tenants for the changing conditions, many of the problems that developed had little to do with tenants' economic status, race, or gender. Problems began to develop in the early 1950s, when many upwardly mobile families still lived in public housing, and they developed similarly among African Americans and whites. In some sites, the problems began to appear after only a few years of operation. Certainly some tenants broke rules and disrespected public and private spaces. Yet many authorities' adopted a top-down management style, fueled by a strong bureaucratic emphasis on the need to maintain a respectable image of public housing and a profound distrust of tenants. Their approach helped to gradually erode tenants' affinity for public housing. The lack of funds devoted to the upkeep of public housing and decisions about site selection also played a critical role in fostering the decline in the standard of living. Yet it was much cheaper and more politically expedient to place the blame for public housing's problems on tenants than it was for authorities to acknowledge and remedy the flaws in their policies.

The growing disaffection among tenants stemmed in part from their interactions with local staff members. Women in particular frequently encountered the PHA's on-site staff of managers, assistant managers, management aides, and maintenance workers whose job was to care for public housing but who often worked at cross-purposes from tenants.[18] The staff's main responsibility was to collect rent and keep properties running smoothly and in good condition.

As in other public institutions, staff members differed significantly in their approaches to their jobs, with some exhibiting more respect for tenants than others. Black staff members were not necessarily more sympathetic to black tenants than white staff members, nor were women always more understanding than men. All managers had to follow policy directives from the central office and they could also create rules to meet specific needs. From the tenants' perspective, what stood out was the sheer number of rules, and the demoralizing and sometimes demeaning enforcement practices. Some staff members tried very hard to help tenants when they faced difficulties, but tenants had virtually no voice in public housing's operations. Most managers neither consulted tenants before implementing new policies nor solicited their suggestions.[19] Theresa Davenport, a tenant at Richard Allen, described clashing with her manager whose "theme song" was "if you don't like it, get out."[20]

The PHA enforced strict housekeeping policies targeted at female tenants. Intended to ensure that the conditions of public housing did not deteriorate, these policies often undermined women's abilities to feel that their apartments were their own. Most notoriously, staff members conducted surprise biannual household inspections. If tenants were not home, the staff let themselves in with pass keys. Myrna Coulter protested: "They come in any time they want."[21] Women who were home when the staff members arrived described a wide range of experiences. Marcelle Blackwell recalled female staff members coming into her apartment, having a "cup of tea," and talking amicably about coming events at Raymond Rosen.[22] Other women complained about staff who inspected much more thoroughly, turning down bedspreads to make sure beds had clean sheets, checking under cupboards for vermin, and judging the cleanliness of toilets and walls. Many women particularly resented the staff evaluating the neatness of their apartments. If they failed to wash their breakfast dishes, pick up toys, or make the beds, they could receive poor grades. Emma Taylor's apartment at Richard Allen received a rating of "fair" when it was inspected because she had certain household chores that she required her children to perform each day and if they did not complete the chores before going to school in the morning, she purposely left the tasks unfinished. The staff member, Alice Moore, refused to take Mrs. Taylor's explanation into account and lowered her score on account of her children's mess. Several of Mrs. Taylor's neighbors shared deep misgivings about Mrs. Moore. Barbara Watson observed that if Mrs. Moore could not "find anything wrong with your place, she starts pulling the beds apart and poking around until she finds something." Mrs. Taylor agreed that Mrs. Moore never "builds you up—always tears you down."[23]

Some women complained that managers' concern with the outward appearance of public housing sabotaged their attempts to create orderly and aesthetically pleasing apartments. Laundry became one of the biggest sources of contention. Many women avoided drying their laundry on the racks in the courtyards, which were often falling apart or located in heavily trafficked areas where clothes got dirtied by children playing. Managers infuriated women by prohibiting them from hanging their laundry out of their windows to dry, a sight that could tarnish public housing's "respectable" image. Unable to hang wet clothes outside, women had to drape them on the furniture in their apartments or on the stair rails in the hallways. Women wanted their homes to feel inviting, and the wet clothes hanging in and around their apartments were an eyesore. Mothers of asthmatic children, who needed to avoid damp conditions, complained that their inability to hang their clothes out of the windows threatened their families' health.[24]

Some managers prevented tenants from personalizing and claiming ownership of the exteriors of their homes. Perhaps nowhere was this more clearly evident than at Raymond Rosen in the late 1950s, when a nearby factory burned down and tenants in the low-rises reused its bricks to edge their lawns. Members of each family made several trips to the factory, carrying armfuls of heavy bricks. They believed that the aesthetic payoffs made their labor worthwhile, reporting that their lawns edged with bricks looked "beautiful," especially when viewed in a row. Raymond Rosen's manager did not agree. Without consulting the tenants, he sent trucks to take the bricks away. Tenants stood powerlessly, while maintenance workers dug up their gardens before their eyes. The conflict shattered tenants' sense of ownership of their surroundings. "It was as if the management staff told us, 'We're letting you live here out of charity,'" explained Marcelle Blackwell. "We no longer felt that the apartments were really ours."[25]

The lack of adequate funding for public housing further diminished tenants' appreciation of their homes. An amendment to the 1937 Wagner-Steagall Act, written by Harry Byrd, the Democratic Senator from Virginia, implemented strict spending restrictions on all new construction.[26] The United States Housing Authority (USHA) pushed cities to reduce costs even further by requiring local authorities to remove all of the "frills" and design innovations from their plans for new public housing.[27] These federal restrictions on construction expenditures weighed heavily on tenants. Over time, many of them ceased remarking on the luxuries in public housing and began to complain about its inadequacies. Concrete floors were extremely cold, and closets without doors had to be in perfect order or else their contents spilled out onto the floors. Without dining rooms, families had to eat in their living rooms. The inadequate cupboard space forced many women to store canned food, dishes, and utensils in their bedrooms. Buildings lacked finished basements for storage, so tricycles, bicycles, and baby carriages usually ended up in the hallways or lodged in the tiny living rooms.[28] Tenants in older buildings resented not having on-site laundry facilities, and residents who had them found them expensive and insufficient because members of the surrounding community frequently made use of them.[29]

The dearth of facilities for children weighed heavily on mothers. Play areas rarely had enough equipment or space. At Raymond Rosen, the two hundred-seat auditorium provided the only indoor recreation space for five thousand tenants. The PHA did not construct a gymnasium at Raymond Rosen because authorities assumed that tenants would be able to use the recreation facilities at the school across the street and at a nearby public recreation center. However, the school did not organize community programs in the afternoons or evenings, and the recreation center was already overcrowded and could not accommodate the thousands of new children from Raymond Rosen. Richard Allen had only two sets of swings and two jungle gyms for its three thousand children. With the nearest public recreation center one mile away and no public parks nearby, children from the surrounding neighborhood also relied on Richard Allen's facilities.[30] In 1952, Richard Allen tenants became so frustrated that they raised funds to install a recreation center and gymnasium in the basement of a nearby church.[31]

The dwindling resources available for the upkeep of public housing had similarly deleterious effects on tenants' morale. Local authorities used the income they collected in rents to pay for salaries, utility bills, maintenance work, and modernization. When tenants' incomes were high, as they were during World War II, securing funding to keep public housing running smoothly was not difficult. However, as the number of two-parent, steadily employed families in public housing declined and the number of poor families increased, the income that the PHA collected from rents dwindled. At the same time, public housing became more expensive to maintain. Buildings and appliances aged, requiring costly repairs and upgrades.[32] As the booming postwar consumer economy made ranges and refrigerators considered luxurious in the early 1940s antiquated by the 1950s, tenants wished for newer items.[33] With little money to spend on upkeep, the PHA restricted the painting of the interior walls in public housing to every four years, even when apartments changed hands. Some tenants had to do the painting themselves. Families moving into apartments with marked-up walls and outmoded appliances did not view public housing as an inviting place to live.[34]

Fueling tenants' growing alienation, managers conserved funds by forcing them to bear some of the costs of public housing's operations. Rents included utilities, but when a manager suspected that a family was using too much electricity, he installed a meter in their apartment and charged them for any use he deemed "excessive." In order to avoid getting stuck with extra electricity bills, some tenants felt compelled to turn off their lights and go to bed early in the evenings.[35] When apartments needed repairs, the PHA typically paid only for relatively inexpensive problems such as busted locks and broken electric switches. Tenants usually had to pay for more expensive repairs and damage deemed to have been caused by their "heedlessness," such as smashed windows, out-of-order toilets, and broken doors. They also had to pay for damage caused by bad weather or other people. Tenants were angry about the expense of repairs, especially since the management prevented them from fixing problems themselves or shopping around for the cheapest handymen.[36]

The PHA's meager expenditures on public spaces inspired similar resentment. When public housing first opened, many tenants tried to keep the exteriors clean. "One of the most spick-and-span spots in Philadelphia these days is the Richard Allen Homes," reported the *Philadelphia Evening Bulletin*, five years after it opened. "What little trash blows around there blows in from the outside and the residents are justifiably proud of the appearance of the area."[37] In an area of only eight city blocks, Richard Allen housed 6,100 people, over three thousand of them children. Yet tenants took such good care of their surroundings that Richard Allen won an award from Philadelphia's Chamber of Commerce and Sanitation Squad for being one of the cleanest spots in the city. Women carefully swept the hallways outside their apartments; reporters noted that in "not a single hallway entered was there any accumulation of trash or even dust."[38] Although not every tenant maintained these high standards, the community ethos in support of cleanliness created generally neat and pleasant public spaces. Tenants in the new public housing that opened in Philadelphia in the 1950s similarly prided themselves on their clean and well-maintained surroundings.[39]

Yet alongside these accounts praising public housing's high standard of living lay evidence of the seeds of future decline. On several premises, the PHA did not support tenants' efforts to maintain public spaces. When people put graffiti on the walls, littered, or vandalized the premises, managers rarely provided much assistance in repairing the damage. One 1957 inspection found the landscape around Richard Allen Homes plagued by "erosion, water pockets, inadequate drainage, irregular surfacing, spindley [sic] plantings, makeshift fencing, [and] bare muddy spots." At Norris, water and urine had accumulated in the stairwells, creating a terrible stench. Even Raymond Rosen had begun to show signs of disrepair after only two years of operation.[40]

Adding to these problems, authorities often located public housing in troubled areas, seeming not to recognize that the boundaries between public housing and these neighborhoods were permeable. During the late 1950s, crime and drug selling became part of life in some of the city's public housing, and the PHA became particularly concerned about the high-rises. "Problems in high-rise structures are mounting," observed PHA executive director Walter E. Alessandroni in 1958. "There is vandalism from outsiders who get into the projects, which have no proper supervision, and nobody is willing to give [the] authority money to do the policing job. Women are raped." Some women began to avoid going out at night because they feared for their safety. In 1958, at Norris, when a group of people waiting for an elevator got frustrated because it was slow to arrive, they yanked the door loose and dropped it down the shaft. Nobody called the police for fear of retaliation.[41] By the 1960s, although African Americans, and especially single mothers, continued to apply for public housing in large numbers because their options in the private market remained limited, many began to doubt that it would improve their lives demonstrably. Once a source of tremendous pride and hope, public housing increasingly became a reflection of their degradation.

NOTES

Introduction

1. Broadly, the literature on European social housing takes one of two approaches: the *convergence* school (emphasizing similarities in response to continent-wide developments) and the *divergence* school (emphasizing differences in welfare systems grounded in social and cultural heritages, particularly between the continental and Anglo-Saxon countries). For *convergence*, see Michael Harloe, *The People's Home?: Social Rented Housing in Europe and America*, Studies in Urban and Social Change (Cambridge, MA: Blackwell, 1995); Bill Edgar, Joe Doherty, and Henk Meert, *Access to Housing: Homelessness and Vulnerability in Europe* (Bristol: Policy Press, 2002); and Christine M. E. Whitehead and Kathleen Scanlon, *Social Housing in Europe* (London: London School of Economics and Political Science, 2007). For *divergence*, see Jim Kemeny, *The Myth of Home-Ownership: Private versus Public Choices in Housing Tenure* (London: Routledge & Kegan Paul, 1981); Jim Kemeny, *From Public Housing to the Social Market: Rental Policy Strategies in Comparative Perspective* (London: Routledge, 1995).

2. Lee Rainwater, *Behind Ghetto Walls: Black Families in a Federal Slum* (Chicago: Aldine Publishing Company, 1970); Katharine G. Bristol, "The Pruitt-Igoe Myth," *Journal of Architectural Education* 44, no. 3 (May 1991); D. Bradford Hunt, *Blueprint for Disaster: The Unraveling of Chicago Public Housing* (Chicago: University of Chicago Press, 2009); William Peterman, "Public Housing Resident Management: A Good Idea Gone Wrong?," *Shelterforce*, November/December 1993.

3. Monica Davey, "In a Soaring Homicide Rate, a Divide in Chicago," *New York Times*, 2 January 2013; Susan J. Popkin, Michael J. Rich, Leah Hendey, Chris Hayes, and Joe Parilla, *Public Housing Transformation and Crime: Making the Case for Responsible Relocation* (Washington, DC: Urban Institute, 2012).

4. Chad Freidrichs, *The Pruitt-Igoe Myth*, State Historical Society of Missouri/First Run Features, 2011.

5. Catherine Bauer, *Modern Housing* (Boston: Houghton Mifflin, 1934); H. Warren Dunham and Nathan D. Grundstein, "The Impact of a Confusion of Social Objectives on Public Housing: A Preliminary Analysis," *Marriage and Family Living* 17, no. 2 (1955); Catherine Bauer, "The Dreary Deadlock of Public Housing," originally published 1957, repr. in *Federal Housing Policy and Programs: Past and Present*, ed. J. Paul Mitchell (New Brunswick, NJ: Center for Urban Policy Research, 1985); John P. Catt, "Experts Critical of Public Housing," *New York Times*, 20 July 1958; William Moore, Jr., *The Vertical Ghetto: Everyday Life in an*

Urban Project (New York: Random House, 1969); David K. Shipler, "Troubles Beset Public Housing across Nation," *New York Times*, 12 October 1969; Rainwater, *Behind Ghetto Walls;* George S. Sternlieb and Bernard P. Indik, *The Ecology of Welfare: Housing and the Welfare Crisis in New York City* (New Brunswick, NJ: Transaction Books, 1973); Rachel G. Bratt, "Public Housing: The Controversy and Contribution," in *Critical Perspectives on Housing*, ed. Rachel G. Bratt, Chester W. Hartman, and Ann Meyerson (Philadelphia: Temple University Press, 1986); John F. Bauman, *Public Housing, Race, and Renewal: Urban Planning in Philadelphia, 1920–1974* (Philadelphia: Temple University Press, 1987); William E. Schmidt, "Public Housing: For Workers or the Needy?," *New York Times*, 17 April 1990; Alex Kotlowitz, *There Are No Children Here: The Story of Two Boys Growing Up in the Other America* (New York: Doubleday, 1991); Michael H. Schill, "Distressed Public Housing: Where Do We Go from Here?," *University of Chicago Law Review* 60, no. 2 (1993); A. Scott Henderson, "'Tarred with the Exceptional Image': Public Housing and Popular Discourse, 1950–1990," *American Studies* 36, no. 1 (1995); Arnold R. Hirsch, *Making the Second Ghetto: Race and Housing in Chicago, 1940–1960* (Chicago: University of Chicago Press, 1998); Gail Radford, *Modern Housing for America: Policy Struggles in the New Deal Era* (Chicago: University of Chicago Press, 1996); Bradford McKee, "Public Housing's Last Hope," *Architecture* 86, no. 8 (1997); Lewis H. Spence, "Rethinking the Social Role of Public Housing," *Housing Policy Debate* 4, no. 3 (1998); John F. Bauman, Roger Biles, and Kristin M. Szylvian, eds., *From Tenements to the Taylor Homes: In Search of an Urban Housing Policy in Twentieth-Century America* (University Park: Pennsylvania State University Press, 2000); Lawrence J. Vale, *From the Puritans to the Projects: Public Housing and Public Neighbors* (Cambridge, MA: Harvard University Press, 2000); Howard Husock, *America's Trillion-Dollar Housing Mistake: The Failure of American Housing Policy* (Chicago: Ivan R. Dee, 2003).

6. D. Bradford Hunt, "How Did Public Housing Survive the 1950s?," *Journal of Policy History* 17, no. 2 (2005); Hunt, *Blueprint for Disaster;* Bristol, "The Pruitt-Igoe Myth"; Edward G. Goetz, *New Deal Ruins: The Dismantling of Public Housing in the U.S.* (Ithaca, NY: Cornell University Press, 2013).

7. Jane Jacobs, *The Death and Life of Great American Cities* (New York: Random House, 1961). For a discussion of Jacobs's earlier writings, see Glenna Lang and Marjory Wunsch, *Genius of Common Sense: Jane Jacobs and the Story of The Death and Life of Great American Cities* (Boston: David R. Godine, 2009); and Anthony Flint, *Wrestling with Moses: How Jane Jacobs Took on New York's Master Builder and Transformed the American City* (New York: Random House, 2009); Bauer, "The Dreary Deadlock of Public Housing."

8. Oscar Newman, *Defensible Space: Crime Prevention through Urban Design* (New York: Collier Books, 1973); Oscar Newman, *Community of Interest* (New York: Doubleday, 1980); Richard Plunz, *A History of Housing in New York City: Dwelling Type and Social Change in the American Metropolis* (New York: Columbia University Press, 1990); Karen A. Franck and Michael Mostoller, "From Courts to Open Space to Streets: Changes in the Site Design of U.S. Public Housing," *Journal of Architectural and Planning Research* 12, no. 3 (1995).

9. Goetz, *New Deal Ruins;* Larry Keating, "Redeveloping Public Housing: Relearning Urban Renewal's Immutable Lessons," *Journal of the American Planning Association* 66, no. 4 (2000).

10. Donald Parson, *Making a Better World: Public Housing, the Red Scare, and the Direction of Modern Los Angeles* (Minneapolis: University of Minnesota Press, 2005); Husock, *America's Trillion-Dollar Housing Mistake;* Bess Furman, "'Socialistic' Tag on Housing Hit," *New York Times*, 10 June 1955.

11. J.S. Fuerst and D. Bradford Hunt, *When Public Housing Was Paradise: Building Community in Chicago* (Urbana-Champaign: University of Illinois Press, 2005); Hunt, *Blueprint for Disaster;* Radford, *Modern Housing for America;* Nicholas Dagen Bloom, *Public Housing That Worked: New York in the Twentieth Century* (Philadelphia: University of Pennsylvania Press, 2008); Vale, *From the Puritans to the Projects;* Lawrence J. Vale, *Reclaiming Public Housing: A Half Century of Struggle in Three Public Neighborhoods* (Cambridge, MA: Harvard University Press, 2002). For liberal scholars' dismissal of public housing as tainted by urban renewal, see Hirsch, *Making the Second Ghetto;* Joel Schwartz, *The New York Approach: Robert Moses, Urban Liberals, and Redevelopment of the Inner City* (Columbus: Ohio State University Press, 1993); Thomas J. Sugrue, *The Origins of the Urban Crisis: Race and Inequality in Postwar Detroit* (Princeton, NJ: Princeton University Press, 1996); Peter Marcuse, "Interpreting 'Public Housing' History," *Journal of Architectural and Planning Research* 12, no. 3 (Autumn 1995): 240–58; Wendell E. Pritchett, *Brownsville, Brooklyn: Blacks, Jews, and the Changing Face of the Ghetto* (Chicago: University of Chicago Press, 2002). Bauman, Biles, and Szylvian, *From Tenements to the Taylor Homes.*

12. Sudhir Alladi Venkatesh, *American Project: The Rise and Fall of a Modern Ghetto* (Cambridge, MA: Harvard University Press, 2000); Edward Goetz, *Clearing the Way: Deconcentrating the Poor in Urban America* (Washington, DC: Urban Institute Press, 2003); Goetz, *New Deal Ruins;* Vale, *Reclaiming Public Housing;* Lawrence Vale, *Purging the Poorest: Public Housing and the Design Politics of Twice-Cleared Communities* (Chicago: University of Chicago Press, 2013). For accounts that focus narrowly on poverty and pathos, see Moore, *The Vertical Ghetto;* Rainwater, *Behind Ghetto Walls;* Jay MacLeod, *Ain't No Makin' It: Leveled Aspirations in a Low-Income Neighborhood* (Boulder, CO: Westview Press, 1987); Kotlowitz, *There Are No Children Here;* Susan J. Popkin, *The Hidden War: Crime and the Tragedy of Public Housing in Chicago* (New Brunswick, NJ: Rutgers University Press, 2000).

13. Goetz, *New Deal Ruins,* 40.

14. Mary Schmich, "Reshaping a Neighborhood," *Chicago Tribune,* 4 July 2004.

15. Nicola Mann, "The Death and Resurrection of Chicago's Public Housing in the American Imagination" (PhD diss., University of Rochester, 2011), 387.

16. David Fleming, "Subjects of the Inner City: Writing the People of Cabrini-Green," in *Towards a Rhetoric of Everyday Life,* ed. Martin Nystrand and John Duffy (Madison: University of Wisconsin Press, 2003), 232.

17. "Perspective: Inner-City School Has Come Around," *Chicago Tribune,* 21 June 1974; Robert Young, "U.S. to Rehabilitate Public Housing," *Chicago Tribune,* 11 July 1978; "Not Everyone Feels Defeated," *Chicago Tribune,* 7 May 1982; Stanley Ziemba, "Study Pushes Tenant Ownership of Cabrini-Green," *Chicago Tribune,* 8 October 1987; Steve Kerch, "Best of Chicago Needs Diverse Eye for Full Expression," *Chicago Tribune,* 6 June 1999.

18. "Cracking Chicago's Wall of Shame," *Chicago Tribune,* 25 July 1988.

19. Wallace Turner, "San Francisco Tackling 'Den of Thieves' Project," *New York Times,* 30 July 1981.

20. These charts use LexisNexis as a search engine and encompass about 40 sources—every newspaper for which the service provides continuous coverage for the full period between 1993 and 2010.

21. For a more extended discussion of public housing stigma, see Lawrence J. Vale, "The Imaging of the City: Public Housing and Communication," *Communication Research* 22, no. 6 (1995): 646–63; and Lawrence J. Vale, "Destigmatizing Public Housing," in *Geography and*

Identity: Living and Exploring the Geopolitics of Identity, ed. Dennis Crow (Washington, DC: Institute for Advanced Cultural Studies/Maisonneuve Press, 1996).

22. National Commission on Severely Distressed Public Housing, *The Final Report of the National Commission on Severely Distressed Public Housing* (Washington, DC: U.S. Government Printing Office, 1992).

23. Goetz, *New Deal Ruins,* 42–43.

24. Michael Katz, *Why Don't American Cities Burn?* (Philadelphia: University of Pennsylvania Press, 2012), 157–58.

Myth #1: Public Housing Stands Alone

1. Lee Rainwater, *Behind Ghetto Walls: Black Families in a Federal Slum* (Chicago: Aldine Publishing Company, 1970); William Moore, Jr., *The Vertical Ghetto: Everyday Life in an Urban Slum* (New York: Random House, 1969).

2. Richard D. Bingham, *Public Housing and Urban Renewal: An Analysis of Federal-Local Relations* (New York: Praeger, 1975).

3. Don Parson, *Making a Better World: Public Housing, the Red Scare, and the Direction of Modern Los Angeles* (Minneapolis: University of Minnesota Press, 2005).

4. Alex Schwartz, *Housing Policy in the United States* (London: Routledge, 2006), 125–26.

5. Gail Radford, *Modern Housing for America: Policy Struggles in the New Deal Era* (Chicago: University of Chicago Press, 1996), 85–102.

6. J.S. Fuerst and D. Bradford Hunt, *When Public Housing Was Paradise: Building Community in Chicago* (Urbana-Champaign: University of Illinois Press, 2005); Joseph Heathcott, "In the Nature of a Clinic: The Design of Early Public Housing," *Journal of the Society of Architectural Historians* 70, no. 1 (March 2011).

7. "Four Vast Housing Projects for St. Louis: Helmuth, Obata and Kassabaum, Inc.," *Architectural Record* 120, no. 2 (August 1956): 182–89.

8. Harland Bartholomew to Mayor Joseph Darst, 27 July 1949, Housing File, 1945–1951, series 1, box 24, Raymond Tucker Papers, Washington University Special Collection.

9. D. Bradford Hunt, *Blueprint for Disaster: The Unraveling of Chicago Public Housing* (Chicago: University of Chicago Press, 2009).

10. John F. Bauman, *Public Housing, Race, and Renewal: Urban Planning in Philadelphia, 1920–1974* (Philadelphia: Temple University Press, 1987).

11. Alexander von Hoffman, "A Study in Contradictions: The Origins and Legacy of the 1949 Housing Act," *Housing Policy Debate* 11, no. 2 (2000): 299–323.

12. For the argument on massive slum clearance, see *The 1947 Comprehensive Plan* (St. Louis, MO: City Plan Commission, 1947).

13. Study reported in the *St. Louis Post-Dispatch,* 27 April 1945. Also see *Plan Commission Annual Report, 1944–1945* (St. Louis, MO: City Plan Commission, 1945), 16.

14. Becky Nicolaides and Andrew Wiese, eds., *The Suburb Reader* (New York: Routledge, 2006), 257–58.

15. Joseph Heathcott, "The City Quietly Remade: National Programs and Local Agendas in the Movement to Clear the Slums, 1942–1952," *Journal of Urban History* 34, no. 2 (2008): 221–42.

16. "Slum Surgery in St. Louis," *Architectural Forum* 94 (April 1951): 128–36.

17. Eugene J. Meehan, *The Quality of Federal Policymaking: Programmed Failure in Public Housing* (Columbia: University of Missouri Press, 1979), 66–69.

18. Thomas J. Sugrue, *The Origins of the Urban Crisis: Race and Inequality in Postwar Detroit* (Princeton, NJ: Princeton University Press, 1996).

19. Colin Gordon, *Mapping Decline: St. Louis and the Fate of the American City* (Philadelphia: University of Pennsylvania Press, 2009), 22, 41–44.

20. Gordon, *Mapping Decline*, 225; Daniel J. Monti, *Race, Redevelopment, and the New Company Town* (Albany, NY: State University of New York Press, 1990).

21. Barbara R. Williams, *St. Louis: A City and Its Suburbs.* (Santa Monica, CA: The Rand Corporation, 1973), 25–28.

22. Sudhir Alladi Venkatesh, *American Project: The Rise and Fall of a Modern Ghetto* (Cambridge, MA: Harvard University Press, 2002).

23. Lee Rainwater, "The Lessons of Pruitt-Igoe," *Public Interest* 8 (Summer 1967): 116–26; Meehan, *The Quality of Federal Policymaking*, 66–69.

24. scar Newman, *Defensible Space: Crime Prevention through Urban Design* (New York: Macmillan, 1972).

25. James Bailey, "The Case History of a Failure," *Architectural Forum* 123 (December 1965): 23; Peter Blake, *Form Follows Fiasco: Why Modern Architecture Hasn't Worked* (Boston: Atlantic Monthly Press/Little, Brown, 1977); Charles Jencks, *The Language of Post-Modern Architecture* (New York: Rizzoli, 1977); Tom Wolfe, *From Bauhaus to Our House* (New York: Farrar, Straus and Giroux, 1981).

26. Arnold R. Hirsch, *Making the Second Ghetto: Race and Housing in Chicago, 1940–1960* (New York: Cambridge University Press, 1983).

27. Schwartz, *Housing Policy in the United States*, 137–44.

28. Susan J. Popkin, et al., *The Hidden War: Crime and Tragedy of Public Housing in Chicago* (New Brunswick, NJ: Rutgers University Press, 2000); Neil Websdale, *Policing the Poor: From Slave Plantation to Public Housing* (Boston: Northeastern University Press, 2001).

29. Katharine G. Bristol, "The Pruitt-Igoe Myth," *Journal of Architectural Education* 44, no. 3 (May 1991): 163.

30. Minoru Yamasaki, "High Buildings for Public Housing?" *Journal of Housing* 9 (1952): 226; Meehan, *The Quality of Federal Policymaking*, 71.

31. Alexander von Hoffman, "Why They Built Pruitt-Igoe," in *From Tenements to the Taylor Homes: In Search of an Urban Housing Policy in Twentieth-Century America*, ed. John F. Bauman, Roger Biles, and Kristin M. Szylvian (University Park: Penn State University Press, 2000), 180–205.

32. Bristol, "The Pruitt-Igoe Myth," 171.

33. Jane Holtz Kay, "Architecture: Pruitt-Igoe Project," *The Nation* 217, no. 9 (September 1973): 284–86.

34. Meehan, *The Quality of Federal Policymaking*, 77.

35. Gordon, *Mapping Decline*, 10–11, 53–57, 214–16.

36. Florian Urban, *Tower and Slab: Histories of Global Mass Housing* (London: Routledge, 2011).

37. Henry Schmandt and George Wendel, *The Pruitt-Igoe Public Housing Complex, 1954–1976* (St. Louis, MO: Center for Urban Programs, Saint Louis University, 1976).

38. Meehan, *The Quality of Federal Policymaking*, 83–84.

39. Gordon, *Mapping Decline*, 189–95.

40. Howard Husock, *America's Trillion-Dollar Housing Mistake: The Failure of American Housing Policy* (Chicago: Ivan R. Dee, 2003).

41. Meehan, *The Quality of Federal Policymaking*, 77.

42. Henry G. Cisneros and Lora Engdahl, eds., *From Despair to Hope: HOPE VI and the New Promise of Public Housing in America's Cities* (Washington, DC: Brookings Institution Press, 2009).

43. Sugrue, *The Origins of the Urban Crisis,* 143–52; William J. Wilson, *When Work Disappears: The World of the New Urban Poor* (New York: Vintage Books, 1997).

44. Hunt, *Blueprint for Disaster,* 221–31, 289–91.

45. Nicholas D. Bloom, *Public Housing That Worked: New York in the Twentieth Century* (Philadelphia: University of Pennsylvania Press, 2008).

46. Meehan, *The Quality of Federal Policymaking,* 77.

47. Radford, *Modern Housing for America,* 107–09; Joseph Heathcott, "Score One for Modernism," *Planning* 72, no. 11 (December 2006): 42.

48. Roger Montgomery, Comment on "Fear and the House-as-Haven in the Lower Class," *Journal of the American Institute of Planners* 32, no. 1 (1966): 31–37.

49. Ibid.

50. Mary Comerio, "Pruitt-Igoe and Other Stories," *Journal of Architectural Education* 34, no. 4 (1981): 26–31.

51. Gordon, *Mapping Decline,* 53–57, 168, 219.

52. Bristol, "The Pruitt-Igoe Myth," 163–71.

Myth #2: Modernist Architecture Failed Public Housing

1. On the phrase "warehousing the poor," see David Fleming, *City of Rhetoric: Revitalizing the Public Sphere in Metropolitan America* (Albany: State University of New York Press, 2009), 154 and chap. 6. In 1990, the chair of the Chicago Housing Authority (CHA) described its projects as "little more than warehouses for the poor"; see *New York Times,* 17 April 1990. On the general public's ambivalence toward housing the poor, see Lawrence J. Vale, *From the Puritans to the Projects: Public Housing and Public Neighbors* (Cambridge, MA: Harvard University Press, 2000).

2. The idea that architecture and planning determine outcomes in housing projects is implied in major works on the history of housing. See, for example, Richard Plunz, *A History of Housing in New York City: Dwelling Type and Social Change in the American Metropolis* (New York: Columbia University Press, 1990); Peter G. Rowe, *Modernity and Housing* (Cambridge, MA: MIT Press, 1993), 218–21. For other critics of architectural modernism, see Charles Jencks, *The Language of Post-Modern Architecture* (New York: Rizzoli, 1977). For a review of the literature on modernist architects as planners, see Nicholas Dagen Bloom, "Architects, Architecture, and Planning," *Journal of Planning History* 7, no. 1 (2008): 72–79.

3. Catherine Bauer, "The Dreary Deadlock of Public Housing," originally published 1957, repr. in *Federal Housing Policy and Programs: Past and Present,* ed. J. Paul Mitchell (New Brunswick, NJ: Center for Urban Policy Research, 1985); Jane Jacobs, *The Death and Life of Great American Cities* (1961; repr., New York: Vintage Books Edition, 1992); Oscar Newman, *Defensible Space: Crime Prevention through Urban Design* (New York: Macmillan, 1972); Oscar Newman, *Community of Interest* (Garden City, NY: Anchor Press, 1980); Tom Wolfe, *From Bauhaus to Our House* (New York: Farrar, Straus and Giroux, 1981).

4. Mary Comerio and Katharine Bristol were the first to make this argument; see Mary C. Comerio, "Pruitt-Igoe and Other Stories," *Journal of Architectural Education* 34, no. 4 (January 1981): 25–31; Katharine G. Bristol, "The Pruitt-Igoe Myth," *Journal of Architectural Education* 44, no. 3 (May 1991): 163–71. See also Alexander Garvin, *The American City: What*

Works, What Doesn't (New York: McGraw-Hill, 1996), 168–70. Garvin writes: "It is wrong to blame the failure of public housing on inadequate design or quality of construction. . . . The real explanation for the failure of specific public-housing projects involves fiscal policies, tenant selection procedures, maintenance practices, and project management."

5. Nicholas Dagen Bloom, *Public Housing That Worked: New York in the Twentieth Century* (Philadelphia: University of Pennsylvania Press, 2008).

6. This chapter draws heavily from the author's work *Blueprint for Disaster: The Unraveling of Chicago Public Housing* (Chicago: University of Chicago Press, 2009).

7. Martin Meyerson and Edward C. Banfield, *Politics, Planning, and the Public Interest: The Case of Public Housing in Chicago* (Glencoe, IL: The Free Press, 1955); Arnold R. Hirsch, *Making the Second Ghetto: Race and Housing in Chicago, 1940–1960* (1983; repr., Chicago: University of Chicago Press, 1998).

8. Alexander Polikoff, *Waiting for Gautreaux* (Evanston, IL: Northwestern University Press, 2006).

9. *Chicago Tribune*, 30 November 1986; Alex Kotlowitz, *There Are No Children Here* (New York: Doubleday, 1991). For other stories of growing up in public housing, see LeAlan Jones and Lloyd Newman, with David Isay, *Our America: Life and Death on the South Side of Chicago* (New York: Scribner, 1997).

10. The Reagan administration had come close to talking over the CHA in both 1982 and 1987, following scathing reports of mismanagement, but HUD ultimately balked at the challenges involved.

11. Lawrence J. Vale, *Purging the Poorest: Public Housing and the Design Politics of Twice-Cleared Communities* (Chicago: University of Chicago Press, 2013); Janet Smith, "The Chicago Housing Authority's Plan for Transformation," in *Where Are Poor People to Live? Transforming Public Housing Communities,* ed. Larry Bennett, Janet L. Smith, and Patricia A. Wright (Armonk, NY: M. E. Sharpe, 2006), 93–124.

12. CHA, *Plan for Transformation,* 6 January 2000; Susan J. Popkin, Michael J. Rich, Leah Hendey, Chris Hayes, and Joe Parilla, *Public Housing Transformation and Crime: Making the Case for Responsible Relocation* (Washington, DC: Urban Institute, 2012).

13. Mark L. Joseph, Robert J. Chaskin, and Henry S. Webber, "The Theoretical Basis for Addressing Poverty through Mixed-Income Development," *Urban Affairs Review* 42, no. 3 (2007): 369–409.

14. CHA Executive Secretary Elizabeth Wood to Alderman George D. Kells, 21 September 1945, City Council file, CHA Subject files, CHA archives. (Note: The CHA maintains control over its historical records, and they are available only through FOIA requests. Photocopies of the documents cited in this article are in the author's possession.)

15. "Experiment in Multi-Story Housing," *The Journal of Housing*, October 1951, 367–69; Julian Whittlesley, "New Dimensions in Housing Design," *Progressive Architecture*, April 1951, 57–68.

16. Public Housing Administration (PHA), "Low-Rent Public Housing: Planning, Design, and Construction for Economy," December 1950. Four years earlier, federal housing officials issued a 294-page publication entitled *Public Housing Design: A Review of Experience in Low-Rent Housing;* it makes only the barest mention of elevator buildings (see p. 100). In a separate federal study, *Livability Problems of 1,000 Families* (PHA, 1945), public housing residents *did* express a preference for one- or two-story structures rather than apartments in multistory buildings. The files of federal officials at this time rarely discussed high-rise design and instead displayed an obsession with costs. For example, see "Address by John Taylor Egan, Commissioner,

Public Housing Administration, at the 17th Annual Conference of the National Association of Housing Officials, Detroit, MI, October 16–19, 1950," box 10, Miscellaneous Records of the Liaison Division, Record Group 196, National Archives II.

17. PHA, "Low-Rent Public Housing"; Catherine Bauer to Gilbert Rodier, 7 February 1952, box 4, outgoing correspondence, Catherine Bauer Wurster Papers, University of California, Berkeley.

18. Elizabeth Wood, "The Case for the Low Apartment," *Architectural Forum*, January 1952, 102.

19. Douglas Haskell, "The Case for the High Apartment," *Architectural Forum*, January 1952, 103–6.

20. *Chicago Sun-Times*, 4 September 1957; *Daily News* (Chicago), 8 March 1958; *Chicago Tribune*, 31 October 1958; telephone interview with Henry F. Leweling (former CHA planner), 13 August 1998, notes in author's possession.

21. Comparing public housing total development costs with suburban housing costs was somewhat misleading, however. Public housing had to absorb greater site costs associated with slum clearance.

22. D. Bradford Hunt, *Blueprint for Disaster: The Unraveling of Chicago Public Housing* (Chicago: University of Chicago Press, 2009), chap. 5.

23. For an example of environmental determinism, see CHA, "Children's Cities" (pamphlet), 1945.

24. CHA, *Monthly Report*, April 1955, available at the Chicago Public Library; CHA to Mayor Richard J. Daley, 19 July 1957, in Mayor's folder, CHA Subject files, CHA archives; CHA, *Official Minutes*, 6 December 1957, CHA files, CHA archives.

25. CHA, *Annual Statistical Reports*, 1951–1960, available at the Chicago Public Library. The CHA's files are shockingly silent on the shift to larger apartments. Basic planning decisions were driven largely by crude, macrolevel understandings of housing need rather than targeted market surveys. Moreover, the decision to program for large families appears driven more by waiting lists than community planning. By the mid-1950s, the CHA was having trouble finding tenants for its small apartments, while its waiting list for large ones soared. In one three-month period in 1957, the CHA reported that fourteen hundred families rejected offers of two-bedroom units at various projects (though the CHA specified neither which projects were rejected by applicants nor the race of the applicants who rejected them). See *Chicago Tribune*, 14 January 1958.

26. Youth density is nearly absent from the literature on planning and public housing. For early hints at the problem, see Anthony F. C. Wallace, "Housing and Social Structure: A Preliminary Survey," reproduced by the Philadelphia Housing Association, 1952, 89; Richard S. Scobie, *Problem Tenants in Public Housing: Who, Where, and Why Are They?* (New York: Praeger Publishers, 1975), 63; Clare Cooper Marcus and Robin C. Moore, "Children and Their Environments: A Review of Research," *Journal of Architectural Education* 29, no. 4 (April 1976): 22–25. Extensive research in the 1970s asked how children adapted to high-rise buildings and public project grounds, especially in Great Britain and Canada. See E. W. Cooney, "High Flats in Local Authority Housing in England and Wales since 1945," in *Multi-Storey Living, the British Working Class Experience*, ed. Anthony Sutcliffe (London: Croom Helm, 1974), 161; City of Vancouver, *Housing Families at High Densities* (Vancouver, BC: Vancouver Planning Department, 1978), 11, 17, 26; Pearl Jephcott, *Homes in High Flats* (Edinburgh: Oliver & Boyd, 1971), 65–67; Alice Coleman, *Utopia on Trial: Vision and Reality in Planned Housing* (London: Hilary Shipman, 1985), 180. Coleman recommends that "there should not

be more than one child under 15 per six adults aged 20 or more in a block of flats." This translates to a youth density of roughly 0.3.

27. U.S. Bureau of the Census, *U.S. Census of Population and Housing: 1960,* Final Report PHC(1)-26, Census Tracts for Chicago, IL, Standard Metropolitan Statistical Area, table P-1.

28. CHA, *Annual Statistical Reports,* 1964–1965, Chicago Public Library. In standard deviation terms, youth-adult ratios in Chicago census tracts containing mostly public housing were 1.9 to 6.3 standard deviations away from the mean in 1960, showing the "off-the-charts" nature of the CHA's youth demographics. The standard deviation calculation uses a definition of youth as 18 or under, due to limitations in census data (at the tract level). See *U.S. Census of Population and Housing: 1960,* Final Report PHC(1)-26, Census Tracts for Chicago, IL, Standard Metropolitan Statistical Area, table P-1. See also Hunt, *Blueprint for Disaster,* chap. 6.

29. CHA, *Annual Statistical Reports,* 1965–1975, Chicago Public Library.

30. *Chicago Defender,* 30 November 1963, 14 December 1963, 15 January 1964, 22 January 1964, 28 January 1964, 4 February 1964, 25 February 1964, 9 March 1964, 31 March 1964, 2 May 1964, and 30 May 1964; *Chicago Tribune,* 27 February 1964.

31. For more on collective efficacy, see the work of Robert Sampson, especially *Great American City: Chicago and the Enduring Neighborhood Effect* (Chicago: University of Chicago Press, 2012). Note that even in Sampson's work, youth densities are either unexamined or taken as a given.

32. *Daily News* (Chicago), 25 April 1959; Mary Wirth, "Interview—Mr. Joe Ford, Supervisor, Robert Taylor Park, Chicago Park District," 18 February 1965, in Mary Bolton Wirth Papers, University of Chicago Special Collections; Alvin Rose to C. L. Farris, 9 December 1960, "Authorities—Miscellaneous" folder, CHA Subject files, CHA archives; *Chicago Defender,* 14 May 1963, 14 December 1963, 6 January 1964, 13 March 1965; *Chicago Tribune,* 9 September 1963, 9 September 1965; Gus Master to William Bergeron, 8 June 1967, CHA Development files, IL 2–37, CHA archives. See also, William Mullen, "The Road to Hell," *Chicago Tribune Magazine,* 31 March 1985.

33. Hunt, *Blueprint for Disaster,* chap. 6.

34. CHA, *Annual Statistical Reports,* 1965–1980, Chicago Public Library; Robert Schafer, *Operating Subsidies for Public Housing: A Critical Appraisal of the Formula Approach* (Boston: Citizens Housing and Planning Association of Metropolitan Boston, 1975).

35. Rhonda Y. Williams, *The Politics of Public Housing: Black Women's Struggles against Urban Inequality* (New York: Oxford University Press, 2004); Roberta Feldman and Susan Stall, *The Dignity of Resistance* (New York: Cambridge University Press, 2004); Sudhir Alladi Venkatesh, *American Project: The Rise and Fall of a Modern Ghetto* (Cambridge, MA: Harvard University Press, 2000); Sudhir Alladi Venkatesh, *Gang Leader for a Day: A Rogue Sociologist Takes to the Streets* (New York: Penguin, 2008); Doreen Ambrose-Van Lee, *Diary of a MidWestern Getto Gurl* (Baltimore: PublishAmerica, 2007).

36. William Moore, Jr., *The Vertical Ghetto: Everyday Life in an Urban Project* (New York: Random House 1969), xv; New York City Housing Authority (NYCHA), "Project Data, Characteristics of Tenants as of January 1, 1968," in NYCHA Archives, LaGuardia Community College. NYCHA figures are for all federal projects, including senior projects, but they were a small fraction of the NYCHA inventory in 1968.

37. U.S. Department of Housing and Urban Development (HUD), *1968 HUD Statistical Yearbook* (Washington, DC: U.S. Government Printing Office, 1969), 269.

38. C. Peter Rydell, *Factors Affecting Maintenance and Operating Costs in Federal Public Housing Projects,* Report R-634-NYC (New York: The Rand Institute, 1970); Frank de Leeuw,

"Operating Costs in Public Housing: A Financial Crisis" (Washington, DC: Urban Institute, 1970).

39. Generally, the criminology literature makes a strong link between declining numbers of youth and reductions in crime. See Alfred Blumstein and Joel Wallman, *The Crime Drop in America* (New York: Cambridge University Press, 2000). However, a sociology dissertation using NYCHA crime data found a strong link between concentrated poverty and crime but did not find a link between youth density and crime. See Tamara Dumanovsky, "Crime in Poor Places: Examining the Neighborhood Context of New York City's Public Housing Projects" (PhD diss., New York University, 1999).

40. Jane Jacobs, *The Death and Life of Great American Cities;* Newman, *Defensible Space.* Jacobs intuitively understood youth density as a planning issue, noting on p. 82 that "planners do not seem to realize how high a ratio of adults is needed to rear children at incidental play. . . . Only people rear children and assimilate them into civilized society."

Myth #3: Public Housing Breeds Crime

1. Howard Husock, *America's Trillion-Dollar Housing Mistake: The Failure of American Housing Policy* (Chicago: Ivan R. Dee, 2003), 1.

2. Wendell E. Pritchett, *Brownsville, Brooklyn: Blacks, Jews, and the Changing Face of the Ghetto* (Chicago: University of Chicago Press, 2002), 152; Garth Davies, *Crime, Neighborhood, and Public Housing* (New York: LFB Scholarly Pub., 2006), 7.

3. Hanna Rosin, "American Murder Mystery," in *Best American Crime Reporting 2009,* ed. Jeffrey Toobin, Otto Penzler, and Thomas H. Cook (New York: Ecco, 2009).

4. Fritz Umbach, *The Last Neighborhood Cops: The Rise and Fall of Community Policing in New York Public Housing* (Newark, NJ: Rutgers University Press, 2011), chap. 1.

5. Brill and Associates, "Victimization, Fear of Crime, and Altered Behavior: A Profile of the Crime Problem in Capper Dwellings" (Washington, DC: U.S. Department of Housing and Urban Development, 1977); Brill and Associates, "Victimization, Fear of Crime, and Altered Behavior: A Profile of the Crime Problem in Murphy Homes, Baltimore, Maryland" (Washington, DC: U.S. Department of Housing and Urban Development, 1977); Brill and Associates, "Victimization, Fear of Crime, and Altered Behavior: A Profile of the Crime Problem in Four Housing Projects in Boston" (Washington, DC: U.S. Department of Housing and Urban Development, 1975); Brill and Associates, "Victimization, Fear of Crime, and Altered Behavior: A Profile of the Crime Problem in William Nickerson Gardens, Los Angeles, California" (Washington, DC: U.S. Department of Housing and Urban Development, 1976); Brill and Associates, "Victimization, Fear of Crime, and Altered Behavior: A Profile of the Crime Problem in Scott/Carver Homes, Dade County, Florida" (Washington, DC: U.S. Department of Housing and Urban Development, 1977); Harold R. Holzman, Karl Roger Kudrick, and Kenneth P. Voytek, "Measuring Crime in Public Housing: Methodological Issues and Research Strategies," *Journal of Quantitative Criminology* 14, no. 4 (1998): 331; Oscar Newman, *Defensible Space: Crime Prevention through Urban Design* (New York: Collier Books, 1973).

6. Minorities and the poor disproportionately live in public housing developments (PHDs); surveys consistently identify these groups as more likely to be victimized. Victim data found at http://www.bjs.gov/index.cfm?ty=pbdetail&iid=4494; current resident data found at http://portal.hud.gov/hudportal/HUD?src=/program_offices/public_indian_housing/systems/pic/50058/rcr; Dennis W. Roncek, Ralph Bell, and Jeffrey Francik, "Housing Projects and Crime: Testing a Proximity Hypothesis," *Social Problems* 29, no. 2 (1982); John E. Farley, "Has Public

Housing Gotten a Bum Rap?," *Environment and Behavior* 14, no. 4 (1982); Arnold R. Hirsch, *Making the Second Ghetto: Race and Housing in Chicago, 1940–1960* (1983; repr., Chicago: University of Chicago Press, 1998).

7. Crime mapping, obviously, neither requires GIS nor commenced with its arrival; however, the labor such mapping required before GIS did discourage researchers. See Keith Hayword, "Five Spaces of Cultural Criminology," *The British Journal of Criminology* 52, no. 3 (2012). For GIS limitations, see Jeffrey Fagan et al., "Crime in Public Housing: Clarifying Research Issues," *National Institute of Justice Journal*, no. 235 (1998): 4.

8. For periodization in public housing, see Edward G. Goetz, *New Deal Ruins: Race, Economic Justice, and Public Housing Policy* (Ithaca, NY: Cornell University Press, 2013), chap. 1. For the phrase "severe distress," see Lawrence Vale, "Beyond the Problem Projects Paradigm: Defining and Revitalizing 'Severely Distressed' Public Housing," *Housing Policy Debate* 4, no. 2 (1993).

9. For Pruitt–Igoe crime, see Lee Rainwater, *Behind Ghetto Walls: Black Families in a Federal Slum* (Chicago: Aldine Publishing Company, 1970), 16, 35, 239–40. See also Jay MacLeod, *Ain't No Makin' It: Leveled Aspirations in a Low-Income Neighborhood* (Boulder, CO: Westview Press, 1987); John Herbers, "The Case History of a Housing Failure," *New York Times*, 2 November 1970. For progressive scholars' intentions and impact, see Roger Montgomery, "Review Symposium: *Behind Ghetto Walls: Black Families in a Federal Slum*," *Urban Affairs Review* 7, no. 109 (1971); Alice O'Connor, *Poverty Knowledge: Social Science, Social Policy, and the Poor in Twentieth-Century U.S. History* (Princeton, NJ: Princeton University Press, 2001), 201. For Pruitt–Igoe as stand-in, see Robin D. G. Kelley, *Yo' Mama's Disfunktional!: Fighting the Culture Wars in Urban America* (Boston: Beacon Press, 1997), 19.

10. Oscar Newman, Defensible Space: Crime Prevention Through Urban Design (New York, NY; Macmillan Press, 1972). Katharine G. Bristol, "The Pruitt-Igoe Myth," *Journal of Architectural Education* 44, no. 3 (May 1991).

11. Umbach, *The Last Neighborhood Cops.*

12. Newman, *Defensible Space;* Joy Ruth Knoblauch, "Going Soft: Architecture and the Human Sciences in Search of New Institutional Forms (1963–1974)" (PhD diss., Princeton University, 2012), chap. 3; Jack Rosenthal, "Housing Study: High Rise = High Crime," *New York Times*, 26 October 1972.

13. Newman, *Defensible Space,* 25.

14. Knoblauch, "Going Soft," 124.

15. D. Bradford Hunt, *Blueprint for Disaster: The Unraveling of Chicago Public Housing* (Chicago: University of Chicago Press, 2009).

16. Knoblauch, "Going Soft," 124–25 and 114; Hunt, *Blueprint for Disaster,* 155.

17. Umbach, *The Last Neighborhood Cops,* 137–46.

18. Ibid. For more recent analysis of screening's impact on safety, see Larry Buron et al., "Interim Assessment of the HOPE VI Program Cross-Site Report" (Bethesda, MD: Abt Associates, 2003). For eviction, see Justin Ready, Lorraine Green Mazerolle, and Elyse Revere, "Getting Evicted from Public Housing: An Analysis of the Factors Influencing Eviction Decisions in Six Public Housing Sites," *Crime Prevention Studies* 9 (1998).

19. W. Victor Rouse, *Crime in Public Housing: A Review of Major Issues and Selected Crime Reduction Strategies,* vol. 1, *A Report* (Washington, DC: Department of Housing and Urban Development, 1978), 75.

20. 45 percent of tenants surveyed by HUD researchers at Baltimore's Murphy Homes believed that tenant selection was a "serious," "fairly serious," or "very serious" cause of crime;

only 11.8 percent identified "environmental improvements" as potentially useful. See Brill and Associates, "Victimization: Murphy Homes, Baltimore," 43–44. For activism, see for example, Umbach, *The Last Neighborhood Cops*, 127. For long-term tenants' perceptions of tenants arriving after loosened screening, see Rhonda Y. Williams, *The Politics of Public Housing: Black Women's Struggles against Urban Inequality* (New York: Oxford University Press, 2004), 132.

21. Tamara Dumanovsky, "Crime in Poor Places: Examining the Neighborhood Context of New York City's Public Housing Projects" (PhD diss., New York University, 1999), 90–115.

22. Harold R. Holzman, Tarl Roger Kudrick, and Kenneth P. Voytek, "Revisiting the Relationship between Crime and Architectural Design: An Analysis of Data from HUD's 1994 Survey of Public Housing Residents," *Cityscape* 2, no. 1 (February 1996): 107–26.

23. For Newman's later work, see Rouse, *Crime in Public Housing*, vol. 1; and Oscar Newman, *Housing Design and the Control of Behavior* (New York: Doubleday, 1980). Newman later (and controversially) argued for quotas on welfare recipients and braided together socioeconomic factors and architectural details as drivers of PHD failure. See Oscar Newman, *Community of Interest* (Garden City, NY: Anchor Press/Doubleday, 1980).

24. James Q. Wilson & George L. Kelling, "Broken Windows," *Atlantic Monthly*, March 1982; Robert J. Sampson, *Great American City: Chicago and the Enduring Neighborhood Effect* (Chicago: University of Chicago Press, 2011).

25. For the failure of these efforts, see Anthony Pate, *An Evaluation of the Urban Initiatives Anti-Crime Program: Final Report* (Washington, DC: Department of Housing and Urban Development, 1984), chap. 2.

26. Harold R. Holzman, Tarl Roger Kudrick, and Kenneth P. Voytek, "Revisiting the Relationship between Crime and Architectural Design: An Analysis of Data from HUD's 1994 Survey of Public Housing Residents," *Cityscape* 2, no. 1 (February 1996): 107–26.

27. Brill and Associates, "Victimization: Capper Dwellings"; Brill and Associates, "Victimization: Murphy Homes, Baltimore."

28. Ibid.

29. Marcus Felson, *Crime and Everyday Life* (Thousand Oaks, CA: Sage Publications, 2002).

30. Langley C. Keyes, *Strategies and Saints: Fighting Drugs in Subsidized Housing* (Washington, DC: Urban Institute, 1992), 28.

31. Farley, "Has Public Housing Gotten a Bum Rap?," 463–64.

32. Roncek, Bell, and Francik, "Housing Projects and Crime," 163.

33. Goetz, *New Deal Ruins*, chap. 1. For social isolation, see William J. Wilson, *The Truly Disadvantaged: The Inner City, the Underclass, and Public Policy* (Chicago: University of Chicago Press, 1987).

34. Davies, *Crime, Neighborhood, and Public Housing*, 24.

35. Dumanovsky, "Crime in Poor Places," 45.

36. Goetz, *New Deal Ruins*, chap. 2.

37. For the timing of crack's arrival and a brief sketch of the consequences, see Roland Fryer et al., "Measuring the Impact of Crack Cocaine" (NBER Working Paper No. 11318, National Bureau of Economic Research, Cambridge, MA, May 2005).

38. Ann Mariano, "Kemp Wants Report on Drugs in Housing Projects," *Washington Post*, 11 March 1989. Holzman, Kudrick, and Voytek, "Revisiting the Relationship between Crime and Architectural Design."

39. The Police Foundation's study of Denver and New Orleans public housing drug crime is discussed in Terence Dunworth and Aaron Saiger, *Drugs and Crime in Public Housing: A Three-City Analysis* (Washington, DC: U.S. Department of Justice, Office of Justice Programs,

National Institute of Justice, 1994), 9–10. Dunworth and Saiger's study itself addresses Los Angeles, Phoenix, and DC.

40. Alex Kotlowitz, "Urban Trauma: Day-to-Day Violence Takes a Terrible Toll on Inner-City Youth," *Wall Street Journal*, 27 October 1987; Mercer L. Sullivan, *"Getting Paid": Youth Crime and Work in the Inner City* (Ithaca, NY: Cornell University Press, 1989).

41. Dunworth and Saiger, *Drugs and Crime in Public Housing*, 33.

42. Katherine Beckett and Theodore Sasson, *The Politics of Injustice: Crime and Punishment in America*, 2nd ed. (Thousand Oaks, CA: Sage Publications, 2004); Jonathan Simon, *Governing through Crime: How the War on Crime Transformed American Democracy and Created a Culture of Fear* (New York: Oxford University Press, 2007); Michelle Alexander, *The New Jim Crow: Mass Incarceration in the Age of Colorblindness* (New York: New Press, 2010).

43. Dunworth and Saiger, *Drugs and Crime in Public Housing*, 30.

44. Adele V. Harrell and Caterina Gouvis Roman, *Predicting Neighborhood Risk of Crime* (Washington, DC: Urban Institute, 1994).

45. Dunworth and Saiger, *Drugs and Crime in Public Housing*, 30–38.

46. Harold R. Holzman, Robert A. Hyatt, and Joseph M. Dempster, "Patterns of Aggravated Assault in Public Housing: Mapping the Nexus of Offense, Place, Gender, and Race," *Violence against Women* 7, no. 6 (June 2001): 662–84.

47. Ibid., 677.

48. Harold R. Holzman, Robert Hyatt, and Tarl Roger Kudrick, "Measuring Crime in and around Public Housing," in *Geographic Information Systems and Crime Analysis*, ed. Fahui Wang (London: Idea Group Publishing, 2005), 324.

49. Ibid., 325.

50. For the persistence and power of such fears, see George Galster, Kathryn Pettit, Anna M. Santiago, and Peter Tatian, "The Impact of Supportive Housing on Neighborhood Crime Rates," *Journal of Urban Affairs* 24, no. 3 (2002): 289–315.

51. Portions of this discussion taken from Davies, *Crime, Neighborhood, and Public Housing*, 24–25, 99, 156; Umbach, *The Last Neighborhood Cops*, 144.

52. Steven R. Holloway and Thomas L. McNulty, "Contingent Urban Geographies of Violent Crime: Racial Segregation and the Impact of Public Housing in Atlanta," *Urban Geography* 24, no. 3 (2003): 194–96.

53. Elizabeth Griffiths and George Tita, "Homicide in and around Public Housing: Is Public Housing a Hotbed, a Magnet, or a Generator of Violence for the Surrounding Community?," *Social Problems*, 56, no. 3 (2009): 489–90.

54. Umbach, *The Last Neighborhood Cops*, 2; Pritchett, *Brownsville, Brooklyn*, 89.

55. This paragraph draws heavily upon Umbach, *The Last Neighborhood Cops*, 144–47.

56. Goetz, *New Deal Ruins*, 42.

57. Dinzey-Flores's research focuses on the intersection of public perceptions of project crime and public policy and so, understandably, her analysis of crime data from Puerto Rico is not a full-fledged statistical study. Notably, her analysis lacks the precision more recent GIS-enabled studies might insist upon. Zaire Dinzey-Flores, "Criminalizing Communities of Poor, Dark Women in the Caribbean: The Fight against Crime through Puerto Rico's Public Housing," *Crime Prevention and Community Safety* 13, no. 1 (2011): 53–73. Dinzey-Flores subjects her data to a more sophisticated analysis in "Fighting Crime, Constructing Segregation: Crime, Housing Policy, and the Social Brands of Puerto Rican Neighborhoods" (PhD Diss., University of Michigan, 2005).

58. Edward G. Goetz, "Where Have All the Towers Gone?: The Dismantling of Public Housing in U.S. Cities," *Journal of Urban Affairs* 33, no. 3 (2011).

59. Studies suggest about 30 percent of former site residents will move back to the redesigned sites; of those who do not return, about 50 percent will move to other public housing, 30 percent will find housing with Section 8 vouchers, and 20 percent will either be evicted for lease violations or relocated without assistance. Xavier de Souza Briggs, Susan J. Popkin, and John M. Goering, *Moving to Opportunity: The Story of an American Experiment to Fight Ghetto Poverty* (New York: Oxford University Press, 2010), 42–43. Goetz, *New Deal Ruins*, 42.

60. Susan J. Popkin, "Beyond Crime Prevention: How the Transformation of Public Housing Has Changed the Policy Equation," *Criminology & Public Policy* 3, no. 1 (2003): 47; Susan J. Popkin et al., *The Hidden War: Crime and the Tragedy of Public Housing in Chicago* (New Brunswick, NJ: Rutgers University Press, 2000); Goetz, *New Deal Ruins*, 70–72.

61. Briggs, Popkin, and Goering, *Moving to Opportunity*, 47–50.

62. Ibid., 90–91, 107–8.

63. Xavier de Souza Briggs and Peter Dreier, "Memphis Murder Mystery? No, Just Mistaken Identity," *Shelterforce*, 22 July 2008. Available at http://www.shelterforce.org/article/1043/memphis_murder_mystery_no_just_mistaken_identity/ (accessed 23 August 2014).

64. Ibid.

65. Susan J. Popkin, Michael J. Rich, Leah Hendey, Chris Hayes, and Joe Parilla, *Public Housing Transformation and Crime: Making the Case for Responsible Relocation* (Washington, DC: Urban Institute, 2012), 5.

66. Umbach, *The Last Neighborhood Cops*, chap. 1.

67. Michel Foucault, *L'Archéologie du savoir* (Paris: Gallimard, 1969), trans. A. M. Sheridan Smith, *The Archaeology of Knowledge* (London: Routledge, 2002).

Myth #4: High-Rise Public Housing Is Unmanageable

1. Height data and national percentage from http://www.nyc.gov/html/nycha/downloads/pdf/hra-advisors-nycha-rehabilitation-replacement-20130816.pdf, 8.

2. New York City Housing Authority (NYCHA), "Guide to Housing Developments," 1965 Box 100A3, Folder 7, New York City Housing Authority Records, LaGuardia Wagner Archives, LaGuardia Community College (NYCHAR); Nicholas Dagen Bloom, *Public Housing That Worked: New York in the Twentieth Century* (Philadelphia: University of Pennsylvania, 2008).

3. Current data retrieved from http://www.nyc.gov/html/nycha/downloads/pdf/superstorm-sandy-testimony-1-17-13.pdf.

4. NYCHA Fact Sheet (2012). Current NYCHA data retrieved from http://www.nyc.gov/html/nycha/html/about/factsheet.shtml.

5. Woodrow Wilson percentages derived from communication with Bradford Hunt and NYCHA Research division.

6. NYHCA, "Information on Kingsborough Houses," November 1941, LaGuardia Papers, Roll 93. New York City Municipal Archives.

7. Chairman Philip Cruise to the *New York Daily News*, 27 February 1957, Box 65C8, Folder 6, NYCHAR, 4–9.

8. G. Swope to Fiorello LaGuardia, 15 January 1942, Box 54E6, Folder 9, NYCHAR.

9. Cyril Grossman interview by Marcia Robertson, 1 August 1990, NYCHA Oral History Project, Box 1, NYCHAR, 28, 45.

10. Edmond Butler to Fiorello LaGuardia, 1 June 1945, LaGuardia Papers, Roll 92A, MA.

11. Cruise to the *New York Daily News*, 4–9; Robert Stern, *New York, 1960* (New York: Monacelli Press, 1995), 901; "Fort Greene Houses Will Be Renovated," *New York Times*, 10 February 1957, 71.

12. Ira Robbins, "Address to the ADA," 13 September 1958, Box 59D3, Folder 5, NYCHAR, 2, 4; Charles Grutzner, "Tiled Lobbies, Closet Doors Give a Modern Look to Public Housing, "*New York Times*, 1 January 1957, 25; NYCHA, "Planning and Designing Public Housing Projects," ca. 1956, Box 72D4, Folder 3, NYCHAR.

13. Charles Preusse, "Organization and Management of NYCHA," September 1957, Box 100A2, NYCHAR, 5.

14. Samuel Zipp, *Manhattan Projects: The Rise and Fall of Urban Renewal in Cold War New York* (Oxford: Oxford University Press, 2010).

15. Grutzner, "Tiled Lobbies, Closet Doors," 25.

16. Elizabeth Lyman, "Tenant Response to a Series of Family Life Discussion Groups in a Public Housing Project," Community Service Society, December 1966, Box 61C5, Folder 8.

17. Raymond Henson interview by Marcia Robertson, 6 August 1990, NYCHA Oral History Project, Box 1, NYCHAR, 14–15.

18. NYCHA, "Project Survey Report, Van Dyke Houses," 1970–1972, Box 66E8, Folder 13, NYCHAR; Ida Posner, Brownsville Public Housing Coordinating Council, Memo, Box 65C2, Folder 6, NYCHAR.

19. NYCHA, "Requests from the Brownsville Community Council, Inc.," 7 April 1970, NYCHA Internal Document, Box 65C2, Folder 6, NYCHAR.

20. NYCHA, "New York City Housing Authority Interim Report on Progress of Target Projects Program," 14 January 1976, Box 76A5, Folder 1, NYCHAR.

21. NYCHA "Broken Glass Replacement," 1973, unpublished memo retrieved from Box 65C1, Folder 1. NYCHAR; NYCHA, "Janitorial Standards," 30 January 1974, unpublished memo retrieved from Box 90C4, Folder 14. NYCHAR.

22. Sidney Schackman to Joseph Christian, 22 November 1974, Box 88B2, Folder 6, NYCHAR; NYCHA Response to HUD Review of Operations, October 1973, Box 62A4, Folder 3, NYCHAR.

23. Bloom, *Public Housing That Worked*, 45–76, 128–51, 245–68.

24. Max Siegel, "Elevator Crisis in City Projects," *New York Times*, 4 July 1973, 1.

25. City of New York, "Mayor's Office of Operations (2012)," CPR: Agency Performing Reports, retrieved from http://www.nyc.gov/html/ops/cpr/html/themes/community.shtml; chart reproduced from http://www.nyc.gov/html/ops/downloads/pdf/mmr0912/nycha.pdf; Bloom, *Public Housing That Worked*, 245–68.

26. Department of Housing Preservation and Development, *Housing New York City 2008*, retrieved from http://www.nyc.gov/html/hpd/html/pr/HVS-Archive.shtml, 476, 489; Department of Housing Preservation and Development, *Housing New York City 2008*, retrieved from http://www.nyc.gov/html/hpd/downloads/pdf/HVS-report-2011.pdf, 447.

27. Office of the Comptroller, *How New York Lives: An Analysis of the City's Housing Maintenance Conditions*, September 2014, retrieved at http://comptroller.nyc.gov/wp-content/uploads/documents/How_New_York_Lives.pdf, 7, 11.

28. City of New York, "Mayor's Office of Operations (2012)."

29. Bloom, *Public Housing That Worked*, 181–200, 220–40, 245–68.

30. http://www.nyc.gov/html/nycha/downloads/pdf/hra-advisors-nycha-rehabilitation-replacement-20130816.pdf; http://www.nyc.gov/html/nycha/html/news/maintenance-and-repair-backlog-action-plan.shtml, retrieved 4 December 2013.

31. http://www.nyc.gov/html/ops/downloads/pdf/mmr0912/nycha.pdf. See also http://www
.nyc.gov/html/nycha/downloads/pdf/hra-advisors-nycha-rehabilitation-replacement-20130816.
pdf; http://www.nyc.gov/html/nycha/html/news/nycha-releases-economic-impact-reports.shtml,
retrieved 4 December 2013.

32. http://www.nyc.gov/html/nycha/downloads/pdf/j11apre.pdf.

33. George L. Kelling and Catherine M. Coles, *Fixing Broken Windows: Restoring Order
and Reducing Crime in Our Communities* (New York: Free Press, 1998).

34. Senator Robert Wagner as quoted in Marcuse, *Public Housing in New York City: History of a Program* (Unfinished manuscript, NYCHA Central Office, 1989), 49.

35. Bloom, *Public Housing That Worked*, 77.

36. Ibid., 82.

37. Ibid., 168–98.

38. D. Bradford Hunt, *Blueprint for Disaster: The Unraveling of Chicago Public Housing*
(Chicago: University of Chicago Press, 2009).

39. Bloom, *Public Housing That Worked*, 168–80.

40. NYCHA Annual Report, "A Clearer Focus," 1962, Box 100A2, Folder 12. NYCHAR.

41. NYCHA Tenant Data, 1 January 1974; data retrieved from NYCHA data books in Peter
Marcuse Personal Data Collection, Columbia University.

42. Hunt, *Blueprint for Disaster*, 185.

43. http://www.nyc.gov/html/nycha/html/news/nycha-releases-economic-impact-reports.
shtml, retrieved 4 December 2013.

44. NYCHA Fact Sheet (2012); current NYCHA data retrieved from http://www.nyc.gov
/html/nycha/html/about/factsheet.shtml; http://www.nyc.gov/html/ops/downloads/pdf/mmr0912
/nycha.pdf; City of New York, "Mayor's Office of Operations (2012)."

45. New York City Center for Economic Opportunity, *The CEO Poverty Measure* (New
York: NYC Center for Economic Opportunity, August 2008), retrieved from http://media.npr.
org/assets/news/2009/09/09/poverty_report.pdf, 3; http://www.nyc.gov/html/nycha/downloads
/pdf/hra-advisors-nycha-economic-impact-20130912.pdf, retrieved 4 December 2013, 8.

46. See various NYCHA performance records on the newly created site, NYCHA Metrics,
https://eapps.nycha.info/NychaMetrics.

Myth #5: Public Housing Ended in Failure during the 1970s

Acronyms for Endnotes

GWR: George W. Romney

HUD: U.S. Department of Housing and Urban Development

LBJ: Lyndon B. Johnson

RA: George Romney Archives at the University of Michigan at Ann Arbor

RN: Richard Nixon

1. See, for example, Alexander von Hoffman, who writes that "when Richard Nixon placed
a moratorium on federal funding for all housing programs in 1973, many felt that it seemed
appropriate to end a bad program" (public housing) as symbolized by the demolition of Pruitt-
Igoe; Von Hoffman, "High Ambitions: The Past and Future of American Low-Income Housing Policy," *Housing Policy Debate* 7, no. 3 (1996): 436. David J. Erickson comments that "in
subsidized housing programs, *both* liberals and conservatives were frustrated with the programs
of the Great Society, and while they disagreed on emphasis, both looked to change the deliv-

ery of social services," and, similarly, that "block grants and 'federalism' are associated with Nixon and conservative politics, but liberals who were disillusioned by earlier urban-renewal programs and perceived HUD inefficiencies were eager to move in this direction as well"; Erickson, "Community Capitalism: How Housing Advocates, the Private Sector, and Government Forged a New Low-Income Housing Policy, 1968–1996," *Journal of Policy History* 18, no. 2 (2006): 170, 175. Louis Winnick argues that public housing had little to do with the moratorium, however, noting that the difficulties with the Sections 235 and 236 programs "prompted" the moratorium; see Winnick, "The Triumph of Housing Allowance Programs: How a Fundamental Policy Conflict Was Resolved," *Cityscape* 1, no. 3 (September 1995): 98.

2. I refer to these policies as "conservative" in that both reducing federal government allocations and shifting power to lower levels of the federal system are hallmark policies of modern American conservatives. Richard P. Nathan, who was assistant director of the Office of Management and Budget between 1969 and 1972, argues that Nixon was a liberal on domestic affairs; Nixon's programs, he argues, expanded federal programs, and his moratorium followed four years of unprecedented investment in expanded housing programs under the 1968 Housing Act. Indeed, new entitlement programs such as the Family Assistance Plan (FAP), had they been implemented, would likely have had a larger impact on reducing American inequality than programs like public housing, which were limited to those who were able to secure a unit. See Richard P. Nathan, "A Retrospective on Richard M. Nixon's Domestic Policies," *Presidential Studies Quarterly* 26, no. 1 (Winter 1996): 155–64.

3. Others have argued that the moratorium's primary cause was not the failure of public housing. Alexander von Hoffman points out that "the real reason [for the moratorium] . . . was fiscal: the Office of Management and Budget . . . had imposed the freeze"; see "History Lessons for Today's Housing Policy: The Politics of Low-Income Housing," *Housing Policy Debate* 22, no. 3 (June 2012): 361. Critics like Von Hoffman underplay the Nixon administration's ideological effort to refashion the federal government away from programs and toward income support and decentralization, which was at the heart of the motivations behind the moratorium. It should also be noted that the controversy over housing integration, which is not discussed here, might have played a role in the decision to enforce a moratorium, as discussed in Chris Bonastia, "Why Did Affirmative Action in Housing Fail during the Nixon Era?: Exploring the 'Institutional Homes' of Social Policies," *Social Problems* 47, no. 4 (November 2000): 523–24.

4. In Los Angeles, the "red scare" empowered conservatives to completely shut down the city's public housing program. Don Parson, *Making a Better World: Public Housing, the Red Scare, and the Direction of Modern Los Angeles* (Minneapolis: University of Minnesota Press, 2005).

5. Eugene Meehan argues that, from the 1950s on, the program suffered from "a mindless concentration on dollar costs that disregarded the long-run cost of poor quality"; see Eugene J. Meehan, *The Quality of Federal Policymaking: Programmed Failure in Public Housing* (Columbia: University of Missouri Press. 1979), 31, 72, 90; Albert M. Cole, chair of the President's Advisory Committee on Government Housing Policies and Programs, *Recommendations: A Report to the President of the United States* (Washington, DC: Government Printing Office, December 1953); Dwight D. Eisenhower, "The President's News Conference," 13 May 1959; Dwight D. Eisenhower, "Veto of the Second Housing and Urban Renewal Bill," 4 September 1959. These presidential addresses, along with thousands of others, are available through the University of California, Santa Barbara's *American Presidency Project*, compiled and frequently updated by John Woolley and Gerhard Peters, and available online at http://www.presidency.ucsb.edu/.

6. In Detroit, just 758 public housing units had been built between 1956 and 1968, but urban renewal policies had resulted in the clearance of eight thousand existing low-income units during the same period; Roger Biles, "Public Housing and the Postwar Urban Renaissance, 1949–1973," in *From Tenements to the Taylor Homes: In Search of an Urban Housing Policy in Twentieth-Century America*, ed. John F. Bauman, Roger Biles, and Kristin M. Szylvian (University Park: Pennsylvania State University Press, 2000), 149; National Advisory Commission on Civil Disorders, *Report of the National Advisory Commission on Civil Disorders* (Washington, DC: U.S. Government Printing Office, March 1968). For contemporary critiques of urban renewal policy, see Herbert J. Gans, *The Urban Villagers: Group and Class in the Life of Italian-Americans* (New York: The Free Press, 1962); Martin Anderson, *The Federal Bulldozer* (Cambridge, MA: MIT Press, 1964); James Q. Wilson, ed., *Urban Renewal: The Record and the Controversy* (Cambridge, MA: MIT Press, 1966); and Jane Jacobs, *The Death and Life of Great American Cities* (New York: Random House, 1961).

7. Leonard Freedman, *Public Housing: The Politics of Poverty* (New York: Holt, Rinehart and Winston, 1969), 84; Joseph Heathcott, "The Strange Career of Public Housing," *Journal of the American Planning Association* 78, no. 4 (Autumn 2012): 360–75.

8. LBJ, "Special Message to the Congress on Housing and Community Development," 27 January 1964; LBJ, "The President's News Conference," 21 May 1966.

9. Republicans and business interests supported Section 23 "in exchange" for the creation of the Rent Supplement program; neither program was funded comprehensively until 1968; Meehan, *The Quality of Federal Policymaking*, 46; Charles J. Orlebeke, "The Evolution of Low-Income Housing Policy, 1949 to 1999," *Housing Policy Debate* 11, no. 2 (2000): 489–520.

10. Kerner Commission, *Report of the National Commission on Civil Disorders*, Washington, DC: Government Printing Office, 1968; Douglas Commission, *Building the American City: Report of the National Commission on Urban Problems*, Washington, DC: Government Printing Office, 1969; and Kaiser Committee, *A Decent Home: The Report of the President's Committee on Urban Housing*, Washington, DC: Government Printing Office, 1969; Rick Perlstein, *Nixonland: The Rise of a President and the Fracturing of America* (New York: Scribner, 2008), 240; Biles, "Public Housing," 157–59; *A Decent Home: The Report of the President's Committee on Urban Housing* (Washington, DC: U.S. Government Printing Office, December 1968); Dona Cooper Hamilton and Charles V. Hamilton, *The Dual Agenda: Race and Social Welfare Policies of Civil Rights Organizations* (New York: Columbia University Press, 1997); *A "Freedom Budget" for All Americans: Budgeting Our Resources, 1966–1975, to Achieve "Freedom from Want,"* (New York: A. Philip Randolph Institute, 1966).

11. See Alexander von Hoffman, "Calling upon the Genius of Private Enterprise: The Housing and Urban Development Act of 1968 and the Liberal Turn to Public-Private Partnerships," *Studies in American Political Development* 27, no. 2 (October 2013): 165–94.

12. For example, in New York City, the John Lindsay administration was pursuing a policy of scattered-site public housing and major renewal projects that included public housing, moderate-income Section 236 apartments, and middle-income state-subsidized units; Freedman, *Public Housing*, 122–23.

13. HUD, *Housing in the Seventies* (Washington, DC: U.S. Government Printing Office, October 1973).

14. Perlstein, *Nixonland*, 359, 393; Glenn Fowler, "No Further Cuts Seen for Housing," *New York Times*, 11 November 1968, 79.

15. This is not to say the Romney would have found himself at home in the Johnson administration. In a speech at Harvard in 1972, he suggested that "the moral basis of reward for

contribution is not unsound or indefensible," and that government subsidies should reflect "compassion and humanitarianism," rather than be provided by right. Memo for GWR, "America's Value Crisis: Egalitarianism or Reward for Contribution—Suggested Background Material for January 28th Harvard Business School Address," 17 January 1972, Memoranda folder (miscellaneous), box 8-P, RA.

16. "Staff Paper: 'The Model Cities Program,'" 5 February 1969, Model Cities folder, box 9-P, RA; Floyd Hyde, memo to GWR, "The Basic Mission, Goals and Objectives of the Model Cities Program and Its Future," 8 February 1969, Model Cities folder, box 9-P, RA; GWR, "Notes on Task Force on Model Cities Report," "Cabinet Meeting, 5 March 1970: Camp David—Model Cities" folder, box 9-P, RA.

17. The task force's members included James Q. Wilson and public-choice economist James M. Buchanan; Edward C. Banfield, *Report of the Task Force on Model Cities* (Washington, DC: U.S. Government Printing Office, December 1969), ii, 1, 13.

18. Charles Orlebeke, interview with the author, 30 March 2012; Ehrlichman Briefing, Draft #5, 26 January 1970, "Budget Misc., Jan. 1970" folder, box 2-P, RA.

19. "Special" revenue sharing became the Community Development Block Grant (CDBG) program. Bruce A. Wallin, *From Revenue Sharing to Deficit Sharing: General Revenue Sharing and Cities* (Washington, DC: Georgetown University Press, 1998); Warren Weaver, Jr., "G.O.P. Asks Halt in Aid to States," *New York Times*, 11 April 1967, 22; "Nixon's Response to Inquiries about His Economic Policies," *New York Times*, 27 October 1968, F14; Concept Paper on Special Revenue Sharing, 2nd Draft, 1 February 1971, "President and Ehrlichman 1971" folder, box 13-P, RA; White House, "Highlights of Revenue Sharing," 10 February 1970, Revenue Sharing folder, box 11-P, RA.

20. Richard P. Nathan, *The Plot That Failed: Nixon and the Administrative Presidency* (New York: John Wiley and Sons, 1975), 19.

21. GWR, memo to RN, 5 January 1971, "1972 Budget Appeals" folder, box 2-P, RA; Richard P. Nathan, letter to GWR, "HUD Restructured Programs Proposals," 6 January 1971, "1972 Budget Appeals" folder, box 2-P, RA; Floyd Hyde, draft memo (administratively confidential), 29 December 1970, Office of Management and Budget (OMB) folder, box 10-P, RA.

22. Conversation between RN, Vice President Agnew, GWR, et al. Cabinet Room, 23 March 1971, 3:00 P.M., Conversation No. 51–2, Nixon White House Tapes, Nixon Presidential Library. Available online at http://www.nixonlibrary.gov/forresearchers/find/tapes/finding_aids/tapesubjectlogs/710323ca051.pdf (accessed 18 December 2012).

23. This bill did not include "special" revenue sharing (CDBG), which Nixon would continue to promote.

24. HUD, "HUD Fiscal Year 1971 Budget Shows Commitment to Housing" (press release), 2 February 1970, "Budget FY '71" folder, box 1-P, RA.

25. The administration ordered a halt on government construction—with an exception made for housing—in August 1969. Floyd Hyde, memo to GWR, "Need for Additional NDP Funding," 12 March 1969, "Budget Material 1969" folder, box 1-P, RA; Nathaniel Eiseman (director, Office of Budget) memo, "Bureau Mark on HUD Budget Review," 13 March 1969, "Budget Material 1969" folder, box 1-P, RA; Robert P. Mayo, memos to GWR, 28 July 1969 and 20 September 1969, "Budget Material 1969" folder, box 1-P, RA.

26. GWR, memo to Conference on HUD Appropriations, "Conference on HUD Appropriations, FY 1970," 13 November 1969, "Budget Appeal 1969" folder, box 1-P, RA; "Urban Renewal Appeal—Affirmative Presentation," 23 December 1969, "Budget Appeal 1969" folder, box 1-P, RA; GWR, draft memo to Caspar W. Weinberger, Deputy Director, OMB, 12 December

1970, OMB folder, box 10-P, RA; GWR, memo to RN, "The Domestic Crisis and the Budget," 12 June 1970, "President and Ehrlichman 1970" folder, box 13-P, RA.

27. GWR, memo to Conference on HUD Appropriations; "Urban Renewal Appeal—Affirmative Presentation," 23 December 1969.

28. Floyd Hyde, draft memo, 29 December 1970.

29. Charles J. Orlebeke, memo to GWR, 14 October 1970, "Budget Misc., 1970" folder, box 2-P, RA; U.S. Conference of Mayors, Committee on Community Development, draft statement, 20 January 1971, "President and Ehrlichman 1971" folder, box 13-P, RA.

30. Richard C. Van Dusen, memo to GWR, 15 August 1969, Memoranda folder, box 8-P, RA; GWR, comment on "Inflation," 13 January 1970, "Cabinet Meeting 1/13/70" folder, box 2-P, RA; Richard C. Van Dusen, memo to John Ehrlichman and George Schultz, "Independent Offices and Department of HUD 1971 Appropriation Bill (H.R. 17548)," 10 July 1970, "Budget Misc., 1970" folder, box 2-P, RA.

31. In this context, Nixon was referring to replacing the Food Stamp program with FAP. RN, "The President's Remarks at the Opening Session of the Conference," White House Conference on Food, Nutrition, and Health, 2 December 1969.

32. The policy was crafted by Daniel Patrick Moynihan; it was never passed thanks to Democratic opposition to work requirements, but the Earned Income Tax Credit of 1975 and Welfare Reform of 1996 can be seen as its descendants. See Brian Steensland, *The Failed Welfare Revolution: America's Struggle over Guaranteed Income Policy* (Princeton, NJ: Princeton University Press, 2007); "41 Years Ago—RN Unveils Family Assistance Plan," *Nixon Foundation*, 10 August 2010. Available online at http://blog.nixonfoundation.org/2010/08/41-years-ago-rn-unveils-family-assistance-plan/ (accessed 15 April 2012).

33. HUD, "Bureau Hearings on FY 1971 Estimates, Housing Assistance Programs" (notes on comments made during meeting), 7 October 1969, "Budget FY '71" folder, box 1-P, RA.

34. Rent subsidies were first provided for elderly public housing residents in the 1961 Housing Act. The rent limit was later raised to 30 percent. Judith Feins et al., *Revised Methods of Providing Federal Funds for Public Housing Agencies: Final Report*, Office of Policy Development and Research, HUD (Washington, DC: U.S. Government Printing Office, June 1994); Richard C. Van Dusen, "The State of the Department," November/December 1972, "HUD's Future" folder, box 7-P, RA.

35. HUD, "Bureau Hearings on FY 1971 Estimates."

36. Eugene A. Gulledge, memo to GWR, 26 August 1970, "Domestic Council—8/27/70—San Clemente" folder, box 6-P, RA; GWR, draft memo to George P. Schultz, 22 September 1970, "Budget Misc., 1970" folder, box 2-P, RA.

37. Irving Welfeld, "Toward a New Federal Housing Policy," *The Public Interest*, no. 19 (Spring 1970).

38. See *Observations on Housing Allowances and the Experimental Housing Allowance Program*, Report to the Congress by the Comptroller General of the United States (Washington, DC: U.S. Government Printing Office, March 1974); Eugene A. Gulledge, memo to GWR, "Experiments in Housing Allowances," 17 August 1971, Memoranda folder, box 8-P, RA; Louis Winnick, "The Triumph of Housing Allowance Programs: How a Fundamental Policy Conflict Was Resolved," *Cityscape* 1, no. 3 (September 1995): 95–121.

39. Romney's initial recommendations, which were brought up to OMB in late 1970, were not immediately considered because of a lack of "enough information about the new approach to make decisions." GWR, draft memo to George P. Schultz, 1970; Lester P. Condon (Assis-

tant Secretary for Administration), memo to GWR, "Cabinet Meeting on the Budget," 4 November 1970, "Budget Misc., 1970" folder, box 2-P, RA.

40. GWR, memo to RN, 30 December 1970, "Budget Misc., 1970" folder, box 2-P, RA.

41. GWR, memo to Caspar W. Weinberger, 17 December 1971, "Budget Material Dec. '71" folder, box 2-P, RA.

42. Caspar Weinberger, memos to GWR, 21 July 1972 and 6 October 1972, OMB folder, box 10-P, RA.

43. GWR, memo to Caspar Weinberger, 28 September 1972, "Budget Misc., Sept.-Dec., 1972" folder, box 2-P, RA.

44. Conversation between RN, John Ehrlichman, and H. R. Haldeman, Camp David, 16 November 1972, 2:23 P.M., Conversation No. 225–39, Nixon White House Tapes, Nixon Presidential Library. Available online at http://www.nixonlibrary.gov/forresearchers/find/tapes/finding_aids/tapesubjectlogs/cdhw225.pdf (accessed 18 December 2012).

45. Albert J. Kliman (Deputy Director, Office of Budget [HUD]), memo to GWR, "Highlights of OMB Hearing on HPMC Programs," 13 October 1972, OMB folder, box 10-P, RA; Albert J. Kliman, memo, "Highlights of OMB Hearing on HPMC Programs, 12 October 1972," 17 October 2012, OMB folder, box 10-P, RA; Albert J. Kliman, memo, "Highlights of OMB Hearing on Housing Management Programs, 16 October 1972," 18 October 1972, OMB folder, box 10-P, RA.

46. Neither Nixon nor his assistant Haldeman understood the situation with Sections 235 and 236; in mentioning the possibility of problems at HUD, Nixon asked, "What is the housing scandal?" and Haldeman responded, "I don't know—there's something all screwed up." Nixon nonetheless remained committed to the reduction in the HUD budget. Conversation between RN and H. R. Haldeman, Camp David, 21 July 1972, 3:05–3:57 P.M., Conversation No. 197–17, Nixon White House Tapes, Nixon Presidential Library. Available online at http://www.nixonlibrary.gov/forresearchers/find/tapes/tape197/197-017.mp3 (accessed 12 November 2013). It should be noted that, in describing the motivations for changing national housing policy, Orlebeke ("The Evolution of Low-Income Housing Policy," 2000), focuses extensively on the anti-housing production findings of the 1971 *President's Third Annual Report on National Housing Goals.* Yet, this report's conclusions do not seem to have influenced the thinking of Nixon himself, whose statements recorded on tape revolve mostly around reducing HUD's budget, not making programs more effective through policy reforms, as the report advocates.

47. Orlebeke, "The Evolution of Low-Income Housing Policy," 499; Von Hoffman, "History Lessons for Today's Housing Policy," 355.

48. Nathan, *The Plot That Failed,* vii, 6.

49. In 1970, President Nixon reportedly asked Romney to serve as ambassador to India, a position the secretary declined. Record of HUD News Conference with GWR, 25 November 1970, "President 12/2/70" folder, box 14-P, RA; GWR, letter to RN, 10 August 1972, "Meeting with the President—8/12/72" folder, box 13-P, RA.

50. GWR, letter to RN, 9 November 1972, "Ehrlichman and President 1972" folder, box 14-P, RA. Conversation between RN and John Ehrlichman, White House Oval Office, 11 August 1972, 11:09–11:11 A.M., Conversation No. 767–18, Nixon White House Tapes, Nixon Presidential Library. Available online at http://www.nixonlibrary.gov/forresearchers/find/tapes/tape767/767-018.mp3 (accessed 18 December 2012). Conversation between RN, GWR, et al. White House Oval Office, 11 August 1972, 11:15 A.M.–12:22 P.M., Conversation No. 767–20, Nixon White

House Tapes, Nixon Presidential Library. Available online at http://www.nixonlibrary.gov/forresearchers/find/tapes/tape767/767-020a.mp3 (accessed 18 December 2012).

51. The moratorium could be imposed by OMB because housing funds were "discretionary," not "mandatory," meaning that the executive branch was ignoring Congress's appropriations and would simply not spend them. It effectively terminated the Model Cities and Urban Renewal programs. Caspar Weinberger, memo to GWR, 15 May 1972, OMB folder, box 10-P, RA.

52. "Notes from Meeting with OMB Staff regarding 1974 Budget Decisions," OMB folder, box 10-P, RA.

53. Letter to Caspar Weinberger, no date indicated, but c. late 1972, OMB folder, box 10-P, RA; GWR, "Notes for Speech in Roosevelt Room," 22 December 1972, OMB folder, box 10-P, RA.

54. Memo from GWR to RN, 28 December 1972, "Budget Misc., Sept.-Dec., 1972" folder, box 2-P, RA; Orlebeke also points out that Romney "strenuously opposed" the moratorium.

55. Romney avoided the term "moratorium" and instead referred to it as a "temporary hold"; Orlebeke, "The Evolution of Low-Income Housing Policy," 501; Michael C. Jensen, "Romney Discloses Halt in Subsidies for New Housing," *New York Times*, 9 January 1973.

56. Certainly part of the explanation for the decision to reduce funding to affordable housing programs was racial tension, a matter that Nixon had exploited with his stand against policies such as "forced" busing or housing integration. Though it may be argued that Nixon's criticisms of the housing programs reflected his view that they benefited urban minorities and therefore were unappealing to his white, suburban base, his public statements on housing did not refer to race explicitly. RN, "State of the Union Message to the Congress on Community Development," 8 March 1973; Christopher Bonastia, *Knocking on the Door: The Federal Government's Attempt to Desegregate the Suburbs* (Princeton, NJ: Princeton University Press. 2008).

57. Eugene L. Meyer, "Plan to Halt Housing Aid Draws Fire," *New York Times*, 31 December 1972, A1; James M. Naughton, "M'Govern Warns of One-Man Rule; Exhorts Liberals," *New York Times*, 22 January 1973, 1; James M. Naughton, "Congress Regards Cuts as Threat to Its Power," *New York Times*, 30 January 1973, 22.

58. ICF, Incorporated, *Impact of Federal Housing Programs on Community Development*, part of the National Housing Policy Review study series prepared for HUD (Washington, DC: ICF, 1973), chap. 3; HUD, *Housing in the Seventies*; R. Allen Hays, *The Federal Government and Urban Housing*, 3rd ed. (Albany: State University of New York Press, 2012), 123–38; James T. Lynn, Prepared Testimony and Questioning, *Hearings before the Subcommittee on Housing of the Committee on Banking and Currency*, House of Representatives, Ninety-Third Congress, First Session, October 9, 10, 11, 12, 16, and 17, 1973.

59. RN, "Special Message to the Congress Proposing Legislation and Outlying Administration Actions to Deal with Federal Housing Policy," 19 September 1973.

60. Robert C. Weaver, Prepared Testimony and Questioning, *Hearings before the Subcommittee on Housing of the Committee on Banking and Currency, House of Representatives*, Ninety-Third Congress, First Session, October 9, 10, 11, 12, 16, and 17, 1973.

61. The vote was 76 to 11. "Senate Passes Housing Bill without a Major Change," *Congressional Quarterly Weekly Report*, 16 March 1974, 691–95; Paul Delaney, "Major Housing Bill to Aid Poor Approved by Senate Committee," *New York Times*, 11 February 1974, 38.

62. "House Passes Omnibus Housing Bill, 321–25," *Congressional Quarterly Weekly Report*, 29 June 1974, 1702–6; Hays, *The Federal Government and Urban Housing*, 146–49; Edward C. Burks, "Ford Signs Bill to Aid Housing," *New York Times*, 23 August 1974, 9; Del-

aney, "Major Housing Bill," 38; Richard L. Madden, "Housing Measure Is Voted by House," *New York Times*, 21 June 1974, 77.

63. If anything, the end to direct federal subsidies for new low-income housing construction came in 1983, when the Reagan administration enforced a switch from the Section 8 New Construction program to the existing housing voucher program. Edward C. Burks, "3 Biggest Cities Would Gain under New Housing Bill," *New York Times*, 20 August 1974, 20.

64. Meehan, *The Quality of Federal Policymaking*, 66.

65. Public housing production expanded again in the late 1970s and then was cut off during the 1980s under the Reagan administration. See Lawrence J. Vale and Yonah Freemark, "From Public Housing to Public-Private Housing," *Journal of the American Planning Association* 78, no. 4 (Autumn 2012): 379–402.

Myth #6: Mixed-Income Redevelopment Is the Only Way to Fix Failed Public Housing

1. Henry Cisneros and Lora Engdahl, eds., *From Despair to Hope: Hope VI and the New Promise of Public Housing in America's Cities* (Washington, DC: Brookings Institution Press, 2009); Lawrence J. Vale and Yonah Freemark, "From Public Housing to Public-Private Housing: 75 Years of Social Experimentation," *Journal of the American Planning Association* 78, 4 (2012): 379–402. In addition to the United States, many countries have attempted to replace public housing or social housing with various forms of "mixed communities." For discussion of examples from the UK, France, the Netherlands, Canada, and Australia, see Gary Bridge, Tim Butler, and Loretta Lees, *Mixed Communities: Gentrification by Stealth?* (Bristol, UK: The Policy Press, 2012).

2. Parts of this chapter draw upon and extend arguments first made in Lawrence J. Vale, "Comment on Mark L. Joseph's 'Is Mixed-Income Development an Antidote to Urban Poverty?'" *Housing Policy Debate* 17, no 2 (2006): 259–69. For an overview and compendium of recent research, see "Mixed Messages on Mixed Incomes," *Cityscape* 15, no. 2 (2013): 1–221. The website of the National Initiative on Mixed-Income Communities also provides an extensive bibliography and other resources, available at http://nimc.case.edu.

3. Peter Marcuse, "Interpreting 'Public Housing' History," *Journal of Architectural and Planning Research* 12, no. 3 (1995): 240–58.

4. Lawrence J. Vale, *From the Puritans to the Projects: Public Housing and Public Neighbors* (Cambridge, MA: Harvard University Press, 2000).

5. William J. Wilson, *The Truly Disadvantaged: The Inner City, the Underclass, and Public Policy* (Chicago: University of Chicago Press, 1987); Vale and Freemark, "From Public Housing to Public-Private Housing."

6. Cisneros and Engdahl, *From Despair to Hope;* Sean Zielenbach, Richard Voith, and Michael Mariano, "Estimating the Local Economic Impacts of HOPE VI," *Housing Policy Debate* 20, no. 3 (2010): 485–522.

7. Edward Goetz, *Clearing the Way: Deconcentrating the Poor in Urban America* (Washington, DC: Urban Institute Press, 2003); Janet L. Smith, "Mixed-Income Communities: Designing Out Poverty or Pushing Out the Poor?" in *Where Are Poor People to Live?: Transforming Public Housing Communities*, ed. Larry Bennett, Janet L. Smith, and Patricia A. Wright (Armonk, NY: M.E. Sharpe, 2006); Loretta Lees, "Gentrification and Social Mixing: Towards an Inclusive Urban Renaissance?," *Urban Studies* 45, no.12 (2008): 2449–70; Bridge, Butler, and Lees, *Mixed Communities.*

8. Susan J. Popkin, Larry F. Buron, Diane K. Levy, and Mary K. Cunningham, "The Gautreaux Legacy: What Might Mixed-Income and Dispersal Strategies Mean for the Poorest Public Housing Tenants?," *Housing Policy Debate* 11, no. 4 (2000): 911–42; Susan J. Popkin, Bruce Katz, Mary Cunningham, Karen D. Brown, Jeremy Gustafson, and Margery Turner, *A Decade of HOPE VI: Research Findings and Policy Challenges* (Washington, DC: The Urban Institute and the Brookings Institution, 2004); Mindy Turbov and Valerie Piper, *HOPE VI and Mixed-Finance Redevelopments: A Catalyst for Neighborhood Renewal* (Washington, DC: Brookings Institution, 2005); Rachel Garshick Kleit, "HOPE VI New Communities: Neighborhood Relationships in Mixed-Income Housing," *Environment and Planning A* 37 (2005): 1413–41; Mark Joseph and Robert Chaskin, "Living in a Mixed-Income Development: Resident Perceptions of the Benefits and Disadvantages of Two Developments in Chicago," *Urban Studies* 47, no. 11 (2010): 2347–66.

9. Mark L. Joseph, "Is Mixed-Income Development an Antidote to Urban Poverty?" *Housing Policy Debate* 17, no. 2 (2006): 209–34; Diane K. Levy, Zach McDade, and Kassie Bertumen, "Mixed-Income Living: Anticipated and Realized Benefits for Low-Income Households," *Cityscape* 15, no. 2 (2013): 15–28.

10. George C. Galster, Jason C. Booza, and Jackie M. Cutsinger, "Income Diversity within Neighborhoods and Very Low-Income Families," *Cityscape* 10, no. 2 (2008): 257–300. The efforts in the United Kingdom to sell off much of the Council Housing stock after 1980 have also sometimes led to communities that are both mixed tenure and mixed income, though often with little social mixing; Reinout Kleinhans and Maarten Van Ham, "Lessons Learned from the Largest Tenure-Mix Operation in the World: Right to Buy in the United Kingdom," *Cityscape* 15, no. 2: 101–17; Ade Kearns, Martin McKee, Elena Sautkina, George Weeks, and Lyndal Bond, "Mixed-Tenure Orthodoxy: Practitioner Reflections on Policy Effects," *Cityscape* 15, no. 2 (2013): 47–67.

11. Wilson, *The Truly Disadvantaged,*1987; Douglas Massey and Nancy Denton, *American Apartheid: Segregation and the Making of the Underclass* (Cambridge MA: Harvard University Press, 1993).

12. Laura Tach, "More than Bricks and Mortar: Neighborhood Frames, Social Processes, and the Mixed-Income Redevelopment of a Public Housing Project," *City & Community* 8, no. 3 (2009): 273–303.

13. Ibid.

14. Alex Schwartz and Kian Tajbakhsh, "Mixed-Income Housing: Unanswered Questions," *Cityscape* 3, no. 2 (1997): 71–92; Paul C. Brophy and Rhonda N. Smith, "Mixed-Income Housing: Factors for Success," *Cityscape* 3, no. 2 (1997): 3–31.

15. Alex F. Schwartz, *Housing Policy in the United States*, 2nd ed. (New York: Routledge, 2010), 307.

16. James E. Rosenbaum, Linda K. Stroh, and Cathy Flynn, "Lake Parc Place: A Study of Mixed-Income Housing," *Housing Policy Debate* 9, no. 4 (1998): 703–40; Lawrence J. Vale, "Comment on James E. Rosenbaum, Linda K. Stroh, and Cathy A. Flynn's 'Lake Parc Place: A Study of Mixed-Income Housing,'" *Housing Policy Debate* 9, no. 4 (1998): 749–56; Chicago Housing Authority, Tenant Selection Plan, Lake Parc Place, Screening and Selection Policy, 2009, available at http://www.thecha.org/filebin/pdf/MixedIncome/LPP_TSP.pdf (accessed August 11, 2012).

17. Ellen Pader and Myrna Breitbart, "Transforming Public Housing: Conflicting Visions for Harbor Point," *Places* 8, no.4 (1993): 34–41; Jane Roessner, *A Decent Place to Live: From Columbia Point to Harbor Point* (Boston: Northeastern University Press, 2000).

18. National Initiative on Mixed-Income Communities, "Social Dynamics of Mixed-Income Communities," State of the Field Scan #1, November 2013, available at http://blog.case .edu/nimc/2013/11/07/State_of_the_Field_Scan_1_National_Initiative_on_Mixed-Income _Communities.pdf.

19. Erin M. Graves, "Mixed Outcome Developments," *Journal of the American Planning Association* 77, no. 2 (2011): 143–53. See also, Robert C. Ellickson, "The False Promise of the Mixed-Income Housing Project," *UCLA Law Review* 57 (2010): 983–1021. For discussion of the limits of income-mixing in Europe and skepticism about the power of "neighborhood effects" on low-income residents, see David Manley, Maarten van Ham, and Joe Doherty, "Social Mixing as a Cure for Negative Neighbourhood Effects: Evidence Based Policy or Urban Myth?," Discussion Paper No. 5634, April 2011, available at http://ftp.iza.org/dp5634.pdf.

20. Joseph, "Is Mixed-Income Development an Antidote to Urban Poverty?"; Mark L. Joseph, Robert J. Chaskin and Henry S. Webber, "The Theoretical Basis for Addressing Poverty Through Mixed-Income Development," *Urban Affairs Review* 42, no. 3 (2007): 369–409; Joseph and Chaskin, "Living in a Mixed-Income Development."

21. Joseph, "Is Mixed-Income Development an Antidote to Urban Poverty?," 222.

22. Vale, "Comment on Joseph."

23. See Joseph, "Is Mixed-Income Development an Antidote to Urban Poverty?," and Joseph, Chaskin and Webber for a full list of community studies that they assessed.

24. James DeFillipis and Jim Fraser, "Why Do We Want Mixed-Income Housing and Neighborhoods? In *Critical Urban Studies: New Directions,* ed. Jonathan S. Davies and David L. Imbroscio (Albany, NY: State University of New York Press, 2010): 136, 138.

25. Dispersal policies have most famously included the Gautreaux public housing antidiscrimination program in Chicago and the Moving to Opportunity demonstration. See Alexander Polikoff, *Waiting for Gautreaux: A Story of Segregation, Housing and the Black Ghetto* (Evanston, IL: Northwestern University Press, 2006); and Xavier de Souza Briggs, Susan J. Popkin, and John Goering, *Moving to Opportunity: The Story of an American Experiment to Fight Ghetto Poverty* (New York: Oxford University Press, 2010).

26. Edward G. Goetz and Karen Chapple, "Dispersal as Anti-Poverty Policy," in Davies and Imbroscio's *Critical Urban Studies,* 153–57, 159; Susan Clampet-Lundquist, "HOPE VI Relocation: Moving to New Neighborhoods and Building New Ties," *Housing Policy Debate* 15, no. 2: 415–48; Karen Gibson, "The Relocation of the Columbia Villa Community: Views from Residents," *Journal of Planning Education and Research* 27, no. 1 (2007): 5–19; Edward G. Goetz, "Better Neighborhoods, Better Outcomes? Explaining Relocation Outcomes in HOPE VI," *Cityscape* 12, no. 1 (2010): 5–31; Victoria Basolo, "Examining Mobility Outcomes in the Housing Choice Voucher Program: Neighborhood Poverty, Employment, and Public School Quality," *Cityscape* 15, no. 2 (2013): 135–53; Kimberly Skobba and Edward G. Goetz, "Mobility Decisions of Very Low-Income Households," *Cityscape* 15, no. 2 (2013): 155–71; Rachel Garshick Kleit, "False Assumptions about Poverty Dispersal Policies," *Cityscape* 15, no. 2 (2013): 205–9.

27. Rosenbaum, Stroh, and Flynn, "Lake Parc Place"; Vale, "Comment on Rosenbaum, Stroh, and Flynn."

28. Vale, "Comment on Joseph."

29. Ibid.

30. Lawrence J. Vale and Erin M. Graves, *The Chicago Housing Authority's Plan for Transformation: What Does the Research Show So Far?* Report prepared for the MacArthur Foundation, 2010, available at http://web.mit.edu/dusp/dusp_extension_unsec/people/faculty/ljv/vale _macarthur_2010.pdf; Erin M. Graves and Lawrence J. Vale, "The Chicago Housing Authority's

Plan for Transformation: Assessing the First Ten Years," *Journal of the American Planning Association* 78, 4 (2012): 464–65.

31. For a full account of Commonwealth's redevelopment, see Lawrence J. Vale, *Reclaiming Public Housing: A Half Century of Struggle in Three Public Neighborhoods* (Cambridge, MA: Harvard University Press, 2002).

32. Lawrence J. Vale, "Public Housing Redevelopment: Seven Kinds of Success," *Housing Policy Debate* 7, 3 (1996): 491–534.

33. Joseph, "Is Mixed-Income Development an Antidote to Urban Poverty?," 220.

34. Edward G. Goetz, *New Deal Ruins: Race, Economic Justice, and Public Housing Policy* (Ithaca, NY: Cornell University Press, 2013), 185.

35. Susan J. Popkin, Mark K, Cunningham, and Martha Burt, "Public Housing and the 'Hard-to-House,'" *Housing Policy Debate* 16, no. 1 (2005): 1–24.

Myth #7: Only Immigrants Still Live in European Public Housing

1. This definition resonates with the one used by CECODHAS Housing Europe (Comité Européen de Coordination de l'Habitat Social—European Coordination Committee on Social Housing). CECODHAS researchers define public housing by affordability, the existence of administrative rules for tenant allocation, a strong link with public policies, and security of tenure. Alice Pittini and Elsa Laino, *Housing Europe Review 2012* (Brussels: CECODHAS Housing Europe, 2011), 22–23.

2. Karl Christian Führer, *Mieter, Hausbesitzer, Staat und Wohnungsmarkt* (Stuttgart: Steiner, 1995), 77–108.

3. In the 1900 *Bürgerliches Gesetzbuch* (Civil Code), apartments were tied to plots, and co-ownership in a multistory building was outlawed—a measure that was meant to diminish lawsuits between neighbors. See *Bürgerliches Gesetzbuch* (Berlin: Guttentag, 1903), §§ 93 and 94. This was only revoked by the 1951 Gesetz über das Wohneigentum und das Dauerwohnrecht [Law on Residential Ownership and Permanent Dwelling Right], *Bundesgesetzblatt* I (10 March 1951), 175.

4. Berlin data: company Infas Geodaten (2010), quoted in "Berlin bleibt die Mieter-Hauptstadt," *BZ* (Berlin), 4 July 2011, and by the Berlin government on its official website, http://www.stadtentwicklung.berlin.de/wohnen/mieterfibel/. London data (2010) by National Housing Foundation, online at http://www.housing.org.uk/news/housing_market_crisis_as_home/full_press_release_on_housing.aspx (both accessed August 2012).

5. 2007 data quoted in Michelle Norris and Nessa Winston, "Does Home Ownership Reinforce or Counterbalance Inequality?" (Dublin: University College Dublin, 2011), online at http://www.ucd.ie/appsocsc/publicationsandresearch/workingpaperseries/ (accessed August 2012).

6. Georg Wagner, *Sozialstaat gegen Wohnungsnot* (Paderborn: Schöningh, 1995), 22, 38.

7. Ibid., 2, 8–12.

8. Ibid., 8–12.

9. In Germany, this concept was brought forward by the planner Edgar Salin and the sociologist Hans Paul Bahrdt. See Edgar Salin, "Urbanität," in Deutscher Städtetag, ed., *Vorträge, Aussprachen und Ergebnisse der 11. Hauptversammlung des Deutschen Städtetages* (Augsburg: Kohlhammer, 1960); and Hans Paul Bahrdt, *Die moderne Großstadt* (Hamburg: Wegner, 1961).

10. Klaus Schroeder, *Der SED-Staat. Geschichte und Strukturen der DDR* (Munich: Bayerische Landeszentrale für politische Bildungsarbeit, 1998), 283; Joachim Palutzki, *Architektur in der DDR* (Berlin: Reimer, 2000), 113–120.

11. Jürgen Dobberke, "Märkisches Viertel, Star der Bauwochen," *Berliner Leben*, no. 9 (1966); Ingeborg Glupp, "Die Trabanten kommen" *Der Abend* (Berlin) 11 July 1966; or Alexander Wilde, *Das Märkische Viertel* (West Berlin: Nicolai, 1989), 126.

12. Hellmut Maurer, "Menschenfeindliche Gettos statt sinnvoller Ordnung," *Frankfurter Rundschau*, 20 January 1969.

13. See for example "Slums verschoben," *Der Spiegel* 22, no. 37 (9 September 1968), 138; "Es bröckelt," *Der Spiegel*, no. 6 (1969), 38–42; or Kurt Wolber, "Leben wie im Ameisenhaufen," *Stern* 23 no. 3 (19 July 1970): 62–77. For a press review, see Alexander Wilde, *Das Märkische Viertel* (West Berlin: Nicolai, 1989), 127. For a comparison between anti-urban-renewal protest in Europe and the United States, see Christopher Klemek, *The Transatlantic Collapse of Urban Renewal* (Chicago: University of Chicago Press, 2011).

14. See, for example, Eberhard Schulz, "Die Hölle ist es nicht—Plädoyer für das Märkische Viertel," *Frankfurter Allgemeine Zeitung*, 10 November 1973; Hermann Wegner, "Märkisches Viertel, August 1975—Wachsendes Heimatgefühl," *Gemeinnütziges Wohnungswesen* 28, no. 9 (1975): 412–14; Thomas Schardt, "Hochhausstadt ist besser als ihr Ruf," *Berliner Morgenpost*, 31 January 1986; "Märkisches Viertel als Vorbild," *Berliner Zeitung*, 12 May 2010.

15. The acceptance of "the slab" is, for example, evidenced by classified ads in which East Germans could legally look for apartment swaps. They are analyzed in Gerlind Staemmler, *Rekonstruktion innerstädtischer Wohngebiete in der DDR* (West Berlin: IWOS-Bericht zur Stadtforschung, 1981).

16. David Clay Large, *Berlin* (New York: Basic Books, 2000), 466.

17. Michel Hubert, *Deutschland im Wandel—Geschichte der deutschen Bevölkerung seit 1815* (Stuttgart: Steiner, 1998), 303 (East) and 325 (West).

18. pi [abbreviation], "'Züge von modernem Sklavenhandel,'" *Berliner Zeitung*, 2 November 1996; Josefine Janert, "Ethnologien untersuchen die Gettos in Berlin und die Regeln, die sie schufen," *Tagesspiegel* (Berlin), 21 February 2000.

19. For a brief overview of "Little Istanbul" in public perception, see David Clay Large, *Berlin* (New York: Basic Books, 2000), 466–69.

20. Approximately 110,000 Turks are registered in Berlin. "Jeder siebte Berliner ist ein Ausländer," *Berliner Morgenpost*, 14 September 2008.

21. Ralf Schönball, "Kreuzberg ist teurer als die City West," *Tagesspiegel* (Berlin), 28 February 2012.

22. For the corresponding law see "Gesetz zur Überführung der Wohnungsgemeinnützigkeit in den allgemeinen Wohnungsmarkt," *Bundesgesetzblatt I*, 25 July 1988, 1093, 1136.

23. Darinka Czischke and Alice Pittini, *Housing Europe 2007—Review of Social, Cooperative, and Public Housing in the 27 EU Member States* (Brussels: CECODHAS Housing Europe, 2007), 52.

24. "Ausverkauf an Großinvestoren," *Focus* (Munich) 20 October 2006. Similar numbers can be found in Dresden (48,000 flats) and many other German cities. For a critical overview of the privatization strategies, see Berliner Mieterverein [Berlin Tenants Association], ed., *Schwarzbuch Privatisierung* (Berlin: Berliner Mieterverein, 2006). See also Hans Jörg Duvigneau [former chief executive of the GSW public housing corporation], "100 Jahre Berliner

Wohnungsbau," public lecture at the Schader-Stiftung, May 2001, online at http://www.schader-stiftung.de/wohn_wandel/340.php (accessed August 2012).

25. "Ausverkauf an Großinvestoren," *Focus* (Munich), 20 October 2006.

26. On the development of public housing in Europe see Czischke and Pittini, *Housing Europe 2007,* online at http://www.bshf.org/published-information/publication.cfm?lang=00 &thePublD=CE5EBB45-15C5-F4C0-992A576CD5800BEB (accessed July 2012).

27. They have risen significantly from the symbolic levels under socialism but remained moderate in a European context.

28. The Berlin government's rent index is at €4.49 per square meter for the East Berlin slab areas in Marzahn. This amounts to €292 monthly, plus an estimated €100 for heating and utilities. For the West Märkisches Viertel, the rent index is at €6.11 per square meter, which would bring the sample flat up to €397 plus heating and utilities (2011 figures); see http://www.stadtent wicklung.berlin.de/wohnen/mietspiegel/ (accessed July 2012).

29. Data by Handwerkskammer [Chamber of Crafts] Leipzig, online at http://www.hwk -leipzig.de/3,0,3359.html (accessed August 2012).

30. Census data from 2005, Senatsverwaltung für Stadtentwicklung, *Monitoring Soziale Stadtentwicklung* (Berlin: Senatsverwaltung für Stadtentwicklung, 2006), 214, available on-line at http://www.stadtentwicklung.berlin.de/planen/basisdaten_stadtentwicklung/monitoring /de/2006/index.shtml (accessed August 2012).

31. Census data from 2004, Senatsverwaltung für Stadtentwicklung, *Monitoring Soziale Stadtentwicklung* (Berlin: Senatsverwaltung für Stadtentwicklung, 2006), available online at http://www.stadtentwicklung.berlin.de/planen/basisdaten_stadtentwicklung/monitoring /de/2006/index.shtml (accessed August 2012).

32. Census data from 2004 for "Berlin" (p. 191), for the neighborhood "Märkisches Viertel" (p. 191), and for the neighborhood "Mariannenplatz" (p. 188), Senatsverwaltung für Stadtentwicklung, *Monitoring Soziale Stadtentwicklung* (Berlin: Senatsverwaltung für Stadtentwicklung, 2006), available online at http://www.stadtentwicklung.berlin.de/planen /basisdaten_stadtentwicklung/monitoring/de/2006/index.shtml (accessed August 2008). The numbers do not include nationalized foreigners or German nationals with foreign parents.

33. Census data from 2004 for the neighborhood "Lipschitzallee," ibid., 191.

34. Census data from 2004, Senatsverwaltung für Stadtentwicklung, http://www.stadtent-wicklung.berlin.de/planen/basisdaten_stadtentwicklung/monitoring/de/2006/tabellen.shtml (accessed August 2012).

35. Census data from 2005, Statistisches Landesamt Berlin, available online at http://www .statistik-berlin.de/framesets/such.htm (accessed June 2008).

36. In 2004, Berlin's unemployment rate for non-Germans was 14.7 compared to 13.9 for Germans. This encompasses all foreigners, including specialized professionals. The disparity is more dramatic in the areas with a high percentage of former "guest workers." The Neukölln district, for example, had 20.2 percent unemployment among foreigners, compared to 16.5 percent among Germans. Census data from 2006, available at http://www.stadtentwicklung .berlin.de/planen/basisdaten_stadtentwicklung/monitoring/de/2006/tabellen.shtml (accessed July 2012).

37. Pittini and Laino, *Housing Europe Review 2012,* 23.

38. Ibid., 19. Severe housing deprivation indicators include overcrowding, lack of sanitary facilities, or structural shortcomings such as a leaking roof.

39. Ibid., 23.

40. Ibid.

41. See Vienna's official website http://www.wien.gv.at/wohnen/wienerwohnen/ (accessed July 2012).

42. Ibid., 23, 56.

43. Ibid., 64; Czischke and Pittini, *Housing Europe 2007*, 68–69.

44. Ibid., 69.

Myth #8: Public Housing Is Only for Poor People

1. Debates over precisely why public housing provision began center on these potential explanations, put forward (in order) by official retrospectives, including: Hong Kong Housing Authority, *An Illustrated Summary of 40 Years of Public Housing Development in Hong Kong, 1953–1993* (Hong Kong: Hong Kong Housing Authority, 1993); Alan Smart, *The Shek Kip Mei Myth: Squatters, Fires, and Colonial Rule in Hong Kong, 1950–1963* (Hong Kong: Hong Kong University Press, 2006), 12–17; Yue-man Yeung and David Drakakis-Smith, "Comparative Perspectives on Public Housing in Singapore and Hong Kong," *Asian Survey* 14, no. 8 (August 1974): 765–66; and Manuel Castells, Lee Goh, and Reginald Kwok, *The Shek Kip Mei Syndrome: Economic Development and Public Housing in Hong Kong and Singapore* (London: Pion Limited, 1990).

2. Quote from Richard Ronald, *The Ideology of Home Ownership: Homeowner Societies and the Role of Housing* (Basingstoke: Palgrave Macmillan, 2008), 183. Literature and debate on the developmental state abounds. For one summary, see Meredith Woo-Cumings, ed., *The Developmental State* (Ithaca, NY: Cornell University Press, 1999).

3. Castells, Goh, and Kwok, 1.

4. Press statement on New Resettlement Policy by Parliamentary Secretary to the Ministry of National Development, 6 January 1964, HDB box 1239, National Archives of Singapore (hereafter NAS).

5. ECAFE Committee on Industry and Natural Resources, Subcommittee on Housing, Building, and Planning, Ninth Session, 2–9 July 1969, HDB box 1239, NAS.

6. Letter from chief architect Teh Cheang Wan to HDB chair Lim Kim San, 23 October 1961, HDB box 1223, NAS. The original document says, "The extent and scope of aid given by the American Government to public housing authorities in America is interesting." When looking at the full context of his memo, however, it becomes clear that Teh was not only referencing public housing but broader federal housing aid to private and public programs.

7. P.D. Kulkarni, Regional Social Development Adviser, "Social Policy Implications of Urban Development and Slum Clearance," ECAFE Committee on Industry and Natural Resources, Subcommittee on Housing, Building, and Planning, Ninth Session, 2–9 July 1969.

8. Lee Sheng-Yi, *The Monetary and Banking Development of Singapore and Malaysia*, 3rd ed. (Singapore: Singapore University Press, 1990): 90–91.

9. "Cities as Modernizers," speech delivered at the inauguration of the World Assembly of Youth Asian regional seminar, 16 April 1967, reproduced in Goh Keng Swee, *The Economics of Modernization* (Singapore: Federal Publications, 1995), 16–26.

10. William S. W. Lim, "Land Acquisition for Housing with Singapore as a Case Study," in *Land for Housing the Poor*, ed. Shlomo Angel, Raymon W. Archer, Sidhijai Tanphiphat, and Emiel A. Wegelin (Singapore: Select Books, 1983), 405.

11. Goh, 16–26.

12. Lee, 90; Addendum to President's Speech, 6 May 1968, Parliamentary Debates, Republic of Singapore, Legislative Assembly Sittings, Official Report, First Session of the Second Parliament, Part I of the First Session, 6 May 1968 to 1 August 1968, vol. 27.

13. Ibid., 119; Housing and Development (Amendment) Bill, Parliamentary Debates, Republic of Singapore, Official Report, First Session of the Second Parliament, Part III, 11 June 1969 to 30 March 1970, vol. 29, 16.

14. Jennifer Robinson, "Power as Friendship: Spatiality, Femininity, and 'Noisy' Surveillance," in *Entanglements of Power: Geographies of Domination/Resistance,* ed. Joanne Sharp, Paul Routledge, Chris Philo, and Ronan Paddison (London and New York: Routledge, 2000), 73; extract from Verbatim Report of Ordinary Meeting of the City Council of Singapore held on 31 August 1956, HDB box 1100, NAS.

15. Attendance figures and costs from Public Relations and Advisory Committee report, 11 January 1961; quote from chairman's speech at opening of HDB exhibition, Microfilm 1244, NAS.

16. The Lands Department did not state what it would display. Summary of Exhibition on Low-Cost Housing by Department, Microfilm 1244, NAS.

17. Accession Nos. 91260, 91270, Photograph Collection, NAS.

18. Oral history of Alan Fook Cheong Choe, interviewed 1 August 1997 and 29 August 1997 by Ms. Cheong Eng Khim, Reel 7, NAS.

19. My italics. "Applicants for Flats: Housing Board Amends Regulations," *Eastern Sun,* 5 August 1967, Microfilm NA 563, NAS.

20. HDB memo from Estates Manager, 6 January 1965, HDB box 1225, NAS.

21. Aline Wong and Leong Wai Kum, eds., *A Woman's Place: The Story of Singaporean Women* (Singapore: The People's Action Party Women's Wing, 1993), 28.

22. Ibid., 3.

23. Ibid., 42–43.

24. Choe, Reel 8.

25. Draft paper, n.d. "Review of Progress of the Sale of Flats Scheme," HDB box 1227, NAS.

26. Secretary, HDB, "National Day Supplement," 26 April 1965, HDB box 1251, NAS.

27. *HDB Annual Report 2008/09,* "Key Statistics," 1. Available online at http://www.hdb .gov.sg/fi10/fi10221p.nsf/Attachment/AR0809/$file/index.html (accessed. 2 January 2013).

28. Stephen H. K. Yeh, "Housing Conditions and Housing Needs," in Public Housing in Singapore: A Multi-Disciplinary Study, ed. Stephen H. K. Yeh (Singapore: Singapore University Press, 1975), 45.

29. Gundy Cahyadi, Barbara Kursten, Marc Weiss, and Guang Yang, "Singapore Metropolitan Economic Strategy Report: Singapore's Economic Transformation," Prague, June 2004, 6, available online at www.globalurban.org/GUD%20Singapore%20MES%20Report.pdf (accessed 20 December 2012).

30. Data extracted from Time Series on Annual GDP at Current Market Prices, Singapore Department of Statistics, available at http://www.singstat.gov.sg/stats/themes/economy/hist /gdp2.html; World Economic Outlook Database, April 2006, International Monetary Fund, available at http://www.imf.org/external/pubs/ft/weo/2006/01/data/dbcselm.cfm?G=2001 (accessed 1 January 2013).

31. Lim Kim San, foreword to Tan Sook Yee, *Private Ownership of Public Housing in Singapore* (Singapore: Times Academic Press, 1998), xi.

32. Chua Beng-Huat, *Political Legitimacy and Housing: Stakeholding in Singapore* (London: Routledge, 1997), 124–141.

33. Chua, "Public Housing Policies Compared: US, Socialist Countries, and Singapore," paper presented at 83rd Annual Meeting of the American Sociological Association, Atlanta, GA, 24–28 August 1988, 12.

34. Belinda K. P. Yuen, Teo Ho Pin, Ooi Giok Ling, *Singapore Housing: An Annotated Bibliography* (Singapore: National University of Singapore Press, 1998), 5–6.

35. The People's Association, *The People's Association, 1960–1990: 30 Years with the People* (Kallang, Singapore: People's Association, 1990), 1–5, 22.

36. Ibid., iii, 22.

37. Manuel Castells, "The Developmental City-State in an Open World Economy: The Singapore Experience," BRIE Working Paper #31, February 1988, 39.

38. Ibid., 6.

39. Sim Loo Lee, "Planning the Built Environment for Now and the 21st Century," in *City and the State: Singapore's Built Environment Revisited*, ed. Ooi Giok Ling and Kenson Kwok (Singapore: Oxford University Press, 1997), 23.

Myth #9: Public Housing Residents Hate the Police

1. Ivy and Renee Alford, interview by author and Nicholas Alford, 15 December 2006, tape of interview in author's possession.

2. United States Commission on Civil Rights, *1961 Report, Book 5: Justice* (Washington, DC: 1961), 5–28; see also Marilynn S. Johnson, *Street Justice: A History of Police Violence in New York City* (Boston: Beacon Press, 2003), 229–34. Victor Gonzalez, interview by author, 17 September 2008, tape of interview in author's possession.

3. For NYCHA's changing architecture, see Nicholas Dagen Bloom, *Public Housing That Worked: New York in the Twentieth Century* (Philadelphia: University of Pennsylvania Press, 2008), chap. 3.

4. Lawrence Friedman, *Crime and Punishment in American History* (New York: Basic Books, 1993), 151, 358–59, 361. See also Samuel Walker, *A Critical History of Police Reform* (Lexington, MA: Lexington Books, 1977); and Eric H. Monkkonen, *Police in Urban America, 1860–1920* (Cambridge, UK: Cambridge University Press, 1981).

5. Morton Bard, "Police Management of Conflicts among People," 8 August 1970, folder 10, box 60E7, NYCHA; prepared remarks by Joseph Christian, 19 November 1973, folder 7, box 65B1, NYCHA.

6. For the percentage of black officers in 1965, see John J. Truta, "A Comprehensive Study of Recruitment of Negroes by the New York City Police Department with Other Law Enforcement Agencies" (master's thesis, Bernard M. Baruch College, 1969), 70. For the ethnicity of HAPD officers in the 1970s, see "Ethnic Survey, Housing Authority Police Department," 15 August 1974, folder 1, box 88B5, NYCHA. Black and Hispanic patrol officers represented 60.6 percent of the patrol force in 1974. For the size of the HAPD relative to other departments, see Joseph Weldon and Robert Ledee, "High-Rise Policing Techniques," ca. 1966, folder 4, box 60E7, NYCHA.

7. For comparative number of minority officers, see W. Marvin Dulaney, *Black Police in America* (Bloomington: Indiana University Press, 1996), app. B. The NYCHA population figures include what the authority estimated to be the one hundred thousand unregistered residents who double up in the same unit with the tenant(s) of record. For racial composition, see NYCHA, "Racial Distribution in Operating Project at Initial Occupancy and on December 31,

265

1960, All Programs," 18 January 1961, manuscript box IVB, NYCHA. For the size of the HAPD in 1975, see Joseph Christian to Hon. Matthew J. Troy, Jr., Chair of Finance Committee, New York City Council, 17 June 1975, folder 1, box 88B5, NYCHA.

8. Gonzalez interview.

9. Joseph Keeney, interview by author, February 2007 and July 2008, tape of interviews in author's possession.

10 Mary and Tricia Alfson, interview by author and Nicholas Alfson, 15 December 2006; Maria Vasquez, interview by author and Christian Nunez and Maria Figueroa, November 2006; Rachael Ryans, interview by author, 3 December 2006; tapes of all interviews in author's possession.

11. Judith Cummings, "230 Inducted as Housing Police; One Is the First Woman Recruit," *New York Times*, 20 November 1973. In 1965, NYCHA centralized both time records and check payments, and record rooms ceased to play this function; see "Centralization of Time Records in Security Headquarters," 10 November 1965, folder 3, box 64C3, NYCHA.

12. Raymond Henson, interview by author, 28 November 2007, tape of interview in author's possession.

13. Richard Schauss, interview by author, 1 February 2008, tape of interview in author's possession.

14. Peter Grymes, interview by author, 10 February 2008, tape of interview in author's possession.

15. William Reid to Hon. James Gaynor, 5 May 1959, folder 3, box 71B7, NYCHA. Average violations reported extrapolated from state-funded projects data for both complaints and Juvenile Record Cards. Using population totals for state-funded projects with HAPD coverage as of 1959, the rate of violations reported to managers was roughly 0.8 per 1,000 project residents. For population totals, see Property Protection and Security Division, "Present Assignments and Additional Personnel Requested," n.d., folder 3, box 71B7, NYCHA. For a list of finable offenses, see "Red Hook Houses," 11 June 1945, folder 2, box 71B7, NYCHA.

16. Arthur Wallander to the Members of the New York City Housing Authority, 1 October 1957, folder 3, box 64E7, NYCHA.

17. Ellen Lurie, "Rough Draft of a Study of the George Washington Houses," 1956, 11-32, folder 13, box 11, Union Settlement Records, Rare Book and Manuscript Library, Columbia University.

18. Occupancy was not complete at Castle Hill until December 1960, but residents started moving in by 1959. For completion dates on NYCHA developments, see Bloom, *Public Housing That Worked*, app. A; Grymes interview.

19. Terri Sheeps, interview by author, 10 February 2007, tape of interview in author's possession; Gonzalez interview; Fritz Umbach, *The Last Neighborhood Cops: The Rise and Fall of Community Policing in New York Public Housing* (Newark, NJ: Rutgers University Press, 2011), chap. 4.

20. Gonzalez interview.

21. Jennie McIntyre, "Public Attitudes toward Crime and Law Enforcement," *Annals of the American Academy of Political and Social Science* 374, no. 1 (1967).

22. New York City Police Department, *Statistical Report: Complaints and Arrests, Crime Analysis Section* (New York: Office of Management, 1960–1982). Until 1968, the lowest grade for arrests was "offenses," but the 1968 revision of the New York State penal code replaced that term with "violation." In 1964, 86,319 of the 190,289 total arrests were for "offenses," but by 1970, of the 250,902 total arrests, only 44,243 were for violations.

23. Annual Statistical Report—1976, 30 March 1977, folder 3, box 89A3, NYCHA.

24. Thomas J. Sugrue, *Sweet Land of Liberty: The Forgotten Struggle for Civil Rights in the North* (New York: Random House, 2008), 327–28.

25. "Riot Flares in Brooklyn Project; 8 Persons Injured, 5 Arrested," *New York Times,* 16 August 1962; "2 Housing Officers Pelted with Bottles by a Harlem Crowd," *New York Times,* 31 August 1974.

26. Max Siegel, "S.I. Broker and 3 Indicted in Damaging Black's Home," *New York Times,* 15 October 1975; George Todd, "Former Cops Guilty of Vandalizing Black Home," *New York Amsterdam News,* 2 October 1976.

27. Cummings, "230 Inducted as Housing Police."

28. "Police Department, HPS # 284," 10 December 1969, and "Police Department, HPS #3," 2 February 1970, both in folder 3, box 62C1, NYCHA.

29. Rhonda Y. Williams, *The Politics of Public Housing: Black Women's Struggles against Urban Inequality* (New York: Oxford University Press, 2004), 6, 8; for the role of tenant patrols as "viable community spokespersons" within NYCHA, see "Tenant Organizations in Public Housing—The Need for Professional Mediation," 6 December, 1976, folder 13, box 90B4, NYCHA.

30. Bonnie Bucqueroux, "Community Policing Is Alive and Well," *Community Policing Exchange* (May-June 1995), http://www.ncjrs.gov/txtfiles/cpe0595.txt.

31. So certain, for example, was Howard Husock, director of public policy case studies at Harvard, that "everyone knows how quickly . . . housing projects . . . in big cities turn into dangerous, demoralized slums," that he neglected even to provide a citation for this sweeping generalization in his *America's Trillion-Dollar Housing Mistake: The Failure of American Housing Policy* (Chicago: Ivan R. Dee, 2003), 1.

32. Although, as José Ramón Sánchez has observed, not until the 1970s would Puerto Rican residency in public housing reflect their share of the city's low-income population, this pattern was much less true in East Harlem. The Johnson Houses, for example, were 25.4 percent Puerto Rican at their initial occupancy in 1949. See José Ramón Sánchez, "Housing Puerto Ricans in New York City, 1945 to 1984: A Study in Class Powerlessness" (PhD diss., New York University, 1990), 563.

33. Ellen Lurie would eventually acquire fame as an activist defending community control in the Ocean Hill–Brownsville strike. See Jerald E. Podair, *The Strike That Changed New York* (New Haven, CT: Yale University Press, 2002), 175.

34. Ellen Lurie, "Los Vigilantes," September 1959, folder 1, box 17, Union Settlement Records, Rare Books and Manuscript Library, Columbia University; Leonard J. Duhl, *The Urban Condition: People and Policy in the Metropolis* (New York: Basic Books, 1963), 249.

35. Patricia Hill Collins, *Black Feminist Thought: Knowledge, Consciousness, and the Politics of Empowerment—Perspectives on Gender* (Boston: Unwin Hyman, 1990); Nancy Naples, "Activist Mothering: Cross-Generational Continuity in the Community Work of Women from Low-Income Urban Neighborhoods," *Gender & Society* 6, no. 3 (1992): 441–63.

36. Lurie, "Los Vigilantes"; Duhl, *The Urban Condition,* 255.

37. Bloom, *Public Housing That Worked,* 192–96; for the number of tenant associations, see William Reid, "Towards a Slumless City: 1954–1965," November 1965, folder 5, box 59D5, NYCHA.

38. Val Coleman, "Tenant Organization in Public Housing—The Need for Professional Mediation," 6 December 1976, folder 13, box 90B4, NYCHA; see also Blanca Cedeno, "Human Relations Committee Meeting from Millbrook House," 19 October 1972, folder 2, box 88B4, NYCHA; Blanca Cedeno to Albert Walsh, 30 November 1967, folder 1, box 70D5, NYCHA.

39. Randall Bennett Woods, *LBJ: Architect of American Ambition* (New York: Free Press, 2006), 710–11.

40. Sugrue, *Sweet Land of Liberty*, 369–74.

41. David Preston "New Expectations for Public Housing: Paper Presented at the 1965 Annual Meeting of the American Orthopsychiatric Association, New York, New York," *American Journal of Orthopsychiatry* 36, no. 4 (1966): 678; David Preston, "Department of Social and Community Services," 1966, 1, box 59D5, NYCHA; Bloom, *Public Housing That Worked*, 236–37, Nancy Naples, *Grassroots Warriors: Activist Mothering, Community Work, and the War on Poverty* (New York: Routledge, 1998), 76–77, 210–11.

42. Les Mathews, "Greenpoint Slaying Laid to Race Strife," *New York Amsterdam News*, 17 December 1960. Tudy's activism, however, long predated the 1960 events described by the *Amsterdam News;* as Tudy recounted, her grandmother took her to protests on 125th Street organized by Adam Clayton Powell, Jr. It is likely that Tudy was recalling Powell's "Don't Buy Where You Can't Work" Harlem campaign. See Colin Campbell, "A Lifetime of Leadership: An Interview with Mildred Tudy," *Greenline*, 10 October 1986, folder 23, box 97, National Congress of Neighborhood Women Records, Sophia Smith Collection, Women's History Manuscripts, Smith College.

43. Harold Berger to Irving Wise, 14 October 1966, folder 10, box 66E8, NYCHA; Harold Berger to Irving Wise, "Follow-up to Cooper Park Houses Community Meeting," 17 October 1966, folder 10, box 66E8, NYCHA.

44. Richard A. Cloward and Frances Fox Piven, *The Politics of Turmoil: Essays on Poverty, Race, and the Urban Crisis* (New York: Pantheon Books, 1974), 24, 21–22, 7–9.

45. For Tudy's record of activism, see Mathews, "Greenpoint Slaying"; Rhea Callaway, "Hi There!," *New York Amsterdam News*, 28 November 1970; "Locals Demand Jobs on Hospital Site," *New York Amsterdam News*, 24 July 1971; "Residents Demand Jobs on Williamsburg Site," *New York Amsterdam News*, 18 December, 1971; "Charge Racism on District 14 School Board," *New York Amsterdam News*, 11 December 1971; "Blacks Fear Exclusion in Williamsburg Housing," *New York Amsterdam News*, 22 January 1972; "Black Principal Ouster May End School Peace," *New York Amsterdam News*, 9 June 1973; "Court Hears Arguments in Woodhull Suit," *New York Amsterdam News*, 19 July 1980; "A Call to Convene the Black Population of New York," *New York Amsterdam News*, 15 May 1982; "Community Service—Mildred Tudy," *New York Amsterdam News*, 28 December 1991. For Tudy's conception of "basic needs" community activism, see Campbell, "A Lifetime of Leadership."

46. Jim Fuerst and Roy Petty, "Public Housing in the Courts, Pyrrhic Victories for the Poor," *The Urban Lawyer* (Summer 1977): 503.

47. For evictions, see relevant tables, folder 13, box 64A4, NYCHA; for population totals, see NYCHA, "Racial Distribution in Operating Project," 18 January 1961; Martin interview; for telegrams, see Tompkins Tenants Association to Walter Washington, 1 June 1967, folder 10, box 66E8, NYCHA.

48. For the first of these, a three-week vigil in 1963, see the discussion of past protests in Manhattanville Improvement Association, press release, 15 April 1968, folder 1, box 64D3, NYCHA; Les Mathews, "New Locks, More Policemen Promised St. Nicholas Houses," *New York Amsterdam News*, 2 April 1966; notice posted in the lobbies at Marble Hill Houses, "Project Families Demand Our Own Lock," 10 March 1967, folder 5, box 65D8, NYCHA; Edith Paris to Sidney Schackman, 8 August 1967, folder 10, box 65E3, NYCHA; Metropolitan Council on Housing, "Rutgers Project Stands Firm to Continue Vigil until Guards Are Place [*sic*] in

Lobby" (press release), 11 August 1967, folder 4, box 64B7, NYCHA; Alfredo Graham to Mr. Roberts, 13 November 1967, folder 4, box 65E4, NYCHA; Simon Obi Anekwe, "Mugged as Others Picket," *New York Amsterdam News*, 18 November 1967; Manhattanville Improvement Association, press release; Ben Gould to Stanley Roberts, 1 May 1968, folder 4, box 60D8, NYCHA; "City School Budget Assailed; Housing Police Funds Allotted," *New York Times*, 24 May 1968; Stanley Roberts to Joseph Christian, "Patterson Houses Delegation at Mayor's Officer," 6 August 1968, folder 7, box 65E1, NYCHA; "Threaten Rent Strike," *New York Amsterdam News*, 8 August 1970; "Potential Tension Situations," 20 November 1970, folder 4, box 70D2, NYCHA; "Potential Tension Situations," 4 December 1970, folder 4, box 70D2, NYCHA; "Potential Tension Situations," 12 December 1970, folder 4, box 70D2, NYCHA; "Potential Tension Situations," 29 January 1971, folder 4, box 70D2, NYCHA; Les Mathews, "Lincoln Project Crime Wave 'Unfounded,'" *New York Amsterdam News*, 20 March 1971; "Tenants Protest Cutbacks," *The Chief*, 12 May 1971; "Project Tenants Threaten Rent Strike," *Long Island Press*, 30 May 1971; "Redfern Tenants Patrol Plans Protest," *Long Island Press*, 30 May 1971; "Project Groups Hits Golar on V-Gals," *Daily News*, 11 November 1971; "Baruch Tenants in a Protest," *New York Post*, 30 November 1971; Arthur Mulligan, "Lindsay Won't Hike Force: Housing Cops," *Daily News*, 11 December 1971; George Todd, "Angry Tenants Group Launches Drive for More Housing Cops," *New York Amsterdam News*, 25 December 1971; "Potential Tension Situations," 14 January 1972, folder 7, box 70D2, NYCHA; "Public Housing Tenants Demand 2,500 More Cops," *New York Amsterdam News*, 5 February 1972; "Bronx Tenants Demand Security," *New York Voice*, 11 August 1972; "Vladeck Tenants Hold Rally," *Daily News*, 21 July 1972; "Tension Report," n.d., but shortly after 3 August 1972, folder 7, box 65C5, NYCHA. See reference to demonstration at Millbrook Houses: "Tenants Demonstrate at Lehman Village Housing," *New York Amsterdam News*, 8 December 1973; "Law Makers Support the Rent Strike," *New York Amsterdam News*, 3 August 1974; Ad Hoc Committee against the New York City Housing Policy to Mayor Beame, 8 November 1974, folder 5, box 88B2, NYCHA; "New York City Housing Authority Police—Federal Program," 12 December 1976, folder 5, box 90B4, NYCHA; Les Mathews, "Manhattanville Tenants Demand Protection," *New York Amsterdam News*, 24 July 1976; Department of Housing and Urban Development, "Dear Friend," 11 May 1977, p. 4, folder 4, box 89E7, NYCHA; "Williamsburg Houses—Security Demonstration," 3 June 1980, folder 1, box 90A4 NYCHA.

49. In a recent dissertation, for example, historian Tamar Carroll addresses Mobilization for Youth's (MYF) 1964 rent strike and lovingly details the activism of a number of women in NYCHA developments from the 1970s onward, but skips over the 1968 rent strikes for more police officers. See Carroll, "Grassroots Feminism."

50. For the history of "section 755" that provided legal protection for striking tenants under certain conditions, see Joel Schwartz, "Tenant Power in the Liberal City, 1943–1971," in *The Tenant Movement in New York City, 1904–1984*, ed. Ronald Lawson and Mark Naison (New Brunswick, NJ: Rutgers University Press, 1986), 134–208; see also Junius Griffin, "'Guerrilla War' Urged in Harlem; Rent Strike Chief Calls for '100 Revolutionaries,'" *New York Times*, 20 July 1964.

51. For rent strikers getting priority for admission to NYCHA, see Michael Lipsky and Margaret Levi, "Community Organization as a Political Resource," in *People and Politics in Urban Society*, ed. Harlan Hahn (Beverly Hills, CA: Sage, 1972), 195–96; Michael Lipsky, *Street-Level Bureaucracy: Dilemmas of the Individual in Public Services* (New York: Russell Sage Foundation, 1980), 63–64; Simon Obi Anekwe, "Call Tenants Vigil a 'Beautiful Thing,'" *New*

York Amsterdam News, 20 April 1968; for Anekwe's career, J. Zamgba Browne, "Simon Anekwe: A True Journalist," *New York Amsterdam News,* 7 December 2000.

52. For MFY's internal decisions, see Schwartz, "Tenant Power in the Liberal City, 1943–1971"; Roberta Gold argues that the Harlem rent strikes were more effective than Schwartz believes them to have been, but she doesn't take issue with his analysis of MFY at the time. See Gold, *City of Tenants* (Seattle: University of Washington Press, 2004), chap. 4.

53. Noel A. Cazenave, *Impossible Democracy: The Unlikely Success of the War on Poverty Community Action Programs* (Albany: State University of New York Press, 2007), 120–21; Griffin, "'Guerrilla War' Urged in Harlem"; Harold H. Weissman and Mobilization for Youth, *Individual and Group Services in the Mobilization for Youth Experience* (New York: Association Press, 1969), 120.

54. N*ew York City Housing Authority v. Medlin,* 57 Misc. 2d 145, 291 N.Y.S. 2d 672 (New York County, 1968); "Tenants of East Side Projects Vow to Continue Rent Strike," *New York Times,* 14 April 1968; "Harlem Tenants Open Vigil to Press Protection Drive," *New York Times,* 5 May 1968; "Tenant Protection Held Outside Scope of Housing Board," *New York Times,* 28 June 1968; David K. Shipler, "City Is Evicting Rent Protesters," *New York Times,* 7 January 1969.

55. For the Young Lords' thirteen-point program, see Lois Palken Rudnick, Judith E. Smith, and Rachel Rubin, *American Identities* (Malden, MA: Blackwell, 2006), 170–73.

56. "Tension Report—Carver Houses," December 1970, folder 4, box 70D2, NYCH; Sánchez, "Housing Puerto Ricans in New York City, 1945 to 1984," 565.

57. "Threatens Rent Strike."

58. For the funding history of the HAPD, see "Comprehensive HUD Review," September 1983, folder 1, box 91C4, NYCHA; for HAPD's size, see New York City Council Resolution, 13 April, folder 4, box 62 C2, NYCHA; and Joseph Garber, "The History, Organization and Structure of the New York City Housing Authority Police Department" (honors thesis, John Jay College of Criminal Justice, City University of New York, 1970). For the population of NYCHA, see "Project Data Statistics (Blue Book)," 1965–1975, box 72A1 and box 72A2, NYCHA. For the size of the NYPD, see New York Police Department, "Annual Reports," 1965–1971, Special Collection, John Jay College of Criminal Justice, City University of New York. For the hiring freeze, see Murray Schumach, "City Ends Freeze on Police, Fire, Sanitation Jobs," *New York Times,* 3 November 1972; Martin Tolchin, "City Puts Freeze on Jobs of Police and Garbage Men," *New York Times,* 27 April 1970.

59. "Minutes of Project Security Problems Meeting," 18 October 1968, folder 5, box 64B7, NYCHA.

60. Walter Washington to Mayor John V. Lindsay, 22 September 1968, folder 5, box 64B7, NYCHA.

Myth #10: Public Housing Tenants Are Powerless

1. I would like to thank Fritz Umbach for inviting me to contribute to this edited collection. This essay is a condensed version of chapter 6: "An Awakening Giant," from Rhonda Y. Williams, *The Politics of Public Housing: Black Women's Struggles against Urban Inequality* (New York: Oxford University Press, 2004), 155–91. By permission of Oxford University Press, USA.

2. See the following essays by Rhonda Y. Williams: "'To Challenge the Status Quo by Any Means': Community Action and Representational Politics in 1960s Baltimore," in *The War on Poverty: A New Grassroots History, 1964–1980,* ed. Annelise Orleck and Lisa Gayle Hazirjian (Athens: Georgia University Press, 2011), 63–86; "The Pursuit of Audacious Power: Rebel

Reformers and Neighborhood Politics in Baltimore, 1966–1968," *Neighborhood Rebels: Black Power at the Local Level,* ed. Peniel E. Joseph (New York: Palgrave Macmillan, 2010), 215–41; "'Something's Wrong Down Here': Poor Black Women and Urban Struggles for Democracy," in *African American Urban History since World War II,* ed. Kenneth L. Kusmer and Joe William Trotter (Chicago: University of Chicago Press, 2009), 316–36; "Black Women, Urban Politics, and Engendering Black Power," *The Black Power Movement: Rethinking the Civil Rights–Black Power Era,* ed. Peniel E. Joseph (New York: Routledge, 2006), 79–103.

3. Author's interviews with Shirley M. Wise, 22 January 1996, 7 February 1996, 23 April 1996, 1 November 1997, 21 June 2002.

4. Wise interviews.

5. Author's interviews with Julia Matthews, 19 December 1996, and Shirley M. Wise.

6. U-JOIN is Union for Jobs or Income Now, established by the Students for Democratic Society's Economic Research and Action Project (SDS-ERAP).

7. Author's interviews with Goldie Baker, 29 January 1997, 15 July 2000, 24 September 2001, 13 October 2001.

8. Author's interview with Clyde Hatcher, 26 May 1998.

9. "Poverty Plan Is Questioned," *Baltimore Afro-American* (hereafter abbreviated as *BAA*), 15 December 1964. On U-JOIN protests, see *Jobs Now Newsletter* of U-JOIN, 8 February and 15 February 1965; "We Call for a Real War on Poverty" (flyer, n.d.), all in Folder 12: Baltimore, Newsletters and Leaflets, 1964, Box 22, Series 2B, SDS Papers, Wisconsin Historical Society (WHS). Also see "Baltimore U-JOIN Report War on Poverty," n.d., submitted by David Harding and Kim Moody; CAP Report submitted by Bob Moore; ERAP Report, n.d., submitted to Rennie Davis, all in Folder 13: SDS Baltimore Reports and Prospectuses, 1964,1965, SDS Papers, WHS.

10. "Why Anti-Poverty Fight Lags," *BAA*, 20 November 1965; George W. Collins, "OEO, CAA React Quickly to Critique," *BAA*, 14 May 1966; "How Council Holds Up Major Poverty Plans," *BAA*, 23 July 1966; "Uncle Sam Advises CAC to Be More Independent," *BAA*, 23 July 1966; "City Council 'Conservatives' Want Poverty Program Control," *BAA*, 18 March 1969.

11. "Poor Speak Out at First Convention; Firm Plans Due in Dec. 18 Meeting," *BAA*, 13 December 1966; A. W. Geiselman, Jr., "Battle Looms in Poverty Program," *Baltimore Evening Sun* (hereafter abbreviated as *BES*), 19 January 1967.

12. Baker interviews.

13. Douglass Homes was formerly part of another "combo" with Somerset Courts. Memo to Robert S. Moyer from Van Story Branch, 30 January 1968, Folder: Douglass Homes—General 1949–1970, Box 11, Series 14, RG 48, Baltimore City Archives (BCA).

14. Eugenia Davis and Matthews interviews; memo to Charles Knight from John Meehan, 1 July 1968, Folder: Douglass Homes—General 1949–1970, Box 11, Series 14, RG 48, BCA.

15. Hatcher interview.

16. Author's interview with Ann Thornton, 28 May 1996.

17. Baker interviews. Also see Eileen Boris, "When Work Is Slavery," in *Whose Welfare?,* ed. Gwendolyn Mink (Ithaca, NY: Cornell University Press, 1999), 36–55.

18. Minutes of the Commission Meeting of the HABC, 6 February 1968, Folder 13, Box 5, Series I, BURHA Collection, University of Baltimore Archives (UBA).

19. Matthews interview. On the Joyce Thorpe case, see Christina Greene, "'Our Separate Ways': Women and the Black Freedom Movement in Durham, North Carolina, 1940s–1970s" (PhD diss., Duke University, 1996), especially chap. 4; "Supreme Court Decides to Rule on Eviction Case," *Baltimore Afro-American,* 18 April 1967. In 2005, Christina Greene's dissertation was published in book form by University of North Carolina Press.

20. Jack Bryan, "Public Housing Modernization," *Journal of Housing* (hereafter abbreviated as *JOH*) 28, no. 4 (1971): 169.

21. "Minneapolis Gets First Modernization OK," *JOH* 25, no. 3 (1968): 153; HUD circular quote in "Philadelphia Authority Contracts with Residents," *JOH* 27, no. 3 (1970): 144; "Tenant-Management Issues," *JOH* 27, no. 10 (1970): 540.

22. Bryan, "Public Housing Modernization," 170.

23. "Tenants Participate in Modernization Programs," *JOH* 26, no. 8 (1969): 419; Wise interviews.

24. Bryan, "Public Housing Modernization," 170; "Tenant-Management Issues," 540.

25. Minutes: Public Housing Tenant Representatives, 16 August 1968, Folder: 1968–69—RAB, Box 13, Series 13, RG 48, BCA.

26. Minutes of the First Meeting of the Resident Advisory Board, 3 October 1968, Folder: 1968–69—RAB, Box 13, Series 13, RG 48, BCA.

27. Bryan, "Public Housing Modernization," 173. Also see memo to Embry from Branch, 16 September 1968, and Minutes of the First Meeting of the Resident Advisory Board, 3 October 1968, both in Folder: 1968–69—RAB, Box 13, Series 13, RG 48, BCA; "Tenant-Management Issues," 536; Steen R. Weisman, "Tenants Council Will Advise City," *New York Times* (hereafter abbreviated as *NYT*), 22 November 1970; and John Herbers, "Tenants Win Policy Voice in Nation's Public Housing," *NYT*, 27 November 1970. On New Haven, Connecticut, community-based tenant organizations, see Edward White, Jr., "Tenant Participation in Public Housing Management," *JOH* 26, no. 8 (1969): 416–19.

28. "Low-Income Groups More Active," *BES*, 27 December 1972.

29. Bryan, "Public Housing Modernization," 171–72.

30. Jean King was a leader at Darst-Webbe and Peabody complexes. See "Public Housing Tenants in St. Louis Have Been on Rent Strike for Six Months, "*JOH* 26, no. 7 (1969): 351–52. Also in Newark, public housing residents led by a group called Poor and Dissatisfied Tenants initiated a rent strike, picketed up to four complexes, and demanded a reduction in the maximum rent of tenants receiving public welfare. Washington public housing tenants also withheld rents, protesting bad upkeep and slum conditions. "Tenant-Management Relations," *JOH* 27, no. 10 (1970): 534–43. On the St. Louis case, see George Lipsitz, *A Life in the Struggle: Ivory Perry and the Culture of Opposition* (Philadelphia: Temple University Press, 1988), 145–71.

31. "Tenants Began Newark Strike," *BES*, 2 April 1970; Sanford J. Unger and Michael Hodge, "Consumers' New Weapon: Rent Strike," *Washington Post*, 26 July 1970; "Newark Tenants Will Defy Court Order," *NYT*, 15 February 1972, and "Tenant Association in Newark Faces Contempt Charges, *NYT*, 24 February 1972; Joseph P. Fried, "'Tenant Power' Is a Spreading Slogan," *NYT*, 19 March 1973.

32. Neil Gilbert describes the War on Poverty's goal as the "democraticization [*sic*] of social welfare" through "transforming clients into constituents." Gilbert, *Clients or Constituencies* (San Francisco: Jossey-Bass, 1970), x, 9, 29–32.

33. Author's interviews with Gladys Spell, 22 October 1993, 4 November 1993.

34. Ibid.

35. Ibid.

36. Author's interview with Rosetta Schofield, 5 November 1993.

37. Jewell Chambers, "Community Leaders Explore Forming Black Unity Front," *BAA*, 16 March 1968.

38. "Deficit of Action Agency Squeezes Out 10 Centers," *Baltimore News American*, 19 March 1971.

39. Baker interviews.

40. Author's interview with Maxine Stephenson, 4 November 1993.

41. David Farber uses "customized wars" in *The Age of Great Dreams: America in the 1960s* (New York: Hill and Wang, 1994), 107.

Myth #11: Tenants Did Not Invest in Public Housing

1. Author's interview with M.B.M., Philadelphia, PA, June 27, 2000. The names of tenants and social workers in this essay are pseudonyms with the exception of the names of people quoted in newspapers.

2. For an overview of public housing in Philadelphia, see John F. Bauman, *Public Housing, Race, and Renewal: Urban Planning in Philadelphia, 1920–1974* (Philadelphia: Temple University Press, 1987). On the origins and importance of the 1949 Housing Act, see Alexander von Hoffman, "A Study in Contradictions: The Origins and Legacy of the 1949 Housing Act," *Housing Policy Debate* 11, no. 2 (2000): 299–326.

3. "First Housing Projects Here Pay Dividends in Happiness," *Philadelphia Evening Bulletin*, 11 June 1949, 6.

4. Bauman, *Public Housing*, 151.

5. Committee on Public Housing Policy, "Basic Policies for Public Housing for Low-Income Families in Philadelphia" (Philadelphia: Philadelphia Housing Association, 1957), 27a. African Americans were overrepresented among applicants prior to the 1950s; see James Wolfinger, *Philadelphia Divided: Race and Politics in the City of Brotherly Love* (Chapel Hill: University of North Carolina Press, 2007), 66.

6. Questionnaires on Public Housing: a collection of completed questionnaires that were sent out to social workers by the Committee on Public Housing in 1956 to get feedback on public housing in Philadelphia, Box 282, Folders 4924 to 4933, Philadelphia Housing Association/Housing Association of the Delaware Valley, 1909–1975, Urban Archives Temple University (hereafter cited as Questionnaires); "Memo to the Files of Committee on Public Housing Policy from Howard W. Hallman," Box 282, Folder 4933, Philadelphia Housing Association/Housing Association of the Delaware Valley, 1909–1975 (hereafter cited as HADV), Urban Archives Temple University (hereafter cited as UATU); Committee on Housing Policy, "Basic Policies for Public Housing," 25–26.

7. Bauman, *Public Housing*, 171. Abbottsford, Passyunk, Bartram Village, Wilson Park, and Schuylkill Falls became nearly half African American by 1968. Liddonfield and Hill Creek remained predominantly white.

8. See Lisa Levenstein, *A Movement without Marches: African American Women and the Politics of Housing in Postwar Philadelphia* (Chapel Hill: University of North Carolina Press, 2009), 98–103. On single mothers' collective efforts to gain admittance to public housing in Durham, NC, see Christina Greene, *Our Separate Ways: Women and the Black Freedom Movement in Durham, North Carolina* (Chapel Hill: University of North Carolina Press, 2005), 135. In 1968, Community Legal Services, a legal aid agency for low-income Philadelphians, helped a group of thirteen unwed mothers win a suit against the PHA challenging the ban on their admission.

9. Bauman, *Public Housing*, 49–51.

10. "The Philadelphia Housing Authority Presents Richard Allen Homes," pamphlet, Folder Richard Allen Homes, 1945–1967, *Philadelphia Evening Bulletin* Newsclipping Collection, UATU.

11. "Laborer with Six Children First Allen Homes Lessee," *Philadelphia Tribune*, 24 February 1942, 1, 2; "New Life Opens for Widow's Child as First Allen Homes Lease Is Signed," *Philadelphia Record*, 25 February 1942, 3; "New Homes, New Health, New Fun, New Happiness," *Philadelphia Evening Bulletin*, 1 August 1942, 8; "Everything Very Wonderful for Rosen Homes Residents," *Philadelphia Tribune*, 2 August 1955, 1, 2; "Rosen Homes Families Finding Happiness in New Apartments," *Philadelphia Tribune*, 6 August 1955, 1, 2.

12. "Glenwood's 1st Tenants Due Tuesday," *Philadelphia Record*, 29 September 1940, 1; "A Preview of Low-Rent Housing," *Philadelphia Record*, 21 August 1940, 2; "New Homes, New Health."

13. "Richard Allen Homes," *Philadelphia Evening Bulletin*, 27 July 1949, 13.

14. Quoted in "New Homes, New Health."

15. Quoted in "New Homes, New Health."

16. "Everything Very Wonderful for Rosen Homes Residents," quotation on 2.

17. Philadelphia Housing Authority, "Report of Activities Conducted in Community Buildings," October 1955, Box 10, Folder 177, Urban League of Philadelphia Records, 1935–1963, UATU; Philadelphia Housing Association, "1955 Report of Community Activities," Box 282, Folder 4920, HADV, UATU; Philadelphia Housing Authority, *Report for 1955*, 8.

18. Philadelphia Housing Authority, *20 Years of Service: The Story of Public Housing in Philadelphia, 1937–1957* (Philadelphia: Gelmans, 1957), 23.

19. Although tenant advisory organizations began in Baltimore in the 1940s, they did not begin in Philadelphia until later. On Baltimore, see Rhonda Y. Williams, *The Politics of Public Housing: Black Women's Struggles against Urban Inequality* (New York: Oxford University Press, 2004), 63–86.

20. Quotation is social worker paraphrasing Mrs. Davenport, Philadelphia Housing Authority, Housekeeping Discussion Group, April 17, 1961, Box 82, Folder 109, Friends Neighborhood Guild, 1922–1980 (hereafter cited as FNG), UATU.

21. Quoted in Gail Levy and Judith Shouse, "Concept of Alienation: A New Approach to Understanding the AFDC Recipient" (Master of Social Service Thesis, Bryn Mawr College, 1965), 39; Anthony F. C. Wallace, *Housing and Social Structure: A Preliminary Survey, with Particular Reference to Multi-Storey, Low-Rent Public Housing Projects* (Philadelphia: Philadelphia Housing Authority, 1956), 64, 79.

22. M.B.M. interview.

23. Social worker quoting tenants in Philadelphia Housing Authority, Family Discussion Group, February 6, 1961, Box 82, Folder 109, FNG, UATU; "What Happens at a Project in a Blighted Area," *Philadelphia Evening Bulletin*, 29 April 1956, sec. 2, p. 5. See also "What Happens When Public Housing Is Erected in a Neighborhood of Privately-Owned Homes?," *Philadelphia Evening Bulletin*, 29 April 1956, 1, 4.

24. Public Housing Authority, Family Discussion Group, 19 February 1961, Box 82, Folder 109, FNG, UATU; "What Happens When Public Housing Is Erected."

25. M.B.M. interview. Similarly, see "Tasker Homes Up in the Air over Curb on TV Antennas," *Philadelphia Evening Bulletin*, 21 July 1958, 33.

26. Gail Radford, *Modern Housing for America: Policy Struggles in the New Deal Era* (Chicago: University of Chicago Press, 1996), 190–92, 200.

27. For an interesting account, see D. Bradford Hunt, "Was the 1937 U.S. Housing Act a Pyrrhic Victory," *Journal of Planning History* 4, no. 3 (2005): 208–9, 213–14.

28. Questionnaires; Philadelphia Housing Authority, Family Discussion Group, April 3, 1961, Box 82, Folder 109, FNG, UATU; Federal Public Housing Authority, National Housing Agency, *The Livability Problems of 1,000 Families* (Washington, DC: FPHA, 1945), 31.

29. Questionnaires; Philadelphia Housing Authority, Family Discussion Group, 1 May 1961, Box 82, Folder 109, FNG, UATU; Philadelphia Housing Authority, *Public Housing: Report to the Community* IV:2 (May 1954), 9.

30. "Low Rent: Richard Allen Homes," 1945, Box 24, Folder Philadelphia Housing Association, YMCA of Philadelphia–Christian Street, 1943–1964, UATU; Philadelphia District Health and Welfare Council, *Use of Community Facilities in Developments of the Philadelphia Housing Authority* (Philadelphia: Philadelphia Health and Welfare Council, 1955); Philadelphia Housing Authority, *Public Housing: Report to the Community* 11:4 (April 1952), 6.

31. Wharton Center, "Rosen-Johnson Housing Neighborhood," draft, n.d., Box 6, Folder 93, Wharton Center Records, 1913–1968, UATU. The problem had a different configuration in more economically stable neighborhoods with better and less crowded recreational facilities. In those cases, tenants frequently were not welcome at nearby recreation centers. See Health and Welfare Council, *Use of Community Facilities.* On recreation space in public housing in Chicago, see D. Bradford Hunt, *Blueprint for Disaster: The Unraveling of Public Housing in Chicago* (Chicago: University of Chicago Press, 2009), 158–64.

32. For an excellent account of Chicago, see Hunt, *Blueprint for Disaster*, 195–200.

33. In 1955, the PHA made plans to replace the fifteen-year-old ranges and fridges at Richard Allen, Johnson, and Tasker; see Philadelphia Housing Authority, *Report for 1955.*

34. Committee on Public Housing Policy, "Basic Policies for Public Housing," 32; "Maintenance Subcommittee Report," Box 286, Folder 5053, HADV, UATU.

35. Health and Welfare Council, Inc., Family Division, Committee on Social Service in Public Housing, Minutes, April 21, 1960, Box 4, Folder 111, Health and Welfare Council Inc., Records, 1928–1966, UATU; Levy and Shouse, "Concept of Alienation," 39. On working-class African American women's protests against utility bills in 1960s Durham, NC, see Greene, *Our Separate Ways*, 183.

36. "What Happens When Public Housing Is Erected?"

37. "A Spick-and-Span Spot," *Philadelphia Evening Bulletin*, 5 June 1947, 14.

38. "Richard Allen Homes"; "Bright Spot in Public Housing," *Philadelphia Evening Bulletin*, 24 June 1948, 20F.

39. "A Spick-and-Span Spot"; "Everything Very Wonderful for Rosen Homes Residents."

40. "Maintenance Committee Report," 29 January 1957, Box 281, Folder 4886, HADV, UATU.

41. Quoted in Bauman, *Public Housing*, 176; "Girls, 9 Molested in Project, At Home; Two Suspects Sought," *Philadelphia Tribune*, 28 July 1959, 13; "600 Quizzed about Murder," *Philadelphia Evening Bulletin*, 17 August 1958, 3; "Man Admits Killing Guard at Project," *Philadelphia Evening Bulletin*, 19 August 1958, 1; M.B.M. interview.

ACKNOWLEDGMENTS

The editors thank, most of all, the many contributors for their hard work on the articles that compose this collection. We also thank Michael McGandy at Cornell University Press for taking a risk on a provocative approach to a familiar topic, and for commissioning helpful anonymous reviews of the manuscript. John Jay College of Criminal Justice, the New York Institute of Technology, and the Massachusetts Institute of Technology provided financial support that allowed this project to be completed. Sections of chapter 9 originally appeared in Fritz Umbach, *The Last Neighborhood Cops: The Rise and Fall of Community Policing in New York Public Housing.* © 2010 by Fritz Umbach. Reprinted by permission of Rutgers University Press. Sections of chapter 10 originally appeared in Rhonda Y. Williams, *The Politics of Public Housing: Black Women's Struggles against Urban Inequality.* © 2005 by Rhonda Y. Williams. Reprinted by permission of Oxford University Press. Portions of chapter 11 originally appeared in Lisa Levenstein, *A Movement without Marches: African American Women and the Politics of Poverty in Postwar Philadelphia.* © 2009 Reprinted by permission of University of North Carolina Press.

CONTRIBUTOR BIOGRAPHIES

JOSEPH HEATHCOTT, Associate Professor of Urbanism at The New School, is President of the Society for American City and Regional Planning History for 2013–2015, and serves on the Editorial Board of the *Journal of the American Planning Association.*

D. BRADFORD HUNT is the Dean of the Evelyn T. Stone College of Professional Studies and Vice Provost for Adult and Experiential Learning at Roosevelt University in Chicago. He is the author of *Blueprint for Disaster: The Unraveling of Chicago Public Housing* (University of Chicago Press, 2009).

FRITZ UMBACH, Associate Professor of History at John Jay College of Criminal Justice (CUNY), is the author of *The Last Neighborhood Cops: The Rise and Fall of Community Policing in New York Public Housing* (Rutgers University Press, 2011).

ALEXANDER GEROULD, Assistant Professor of Criminal Justice at San Francisco State University is the coauthor of Vold's *Theoretical Criminology*, 6th Edition, (Oxford University Press, 2010) and coauthor with Kermit Alexander and Jeff Snipes of *The Valley of the Shadow of Death* (Atria Books, Forthcoming 2015).

NICHOLAS DAGEN BLOOM, Associate Professor of Social Science at the New York Institute of Technology, is the author of many books on urban affairs including *Public Housing That Worked: New York in the Twentieth Century* (University of Pennsylvania Press, 2008).

YONAH FREEMARK is a project manager at Chicago's Metropolitan Planning Council, where he focuses on transit-oriented development, affordable housing strategies, and public transportation. He holds degrees in city planning and transportation from the Massachusetts Institute of Technology.

LAWRENCE J. VALE, Ford Professor of Urban Design and Planning at the Massachusetts Institute of Technology, is the author of many works in planning and urban affairs including *Reclaiming Public Housing* (Harvard University Press, 2002) and *From the Puritans to the Projects:* (Harvard University Press, 2000; repr., 2007), and *Purging the Poorest* (University of Chicago Press, 2013).

FLORIAN URBAN, Professor and Head of History of Architecture and Urban Studies at the Mackintosh School of Architecture, Glasgow School of Art, is the author of *Tower and Slab: Histories of Global Mass Housing* (Abingdon: Routledge, 2011).

NANCY KWAK, Assistant Professor of History at the University of California, San Diego. Her forthcoming book is *Homeownership for All: American Power and the Politics of Housing Aid post-1945* (University of Chicago Press, 2015).

RHONDA Y. WILLIAMS, Associate Professor of History at Case Western Reserve, is the author of *The Politics of Public Housing: Black Women's Struggles against Urban Inequality* (Oxford University Press, 2004).

LISA LEVENSTEIN, Associate Professor of History at the University of North Carolina–Greensboro, is author of *A Movement without Marches: African American Women and the Politics of Poverty in Postwar Philadelphia* (University of North Carolina Press, 2009).

INDEX

Page numbers in italics refer to figures. Page numbers in bold refer to tables.

academic research, public housing: effects
    of, 11, 19, 40–41, 64–78, 89–90; new
    public housing scholarship, 5, 19–20,
    78–89; role of funding in, 69, 74, 76–78,
    85–86
Alessandroni, Walter E., 234
American Civil Liberties Union (ACLU),
    50
Architectural Forum, 53–54
architecture and design, 21–22, 33–35,
    47–48, 51–55; as cause of crime, 66–71;
    child rearing and, 52–55; determinism,
    56, 69–71, 90, 91, 240n2; in Germany,
    157, 161–63; modernization, 182–85,
    217–18; narrative of decline and, 47–48,
    64; in New York, 52, 99–101; in Philadel-
    phia, 226–27; types of, 4; youth density
    and, 56, 61, 63
Asia, public housing in, 3–5, 175–76
Atlanta public housing, 82, 88; Techwood
    Homes, *3*, 34
Austria, public housing in, *172*

Baltimore public housing, 27–28, 34, 76,
    206–15, 217–22; Douglass Homes, 212–14,
    217, 271n13; Lafayette Courts, 212–14,
    217; Murphy Homes, 72–73, 219–21;
    projects, origin date, 206–7; Somerset
    Courts, 271n13; white flight in, 38
Bard, Morton, 191

Bartholomew, Harland, 34–36, 41
Baruch College, 109
Bauer, Catherine, 9, 47
Berlin public housing, 155–59, 161–69;
    Ernst-Reuter-Siedlung, 160; Falkenha-
    gener Feld, 161; Gropiusstadt, 161;
    Heinrich-Heine-Viertel, 155; Hellersdorf,
    163; Hohenschönhausen, 163; Märkisches
    Viertel, 155, 162; Marzahn, 155, *162*, *163*
Bezalel, Ronit, documentaries, 18
Black Student Union, 219
Bloom, Nicholas Dagen, 22–23, 43–44, 48,
    198
Boston public housing, 34, 39; Common-
    wealth, 149–53; Harbor Point, 145
Branch, Van Story, 217
Bristol, Katharine, 41
Brooke, Edward, 20, 131
Brown v. Board of Education, 37

Cabrini-Green, 2, 18, 55, 143; "notorious"
    description, 12–14
Carroll, Tamar, 269n49
Carter, Walter P., 210
Castells, Manuel, 176
Central Provident Fund (CPF), 178–180,
    183–184
CHA. *See* Chicago public housing
Chicago Defender, 57
Chicago Park District public pools, 60

Chicago public housing, 48–55, 241n10, 255n46; Cabrini-Green, 2, 12–13, 18, 55, 143; family size, 242n25; governance structure, 32–33; Henry Horner Homes, *51*; Jane Adams Houses, *2*; Lake Park Place, 144, 148; Loomis Courts, *53*; Plan for Transformation, 6, 50–51, 149; Robert Taylor Homes (*see* Robert Taylor Homes); Rockwell Gardens Day Care Center, *60*; site selection, 34, 48–50; Stateway Gardens, *54*; tenant representation, 218; Villages at Westhaven, *51*; welfare rates, 112

Chicago Tribune, 12–14, 50

Cincinnati public housing, governance structure, 32–33

Cisneros, Henry G., 43, 50

Cleveland public housing, 34, 38, 74

Cloward, Richard, 200–201

collective efficacy, 223–34, 273n8; definition, 57; in New York public housing, 187, 189, 192, 196; and youth density, 57–63

Community Action Agency (CAA), 210–14, 217, 221

Community Action Commission (CAC), 211

Conference of Mayors, 129

Congress of Racial Equality (CORE), 210–11

contagion effect, 147

convergence school, 235n1

crime and disorder, 6, 98–99, 234; cause(s) of, 82–90; government role, 60–61; social versus legal definition, 64; statistical evidence, 66–67, 71–73, 77–78, 88–89, 244n6; tenant activism and, 196–205, 211; victimization surveys, 66, 72, 78–80; youth density and, 56–57, 61–63, 94, 244n39

crime studies, methodological issues, 74–81

criminology, 65–66, 71–73, 78–81, 83–85, 87, 244n39

culture of poverty, 67

Dagen, Irving, 44

Darst, Joseph, 36, 41

Davies, Garth, 65, 75, 82

Davis, Dantrell, 13

decline, narrative of, 1, 18–19, 250n1, 267n31; due to architecture and design, 47–48, 64; due to crime and disorder, 64–71, 83; evidence against, 5, 19–28, 40–45; media portrayals and, 11–18, 50; origin, historical, 8–10; and policy, 121–22; Pruitt-Igoe, 40–46

Defensible Space. See Newman, Oscar

DeFilippis, James, 146

demographic composition, public housing: post–World War II, 38; single-parent families, 57, 226; youth density, 48, 56–63

Department of Housing and Urban Development (HUD), 9–10, 50, 108, 255n46; Chicago Housing Authority (CHA), takeover of, 241n10; Federal Housing Administration (FHA), 36, 39, 43; moratorium, 24–25, 121–22, 132–38, 250n1; promoting activism, 216; public housing studies, 72–73, 76, 78–79, 133, 245n20; site selection, 50

Detroit, 38, 42, 252n6

Dinzey-Flores, Zaire, 84, 247n57

divergence school, 235n1

Dumanovsky, Tamara, 71, 80, 244n39

Eisenhower, Dwight D., 122

Embry, Jr., Robert C., 217

environmental determinism, 56, 69–71, 90, 91, 240n2

Erickson, David J., 250n1

Europe, 3–5, 157–58, 169–72

Family Assistance Plan (FAP), 130–31, 133, 251n2, 254n31

family structure, 21–22, 57, 62, 115, 182

Farley, John, 74

Federal Housing Administration (FHA), 36, 39, 43

finance of housing projects, 242n21; federal funding, 33, 36, 55, 224, 231–32; poverty, role of, 212–13; in Singapore, 178–79; tenant rent, 20, 60–61

First Urban Renewal Program (Germany), 164

Fleming, David, 12

Foucault, Michel, 89
Fraser, Jim, 146
Freedman, Leonard, 123

Garvin, Alexander, 241n3
Gautreaux cases, 50
Gautreaux Project, 86
geographic information system (GIS), 67, 79–80, 245n7
Germany, 158–161
Goetz, Edward, 12, 18, 84–85, 147, 151
Goh, Lee, 176
Goh Keng Swee, 177–78
governance, public housing, 32–33
Great Society, 250n1
Griffiths, Elizabeth, 82–83

Haskell, Douglas, 54
Hatcher, Clyde, 210–11, 213
Hawryluk, Agnes, 227
Hirsch, Arnold, *Making the Second Ghetto*, 11, 40, 50
Holloway, Steven, 82
Holzman, Harold, 66, 71, 79–82
HOPE VI, 9–10, 46, 87–89, 248n59; definition, 85, 141
Housing Act of 1937, 32–36, 40, 44, 140, 206, 231–32. *See also* Wagner-Steagall Act
Housing Act of 1949, 35–36, 122, 207
Housing Act of 1954, 122
Housing Act of 1965, 123
housing authority. *See public housing in specific cities*
Housing Development Board (HDB), 177, 179, 180–186
Houston public housing, governance structure, 33
HUD. *See* Department of Housing and Urban Development
Hunt, D. Bradford, 43, 69, 111
Husock, Howard, *America's Trillion-Dollar Housing Mistake*, 10, 43, 64–65, 267n31

immigration, 154, 164–66, 168–69, 262n36
international comparison, 3–5, 154–55, 175–76, 186

Jacobs, Jane, 8–9, 47, 63, 244n40
Jencks, Charles, 40–41
Johnson, Lyndon, 69, 123–24, 136, 198
Johnson, Margaret E., 217
Johnson administration, 124–25
Joseph, Mark, 145–46, 150, 152
Journal of Housing, 218

Kay, Jane Holtz, 41
Kelley, Robin, 67
Kemp, Jack, 46, 76
Keyes, Langley, 74
King, Jean, 218, 272n30
Knoblauch, Joy, 69–70
Kotlowitz, Alex, *There Are No Children Here*, 50, 62
Kwok, Reginald, 176

Lane, Vincent, 144
Law Enforcement Assistance Administration (LEAA), 69
Le Corbusier, 40, 122, 157
Lee Kuan Yew, 177
Legal Aid, 217
Lively, Walter H., 210, 221
Los Angeles public housing, 78, 82–83, 251n4; governance structure, 33
Los Angeles Times, 13–18
Los Vigilantes, 197

maintenance, 95–99, 217–18, 232–33, 102–10; deferred, 12, 39; by tenants, 223–24, 233
management practices, 95, 103–8, 110–18, 192; eviction, 116, 200–201, 214–15; and race, 219, 221; staffing level, 96–98, 102, 107, 213; tenant-staff relations, 212–14, 229–31
Mann, Nicola, 12
McMillan, Benjamin, 219, 221
McNulty, Thomas, 82
Meehan, Eugene, 42, 44, 138, 251n5
Minneapolis, 216
mixed-income housing, 9–10, 25, 51, 141–48, 152–53, 257n1; in Boston, 149–51; definition, 141–45
Mobilization for Youth (MFY), 201–3

Moses, Robert, 99
Moving to Opportunity (MTO), 85–87, 147
myth, definition, 6

Nathan, Richard P., 127, 251n2
National Industrial Recovery Act, 34
National Institute of Justice (NIJ), 77
National Institute of Mental Health (NIMH), 67
Netherlands, public housing in the, 154
Newman, Oscar, *Defensible Space,* 9, 41–42, 47, 79; and collective efficacy, 63; in myth, 67–72; and Van Dyke Houses, 101
New Orleans public housing, 62, 92
Newton, Joel, 213–14, 221
New York City Housing Authority Police Department (HAPD), 189–96, 199, 203; minorities in, 191
New York City public housing, 93–96; architecture and design, 52, 99–101; Brownsville Houses, 68, 102; Claremont Village, 100; collective efficacy, 187, 189, 192, 196; Coney Island Houses, 92; Cooper Park, 199; East River Houses, *92;* Fort Greene Houses, 98–99; George Washington Carver Houses, 203; governance structure, 32–33; Harlem River Houses, 98; James Weldon Johnson Houses, 100, 103, 192; Lexington Houses, 197; management practices in, 91, 93, 96–110, 192; policing in, 83–84, 189–205; Polo Grounds Towers, 91, 99; Queensbridge Houses, 100; rent strike, 202–3, 269n49; St. Louis, contrast to, 42; tenant activism, 196–205; tenant organizations, 197–98; tenant representation, 217–18; Van Dyke Houses, 68, 100–2; violent and property crime in, 73; Welfare rates, 112; Whitman Houses, 203; Williamsburg Houses, 98; Woodrow Wilson Homes, 61, 94, 100; youth density in, 61–62
New York Times, 13–18, 68, 109
1968 Civil Rights Act, 39
Nixon, Richard, 121, 130
Nixon administration: and devolution, 125–29; moratorium, 24–25, 121–22,

132–38, 250n1, public housing critique, 130–32; public housing policy, 121–122
NYCHA. *See* New York City public housing
NYCHA v. Medlin, 202

Office of Economic Opportunity, 198–99
Office of Management and Budget (OMB), 128–34, 256n51
Olugbala, 219, 221
Orlebeke, Charles, 129, 255n46

Parker, Mattie, 211
People's Action Party (PAP), 177–78, 180, 182–84
Perlstein, Rick, 125
PHA (Philadelphia Housing Authority). *See* Philadelphia public housing
PHA (Public Housing Administration), 52
PHAs (public housing authorities), definition, 32
PHD (public housing development), definition, 64
Philadelphia Evening Bulletin, 228, 233
Philadelphia public housing, 223–34; architecture and design in, 226–27; demographics of, 225; governance structure, 33; James Weldon Johnson Homes, 226; Norris, 234; origin dates, 224–25; Raymond Rosen, 224, 228–29, 231; Richard Allen Homes, 226, *227,* 228, 233; site selection, 35; tenant representation, 218
Phoenix public housing, 78
Pittsburgh public housing, 218
Piven, Frances Scott, 200–201
Plan for Transformation, 6, 50–51, 149
police strategies, 71; community policing, 190; order-maintenance policing, 193–94; radio motor patrol, 190–91
political views, 2, 6, 8, 250n1; conservative, 10, 130–132, 251n2; liberal, 11
Popkin, Susan, 85, 88–89
private sector, role of, 3, 123–124, 166–167
Pruitt-Igoe, 2, 4, 14, 19, 21, 38, 40–46, 67–68, 72, 91, 101, 136, 155; comparison, 155; in myth, 6, 31–32; origin, historical, 37; youth density, 61

Pruitt-Igoe Myth, The, 6
public housing, definition, 157, 260n1
Public Housing Drug Elimination Program, 77, 78
public housing policy, federal, 2–4; 1949–1970, 122–25; under Johnson administration, 124–25; under Nixon administration, 121–22, 125–38; race and, 50–51
Public Works Administration (PWA), 34, 44, 140

race: and Housing Act of 1949, 36, and Jim Crow laws, 206–7; and New York public housing, 195; and public housing, 4–5, 11, 40, 256n56; and site selection, 34, 37, 48–50; and tenant activism, 209–10, 219–22; and tenant selection, 50; and white flight, 39
Rainwater, Lee, 44, 67, 72
RAND Corporation, 39
Research Triangle Institute (RTI), 78–79
Resident Action Committee (RAC), 212–15, 218
Residents in Action, 218
Robert Taylor Homes, *49,* 55, 56; comparison, 155; collective efficacy in, 58–59; tragic deaths in, 57, *58*
Romney, George, 121, 126–29, 131–34
Roncek, Dennis, 74
Rosin, Hanna, 65, 87–88

San Francisco public housing, 13–14, 144–45
Schmandt, Henry and George Wendel, 42
Schmich, Mary, 12
Schwartz, Alex, 144
Schofield, Rosetta, 214, 220–21
Singapore public housing, 176–86; consumption and, 180–183; public policy, 176–180; Tiong Bahru, 177
site selection, 33–34, 48–50, 225
slums. *See* tenements and slums
social ecology, definition, 72
social exclusion, 8
social strain (theory), 67

Soul School, 219–20
Spencer, Mildred and Joseph, 223–24
staffing practices. *See* management practices
Stephenson, Maxine, 221
St. Louis, city and county, 38–39
St. Louis public housing, 35–46; Blumeyer Homes, 37; Carr Square Village, 35; Clinton-Peabody, 35; Cochran Gardens, 36–37, 44; Darst-Webbe, 37; governance structure, 32–33; Pruitt-Igoe (*see* Pruitt-Igoe); rent strike, 218; site selection, 34, 37; Vaughan-Taylor Homes, 37, 44; Wendell O. Pruitt Homes, 37 (*see also* Pruitt-Igoe); William Igoe Apartments, 37 (*see also* Pruitt-Igoe)
Super Storm Sandy, 91–92

Teh Cheang Wan, 177
tenant activism, 196–205, 269n49; black nationalism and, 219–22; black women and, 208, 217–19, 223–26; causes of, 209–10; federal support for, 216–17; motivations and incentives for, 207–8; organizers, role of, 210–12; rent strikes, 202–203, 218
tenant organization. *See specific names of organizations*
tenant rights and representation, 215–18
tenant selection, 42–43, 50, 75, 226
tenements and slums, contrast with public housing, 5, 8, 140, 206–7
Thorpe v. Housing Authority, 215
Tier System, 112
Tita, George, 82–83
Turnkey Program, 37, 124–25

Ulbricht, Walter, 161
United States Housing Authority (USHA), 32–36, 40, 44, 140, 206, 231–32
urban decline, 38–39, 45, 94; deindustrialization, 20–21, 38, 75–76, 77
Urban Renewal Program (United States), 122, 126–28
USHA. *See* United States Housing Authority

utopian narrative, 1–2, 225–26; crime and, 65; critiques of, 6, 9–18 (*see also* decline, narrative of); in Europe, 157–58; family, 56; origin, historical, 7–8

Van Dusen, Richard C., 129
von Hoffman, Alexander, 251n3

Wagner, Robert, 36, 110
Wagner-Steagall Act, 32–36, 40, 44, 140, 206, 231–32. *See also* Housing Act of 1937
"warehousing the poor," 240n1
War on Poverty, 211
Washington, DC, public housing, 72–73, 78

Washington Post, 13–18
Weaver, Robert C., 123, 136
Welfeld, Irving, 131
Williams, Rhonda Y., 196
Wolfe, Tom, 47–48
Wood, Elizabeth, 9, 52–54
Wylie, Rose, 218

Yamasaki, Minoru, 37, 41
Young Lords Organization (YLO), 203
youth density, 56–63, 242n26, 244n40; comparison, city-level, 62

Zipp, Samuel, 99

Lightning Source UK Ltd.
Milton Keynes UK
UKOW04f2330300915

259563UK00002B/39/P